This book brings a surprisingly wide range of intellectual disciplines to bear on the self-narrative and the self. The same ecological/cognitive approach that successfully organized Ulric Neisser's earlier volume *The Perceived Self* now relates ideas from the experimental, developmental, and clinical study of memory to insights from postmodernism and literature. Although autobiographical remembering is an essential way of giving meaning to our lives, the memories we construct are never fully consistent and often simply wrong. In the first chapter, Neisser considers the so-called false memory syndrome in this context. Other contributors discuss the effects of amnesia, the development of remembering in childhood, the social construction of memory and its alleged self-servingness, and the contrast between literary and psychological models of the self. Jerome Bruner, Peggy Miller, Alan Baddeley, Kenneth Gergen, and Daniel Albright are among the contributors to this unusual synthesis.

Emory Symposia in Cognition 6

The remembering self

The remembering self
Construction and accuracy
in the self-narrative

Edited by

ULRIC NEISSER
and
ROBYN FIVUSH

CAMBRIDGE
UNIVERSITY PRESS

PUBLISHED BY THE PRESS SYNDICATE OF THE UNIVERSITY OF CAMBRIDGE
The Pitt Building, Trumpington Street, Cambridge CB2 1RP, United Kingdom

CAMBRIDGE UNIVERSITY PRESS
The Edinburgh Building, Cambridge CB2 2RU, UK   http://www.cup.cam.ac.uk
40 West 20th Street, New York, NY 10011-4211, USA   http://www.cup.org
10 Stamford Road, Oakleigh, Melbourne 3166, Australia

First published 1994
Transferred to digital printing 1998

Printed in the United States of America

Typeset in Baskerville

A catalogue record for this book is available from the British Library

Library of Congress Cataloguing-in-Publication Data is available

ISBN 0-521-43194-8 hardback

Contents

Folk –

Preface

Several independent lines of thought come together in this book. The first of these is an ecological/cognitive analysis of the self that was initially proposed by one of us (Ulric Neisser) in 1988. Five different sources of self-relevant information were identified in that analysis and described in terms of the different "selves" that they establish. The "ecological" and "interpersonal" selves, based on perception, have been considered in a preceding volume called *The Perceived Self.* The "private" and "conceptual" selves will be the subject of a volume currently in preparation. Here we are concerned with what was initially called the "temporally extended" self – that is, with memory and the self-narrative.

The second group of ideas that animates this book comes from recent studies of memory development. The research of the last few years, including our own (Robyn Fivush), has made it obvious that remembering does not just happen. Instead it is a skill that must be learned, a socially motivated activity with a specific developmental history in early childhood. This means that the remembering *self* has a course of development too, one that is explored in several of these chapters.

Our third theme is one of the more prominent currents in late 20th-century intellectual life. The concept of narrative has recently become important across a surprisingly wide range of disciplines. The seven fields listed on the contributor information page of the *Journal of Narrative and Life History* – anthropology, education, folklore studies, linguistics, literary criticism, psychology, and sociology – are just the tip of the iceberg; history, philosophy, and theology are among many that could be added. One of the key ideas in this movement is that narratives are not fixed or static; rather, they change with every retelling. Many contributors to this volume remind us that this is especially true of *self*-narratives. There is not just one single "remembered self," permanently established by some fixed set of memory traces. Different occasions must, should, and do elicit different accounts of the past. Our title, *The Remembering Self,* was chosen to emphasize that flexibility.

If we had written this preface two years ago, our list of underlying themes might have ended at this point. In that brief time, something remarkable has happened in America. The accuracy of the self-narrative is no longer of interest only to scholars: It has become front-page news. This is because of a striking increase in what seem to be recollections of childhood sexual abuse, often recalled for the first time – decades after the alleged events – in the course of psychotherapy. Although some of these recollections are surely valid, we believe that many others are not. The term *false memory syndrome* has recently been coined to describe such cases. Because this issue had not surfaced at the time of the conference on which the present volume is based, most of our contributors do not discuss it. Nevertheless, as Neisser argues in the introductory chapter, it lies very close to the core of the issues with which this book is concerned.

A grant from the Mellon Foundation to Emory University has made it possible to convene a series of conferences on different aspects of the self. The third of these meetings, convened by the Emory Cognition Project in January 1991, dealt with "The Remembered Self." It was remarkably successful, beginning with Daniel Albright's brilliant contrast between literary and psychological models of the self (chap. 2 of this volume) and continuing in the same vein of interdisciplinary exploration for two and a half days. All the major contributions to that conference are included here, along with a new introductory chapter.

Although this is only the second of our volumes on the self, it is the Sixth Emory Symposium on Cognition. Like all the others, it brings ecological and developmental perspectives to bear on a significant problem in cognitive psychology. Also like all the others, it is essentially interdisciplinary in its orientation: We believe that psychologists have a lot to learn from colleagues in other fields. Certainly we ourselves have learned a great deal from the contributors to this symposium. We are deeply grateful for their contributions, their insights, and their friendship. And also, alas, for their patience: Once again it has taken much too long to get the show on the road!

But here it is at last. Like the narratives that form its subject matter, *The Remembering Self* is not intended simply as a record of a significant past event (the 1991 conference). It is also aimed at the future, shaped to a purpose. We hope it will contribute to the ongoing theoretical exchanges – about truth and falsehood, memory and development, the self and self-knowledge – that make the ecological study of cognition so interesting. If that happens, we will be more than satisfied.

Contributors

Daniel Albright is Professor of English at the University of Rochester.

Alan Baddeley is the Director of the Applied Cognitive Psychology Unit in Cambridge, England.

Craig R. Barclay is Professor of Education at the University of Rochester.

Jerome Bruner is Research Professor at New York University.

Roger Buehler is Assistant Professor of Psychology at Simon Fraser University.

Rebecca A. Eder is Assistant Professor of Psychology at the University of California at Davis.

Robyn Fivush is Associate Professor of Psychology at Emory University.

Kenneth J. Gergen is Professor of Psychology at Swarthmore College.

William Hirst is Professor of Psychology at the New School for Social Research.

April E. Metzler is Assistant Professor of Psychology at Lehigh University.

Peggy J. Miller is Associate Professor of Psychology at the University of Illinois at Urbana.

Ulric Neisser is Robert W. Woodruff Professor of Psychology at Emory University.

Greg J. Neimeyer is Associate Professor of Psychology at the University of Florida.

Edward S. Reed is Associate Professor of Psychology at Franklin and Marshall College.

Michael Ross is Professor of Psychology at the University of Waterloo in Canada.

Willem A. Wagenaar is Professor of Psychology at the University of Leiden in the Netherlands.

Eugene Winograd is Professor of Psychology at Emory University.

The remembering self

1

Self-narratives: True and false

ULRIC NEISSER

Human beings exist through time, just as everything else does: One thing happens after another. But unlike anything else, people remember what happened to them – some of it, anyway. This is a remarkable achievement. The remarkable thing is not just that past events influence the present (which happens in all biological systems) but that they are explicitly reconstructed by the person who experienced them. By definition, such reconstructions are examples of *episodic memory*. If the remembered event seems to have played a significant part in the life of the rememberer, it becomes an example of *autobiographical memory* and may form part of a *life narrative*. Life narratives are significant because they are one way of defining the self.

This book has two goals: to explore the relations between remembering and the self, and to see those relations in proper perspective. Life narratives are often described as if they were the chief or even the only ingredient of the self: "They [life narratives] are the basis of personal identity and self-understanding and they provide answers to the question 'Who am I?'" (Polkinghorne, 1991, p. 136). This claim goes too far: Self-knowledge depends on perception, conceptualization, and private experience as well as narrative (Neisser, 1988). Self-narratives are *a* basis but not *the* basis of identity. It is appropriate, then, that the present volume is only one of a series devoted to self-knowledge and the self. An earlier book (Neisser, 1993a) was concerned with ecological and interpersonal perception; the self-concept will be considered in a subsequent volume.

However important those other sources of self-knowledge may be, they are not our focus here. This book is concerned with the remembering self: with self-narratives and whether to believe them, with the functions of those narratives and what happens without them, with the social and individual determinants of what is recalled and what is forgotten, with skills of remembering and how those skills are acquired. In the chapters ahead these issues are addressed by a talented and diverse group of contributors; first it is appropriate to present some views of my own.

1

1

Narrative and reality

Not all self-narratives are true. Even when people strive for accuracy, what they remember may not be just what happened. In episodic memory we must distinguish: (1) the actual event; (2) the event as it was experienced by the individual in question; (3) the subsequent act of remembering it; and (4) the remembered event, that is, the particular version of (1) that is established by (3). The analogous categories in autobiographical memory are: (1) actual past events and the *historical self* who participated in them; (2) those events as they were then experienced, including the individual's own *perceived self* at the time; (3) the *remembering self*, that is, the individual in the act of recalling those events on some later occasion; and (4) the *remembered self* constructed on that occasion. Moreover, self-narratives do not rely on episodic memory alone. People often begin narratives with their own birth, although they do not remember it; sometimes they even start with the deeds of their ancestors. Later events may also be reported without being actually remembered, if the narrator is sufficiently sure of them.

These distinctions seem rather obvious to me, but in fact they are controversial. Not everyone agrees that it is useful to speak of real historical events, or of a "historical self." The British psychologists Derek Edwards and Jonathan Potter, for example, note that "the epistemological status of 'original events' is problematic" (1992, p. 204). They see little point in postulating such events, which can never be definitely established anyway. The ordinary course of life rarely generates objective records. Even when a record happens to exist (e.g., a tape recording; cf. Neisser, 1981), it is often susceptible to more than one interpretation. According to Edwards and Potter, reality is not so much something against which memories can be checked as something established by those memories themselves. "Everyday conversational remembering often has this as its primary concern – the attempt to construct an acceptable, agreed, or communicatively successful version of what really happened" (1992, p. 210).

This postmodern approach to the study of memory is not without its critics (cf. Edwards, Potter, & Middleton, 1992; with replies by Baddeley, 1992; Hyman, 1992; Neisser, 1992; and others). The main thrust of the critique is that it *does* matter what really happened. To manage the present or survive the future, we often need an honest account of the past. Even when no such account is available, we must still *believe* that the past consisted of some definite set of events that have had specific consequences for the present. Otherwise, why would we think of the present as having consequences for the future? How would wild fabrication be different from sober report? Perhaps most important, how would false allegations and accusations differ from those that are true?

Recollections and accusations

The problem of false accusation first became salient for psychologists in the work of Sigmund Freud. In the early years of his practice, Freud noticed something remarkable: All his hysteric patients recovered vivid memories of childhood sexual experience at some point in their analyses. His initial interpretation (Freud, 1896/1985) was that repressed memories of such experiences, in combination with less repressed later events, were the underlying cause of their illness. Soon afterward, however, he decided that the patients must have been recalling fantasies rather than real experiences. It was those fantasies, again in combination with later memories, that produced the symptoms of hysteria.

In terms of Freud's overall theory, this was a relatively small change. Even in the first interpretation he had insisted that the basic cause of hysteria was not the event itself but its mental representation: "The matter is not merely one of the existence of the sexual experiences, but that . . . the scenes must be present as *unconscious memories;* only so long as, and in so far as, they are unconscious are they able to create and maintain hysterical symptoms" (Freud, 1896/1985, p. 280; italics in original). In fact, however, this revision has had momentous consequences. From that time onward, psychoanalysts have systematically sought the origins of mental illness in early fantasy rather than in concrete life experience.

Just why Freud abandoned the "seduction theory" so easily is a hotly disputed question (Masson, 1985). I will not enter that dispute here; the real facts of the matter (i.e., whether the reported sexual experiences actually happened) are forever beyond our reach. Unfortunately, however, the issue is of much more than historical interest today. Very similar reports – apparent memories of sexual traumas that were experienced in childhood and then long forgotten – are often given by patients today. A full century after Freud's initial investigations, it is still hard to be sure what they mean.

These sexual-abuse memories appear during psychotherapy, often together with participation in "incest survivor" groups. Often they strike the patient as surprising, having "emerged" for the first time during the therapy itself. This fact does not arouse the therapist's skepticism; on the contrary, it is usually taken as evidence that the memories must have been very deeply repressed. With the lifting of that "repression," many terrible recollections may appear. At that point, the presumptive experience of childhood sexual abuse becomes the turning point of the patient's life narrative. (See Bruner, chap. 3 of this volume, for more on turning points.) She (most of the patients are women) now sees herself as victim; formerly beloved family members are seen as perpetrators. Accusations are made, lives changed, families broken up; legal action may be undertaken. The sheer number of such cases is remarkable. The False Memory Syndrome (FMS) Foundation, set up in 1992 as a support group for persons accused in this way, received thousands of calls for help in its first year of operation.

Are these accusations justified? For therapist and patient, the vividness of the memories and the coherence of the narrative that they support seem to be self-validating. Nevertheless, they may be far less plausible to outsiders. The alleged perpetrators typically deny everything: The accusations seem to take them by surprise and their friends may warmly defend their characters. In addition, the reported abuses are often wildly implausible. In an FMS Foundation (1993) survey, 18% of the narratives include "satanic cult" stories – bizarre torture rituals conducted by robed figures, children made pregnant to produce babies for human sacrifice, infants killed and eaten. In other cases the events are described as occurring so openly and often, with so many people, that it seems impossible they could have gone unnoticed. In one case the victim reported that her father and his poker buddies used to rape her routinely, every weekend, with the collusion of her mother (Wright, 1993). Then, apparently, normal family life would resume.

Patients like these are dominated by their remembered selves. Their current life problems are interpreted as resulting from their awful past experiences. They may recall those experiences in rich detail; when this happens, the vividness of the memories is taken as strong evidence for the narrative they support. Oddly, however, patients can also be convinced that they were sexually abused in childhood without remembering very much at all. Recalling/imagining just the faint touch of a hand, or having an indefinite feeling that "something bad was done to me," is often enough to confirm the therapist's abuse hypothesis. These minimal fragments often lead to further suggestions: "Tell me what that bastard did to you!" Because strong conviction is contagious, the patient may accept the therapist's interpretation without actually recalling any specific memories to substantiate it. A "remembered self" constructed in this way is based less on the patient's own life experiences than on whatever incest narratives the therapist takes to be prototypical. Albright (chap. 2 of this volume) might want to call it a "plagiarized self" instead.

The acute reader will have detected a skeptical note in this discussion. I believe that many of these memories are confabulated, many of the accusations false. In some cases, my disbelief rests on the implausibility of the narratives themselves. There is scarcely more evidence of the existence of satanic cults as described than of flying saucers; any suggestive situation that elicits such bizarre stories must be regarded with considerable skepticism. Here, the key elements of the situation seem to be (1) a distressed patient urgently seeking an explanation of her problems, and (2) a strong therapist who expects to find that explanation in a sexual-abuse narrative. The dynamics of this situation provide the answer to a question that is frequently asked: Why would anyone make up such terrible things if they weren't true? It is because they are essential to a narrative in which both parties are heavily invested.

I am also suspicious of the unusual form of "repression" that must be postulated to make these stories true: The events occur regularly for years, are then forgotten for decades, and finally reappear in florid detail. Although child abuse certainly does occur – more often than we like to think – I am inclined to believe that it is usually remembered rather than forgotten. Victims of other traumas – concentration camp survivors, Vietnam War veterans, eyewitnesses to murder – rarely repress them in this way. On the contrary, they may be haunted by their experiences for years.

The prevalence of error

Cases like these raise significant questions for students of memory. Is it really possible for vivid recollections to be completely fabricated? Isn't there a "grain of truth" in even the most distorted memory? And on the other hand, does the existence of false memories mean that no memory can ever be trusted? Are all our recollections wrong? To what extent?

The answer to the first question is simply *yes*. People can indeed have convincing memories of things that never happened. This has long been known for suggestions made in hypnosis (e.g., Laurence & Perry, 1983), but it can also happen without any hypnotic involvement. Richard Ofshe (1992) recently suggested a novel memory of sexual abuse to a man who had already been arrested for, and confessed to, many other bizarre abusive acts. The suggestion was readily accepted, and an elaborated version of the suggested experience was soon incorporated into the "perpetrator's" self-narrative. A very different set of examples comes from recent work by Elizabeth Loftus (1993). Using plausible suggestions made by trusted relatives, Loftus has successfully implanted false recollections of *having been lost in a shopping mall when a child* into the memories of normal adults. Her subjects, who soon elaborate these "memories" in plausible ways, are fully convinced that the event actually happened. A similar dynamic was probably responsible for Jean Piaget's (1962) famous memory of a childhood kidnapping attempt that later turned out to have been a complete fabrication.

Another recent study is worth mentioning because it shows that false memories can appear even without explicit suggestion. On the morning after the space shuttle *Challenger* exploded in 1986, I asked a group of Emory students to record how they had first heard the news on the preceding day. Three years later, the 44 who were still on campus were again asked to recall how they had heard about *Challenger*, and to rate their confidence in various aspects of that memory (Neisser & Harsch, 1992). About a quarter of those accounts, including many reported with high confidence, were entirely wrong. One subject, who in fact had first heard about the disaster from fellow students in class, later recalled being stunned by the news while watching TV with her roommate. Another, who had actually heard the news from friends at lunch in the cafeteria, remembered how "some girl came running down the hall screaming 'The space shuttle just blew up.'" In subsequent interviews, we showed the subjects their original 1986 questionnaires. Even then they were reluctant to abandon their incorrect memories: "Yes, that's my handwriting – but I still remember it this other way!" Established self-narratives are very hard to change.

What about the notion that there is "a grain of truth" in every memory? Freud, of all people, seems to have believed this. He thought of psychoanalysis as comparable to archaeology (Freud, 1937/1964), a science that retrieves genuine fragments from the past and constructs essentially valid scenarios of ancient events. (At first sight this seems to conflict with his earlier rejection of the seduction theory, but the contradiction is only apparent. The truth-grains in which Freud believed were fragments of fantasies or images, not memories of actual events.) As Donald Spence (1982) has shown, this claim reflects a basic confusion between "narrative truth" and "historical truth." Images and memories are never simply "observed" by the patient and then "reported" to the analyst, as the archaeological metaphor would imply. They are always constructs, shaped by the shared need to establish a psychoanalytically satisfactory narrative of the patient's mental development.

In denying that memories must contain grains of truth, I do not mean to deny that they have comprehensible causes. Sometimes those causes are obvious. The subject who falsely remembered first learning about *Challenger* from TV, for example, had probably watched television coverage of the disaster later that day. It is harder to guess the origin of the mythical girl who ran screaming through the dorm, but she too must have started somewhere. (I am tempted by Freud's fantasy hypothesis in this case. Perhaps the subject herself felt like screaming, and transformed her feeling into an image that eventually became a memory.) False memories of childhood sexual abuse also have their sources, but those sources need not lie in the actual childhood of the patient. It is often supposed that "something must have been going on" to give rise to such a memory, but this assumption is not justified. It is at least as likely that the underlying ideas were acquired later, perhaps in adult life.

The fact that *some* memories can be dramatically mistaken does not mean that *all* memories are wrong. That would be impossible. Many recollections concern events that have present consequences: I remember my wedding, and am still married; remember moving to Atlanta and still live there. Such consequences do not guarantee the accuracy of details, which may indeed be mistakenly remembered, but they do constrain the main outline of the narrative. In addition, many recollections involve other people. We may have to construct an "agreed or communicatively successful version of what really happened" (Edwards & Potter, 1992, p. 210) with someone else who was there too. The process of construction may uncover real differences, but it usually reveals substantial consensus as well.

In recent years a number of psychologists have conducted "diary studies," in which subjects record their experiences on a daily basis and later test their memories of those experiences (Linton, 1982; Wagenaar, 1986, and chap. 10 of this volume; Brewer, 1988; White, 1989; Larsen, 1992; Hirst, chap. 14 of this volume). These studies show a good deal of forgetting, but not much misremembering: There are very few overt errors or confabulations. Diarists may be unusually dependable people, or – as Eugene Winograd observes in chapter 13 of this volume – they may just be unusually careful because they know their memories will soon be checked.

Another relevant line of research focuses on memory in young children. Two-, 3-, or 4-year-olds can be asked to recall specific life events: holidays, trips to the zoo, and the like (e.g., Fivush, Gray, & Fromhoff, 1987; Fivush & Hamond, 1990). Experimenters trained to be sympathetic and yet not suggestive can elicit a surprising amount of information about the past, even from very young subjects. Although most of the memories are fragmentary and incomplete, they rarely include confabulations or serious errors. This does not mean that young children are always right; on the contrary, they are very vulnerable to suggestion (Ceci & Bruck, 1993). That vulnerability is important for understanding a different set of child-abuse accusations, those based not on long-delayed recollections by adults but on contemporary accounts given by the children themselves. Some of those accounts are certainly valid, but others are just the product of prolonged and suggestive interrogation. Children's memory, like that of adults, is more or less on the mark in many situations but vulnerable to suggestion in others.

2

The oblivious self

In short, autobiographical memory is best taken with a grain of salt. The self that is remembered today is not the historical self of yesterday, but only a reconstructed version. A different version – a new remembered self – may be reconstructed tomorrow. *How* different? I myself am biased toward continuity, and tend to think of most remembered selves as fairly stable from one day to the next. Perhaps my bias is predictable: don't psychologists always hope to find order in behavior? In any event, it is not a universal preference. Many literary accounts of human nature are very different: chaotic, mysterious, full of surprises. The contrast between these attitudes can be very sharp. In Daniel Albright's memorable phrase (chap. 2 of this volume), "Literature is a wilderness, psychology is a garden."

Albright's chapter 2, which I hope you will read next, is a tour de force – one of the most original contributions ever made to a symposium on memory. It begins with what he calls "the brokenness of memory." The remembered self is radically incomplete; it "begins and ends in a state of nothingness, and from beginning to end is riddled with nothingness." Childhood amnesia – "Alzheimer's other disease" – is only its most obvious gap: The self might be better called "oblivious" than "remembering." Rememberers must gloss over vast empty spaces, like the miles between unconnected bits of a great Chinese Wall. Yet oblivion is not always undesirable: On the contrary, it establishes a kind of absolute freedom that memory denies.

Albright is suspicious of the unity and coherence implied by the word *self.* We are more plural than that, divided against ourselves, discontinuous. "The human self is crazily mutable; my face may seem impassive, but beneath the calm exterior I am shifting, shifting, shifting, growing unrecognizable from moment to moment" (sec. 2). Albright is not the only contributor to this volume who emphasizes the multiplicity of the self. The same theme turns up in several other chapters, including Edward Reed's concluding comparison between memory and perception (chap. 15). Where perceiving is an essentially unitary act (at any given time, each individual is embedded in the environment in one particular way and perceives exactly that), memory is always dual. Reed describes autobiographical memory as "the me-experiencing-now becoming aware of a prior-me-experiencing its (prior) environment." This is exactly the duality of the remembering and the remembered self.

We met the remembering and remembered selves earlier in this chapter. It is time now to meet their more famous cousins, the *I* and the *me*.

These concepts were first introduced by William James (1890) and later elaborated by G. H. Mead (1934). *I* is the subject himself/herself. In Mead's analysis *I* is the doer; it is always the *I* who acts or speaks or knows anything. The *me*, in contrast, is just something known by the *I*. Essentially, it is a (socially generated) mental representation of the self. Many aspects of the *me* are included in what I have elsewhere called the *conceptual* self (Neisser, 1988), but others with a more narrative form constitute the remembered self. In this context the *I* is the remembering self, inventor and constructor of the remembered *me*. But here too, Albright enriches our thinking. He argues that we can also reverse these definitions, regarding the remembered self as the inventor and the present self as its continuing invention. Is *he* not now the (albeit imperfectly realized) object that was intended long ago by the young Dan Albright?

The multiplicity of narrative

Jerome Bruner (1986, 1990) is psychology's most eloquent advocate of the narrative mode. Nevertheless, he is keenly aware of the ambiguities involved. In chapter 3, Bruner specifically rejects the term "remembered self." For one thing, actual self-narratives are not so dependent on memory as it implies. "The crucial cognitive activities involved in self-construction seem much more like 'thinking' than 'memory'" (sec. 1). For another thing, there is the multiplicity of the selves that we remember. Self-narratives vary from one occasion to the next, one audience to the next, one mood to the next. Moreover, they are always shaped by implicit theories of narrative and narration. It is because of those theories, for example, that crucial turning points so often appear in life narratives – probably much more often than in life itself. Bruner also introduces another important concept, one that students of false sexual-abuse memories may find especially useful. Conceptions of narrative often lead us to emphasize our own "agency" (the effect of choices we made ourselves), but they can occasionally produce "victimicy" as well. That is, sometimes the best life narrative is one in which we seem to be the helpless victim of choices made by someone else.

Bruner and Albright and Reed are not the only ones with reservations about the singleness of the self. Such reservations are expressed even more strongly by Craig Barclay in chapter 4. Barclay, a longtime student of the vicissitudes of memory, is especially concerned with the affective aspects of recall. "Remembrances that become selves are pregnant with meanings: Meanings are bound together by the emotional life of individuals interconnected with the lives of others." In addition, Barclay emphasizes that autobiographical remembering is typically a matter of skillful improvisation rather than direct retrieval. The results of these improvisations are *protoselves*, selves in the making, new on every occasion, innovatively adapted to the present circumstances and emotional needs of the individual.

In chapter 5, Kenneth Gergen goes even further than Barclay in emphasizing the importance of social context. He begins by describing two extreme positions in the study of memory. For what he calls *psychological essentialism*, memory is a self-contained process within the mind (or the brain). This is, indeed, the underlying assumption of most modern memory research. Such research has been productive in many ways, but it has little to say about the issues discussed in this volume (e.g., about the accuracy of recall). The other position is that of *textual essentialism*. For postmodern thinkers like Barthes and Foucault, only texts matter; "person" and "self" are not even useful categories. Although I myself have never understood how to take this view seriously, Gergen apparently does. Therefore, he sees a need to compromise between these two alternatives. To this end he proposes *social constructionism*, a position in which "accounts of memory gain their meaning through their usage, not within the mind nor within the text but within social relationships."

Gergen is probably the leading psychological exponent of postmodern epistemology, so his willingness to make such a compromise – even to find a place for "the kinds of experimental explorations that have been the hallmarks of psychology as a science" (chap. 5) – is important. In a roughly reciprocal way, I hope to find a place (in my own ecological/cognitive framework) for social constructionist accounts of the self. Many selections in this book can be seen as attempts to do just that. Nevertheless, no theory based only on social process and socially constructed memory can do full justice to self-knowledge. People are perceivers as well as rememberers. At all times we can directly see (and hear and feel) where we are and what we are doing; even whether we are socially engaged (Neisser, 1993b). However accurately or inaccurately we may recall or reconstruct the past, *this/here/now* is the present state of affairs for us. On the other hand, perception and the present are not always the individual's most important concern. Wherever we happen to be here and now, we can still be caught up in some compelling memory from long ago and far away. Like it or not, then, self-knowledge is intrisically multimodal. It cannot be reduced to any single source of information.

Given the constructive nature of social recall, one might expect to find wide individual differences in its constructions. Do some people remember their experiences more fully than others? Vary their accounts more freely from one social setting to the next? Bias them in a more self-serving way? Construct different kinds of narratives about them? There has been surprisingly little work on these questions, but Greg Neimeyer and April Metzler make a good start in chapter 6. They focus on a dimension of individual difference that is particularly applicable to young people of college age, a dimension that derives from the work of Erik Eriksen. At any given point in time, a person may be in one of four "identity statuses" (Marcia, 1966). *Diffuse* individuals do not have stable commitments to any set of values; *Foreclosed* individuals have committed themselves prematurely; *Moratorium* and *Achieved* individuals are actively seeking self-relevant information to establish or confirm such commitments. In Neimeyer and Metzler's computer-controlled experiment, subjects from the two information-oriented groups generated the most autobiographical memories while Diffuse subjects produced the fewest. There were also specific patterns across groups in the recall of positive and negative experiences, as well as in the impact of memories that disconfirmed the subject's own self-perceptions.

The development of the remembering self

Remembering is a skill, first learned by young children in social settings. We all begin, in childhood, by remembering with and for other persons; only later are we able to spin narratives just for ourselves. Memory is where social constructionism and developmental psychology meet. On the one hand, Gergen's (chap. 5 of this volume) claim about the social nature of remembering applies especially well to children. On the other hand, Vygotsky's (1978) claim that all intellectual skills appear first in social settings applies especially well to remembering. It is appropriate, then, that three chapters of this book deal with the development of the remembering self.

The existence of parental memory "styles" – different ways of talking with one's children about past events – has been known for some time. Some mothers are more *elaborative* in such contexts, while others are more *repetitive* (Engel, 1986; Fivush & Fromhoff, 1988). In chapter 7, Robyn Fivush shows that children's own modes of recall – how they themselves describe past events – depend on the styles to which they have been exposed. As might be expected, the children of elaborative mothers are later more elaborate in recalling their own experiences.

Fivush also reports another, less expected result. It turns out that parental memory styles vary with the gender of the child who is being addressed. Mothers of daughters discuss the past in more elaborative ways than mothers of sons; what's more, they interpret the past differently. These differences are especially marked when the topic of discussion is an emotional event. In recalling some frustrating experience (when a playmate broke their child's toy, for example), mothers of girls often say something like "It made you sad, didn't it?" Mothers of boys, in contrast, are likely to tell their sons, "It made you angry." These findings may be giving us an early and important glimpse of the processes by which gender roles are established.

Fivush's observations remind us of what might be considered a special kind of "remembered self": A's past experience as it is interpreted for A by B. This happens often in everyday life, and regularly in psychotherapy. Many therapists take the reframing and reinterpretation of the patient's life experiences as a major part of their responsibilities. Our earlier discussion of false memories makes it clear that such reinterpretations can be powerful indeed! Nevertheless, the authority of parents in interpreting the past for their children must be even more powerful. Not only is the parent–child relationship intrinsically an asymmetric one, but the parent often has the added authority of having shared the very same experience. This is inevitable, and I do not mean to deplore it. Parents cannot help interpreting the world for their children; indeed, they must do so if culture is to be transmitted to the next generation.

The process of interpreting the past is not always subtle or unconscious. On the contrary, as Peggy Miller notes in chapter 8, it may be very deliberate. "The flow of social and moral messages is relentless in the myriad small encounters of everyday life." In the working-class families that Miller studied, mothers constantly tell stories about the past. No such story is without its moral: "A neutral story about the self is virtually inconceivable." At first (when the children are very young) the mothers just talk around them. A little later, they start to talk about the child's own exploits; eventually the child joins in. The stories that the children tell are not fixed or memorized; no two tellings are ever identical. Their "elaborative" mothers encourage them: They are proud of their elaborative children.

As Rebecca Eder points out in her commentary (chapter 9), children tell stories for a purpose. Often their stories include a strong element of self-presentation: The child is trying to create a particular impression on its listeners. This observation implies that the self is not established for the first time by the act of telling the stories themselves: To be worth presenting in a certain light, it must already exist. In general, autobiographical memory presumes the prior existence of a conceptual self – of the very *me* whose experiences are being remembered. This poses no theoretical difficulties, however; we already know that the basic self-concept appears in development long before the first stirrings of episodic memory. Following Michael Tomasello, I would put its appearance not long after the development of joint attention – that is, at around 9 months of age (Neisser, 1993b; Tomasello, 1993). In contrast, genuine remembering becomes possible only in the third year or later (Miller, chap. 9 of this volume; Fivush & Hudson, 1990).

Self-centered memories?

Everyone seems to believe that memory is biased in favor of the self (e.g., Greenwald, 1980), but there are few systematic studies to support this claim. The claim itself is rather vague: What kinds of mnemonic transformations would count as examples? It is often suggested that people remember "pleasant" experiences more readily than "unpleasant" ones, but early studies of the issue were so plagued by methodological problems that it has been all but abandoned (Rapaport, 1959). Albright's discussion of "subjectivity" in this volume makes it painfully clear that the real biases of memory are far too subtle to be captured by such a crude dichotomy. Another example of the same general claim (that memory is self-serving) is the casually held but common assumption that people remember their own contributions to a conversation better than those of other participants. In an empirical study of memory for seminar discussions, Ira Hyman and I found that this claim is much too simplistic (Hyman & Neisser, 1992).

Recent diary studies of memory have opened up a new approach to this question. In what may be the most systematic of these studies, Willem Wagenaar (1986) did find that events rated as "pleasant" were somewhat better recalled than those rated "unpleasant." This finding seems straightforward enough, but it actually obscures an important distinction. In chapter 10, Wagenaar takes a crucial further step. In addition to classifying the events as "pleasant" or "unpleasant," he now also classifies them as "self-related" or "other-related." For example, an event in which he himself behaved badly (in his own judgment) would be scored as "unpleasant/self-related." In contrast, the funeral of a friend's daughter would be "unpleasant/other-related." The results were clear: Unpleasant/self-related events were remembered *better* (not worse) than anything else. Wagenaar's interpretation of these results is discussed by Alan Baddeley in chapter 12, so I will not consider it here. I cannot help wondering, however, whether his finding is widely generalizable. It may just apply to relatively self-critical individuals, such as Wagenaar himself.

No modern psychologist has addressed the problem of memory distortion more systematically than Michael Ross. Ross (1992; see also chap. 11 of this volume) has proposed and tested a very specific theory of one class of memory errors. He suggests that when people are asked to recall some past characteristic or trait – their political opinions 10 years ago, how bad their headaches used to be – they estimate the answer on the basis of two sources of information. The first of these is their *present* standing on the trait; the second is an implicit theory of how the trait is likely to have changed with time. Asked to recall a former political stance, for example, most people apply a "no-change" theory and remember it as similar to their attitude today. Asked what their reading speed was last month – before the start of the study skills course that they have just now completed – they begin with the implicit hypothesis that the course must have been effective. Using that assumption, they recall their earlier reading speed as lower than the speed they have now.

This idea – that accounts of the past are driven by implicit theories of stability and transformation – has implications for many different domains. The abuse narratives discussed above are a case in point: They depend on the theory that adult life problems reflect histories of childhood victimization. Similar implicit theories appear in other contexts. The unhappy childhoods often recalled by clinically depressed patients, for example, cannot be taken at face value. Ross and Buehler (chap. 11 of this volume) show that folk theories of the origin of depression contribute to such accounts in predictable ways. In a different vein, they also consider the shared recollections of married couples – recollections that often reflect implicit theories of the relationship itself. (One interesting aspect of those theories is the belief that wives have better memories than husbands; cf. Ross & Holmberg, 1990.)

Like Albright, Bruner, and Gergen, Ross and Buehler know that recollections are shaped by narrative convention. They are also concerned with the *functions* of those recollections. For example, why does writing an account of a traumatic event sometimes produce positive psychological effects? Perhaps most interesting of all, they wonder why people find some narratives more believable than others. What makes a story credible? Indeed, why do we credit our *own* stories in preference to accounts given by others? Ross and Buehler's explanations of this preference seem plausible – not only to me but also to Eugene Winograd, who comments on their contribution in chapter 13. Winograd's thoughtful commentary revisits many of the themes that have been touched on in this introduction, and presents a further example.

Is memory necessary?

William Hirst's reflections on amnesia in chapter 14 may come as a shock to narrativists. The "anterograde" amnesics he studies are essentially incapable of acquiring new information, whether about themselves or anything else. To demonstrate that incapacity Hirst enlisted them in a kind of diary experiment, the first such study ever run with amnesics. Each subject carried a "beeper," and wrote down what he or she was doing whenever the beeper went off. Unsurprisingly, they remembered virtually none of those experiences later on. Such amnesics have no current autobiographical memories and no ongoing self-narratives: They are not "remembering selves" in the current sense at all. Nevertheless each of them has, and is aware of having, an obvious and distinct identity.

Devoid of memories, these patients are not devoid of feelings. In particular, they are often depressed about the impoverishment of their lives that amnesia has produced! They know what they have lost, even though they cannot remember it. They do not need to remember it, because the circumstances of their lives make it obvious every day. You might say (indeed, Hirst does say) that the social situation remembers it for them. On this point at least, he is in accord with the social constructionist view shared by many other contributors to this volume. Information is to be found in the social world that individuals establish together, not just in their separate heads. Precisely for that reason, selves are not supported by narrative alone.

In the mental life of such an amnesic, someone is "at home" (i.e., there is conscious self-awareness) although no one is remembering. How many individuals are "at home" when remembering does take place? According to Edward Reed (chap. 15), there are at least two. This claim is Reed's way of solving a problem with which I myself have much sympathy: the problem of the relation between perception and memory. As J. J. Gibson's biographer (Reed, 1988), Reed is even more committed to the ecological approach than I am. Unfortunately, Gibson's (1966, 1979) ecological approach to perception is difficult to generalize to other domains. By definition (Gibson's definition), perception is based on the ongoing activity of organisms that are in direct contact with their environments. Also by definition, that is exactly what memory is not.

My own solution to this problem has been to make a sharp distinction. Perception is one thing – direct, embedded, realistic, and veridical; memory is quite another thing. Unwilling to accept this distinction, Reed tries to use the same conceptual apparatus for both activities. He does it by giving up the unity of the self that is experienced in perceiving: "*Perception is to self as memory is to selves.*" He regards this as a radical move. In my view it doesn't work out that way: His duality is not very different from Mead's *I* and *me*, or even from the remembering and remembered selves. But Reed does take it in a different direction than Mead did, noting the similarity between this duality and other interesting bifurcations of experience. In *akrasia*, for example, there is one self who intends and another who acts; in *empathy*, one self who shares someone else's feeling and another who is aware of it; in *shame*, one who has done something regrettable and another who, in the role of an outsider, condemns it. For Reed, all these conditions have something interesting and fundamental in common with remembering itself. Maybe they do.

The temporally extended self

In an earlier discussion of these problems (Neisser, 1988), I introduced the concept of the "temporally extended self." It was that self which filled out the full set of five, keeping company with the ecological, interpersonal, private, and conceptual selves. Temporal extension was a usefully vague idea, innocent of the later distinctions that now seem so important – between remembering and remembered selves, for example, or between narratives and other ways of knowing the past. It does not even distinguish between the past and the future! (People are "temporally extended" in both directions: into the past via memory and into the future via anticipation.) For those very reasons, however, it may still have its uses. Hirst's amnesics, with inadequate self-narratives and no remembered selves, are still keenly aware of being extended in time. They know there was a yesterday, though they have forgotten it; they know all too well that there will be a tomorrow, in which they will be just as amnesic as they are today.

All of us know about yesterday and today and tomorrow. We have known it for a long time – perhaps since we were 2 or 3 years old, though it didn't seem important then. Knowing it, each of us is a special kind of self: a *human* self, to introduce one last and redundant category. The ecological and interpersonal selves established by perception are vital to us, but they are limited to the here and now. To be human, I think, means also to know that we have a past and a future. Of course it means much more than that: self-concepts and moral decisions and private consciousness and many other things are patiently waiting for the next volume of this series to come out. Nevertheless the sense of being in time, of living through time, has a special and central status in human lives. Dan Albright (chap. 2 of this volume) puts it better than I ever could. "Our lives would be intolerable," he says, "without some predicate, some ballast of identity, to provide a context for the wisps of thought and action that constitute our instantaneous selves. We may be small in space, but . . . we are each of us giants in the dimension of time."

REFERENCES

Baddeley, A. (1992). Is memory all talk? *The Psychologist, 5,* 447–448.
Brewer, W. F. (1988). Memory for randomly sampled autobiographical events. In U. Neisser & E. Winograd (Eds.), *Remembering reconsidered: Ecological and traditional approaches to the study of memory* (pp. 21–90). Cambridge University Press.

Bruner, J. (1986). *Actual minds, possible worlds.* Cambridge, MA: Harvard University Press.

Bruner, J. (1990). *Acts of meaning.* Cambridge, MA: Harvard University Press.

Ceci, S. J., & Bruck, M. (1993). Suggestibility of the child witness: A historical review and synthesis. *Psychological Bulletin, 113,* 403–439.

Edwards, D., & Potter, J. (1992). The Chancellor's memory: Rhetoric and truth in discursive remembering. *Applied Cognitive Psychology, 6,* 187–215.

Edwards, D., Potter, J., & Middleton, D. (1992). Toward a discursive psychology of remembering. *The Psychologist, 5,* 441–446.

Engel, S. (1986, April). *The role of mother child interaction in autobiographical recall.* Paper presented at the Southeastern Conference on Human Development, Nashville, TN.

Fivush, R., & Fromhoff, F. A. (1988). Style and structure in mother–child conversations about the past. *Discourse Processes, 11,* 337–355.

Fivush, R., Gray, J. T., & Fromhoff, F. A. (1987). Two-year-olds talk about the past. *Cognitive Development, 2,* 393–407.

Fivush, R., & Hamond, N. R. (1990). Autobiographical memory across the preschool years: Toward reconceptualizing childhood amnesia. In R. Fivush & J. A. Hudson (Eds.), *Knowing and remembering in young children* (pp. 223–248). Cambridge University Press.

Fivush, R., & Hudson, J. A. (1990). *Knowing and remembering in young children.* Cambridge University Press.

FMS Foundation (April 16, 1993) *Family survey: Partial report.* Philadelphia: False Memory Syndrome Foundation.

Freud, S. (1964). Constructions in analysis. In J. Strachey (Ed.), *Collected papers of Sigmund Freud* (Vol. 23, pp. 257–269). London: Hogarth Press. (Original work published 1937)

Freud, S. (1985). The aetiology of hysteria. Reprinted in J. M. Masson *The assault on truth,* pp. 259–290. New York: Penguin. (Original work published 1896)

Gibson, J. J. (1966). *The senses considered as perceptual systems.* Boston: Houghton Mifflin.

Gibson, J. J. (1979). *The ecological approach to visual perception.* Boston: Houghton Mifflin.

Greenwald, A. G. (1980). The totalitarian ego: Fabrication and revision of personal history. *American Psychologist, 35,* 603–618.

Hyman, I. E., Jr. (1992). Multiple approaches to remembering. *The Psychologist, 5,* 450–451.

Hyman, I. E., Jr., & Neisser, U. (1992). The role of the self in recollections of a seminar. *Journal of Narrative and Life History, 2,* 81–103.

James, W. (1890). *Principles of psychology.* New York: Henry Holt.

Larsen, S. F. (1992). Potential flashbulbs: Memories of ordinary news as the baseline. In E. Winograd & U. Neisser (Eds.), *Affect and accuracy in recall: Studies of "flashbulb" memories* (pp. 32–64). Cambridge University Press.

Laurence, J. R., & Perry, C. (1983). Hypnotically created memory among highly hypnotizable subjects. *Science, 222,* 523–524.

Linton, M. (1982). Transformations of memory in everyday life. In U. Neisser (Ed.), *Memory observed: Remembering in natural contexts* (pp. 77–91). New York: Freeman.

Loftus, E. F. (1993). The reality of repressed memories. *American Psychologist, 48,* 518–537.

Marcia, J. E. (1966). Development and validation of ego-identity status. *Journal of Personality and Social Psychology, 3,* 551–558.

Masson, J. M. (1985). *The assault on truth.* New York: Penguin.

Mead, G. H. (1934). *Mind, self and society.* Chicago: University of Chicago Press.

Neisser, U. (1981). John Dean's memory: A case study. *Cognition, 9,* 1–22.

Neisser, U. (1988). Five kinds of self-knowledge. *Philosophical Psychology, 1,* 35–59.

Neisser, U. (1992). The psychology of memory and the socio-linguistics of remembering. *The Psychologist, 5,* 451–452.

Neisser, U. (Ed.). (1993a). *The perceived self: Ecological and interpersonal sources of self-knowledge.* Cambridge University Press.

Neisser, U. (1993b). The self perceived. In U. Neisser (Ed.), *The perceived self: Ecological and interpersonal sources of self-knowledge* (pp. 3–21). Cambridge University Press.

Neisser, U., & Harsch, N. (1992). Phantom flashbulbs: False recollections of hearing the news about *Challenger.* In E. Winograd & U. Neisser (Eds.), *Affect and accuracy in recall: Studies of "flashbulb" memories.* Cambridge University Press.

Ofshe, R. J. (1992). Inadvertent hypnosis during interrogation: False confession due to dissociative state, misidentified multiple personality and the satanic cult hypothesis. *International Journal of Clinical and Experimental Hypnosis, 40,* 125–156.

Piaget, J. (1962). *Play, dreams, and imitation in childhood.* New York: Norton.

Polkinghorne, D. E. (1991). Narrative and self-concept. *Journal of Narrative and Life History, 1,* 135–153.

Rapaport, D. (1959). *Emotions and memory.* New York: International Universities Press.

Reed, E. S. (1988). *James J. Gibson and the psychology of perception.* New Haven, CT: Yale University Press.

Ross, M. (1989). Relation of implicit theories to the construction of personal histories. *Psychological Review, 96,* 341–357.

Ross, M., & Holmberg, D. (1990). Recounting the past: Gender differences in the recall of events in the history of a close relationship. In M. P. Zanna & J. M. Olson (Eds.), *Self-inference processes* (pp. 135–152). Hillsdale, NJ: Erlbaum.

Spence, D. P. (1982). *Narrative truth and historical truth: Meaning and interpretation in psychoanalysis.* New York: Norton.

Tomasello, M. (1993). On the interpersonal origins of self-concept. In U. Neisser (Ed.), *The perceived self: Ecological and interpersonal sources of self-knowledge* (pp. 174–184).

Vygotsky, L. (1978). *Mind in society: The development of higher psychological processes.* Cambridge, MA: Harvard University Press.

Wagenaar, W. (1986). My memory: A study of autobiographical memory over six years. *Cognitive Psychology, 18,* 225–252.

White, R. T. (1989). Recall of autobiographical events. *Applied Cognitive Psychology, 1,* 127–135.

Wright, L. (1993). Remembering Satan. *The New Yorker,* May 17, pp. 60–81; May 24, pp. 54–76.

2

Literary and psychological models of the self

DANIEL ALBRIGHT

Literature is a wilderness, psychology is a garden. To a literary critic, the categories of the psychologist often look impossibly spruce and well kempt: a hierarchy of brains, graduating from the limbic reptile to the cortical human; a hierarchy of orifices, graduating from the juvenile oral and anal to the adult genital; a hierarchy of selves, graduating from the vegetable self, dumbly growing in its plot, to the master self that coordinates and supervises all the lower selves. The literary critic is inclined to regard all these neatly cut divisions as mythologies, not truths; as beliefs designed not to describe reality but to increase the power, prestige, and earning capacity of psychologists. But I imagine that psychologists (who seem to be more polite than literary critics) whisper behind closed doors characterizations of literary critics equally unfavorable – that literary critics have a vested interest in keeping all texts mysterious, in denying the possibility of truth or insight or wisdom, in reducing all human life to a thicket of darkly intersecting, self-contradicting systems of signs, a jungle in which literary critics, blindly refusing the existence of eyesight, will nevertheless volunteer (for a fee) to act as guides. Furthermore, I imagine that psychologists, though they have sometimes looked for inspiration or confirmation to the masterpieces of literature, sometimes shake their heads or stare at the ceiling or mutter to themselves at the notions of human identity to be found among poets and novelists – such ranting, such willful incoherence, so much that is extraneous, undigested, or formulaic. In this essay I will try to explain the causes of this split between the psychological and the literary, and to speculate on whether literary constructions of selfhood might be of use to psychologists. In this task I am handicapped by the fact that, when I speak of psychology, I speak as a fool. It is possible that out of the fool's mouth will come wisdom, but Las Vegas advises betting against it.

Part of the divergence between psychology and literature can be explained by a difference of purpose: Roughly speaking, the purpose of psychology is psychiatric, to cure; the purpose of literature is ethical, to justify. When I read psychological treatises, I'm often struck by an assumption, often quite tacit, that the self is by nature whole, healthy, adjusted, and organized, and if (as is usually the case) the self manifests obvious flaws, the psychologist tends to explain this as a deviation, not as a situation to be taken for granted. It is a rare psychologist who lacks a vision of sanity; but this is precisely the condition we meet in many of the authors of classical literature. One of the reasons that Freud's late book *Civilization and Its Discontents* (1930) is popular among English teachers is that Freud there claims that neurosis is a necessary consequence of civilization, that self-realization and self-deformity are inextricably one; mental health is therefore a vain dream. This is exactly the message of Conrad's *Heart of Darkness* (1899), a frightening book that teaches that it is the *best* ideals of civilization that most fully corrupt; it is the message of Rimbaud's program for his poetry, which he described (in his letter to Paul Demeny, May 15, 1871) as self-mutilation, using a metaphor from a novel of Victor Hugo's in which gypsies maim children in order to create freaks for a freak show (Rimbaud, 1966, p. 306). Of course, if a few psychologists have the outlook of novelists, there are also a few novelists who have the outlook of psychologists. D. H. Lawrence, for example, not only wrote two books about the unconscious but developed an elaborate program for restoring the lost sanity of Western man – a silly program of abolishing literacy among the masses and asking men to wear red trousers and to work no more than four hours per day (see, for example, *Lady Chatterley's Lover* [1928], chap. 15). But, for the most part, the notable writers of recent times have said, in effect, we *are* our disease; to cure us would destroy us. This may be one explanation for the popularity of a medievally severe Christianity among such writers as T. S. Eliot: Whatever the defects of Christian theology, it does not teach that man is naturally healthy; instead it offers a vision of original sin – *inter urinas et faeces nascimur.* To literary minds, good psychic health has seemed almost an affront to human dignity, as if mankind is too rich, too capricious, too absurd, too magnificently corrupt, to be confined to some psychiatric schema of sanity; human faculties overflow limits, overflow categories and hierarchies. Especially during the last two centuries, literature has justified mankind by exalting its disorder, its superabundance. The point of James Joyce's *Ulysses* (1922) is not that Leopold Bloom's life is a low parody of Odysseus's, but that Bloom's life is far more interesting than Odysseus's, his journey – though constrained by a few city blocks and a span of 18 hours – more marvelous and praiseworthy. Though Bloom is impotent except when masturbating and his appetite for food is improved by the smell of urine, Joyce presents him as no less heroic for his psychopathology.

So, in a sense, literature tends to deny the possibility of psychology, if psychology requires a knowable, organizable picture of the mind; or, to put it another way, literature insists that psychology is an art, not a science. (Perhaps some psychologists would also agree with this characterization.) Literature is particularly suspicious of the remembered self, what Ulric Neisser (1988) calls the extended self. As Neisser notes, anyone who asks himself the question Who am I? will offer not only social and physical information – I am so-and-so's husband and I have a scar on my right hand – but also historical information. One might say that each of us carries around a videotape of our identity, or a kind of time-doll, painted with our own features, continually taking shape from infancy onward, continually becoming inflected by significant experiences, until it triumphantly culminates in our present form. We feel an amazing intimacy with this time-doll – not only do we cherish it as the dearest thing in our lives, but it cherishes us as well, it supports us, it defends us against the thinness, boredom, and futility of the immediate present, where no one is hugging us and we are in a lecture hall droning on or listening to someone else droning on. Our lives would be intolerable without some predicate, some ballast of identity, to provide a context for the wisps of thought and action that constitute our instantaneous selves. We may be small in space, but, as Proust noted, we are each of us giants in the dimension of time: "I should not fail to portray man, in this universe, as endowed with the length not of his body but of his years and as obliged . . . to drag them with him wherever he goes" (Proust, 1981, Vol. 3, p. 1104). However, this remembered self is a fragile construction. Proust and other writers have gone to astonishing lengths to strengthen and solidify it; but no matter how tight its sinews, how well articulated its joints, the time-doll is just a doll, and cannot be a complete, coherent human being, cannot relieve us of the responsibility for further thought and action, further investigation of ourselves, further development of ourselves. When we read works of fiction, we are always beguiled with the possibility that we are ourselves fictions, that the things we believe about ourselves are preposterous inventions – we wonder whether we are defective, not-too-imaginative novelists who have labored all our lives over the development of one expensive character, ourselves. Perhaps this literary notion renders psychology impossible. I'm not sure, for example, whether Freud could have developed psychoanalytic theory without asking himself whether hysterical women who reported abuse by the fathers were lying or telling the truth; but, if the self is genuinely fictitious, then *it is irrelevant whether such abuse actually occurred* – there no longer exists a distinction between verifiable and unverifiable memories. On the other hand, perhaps psychology can continue to diagnose and attempt to cure the self, even if the self is wholly fictitious, a plume of smoke that assumes an illusory solidity, an impressive volume, when beheld from a great distance. If a psychotherapist can convince the unhappy part of me that it is unreal, perhaps I can be happy. Perhaps psychology can survive and even prosper as a branch of fantastic literature. But I imagine that many psychologists will resist this trend, and retain the concept of the self's reality and integrity.

The literary attack on the concept of a remembered self comes principally from three directions: (1) the brokenness of memory, (2) the difficulty of affirming that all memories pertain to the same self; and (3) the impossibility of pretending that a subject is an object. All three of these attacks tend to dissolve the self, to expose it as fictitious, artificial, quaintly contrived.

1. The interrupted self

The clearest sign of the fragility, the lack of a proper foundation, of the remembered self is the fact that it begins and ends in a state of nothingness, and from beginning to end is riddled with nothingness. The first requirement for a theory of the remembered self is a theory of oblivion. In a dim way we have a linear sense of personal evolution, much enhanced since the invention of photography; sometimes, but seldom, we are uncomfortably aware that experiences that ought to have been memorable somehow have become erased from the record. The traditional psychoanalytic explanation for these gaps (or at least for some of them) is that we repress certain memories, make neurotic adjustments of circumstance in order to prevent a general loss of function. W. H. Auden nicely described this process in "In Memory of Sigmund Freud":

> He wasn't clever at all: he merely told
> the unhappy Present to recite the Past
>   like a poetry lesson till sooner
> or later it faltered at the line where
>
> long ago the accusations had begun,
> and suddenly knew by whom it had been judged . . .
>   (Auden, 1976, p. 216)

The psychoanalyst assumes, then, that the holes in the memory line represent particularly explosive, significant matters, and that the sanest man has the completest, most factually correct memory. It is not surprising that some poets, novelists, and other imaginative people have looked with scorn at this ideal Freudian dullard, who can attain great feats of self-recall only by draining his memories of all electric charge.

Furthermore, it is possible that the gaps in the remembered self simply overwhelm the memories. In 1917 Franz Kafka wrote a parable about the building of the Great Wall of China: It was constructed not consecutively, but in short stretches scattered over its entire length; the workers slowly labored to connect these segments, but never succeeded (Kafka,

1970, pp. 83–97). It is possible that the remembered self is like Kafka's wall, consisting more of holes than of bricks. Judging from the evidence of autobiography, it is difficult to provide more than a few erratic flashes of event; nothing makes us more suspicious of the autobiographer's veracity than a smooth, consecutive narration. T. S. Eliot lamented, in 1933, that memory is but a "few meagre arbitrarily chosen set of snapshots . . . the faded poor souvenirs of passionate moments" (Eliot, 1964a, p. 148), and even declared, in "The Dry Salvages,"

> That the future is a faded song, a Royal Rose or a lavender spray
> Of wistful regret for those who are not yet here to regret,
> Pressed between yellow leaves of a book that has never been
>   opened.
> (Eliot, 1953, p. 134)

In other words, the future, like the past, will be nothing more than a state of interrupted amnesia; the experiences that we have not yet experienced are in a sense predecayed, waiting for the scrapbook where all pictures have lost their true colors. The time-doll will extend into a future every bit as spongy, friable, lethargic, and cramped as the past. Kafka once told a young friend that people shouldn't greet one another on the street by saying, "How are you?"; instead, they should say, "How are you withering? How goes your esteemed decomposition?" (Janouch, 1971, p. 125).

The great writers are not only expert in memory; they are also expert in oblivion. Even Tennyson, not usually considered a radical poet, yearned strangely after a complete dismissal, a rejection of the remembered self. Two of his best poems, "The Lotos-Eaters" (1832; revised 1842) and "Enoch Arden" (1864), concern island dwellers who lose all sense of their prior, civilized lives, and dwindle into a state at once subhuman and superhuman. Enoch Arden, marooned on a desert isle after his ship sinks, eventually loses the capacity for language; he is finally discovered

> Brown, looking hardly human, strangely clad,
> Muttering and mumbling, idiotlike it seemed,
> With inarticulate rage, and making signs . . .
> (Lines 634–636; Tennyson, 1969, p. 1145)

The Lotos-Eaters remain able to speak, but their speech shows a continual contempt for those will not join them in their state of willed autistic stupor. They eat their drug, they stare hypnotized by the waves rolling onto the shore, they live as if already dead:

>   if his fellow spake,
> His voice was thin, as voices from the grave;

And deep-asleep he seemed, yet all awake,
And music in his ears his beating heart did make.
            (Lines 33–36; Tennyson, 1969, p. 431)

The Lotos-Eaters regard themselves as gods:

Let us swear an oath, and keep it with an equal mind,
In the hollow Lotos-land to live and lie reclined
On the hills like Gods together, careless of mankind.
For they lie beside their nectar . . .
. . . they smile in secret, looking over wasted lands,
Blight and famine, plague and earthquake, roaring deeps and fiery
    sands,
Clanging fights, and flaming towns, and sinking ships, and praying
    hands.
But they smile, they find a music centred in a doleful song
Steaming up, a lamentation and an ancient tale of wrong,
Like a tale of little meaning though the words are strong;
            (Lines 153–156, 159–164; Tennyson, 1969, p. 437)

I believe that Tennyson wrote here one of the finest descriptions of the oblivious self, the self that attains divine apathy, divine athambia, by relinquishing every vestige of history, family, culture. In some ways the remembered self, though it offers us pleasure and sustenance, is always a liability to our pride, our egotism. We want the self to be absolute, inviolable, its own law; and the remembered self can never be absolute – it has suffered too many humiliations, it is crammed too full of examples of its own impotence. To the remembered self there adhere a thousand filaments, connecting it to other people, people from whom it can never claim perfect independence. The oblivious self can be criticized on many grounds – as Bettelheim (1967, pp. 233–339) noted in his case study of "Joey," autistic children grow utterly impoverished by building foot-thick walls around themselves. But there is something gratifying about oblivion as well. One of the most luminous, energetically calm passages in modern music occurs in Stravinsky's *Perséphone* (1934), accompanying a text (by André Gide) that describes how the souls of the newly dead drink the waters of Lethe and forget their previous lives; and similar evocations of amnesiac purity and lucidity of being can be found in many places. The Lotos-Eaters' song seduces to some degree all of us.

Tennyson derived the episode of the impassive gods who relish the spectacle of human misery from Lucretius's *De Rerum Natura*, Book 3, an episode that has appealed to many writers, including Matthew Arnold and Virginia Woolf as well. There is a famous meditation in Woolf's novel *To the Lighthouse* (1927), in which the heroine, Mrs. Ramsay, knits a stocking and feels herself becoming detached from the worry and frenzy of family life:

To be silent; to be alone. All the being and the doing, expansive, glittering, vocal, evaporated; and one shrunk, with a sense of solemnity, to being oneself, a wedge-shaped core of darkness, something invisible to others. Although she continued to knit, and sat upright, it was thus that she felt herself; and this self having shed its attachments was free for the strangest adventures. When life sank down for a moment, the range of experience seemed limitless. . . . There were all the places she had not seen; the Indian plains; she felt herself pushing aside the thick leather curtain of a church in Rome. This core of darkness could go anywhere, for no one saw it. . . . There was freedom, there was peace, there was, most welcome of all, a summoning together, a resting on a platform of stability. Not as oneself did one find rest ever, in her experience (she accomplished here something dexterous with her needles) but as a wedge of darkness. Losing personality, one lost the fret, the hurry, the stir. . . . (Woolf, 1955, pp. 95–96)

Woolf here suggested that the remembered self and the oblivious self can attain a remarkable co-presence. There is a little Lucretian god inside each of us, at all times, lolling on his private cloud and faintly smiling at the general tragedy of human life; it takes only an instant of tranquillity to liberate him. At the bottom of personality is a depersonalized entity, a wedge of darkness, evidently more real, more stable, more omnipresent, than the various fabrications built on top – the social self, the remembered self. According to Woolf, we each of us move continually, easily, back and forth between the ordinary self and the self that the ordinary self embarrasses – between the time-doll and a doll that has no face. This wedge of darkness does not discredit the remembered self, but, by offering an exhilarating alternative model of identity, it makes the remembered self less engrossing, more dispensable. I am sure that Woolf tended to regard the remembered self as accident, the wedge of darkness as essence: The spookiest moment in *To the Lighthouse* comes when a postimpressionist painter, in no way privy to Mrs. Ramsay's meditations, chooses to portray her, while she sits by her window reading to her young son, as a purple triangle (Woolf, 1955, pp. 81, 299). In this manner the overt visual self and the fundamental self converge as an abstract geometrical shape, whose simplicity puts to shame the thousand inflections and subtleties of the self we remember.

But the greatest liability of the remembered self, as I understand it, lies in its origin. The remembered self always appeals to the biological model; even if we fail to make exact correlations between recalled events and the exact degree of development of our bodies, we assume that such correlations exist and are important. The remembered self is, one might say, a colored image of the physical body altering through time and impinging on circumstance. Indeed, if a memory is not directly grounded on the sensorium, does not directly summon up some phantom of the body that experienced the original event, we usually do not use the word memory; we call it an idea, a dream, a vagrant feeling. Memories gain precision to the degree that we can conjure up the rememberer, on a certain day and in a certain place; without a biophysical presence, a memory is a dim ghost lacking a house to haunt.

The biological model of the remembered self is comforting in many ways, especially because it offers the certainty of continuity. As we have seen, the remembered self contains huge gaps; but the body, we know, has been continuously in existence since the day of our birth, and affirms the unity of being that memory fails to affirm. We graft our remembered self, a comparatively flimsy construct, onto our physical body, which, whatever its defects of health and talent, has been triumphantly persistent through the span of our lives; and much of our so-called remembered self is merely the illusion of continuity derived from the physical body and from logical deductions that connect one remembered experience to the next. I see myself at the age of 7, being lifted onto a horse; I see an adult put a spoon in my hand, and balance an egg on that spoon; I see in my mother's house the ribbon I got for coming in 23rd out of 23 in the race. I can imagine the rest of the scene – the horses led to the starting line, the egg immediately falling off my spoon, the general derision – but this is purely factitious, a pseudo-memory derived by filling in the blanks, because I assume that somehow there was an *I* there to connect the scenes that I can remember. I wonder how many of my memories I can confidently say are not pseudomemories, imaginations of unremembered memories.

But there is one significant failure in the biological model: Biology offers us a lucid explanation for our origins, but memory cannot; it is hard even to pretend that the remembered self extends backward much before the age of 2. Biology tells us that we existed long before that – our father seems to have done something to our mother, fertilizing an egg from which we grew. But what is the egg from which the remembered self hatches? The unlucky truth, I believe, is that there isn't any: Our memories begin, not in a feeling of pregnant indiscriminate fullness of being, but in a few faint wisps, contrails of the jet long since vanished from the sky. Memoirists who describe their first memories usually speak of the trivial or the embarrassing: Gide sitting under a table with another little boy, inspecting penises (Gide, 1963, p. 3); Yeats sitting on someone's knee, fearful when a servant tells him that a messenger lad intends to blow up the town (Yeats, 1965, p. 1); Joyce (if the first page of *A Portrait of the Artist as a Young Man* [1916] is true of his own life) hearing nursery tales and wetting his bed. Only a few memoirists report a conspicuously happy first memory – the baby Goethe, for example, throwing plates out of a window and watching them crash on the pavement. For the most part, when we look backward to our origin, we find a sort of juvenile senility, Alzheimer's other disease, a frustrating, inconsequential, nearly meaningless set of stray impressions. This is the very ground of the re-membered self, a species of quicksand. There is a tendency among certain authors to supply the illusion of an egg or embryo for the remembered self by a kind of literary trickery; notice the metaphors in Virginia Woolf's description of her first memory:

> If life has a base that it stands upon, if it is a bowl that one fills and fills and fills – then my bowl without a doubt stands upon this memory. It is of lying half asleep, half awake, in bed in the nursery at St. Ives. It is of hearing the waves breaking, one, two, one, two, and sending a splash of water over the beach; and then break-ing, one, two, one, two, behind a yellow blind. It is of hearing the blind draw its little acorn across the floor as the wind blew the blind out . . . of feeling the purest ecstasy I can conceive. . . . the feeling . . . of lying in a grape and seeing through a film of semi-transparent yellow. . . . (Woolf, 1976, pp. 64–65)

This is brilliantly written, but unconvincing; the vision of one's infant self as a kind of grapeseed lying in an amnion of light seems imported by an adult sensibility. It is hard not to patronize one's own origin, hard not to invest it with pomp.

I wonder whether the role of infantile amnesia in psychology and intel-lectual history has been given its due. It is possible that the human race would have a different concept of itself if people could remember back to the womb – in that case the remembered self might deserve more pres-tige. A few people, such as Salvador Dali and Samuel Beckett, claim to remember experiences before they were born; and, with the popularity of the sonogram, I expect fetal life to become increasingly memorable – photography is an immense aid to memory. But for most of us there is only a void at the beginning; and even Beckett and Dali do not remember the instant of their conception. Because of infantile amnesia, we know that there is a self that is completely unremembered; and from this origi-nal separation of memory and being the most remarkable philosophical fictions can be derived. Aristotle's concept of the soul, the seat of affect; the Hindu and Christian concept of the soul, a naked shred of identity surviving after death, though possibly much deformed by life; Locke's *tabula rasa;* Lacan's stage before the mirror stage; all these philosophies assume that the remembered self is inscribed upon an unremembered self. In many of these philosophies, the pure, potent subself lies in much danger of contamination as it falls into history, into memory: how often Christianity tends to sentimentalize the fetus, despite the fact that such sentimentality contradicts the Christian doctrine of original sin; how much Jacques Lacan (1977, p. 48) shudders at the thought that the baby will recognize its image in the mirror, will turn into a "slave of language" swaddled, stifled in self-images, will trade its divine indeterminacy of be-ing for the prison of a finite, objective self, "the armour of an alienating identity" (Lacan, 1977, p. 4). Indeed it is possible that every myth of the fall of man depends on infantile amnesia as a vacant surface on which to imagine an unfallen state. If this is admitted, then the remembered self consists chiefly of the record of our estrangement from the good – in a sense, our estrangement from ourselves.

To an unreligious man the state of infantile amnesia may represent the dangerous possibility that the infant within us can swallow up our evolved, adult self; we may forget ourselves into a kind of morbid and childish self-extinction. Freud, for example, wrote that "we must not fail to observe that the existence of infantile amnesia provides a new point of comparison between the mental states of children and psychoneurotics . . . the sexuality of psychoneurotics has remained at, or been carried back to, an infantile stage. . . . It may be said that without infantile amnesia there would be no hysterical amnesia" (Freud, 1962, pp. 41–42). I wonder whether Freud might have concluded that infantile amnesia was the ultimate locus of the principle of Thanatos. But to a religious man, the remembered self must be interrupted, superseded, by appeals to the unremembered self, the oblivious self, the self not alienable from reality. To some extent, the function of art, like religion, is to invoke wonder; and wonder may be nothing more than the emotion caused by a glimpse of what is not yet comprehended, grasped – a retrieval and simulation of the infantile prelinguistic mind in which nothing is securely remembered because nothing can be encoded in language. In this way the artist is complicit with oblivion, working in penumbral regions of thought and feeling slowly being mastered, incorporated into the lucid and memorable.

But I do not want to do what I accuse others of doing – that is, sentimentalizing oblivion, infantile amnesia. The amnesiac self, like the remembered self, is best regarded as a construction, a fiction. The empty billboard onto which the sign is glued is itself only another sign, not some magical pre-semiotic condition that upholds or stabilizes the toothpaste advertisement, the grim face of the Republican candidate for sheriff, or the notice of the coming strawberry festival.

2. The plural self

We now come to a second vulnerability of the remembered self, its unity. We like to think that all our memories pertain to a single self; that we clasp intimately one doll, accreting and mutating over time. Of course, many works of literature, philosophy, and psychology deny the singularity of the self; but we do not like to think of ourselves as essentially plural. In one production of *Hamlet*, Hamlet was played by eight actors, all on stage at once, dividing Hamlet's lines among them and responding differently to the other characters' words and actions. But one Daniel Albright is enough; I don't want competing selves in my house, eating my food and spilling crumbs on my floor.

And yet, when I try to account for my inner life – my conflicting desires, my moments of decision – I tend to see it as a drama with several actors, each a fraction of myself. There is a literary term for this: *psychomachia*, soul-battle, named after an old poem by Prudentius. Much great literature is written in psychomachia form, such as the 15th-century morality play *Everyman,* or the House of Alma episode of Spenser's *The Faerie Queene* (1596). In the simplest kind of psychomachia, a devil painted with my features whispers in one ear, and an angel in the other; but a psychomachia may have a cast not just of three, but of thousands. Classical psychoanalysis also tends to populate the mind's theater with warring selves, figments of identity; Auden wrote a nice parody of this, combining Freud, *Everyman,* and a subway scene in which a woman steps on one's toe:

SELF: (*in whom the physical sensation of pain has become the mental passion of anger*):
    "Care for my anger! Do something about it!"
COGNITIVE EGO: "You are angry because of the pain caused by this large lady
    who, carelessly but not intentionally, has trodden on your corn. If you
    decide to relieve your feelings, you can give her a sharp kick on the
    ankle without being noticed."
SELF: "Kick her."
SUPER-EGO: . . . "Unintentional wrongs must not be avenged. Ladies must not
    be kicked. Control your anger!"
LADY: (*noticing what she has done*):
    "I beg your pardon! I hope I didn't hurt you."
SELF: "Kick her!"
SUPER-EGO: "Smile! Say 'Not at all, Madam.'"
VOLITIONAL EGO: (*to the appropriate voluntary muscles*):
    either "Kick her!"
    or "Smile! Say 'Not at all, Madam.'" (Auden, 1962, pp. 111–112)

Each of us, then, comprises (among other selves) a hothead and a dispassionate prissy fellow, a Jack Klugman and a Tony Randall, pressing their competing claims before some neutral adjudicator.

And yet, these divisions of identity do not seem particularly troubling. Even if Auden's comic skit were changed into a serious drama of temptation, in which personifications of envy, greed, and lust struggled for control of the soul's mansion, this schema would not disturb one's sense of one's own integrity. I will not fly off into pieces if impulse and restraint war within me; indeed, if they did not, I would not find myself to be recognizably human.

There are works of literature, however, which do assault one's innermost feeling that one's experiences and memories refer to a single person. "Je est un autre," says Rimbaud (1966, p. 304) – "I is somebody else";

he goes on to note that the soul must make itself monstrous. Kafka (1970, p. 175) puts the matter quite explicitly: "There exist in the same human being varying perceptions of one and the same object which differ so completely from each other that one can only deduce the existence of different subjects in the same human being" ("Reflections," No. 68); and Kafka's fiction disorients the reader precisely because the complacent, day-to-day self is continually getting unselved, metamorphosed into a dungbeetle or compelled to undergo some other unpleasant sort of transfiguration. Kafka's reflection on the plural self is also corroborated by T. S. Eliot, who, before attempting a career as a man of letters, wrote a Ph.D. dissertation on philosophy; indeed if World War I had not prevented him from returning to Harvard to defend it, Eliot might have had an academic career as a professor of philosophy. In his dissertation Eliot (1964b, p. 79) claims that "the soul is, in fact, the whole world of its experience at any moment" and, furthermore, the soul varies continually with its experience. If a bird cheeps, if a fluorescent light flickers, my world changes, and I change commensurately; I am always turning into someone else. Eliot (1964b, p. 91) even makes the astonishing claim that the difference between myself at one instant and myself at another instant is no less than the difference between myself and Ulric Neisser, or between Ulric Neisser and Sophia Loren. The human self is crazily mutable; my face may seem impassive, but beneath the calm exterior I am shifting, shifting, shifting, growing unrecognizable from moment to moment. Eliot (1962, pp. 37–42) embodied this philosophy in a famous poem, in which a woman remembers an exhilarating sled ride, and a Cornish sailor sings of the wind blowing him homeward, and we hear the most elegant, the most intelligent "Shakespeherian Rag" (*The Waste Land* [1922]). The original title of *The Waste Land* was *He do the Police in Different Voices,* a line by Dickens describing a half-wit in *Our Mutual Friend* (1865) who liked to use vocal impersonations when reading the newspaper out loud. The original title is certainly less grand and imposing than the one we know, but it provides the important interpretative clue that the whole poem is an act of continuous impersonation – the ideal reciter is someone like Richard Pryor or Rich Little, capable of switching instantly from one voice to another, from a German countess to the prophet Ezekiel to the sailor in the first act of Wagner's *Tristan und Isolde* to an Englishman consulting a fortune-teller. The soul *is* the world of its experience, and the world of its experience is huge and shapeless; every finite personality is just a still frame in a film that includes all selves.

We have seen that one alternative to the remembered self is the oblivious self, the doll with no face; here we have a second alternative to the remembered self – the plural self, the doll with all conceivable faces, pure silly putty. According to this model, the remembered self is simply a cold, puny, arbitrary selection from a dazzling array of possible selves – there is no line of demarcation between memory and fantasy, between selves that we have been and selves we might be. In his dissertation, Eliot (1964b, pp. 112, 147) notes that hallucinations are every bit as real as anything else: "Reality contains irreducible contradictions and irreconcilable points of view," and we are all engaged in the painful struggle to put together "jarring and incompatible" selves, jarring and incompatible worlds. In a late poem Eliot described how our lives fork backward into memory and fantasy, fantasy no less real, no less significant than memory:

> Footfalls echo in the memory
> Down the passage which we did not take
> Towards the door we never opened
> Into the rose-garden.
> ("Burnt Norton" [1936],
> Eliot, 1958, p. 117)

The remembered self, then, is not linear, but a matrix ramifying backward in all directions, a garden of forking paths that converge in the present.

For many authors, the self is less a single determinate human shape than a quarry from which any human shape can be cut. Browning, in the 19th century, made his collected poems a kind of museum or psychiatric encyclopedia in which almost any character type, any healthy or deviant personality, can be found. But in some of his best poems he presents, not a finished, developed portrait or case history, but a loose, disorganized human entity, a simulacrum of his own creative energy. Such is Fra Lippo Lippi, a Renaissance painter (as Browning depicted him in 1855) too wild and ravenous to be confined to a particular set of character traits; and such is Browning's Caliban, whose ego, though vehement, is so muddled and messy that it speaks in the third person:

> 'Will sprawl, now that the heat of day is best,
> Flat on his belly in the pit's much mire,
> With elbows wide, fists clenched to prop his chin.
> And, while he kicks both feet in the cool slush,
> And feels about his spine small eft-things course,
> Run in and out each arm, and make him laugh:
> And while above his head a pompion-plant,
> Coating the cave-top as a brow its eye,
> Creeps down to touch and tickle hair and beard
>
>   .   .   .   .
> [He] talks to his own self, howe'er he please. . . .
> ("Caliban upon Setebos" [1864], lines 1–9, 15;
> Browning, 1981, Vol. 1, p. 805)

Caliban is, so to speak, one huge tickle, an ideal specimen of polymorphous perversity, a human amoeba. Like Browning himself, he is a blob in whom all personalities are latent; silly putty given a voice and some theological speculations (not surprisingly, Caliban dreams of a God who looks exactly like Caliban).

Browning was the first of many poets who specialized in constructing a wide variety of masks for themselves; and his successors were more explicit than Browning himself about the poet's relation to his masks. Ezra Pound modeled his life's work, the *Cantos*, on Browning's *Sordello* (1840); in one of Pound's letters (from 1920) we find a strong statement of the poet's sense of the unstructuredness of his personality:

While "Homage to S. Propertius", Seafarer, Exile's Letter, and Mauberley [these are all poems in which the poet wears a historical mask] are all "me" in one sense; my personality is certainly a great slag heap of stuff which has to be excluded from each of this [*sic*] crystalizations. And an expression of the "personality" wd. be a slag heap and not art. (Pound, 1982, p. 42)

It was Pound who popularized the term *persona* in literary criticism – the Latin word for mask, derived from *per* + *sonare*, something spoken through; and clearly Pound conceived every mask as a kind of machine for specifying a precise vocal tone out of a whole spectrum of possibilities. Long before Pound's time, John Milton described the creation of the universe as a process of retraction: In the beginning God filled the universe, but withdrew himself in order to provide room for the stars and the planets, room for the operation of human free will. As God the Father says to the Son, riding into Chaos:

> Boundless the Deep, because I am who fill
> Infinitude, nor vacuous the space.
> Though I uncircumscrib'd myself retire,
> And put not forth my goodness, which is free
> To act or not, Necessity and Chance
> Approach not mee, and what I will is Fate.
>   (*Paradise Lost* [1674],
>   Book 7, lines 168–172; Milton, 1957, p. 350)

Similarly Pound conceives human personality as a process of retraction: We suppress extraneous parts of our being in order to show some lithe, smooth, shapely, consistent mask to the outer world – and perhaps to ourselves as well. How much of our remembered self is carefully, scrupulously edited in order to conform to some vision of how we would like our self to appear? If we speak of a remembered self, we should also speak of an editorial self that consciously or unconsciously selects the memories that wrap us round with the sense of our dignity, our erotic

power, our nonchalance, our good will toward mankind, all those pleasures that our self-consideration craves.

But, as I have said, we like to be relieved of the burden of a remembered self from time to time, and literature is the most excellent of es-
capes, for the reader as well as the writer. We have seen that oblivion
provides a relief from the remembered self, but a similar relief is provided by substituting alternative remembered selves for our own – and
such substitutions can be easily achieved by reading poems and novels.
T. S. Eliot (1964b, p. 124) said in his dissertation that "no really 'vital'
character in fiction is altogether a conscious construction of the author.
On the contrary, it may be a sort of parasitic growth upon the author's
personality, developing by internal necessity." Similarly, Carl Jung once
said (in a lecture of October 1935 that changed the course of Samuel
Beckett's career – see Bair, 1978, p. 208) that a novelist's characters were
simply the author's psychological complexes, elaborated into little sub-
personalities of their own (Jung, 1968, pp. 80–81). One might go further
and suggest that every novel is a spell designed to implant this parasite,
to transfer the psychological complex, into the reader's sensibility. The
novel's essential effect is this pleasing intimacy between reader and character, as if the reader were offered a parallel world in which he was to
watch himself evolve in some unexpected way. Just as an amputee may
feel phantom sensations in an absent arm or leg, so we are capable of
evolving phantom sensibilities that grope outward toward experiences
that never happened to our usual selves. Our remembered selves are
everywhere informed by and dependent on literary concoctions, sometimes quite flimsy and absurd literary concoctions, and it is possible to be
uncertain of the exact boundaries of our affective systems – just where
our own memories end and literary pseudomemories begin. Not all of us
would go so far as Oscar Wilde (1973, p. 976), who claimed, "One of the
greatest tragedies of my life is the death of Lucien de Rubempré [a character in a Balzac novel]"; but we all know intelligent people who seem to
enact in their daily lives scenes from novels – sometimes even Harlequin
romances.

The remembered self consists partly of images, but it is also highly verbal in nature, an affair of aggregated tonalities. I recently listened to a
tape recording of myself at the age of 17, and found it an amazing experience; the mere cadences of my own voice, speaking a time dialect utterly
foreign to me now, brought back, not a flood of memories, but a kinesthetic sense of a lost self – how I once held my body when I walked, how
I gestured when I spoke. Sometimes when I read poems I feel a fainter
version of a similar sensation – the illusion that, by speaking a poem of
Wordsworth's to myself, I feel what it was like to live inside Wordsworth's
body, tall, extremely strong, slightly shambling and loose-jointed – as if

Wordsworth's whole person, whole body image, could be conveyed through the tone of his words. A poem, in this sense, is a kind of sensibility machine, recasting the mind that reads it into an alien shape. I have read that schizophrenics who hear voices can silence those voices simply by holding their mouths open – which suggests that imaginary voices that threaten or cajole are simply sublaryngeal phantoms, elaborate externalizations of mutterings under the breath. In a less pathological way the reader of poetry, the bathtub baritone, experiments with new personages to add to the chorus of remembered selves; for we fork backward, not only down the path of the official remembered self, not only down the paths of the selves we might have been if we had married our high school sweetheart or entered the Revlon management training program, but down the paths of Pip, Stephen Dedalus, Elizabeth Bennet, and Don Giovanni as well. To some extent the remembered self is simply the quoted self, the plagiarized self.

But it is easy to sentimentalize the plural self – "Do I contradict myself? / Very well then I contradict myself, / (I am large, I contain multitudes)" (Whitman, 1959, p. 68: "Song of Myself" [1855]) – and I want to avoid that. The plural self is as fragile and dubious as the singular self; fantasy and literature cannot provide the authenticity of being that memory fails to provide. To insist that the self is singular or that the self is plural is to fall into error – indeed the self that is either too singular or too plural is likely to be diseased. On one hand lies neurotic rigidity, repetitiousness of behavior; on the other lies multiple personality disorder – the division of the self into a personality that fights, a personality that flees, a personality that destroys, a personality that cherishes, a whole congeries of terrified half-selves. (I have read that a single person can be so fissile that one personality has allergies, or heart arrhythmia, while other personalities do not.) It is perhaps harder to see that excessive unity of self can be as harmful as disunity; but one study of autopsies of schizophrenic brains showed that the corpora callosa (connecting the two hemispheres of the brain) were abnormally thick, as if the unicameral mind, all functions integrated, were an especially sick mind. But I must not appeal to physiology, especially when my source is that learned journal *Psychology Today;* it is enough to point out that every model of the self is potentially a prison that inhibits self-development; every idea about the self is potentially a weapon that can be turned against it.

3. The subject as object

So far we have examined how the self has been conceived, or misconceived, in conformity to certain ideals: first, the biological model, and second, the arithmetical model. Now we come to the third and final category of vulnerable models of selfhood: the grammatical. Grammar posits two modes of the self, the nominative and the accusative: I and me. Psychology, like philosophy, tends to demote the self, especially the remembered self, to the accusative: The remembered self is a kind of concrete aggregate of *me's*, the totality of all predicates that have gathered themselves around the rememberer, the *I*. Now the division between the rememberer and the remembered seems so natural, so fundamental, that it may seem as if it is impossible to conceive any theory of self that lacks it; as Jorge Luis Borges (1977, p. 123) has said, "Memory . . . makes of anyone both a spectator and an actor." But I believe that the remembered self cannot be treated strictly in the accusative, strictly as an object: Subjectivity keeps leaking into it, no matter how hard we try to confine the subject to the nominative realm.

Again all models of the self derived from portraiture, sculpture, or photography are misleading, because an image can be treated as a genuine object. But the remembered self can never be opaque as a scientist would like; instead of remaining fixed in one place as a sensible thing, susceptible to study and analysis, the remembered self is disturbingly translucent. I will offer two brief examples, one from my own experience, one from literature. Somehow I know, or think I know, that two of my memories refer to events earlier than those referred to in all other memories. In one of them I am wearing short pants, sitting on the tickly wicker bench seat of a train car, and playing with a foam rubber lobster. In the other I am getting out of my bathtub at home, reaching up to a towel folded over a bar too high to be grasped, and thinking that some day I will be tall enough to get that towel. Of the rubber lobster I have nothing to say, but my other first memory is suggestive: At the beginning of time I see myself in the act of seeing myself, in the act of imagining a future in which I will be different. Instead of a snapshot, memory provides a permeable vista endlessly adjusting its focus, endlessly adjusting its focuser; I behold myself beholding another myself beholding another myself in infinite regression. Introspection does not float on memory, it sinks into it; time is a surface without surface tension, and the self deliquesces into a series of transparencies, half subjects and half objects, each a spectator and an actor, an aptote without a definite grammatical case. The remembered self is a jellyfish little distinguishable from the water world that surrounds it, from its prior and future states of being. Borges liked to recall his father's theory of memory: that we do not remember an event, but instead remember the last time we remembered that event:

"I have no memories whatever, I have no images whatever, about my childhood, about my youth.["] And then he illustrated that, with a pile of coins. He piled one coin on top of the other and said, "Well, now this first coin, the bottom coin, this would be the first image, for example, the house of my childhood. Now this second would be a memory I had of that house when I went to Buenos Aires. Then the third one another memory and so on. And as in every memory there's a slight distortion, I don't suppose that my memory of today ties in with the first images I had," so that, he said, "I try not to think of things in the past because if I do I'll be thinking back on those memories and not on the actual images themselves." And then that saddened me. To think maybe we have no true memories of youth. (Burgin, 1970, p. 26)

This may not be a sound theory, but as a metaphor it is revealing: Past events do not lie brightly, overtly before our gaze, but are instead swaddled in a thick tissue of prior recalls and prior recallers, each adding colors and shadows to the original. Borges's father was sad because each act of memory estranged him further from the past he wished to recall; but in another sense he was appropriating his past, making it more truly his own, even as he distorted it; by his analogy, he was increasing his store of wealth, his coin supply, as he multiplied counterfeits of his prior selves. He was inserting himself as rememberer, as a subject, into his personal history; this subjectivity may express itself chiefly by distorting what it studies, but it is still a kind of personalizing, a warming of the bare bones of things. The remembered self always retains a certain nominativeness, a sense of its capacity to choose, discriminate, evaluate, decide; its choices, its discriminations, its evaluations, its decisions, have all long since been made and dismissed, but its ego force, its feeling of consequentiality, nevertheless remain. The little boy who struggled to reach the towel is now a man who grasps towels without much difficulty; but, in memory, all these states, the little boy, the man whom the little boy dreamed of becoming, the man as he now is, coexist on a single deep-focused plane, a plane not like a photograph or a painting because the spectator dwells inside the action at which he stares.

But I promised a literary as well as a personal example, and here it is – a passage from Virginia Woolf's "The Mark on the Wall" (1921), a story or meditation in which a woman woolgathers while staring at a speck of something above her fireplace mantel:

I wish I could hit upon a pleasant track of thought, a track indirectly reflecting credit upon myself, for those are the pleasantest thoughts, and very frequent even in the minds of modest mouse-coloured people, who believe genuinely that they dislike to hear their own praises. They are not thoughts directly praising oneself; that is the beauty of them; they are thoughts like this:

"And then I came into the room. They were discussing botany. I said how I'd seen a flower growing on a dust heap on the site of an old house in Kingsway. The seed, I said, must have been sown in the reign of Charles the First. What flowers grew in the reign of Charles the First?" I asked – (But I don't remember the answer.) Tall flowers with purple tassels to them perhaps. And so it goes on. All the time I'm dressing up the figure of myself in my own mind, lovingly, stealthily, not openly adoring it, for if I did that, I should catch myself out, and stretch my hand at once for a book in self-protection. Indeed, it is curious how instinctively one protects the image of oneself from idolatry or any other handling that could make it ridiculous, or too unlike the original to be believed in any longer. (Woolf, 1949, p. 40)

The remembered self here is a figure with a built-in capacity for self-modification: It shapes itself discreetly, elegantly, in order to conform to the rememberer's desire to think well of herself. The rememberer is not the subject and the remembered self is not the object; instead, both are dancers cooperant to a warm glow of self-satisfaction. The rememberer must maintain that she does not voluntarily shape the remembered self in order to suit her – that would be too gross a fiction; she must attribute this will to be admirable, to make a *bella figura* in one's own sight, to some delegate, some subself, halfway between her consciousness and her remembered self. Shaping force, subjectivity, does not inhere entirely in the present – it extends backward over the whole field of memory. There are few passages in literature that better describe the tenderness, the reverence, the slight bad faith, with which we treat our remembered self, allow it to develop pretty features as if by its own desire. We pretend that the remembered self is an object, achieved, neutralized, almost dead, because we want to have power over it – we want to be masters of ourselves. But, as Woolf suggested, and Proust suggested still more strongly, the remembered self is far from docile, obedient; it can dominate, can overwhelm, the rememberer.

I wonder whether, in philosophy, psychology, and literature alike, we do not tend to give too much prestige to the subject, and not enough to the object. Just as there is a subjective tint in the remembered self, so there is a good deal of objecthood, thinglikeness, in the consciousness. If we were really pure subjects, as Jean-Paul Sartre thought, our freedom would be unlimited, in no wise constrained by our previous actions; but who, besides Sartre, would live or even want to live without momentum or inertia, as an arbitrary autochthon? It is possible that Lacanian therapy, which tries to persuade the patient that all personality is paranoia (see Schneiderman, 1983, p. 150), that all self-image is self-alienation, self-imprisonment, is not likely to be effective in all cases. This is, perhaps, Lacan's error: to believe that there is some component of identity that remains pure, inviolate, behind the armor of personality; some component of identity that remains forever alienated from the assumed self-image. But it seems more likely to me that every part of the self, even the most metaphysically invulnerable, is subject to experience, deformity. Experience has altered the rememberer as well as the remembered self: Memory has its eyelids and its sphincters, its plugged canals, just like our external organs, and our mode of remembering has been reshaped along with the content of our memories. Much reading can either weaken the eyes or improve reading speed; but in either case the way we see has altered, along with the objects that we see; and the same is true of remembering. We identify ourselves with some caricature of the remembered self – a kind of self-imago (compare Lacan, 1977, p. 5) – and that mask in turn obscures and highlights, changes, the remembered self that the rememberer contemplates.

Philosophy and literature have often exalted the subject by claiming that it is above or beyond knowledge: Schopenhauer (1950, Vol. 2, p. 412), for example, loftily announces: "The knower himself, as such, cannot be known; otherwise he would be the known of another knower." And Beckett dedicated his masterwork, the trilogy of novels, to the elusiveness of the subject, the untellability of the teller: in *The Unnamable* (1953), the unnamable subject experiments with various objectifications of itself – a one-legged world wanderer named Mahood, an armless and legless version of the same man who sits in a jar in order to advertise a restaurant, and a naked infant named Worm at the center of an arena – but at length discards each of these representations of itself, all representations of itself. The desire to be nobody – as a later Beckett hero puts it, "here I come again . . . the square root of minus one, having terminated my humanities" (Beckett, 1967, p. 128) – sounds like an abject desire, but it is really a kind of pride: No finite self could do justice to my plasticity, my freedom, my dilation of being. Beckett's heroes are mutilated nobodies, but never humble nobodies, never mere nobodies; they aspire not just to be *nemo* but to be *nemissimo*. My own guess it that it is idle to pretend that the knower can't be known, that the teller can't be told; the knower *can* be known, to the exact extent that the known can be known, for subject and object are not susceptible to rigid dichotomy. If you ask my family and my friends who I am, their information will not be complete, but it will be correct. In other words, *I* is *me*.

I can add one last argument to show that the categories of subject and object are not strictly applicable to human beings – that the split between *I* and *me* is somewhat a sham. There is a sense in which the remembered self is the inventor, and the present self is its invention – I am the object intended by my prior self, probably an imperfectly realized object. I remember the adolescent who wished to go to college, to become a college teacher himself, and I have followed the path that he determined; he was in a sense nominative, I am in a sense accusative. As Wordsworth (1969, p. 62) put it in "My Heart Leaps Up" (1807), the child is the father of the man.

Throughout this essay, I have been rehearsing, and to some extent agreeing with, certain literary ideas that attack conventional notions of the self. But we need both the conventional notion of the self and the attack upon it – the attack must never vanquish it once and for all. There is a place for the conventional notion of the self: It is convenient and necessary to regard one's past as a settled image, objectified and bulky. The best metaphor I can find for the conventional notion of the remembered self is a kind of sculpture produced, not by cutting away stone or by shaping metal, but by adding little pieces to a central armature, like the head of John F. Kennedy in the Kennedy Center in Washington, which appears to have been assembled by gluing together little bits of bronze popcorn. Every day I add another few bits to my portrait-bust of myself – or life glues those bits on for me, whether I choose them or not. But there is another, less conventional image of the remembered self, radically subjective, a self in a condition of free fall, sheer vertigo. In this sense I am not a grounded, reasonable thing, but I am a falling body, and I am the gravity that pulls me down, and I am the air that buffets me into various shapes. The conventional vision of self offers me security; the unconventional one frightens me and frees me. Perhaps to psychologists all these metaphors – Woolf's and Borges's and Eliot's and especially mine – will seem inadequate, beneath the level of discourse on which solid insight can be founded. But it is arguable, even without recourse to metaphor, that metaphors are the only proper way to describe the remembered self, since memory itself is only a metaphor, a dim surrogate for past time that can never be recovered, never embodied, never made to sit still.

REFERENCES

Auden, W. H. (1962). *The dyer's hand.* New York: Random House.
Auden, W. H. (1976). *Collected poems* (Edward Mendelson, Ed.). New York: Random House.
Bair, Deirdre (1978). *Samuel Beckett: A biography.* New York: Harcourt Brace.
Beckett, Samuel (1967). *Stories and texts for nothing.* New York: Grove Press.
Bettelheim, Bruno (1967). *The empty fortress.* New York: Free Press.
Borges, Jorge Luis (1977). *The book of sand.* New York: Dutton.
Browning, Robert (1981). *The poems* (John Pettigrew, Ed.). New Haven, CT: Yale University Press.
Burgin, Richard (1970). *Conversations with Jorge Luis Borges.* New York: Avon.
Eliot, T. S. (1953). *The complete poems and plays, 1909–1950.* New York: Harcourt Brace.
Eliot, T. S. (1964a). *The use of poetry and the use of criticism.* London: Faber & Faber.
Eliot, T. S. (1964b). *Knowledge and experience in the philosophy of F. H. Bradley.* New York: Farrar, Straus.
Freud, Sigmund (1962). *Three essays on the theory of sexuality* (James Strachey, Trans.). New York: Basic.
Gide, André (1963). *If it die* (Dorothy Bussy, Trans.). New York: Vintage.
Janouch, Gustav (1971). *Conversations with Kafka* (Goronwy Rees, Trans.). New York: New Directions.
Jung, C. G. (1968). *Analytical psychology, its theory and practice.* New York: Pantheon.

Kafka, Franz (1970). *The great wall of China* (Willa and Edwin Muir, Trans.). New York: Schocken.

Lacan, Jacques (1977). *Écrits: A selection.* New York: Norton.

Milton, John (1957). *Complete poems and major prose* (Merritt Y. Hughes, Ed.). New York: Odyssey.

Neisser, Ulric (1988). Five kinds of self-knowledge. *Philosophical Psychology,* 1, 35–59.

Pound, Ezra (1982). *Pound/Ford: The story of a literary friendship* (Brita Lindberg-Seyersted, Ed.). New York: New Directions.

Proust, Marcel (1981). *Remembrance of Things Past* (C. K. Scott-Moncrieff, Terence Kilmartin, & Andreas Mayor, Trans.). New York: Random House.

Rimbaud, Arthur (1966). *Rimbaud: Complete works, selected letters* (Wallace Fowlie, Ed.). Chicago: University of Chicago Press.

Schneiderman, Stuart (1983). *Jacques Lacan: The death of an intellectual hero.* Cambridge, MA: Harvard University Press.

Schopenhauer, Arthur (1950). *The world as will and idea* (R. B. Haldane & J. Kemp, Trans.). New York: Scribner's.

Tennyson, Alfred (1969). *The poems of Tennyson* (Christopher Ricks, Ed.). London: Longmans, Green.

Whitman, Walt (1959). *Complete poetry and selected prose* (James E. Miller, Jr., Ed.). Boston: Riverside Editions.

Wilde, Oscar (1973). *Complete works of Oscar Wilde* (Vyvyan Holland, Ed.). London: Collins.

Woolf, Virginia (1949). *A haunted house and other short stories.* New York: Harvest Books.

Woolf, Virginia (1955). *To the lighthouse.* New York: Harvest Books.

Woolf, Virginia (1976). *Moments of being: Unpublished autobiographical writings* (Jeanne Schulkind, Ed.). New York: Harcourt Brace.

Wordsworth, William (1969). *Poetical works* (Thomas Hutchinson & Ernest de Selincourt, Eds.). Oxford: Oxford University Press.

Yeats, W. B. (1965). *The autobiography of William Butler Yeats.* New York: Collier Books.

3

The "remembered" self

JEROME BRUNER

1

The expression *the remembered self* is, I suspect, a cunningly designed oxymoron – rather like, say, the title of a recent book, *The Remembered Present* (Edelman, 1990), which also poses a conceptual challenge. I gladly accept the challenge, for I shall want to argue in what follows that Self is not an entity that one can simply remember, but is, rather, a complex mental edifice that one constructs by the use of a variety of mental processes, one of which must surely be remembering. I shall want to concentrate in what follows on the nature and course of these construction processes and upon some of the conditions that guide and constrain them.

Obviously, one of these processes is selective memory retrieval. But what sorts of criteria guide the selectivity? One set of them must surely be derived from some sort of "need" to emphasize *agency*, to recover memories related to the initiation of relatively autonomous acts governed by our intentional states – our wishes, desires, beliefs, and expectancies. This would be quite consistent with what has come to be called the "primary attribution error" (or "tendency") according to which we attribute behavior not to circumstances but to dispositions and motives (cf. Griffin & Ross, 1991). And though we know that this tendency is more likely to be operative in judging and predicting others than in doing the same for ourselves, it is still a potent tendency in the latter case. The claim, simply, is that Self is a concept one of whose defining properties is agency.

But this criterion also has, as it were, its flip side: Let us call it *victimicy*. If our Self-concept cannot be constructed by assembling and conceptualizing instances of our own agentive acts, then it can be constructed according to the same principle by attributing it to the agency of *another*. According to this view, we construct a victim Self, by reference to memories of how we responded to the agency of somebody else who had the power to impose his or her will upon us directly, or indirectly by controlling the circumstances in which we are compelled to live. And by this maneuver we create a kind of "reactive agency" – as rebel, resistance fighter, Uncle Tom, or James Dean. Obviously, there are other ways of meeting the criterion of Self as agentive, many of them attributable to cultural learning (cf. Tomasello, Kruger, & Ratner, 1993), such as those recently discussed by Markus and Kitayama (1991) in connection with Japanese culture or by Steele (1988) in connection with "racial stigmatization." But even in the case of the Markus and Kitayama study, indicating that the agentive quality of Self is reduced in Oriental cultures, the role of "optionalality" is still central.

Another property of Self as a concept is its tendency toward consistency, which leads us to the suspicion that Self-construction is a form of schematizing in Bartlett's (1932) sense, subject to such processes as assimilation and other forms of "smoothing." But, as we shall see later, agency and schematization often clash. People change, get new goals or reject old ones, do not remain the same. When such sharp changes occur, we find in studies of spontaneous autobiographical accounts, there is a strong tendency to segregate the "periods of life" concerned and make each schematically consistent in its own terms. I shall return to this topic later when considering the ubiquitousness of "turning points" in spontaneous autobiographies marked by accounts of a "changed Self." Turning points are by no means limited to religious conversion or to radical politicization, and are most often humdrum – like breaking away from family or divorcing a bully. Indeed, it may well be that the culture's canonical forms for characterizing the seasons of a life encourage such subjective turning points.

A third criterial attribute of the Self-concept seems to be in conflict with, if not to contradict the first criterion, agency. For while people (at least in our culture) think of Self as proceeding "from the inside out," they also tend to think of their own Selves as not radically different from the Selves of others who, in some commonsense way, are "like" them. Self seems also "outside in." Few people think they are totally "unique" or self-directed. They characterize themselves as sharing canonical traits that, on closer inspection, suggest shared values. Asked what they are like, people will tell you that they are reasonably kind, reasonably honest, reasonably hard-working – all variants of a more general notion of being reasonably "decent" just like the others. One wonders whether this is not a manifestation of what Griffin and Ross (1991) call the "consensus error" (and again, I prefer the term "tendency"), according to which people think that just about any "normal" person like them would do what *they* would do under like circumstances. To be sure, most people do not "live with" the felt contradiction between a feeling of communality and of autonomy – though they recognize the plight when depicted by, say, Willy Loman in *Death of a Salesman*. Perhaps the potential conflict is managed by the well-known tendency to see one's "own" reference group as somehow sharing one's character more than "other" groups (cf. Tajfel, 1978).

Let me briefly note another property of Self as we encounter it in ourselves and in others. It is "storied," or narrative, in structure. When you ask people what they are really like, they tell a great many stories involving the usual elements of narrative (cf. Burke, 1945; Bruner, 1990): there is an *agent* engaged in *action* deploying certain *instruments* for achieving a *goal* in a particular *scene,* and somehow things have gone awry between these elements to produce *trouble.* The stories they tell, moreover, are genre-like: One encounters the hero tale, the *Bildungsroman,* the tale of the victim, the love story, and so on. If one ever doubted Oscar Wilde's claim that life imitates art, reading autobiographies lessens the doubt.

Finally, let me mention a perennially puzzling aspect of Self: Self-depiction varies as a function of the interlocutor to whom the account is given. And this can surely not be *just* a recital effect, for we have all experienced "feeling like" a different person when with, say, our children, our boss, our rivals or colleagues. This has led several thoughtful scholars to propose that Self is, as it were, a dialogic idea or, as with Goffman (1959), a dramaturgic one. Self is also contingent on the role one is playing, or more properly the multiple roles one plays, not all of them being amenable to simultaneous performance. This, of course, is the view initially made famous by George Herbert Mead (e.g., 1934).

What I have said thus far suggests that Self is a conceptual structure, a system for categorizing selected memories, for engendering expectations, for judging fitness, and so forth. The crucial cognitive activities involved in Self-construction seem much more like "thinking" than "memory." We say to people in times of comeuppance, "Who do you *think* you are?" And expressions like *"Remember* who you are!" seem more directed to reminding us of status than of Self. Now if Self is principally a product of thought – even if it does operate on stored memory, as most thought does – we may expect that the best guide to understanding the construction of Self would be to follow the procedures that have led us to understand the operations of thought rather than to concentrate upon Self as a form of remembrance.

So if I may voice one objection to the expression *the remembered Self* it is that it may mislead us into doing studies of people remembering events in their life in the expectation that such remembering constitutes Self-construction.

2

I want to change tack now. I want to consider some particulars involved in trying to "remember" Self, and particularly in trying to reconstruct it from the past. For example, I can remember a good many things about the period from my 10th to my 12th year – like the names of teachers such as Miss Macadam, Miss Davis, Mrs. Orcutt, and Major Connally, to be precise, particularly Mrs. Orcutt, who introduced us to the idea that beneath the visible surface of everything there could be found a less obvious but not directly discernible regularity that was "truer" or "better" or altogether more OK than what you merely saw. She either changed my life or, possibly, I was simply entering Piaget's stage of formal operations and she personified that oceanic event. No matter. It certainly must have changed my way of looking at my Self, whatever we may take that term eventually to mean. For I began looking around for things in the world that matched her intuitive account of the equation of the Brownian movement of molecules with temperature. For example, I even invented two kinds of "waves" in the ether to account for why a pile driver I saw a mile down the shore could be seen hitting its piling before it could be heard to be doing so.

There are some other salient features in how my remembered Self in this account is structured. For one, it is grammatical in the deep sense: more specifically it contains sentences dominated by first-person pronouns marked by features like +agent, +experiencer, +recipient. The sentences are drenched in indexicality. They presuppose that the hearer knows the layout being discussed, and that he will recognize the distinction between expressions dominated by mental verbs for inner states (like *looking for*) and those dominated by existential ones referring to a "world" (like *is located on* . . .). All these imply an astonishing amount of ordering of material "extracted" from memory.

The utterances, moreover, conform fairly well to the Labovian narrative structure. There are canonical starting states (Mrs. Orcutt's version of "deep understanding"), precipitating events (the disjunction of visual and auditory cues at a mile's remove), resolutions (two kinds of waves), a coda in the form of a stance marker ("I *even* invented"), and an evaluative term placed independently of the narrative clauses (I *matched* what my teacher had done).

Moreover, my account is couched in terms that I could not possibly have known at the time of the encounter so as, doubtless, to obscure the preconceptual innocence of the 12-year-old protagonist. The child *then* is being vastly mauled by my sense of what I am now, and I must find some way of turning that 12-year-old kid with his caulking iron into a grownup professor.

But that only begins to scratch the surface. What about the "historical influences" affecting my reconstruction? Why, you may ask, is the account so built around the notion of "finding out" and "getting to the underlying structure"? I certainly did not invent the structure. It is very much part of "American culture" and I can find analogues of it as far back as Jonathan Edwards – even though I had never heard about him when I was 12. Indeed, he has given me some useful hints about my own Self (cf. Bruner, in press–b). While ministering to a frontier congregation in Northampton, Massachusetts, in the 17th century, Edwards came upon a back copy of the *Proceedings of the Royal Society* containing an account of Newton's prismatic demonstration of the spectral composition of white light. He was obviously thrilled. The following Sunday, he announced in a sermon to his parishioners that Man had unlocked another of God's secrets and that they too, by taking pious but independent thought, could do the same. I assume he was trying in his way, much as Mrs. Orcutt might have been trying in hers, to change his parishioners' Selves. There is a long distance between the deistic culture of Edwards's 17th-century western Massachusetts and the secular middle-class culture of my exurban Long Island in the 20th. Yet, how shall we account for the isomorphism in the two stories? Is the formulation of *my* narrative (and the memory retrieval and schematization programs it set in motion) in the same cultural tradition? Most historians would say it was, and are we to deny them?

3

Now let me work from the bottom up with some still tinier details, a flashbulb memory, to be precise. I can recover with vivid and fresh detail an episode with a caulking iron I bought when I was 12 with which I repaired a leaky rowboat under the tutelary eye of one Frank Henning, who ran the dock where we water-struck kids hung out. He and I put the newly caulked boat back into the water by the dock to "soak up" overnight. The flashbulb has to do with the surge of pride I felt when, returning the next morning, I found that the caulked boat had not wept so much as a drop of water overnight: In memory, it was bone dry. Plainly, and even without benefit of free association, this is a flashbulb memory featuring successful agency – unalloyed competence, as Robert White (1959) would put it. Yet, I ask, is it *really* an accurate memory? As we all know, we have good reason to be suspicious of flashbulb memories. I have to conclude on sheer physical grounds that there are some unlikely things in my flashbulb memory. The memory boat, for one, is a beautiful thing, slender and graceful as a Whitehall pulling wherry, though "in fact" it had to have been one of those heavily planked clunker rowboats like the rest of the fleet of graceless for-hire boats at Henning's dock. I also know, from years of experience since, that it could not have been dry as a bone the next morning: Caulked boats don't take up that fast. So, can I simply write off these particular idealizations as a routine example of Bartlettian memory change? I think not.

What is involved in these memory idealizations? Doubtless, it involves "sharpening, leveling, and assimilation" in the classic sense. But it also exemplifies, I want to argue, a feature of Self-construction. For in order to construct an idealized agentive Self, we need the "sympathetic weather" of a world appropriate to it. And just as Bartlett's (1932) subjects created sympathetic weather to go with their recalled version of the "War of the Ghosts" story, so I apparently need a graceful and bone-dry wherry to go with my construction of a competent, agentive 12-year-old Self – a somewhat snobbish one at that. (What I should reveal is that much later in life, I became a great admirer of classic pulling boat designs, and even owned a replica of one such for some years.)

This suggests some sort of "master process" that is involved in synoptically reconstructing Self, as though there were a "writer" of a "continuous" autobiography concerned not only with getting things mnemonically as "right" as possible, but with providing continuity between the then-and-there and the here-and-now, as I noted above. Not only does that "writer" have to remember, but to do so in a version that assimilates that agentively preoccupied 12-year-old to the current me sitting before my word processor. To do this, the autobiographical "writer" in question needs a time-bridging narrative to preserve continuity. And so the innocent change in the flashbulb to a bone-dry and nimble pulling boat.

The closest theoretical model I can propose to account for the processes involved is Vladimir Propp's (1968) discussion of how a story structure as a whole converts its constituent parts into what he calls "functions" – segments that fulfill narrative functions within the whole. The "story" of Jerome Bruner becomes one of competence characterized by an assuring quality of elegance. Once we develop a workable narrative "theory" about how Self developed, we are prepared to shape even our flashbulb fragments of its history in congruence with it. And these construals affect not only our own agency but the world upon which that agency is brought to bear. This is probably what happens when we begin shaping ourselves in conformity with the "legend" or reputation that others tell us we have achieved. It is an old theme in literature – witness Brick in *Cat on a Hot Tin Roof* or the figures of Bonnie and Clyde in the film of that name.

But that is too once-for-all an account of the matter. For notoriously, stories have a way of changing with circumstances and, notably, with the interlocutor to whom they are being told. It would seem, indeed, that we construct not just a single or main Self-narrative, but a set of them – something like a cast of characters, as Freud (1950) once suggested. Hazel Markus and Paula Nurius (1986) have recently proposed that we have accessible a small squad of Possible Selves, each based on a somewhat different working over of the past: what we would *like* to be, what we *fear* becoming, and so on. They also postulate a Now Self (or Selves) who carry out the mundane transactions of daily life. I have argued elsewhere (Bruner, in press – a) that the compartmentalization of bureaucratized modern life probably leads to a certain disconnection among the so-called Now Selves, even to the point of producing multiple personality syndrome. And the multiple Selves probably relate to the reference groups to whom we orient, some of them general (like one's "social class") and some quite punctate (like the image of one's father). I suspect that the manner in which an interlocutor (real or imagined) alters a teller's Self narrative is consistent with the reference group the interlocutor represents in the teller's mind's eye. And the power to alter is proportional in some manner to the teller's identification with that reference group. All of which is probably an oversimplification, but I mention it here more in the spirit of trying to locate a question than of providing an answer to it. I suspect, finally, that the preexistence of alternative Self-concepts in the Markus-Nurius sense makes people the more susceptible to the effects produced by dialogic partners on our Self-narratives. To sum it up with a literary example, would the Hamlet who did all that dueling at his university have characterized his Self dilemma to his sword-happy classmates as he did later in the famous soliloquy when, "sicklied o'er with the pale cast of thought," he now questioned "Whether 'tis nobler in the mind to suffer / The slings and arrows of outrageous fortune, / Or to take arms against a sea of troubles"?

4

Susan Weisser and I (Bruner & Weisser, in preparation) have been studying spontaneously spoken autobiographies and I want finally to revisit some of the topics already discussed in the light of what we have been finding.

The first concerns the startling consistency of these lives as told. The continuity and inherent congruence that our respondents impose on their told lives, while not a surprise from a "commonsense" point of view, should not be taken for granted. Could there be any human activity in which the drive to reduce cognitive dissonance is so great as in the domain of "telling about your life"? The stratagems employed for weaving webs across translocations and dislocations, the degree to which memory search is guided by these stratagems, the absence of discomfort about what must have been glaring discontinuities, the extent to which culturally familiar narrative forms promote this seeming unity in multiplicity – all these give remarkable testimony to Leon Festinger's (1957) powerful insight about dissonance reduction as a principal engine in cognitive functioning.

One may ask some such question as, Did the people involved actually *experience* their lives in this way, or is this just in the telling? But this is surely a question that begs the question. For the story form affects the organization of experience just as surely as it affects memory recall – or as Henry James once put it, "adventures happen to people who know how to tell it that way." The narratives used to form our Self-depictions now are surely not totally alien to the ones used in construing experience then. More likely, they are simply later editions – honed, better narrativized, mitigated as required. The 12-year-old I evoked in my autobiographical fragment was, I suspect, already underestimating how much the boat had leaked overnight, work finally completed in the later flashbulb memory.

The "feel" of agency in our lives is, I suspect, what is most likely to undergo exaggeration in the remembering. It is difficult to find examples in our autobiographical corpus of people reporting themselves as mere sports of fortune and circumstances. One exception was a subject who reported a temporary fugue state, but she carefully "medicalized" it as such. And indeed, it seems to require real pathology to alter this sense of ubiquitous agency, as with autism, in which the capacity for telling and understanding narrative is deeply impaired (Bruner & Feldman, in press). With the impairment of the capacity to tell narratives (which either produces or accompanies their impaired "theory of mind"), autists give typically nonagentive accounts of themselves and their lives. Francesca Happe (1991) reports, for example, that the written autobiographies of high-level autists tend to be strikingly "external," very much written, as it were, on the landscape of action, eschewing the landscape of consciousness. Textually, their accounts are impoverished in mental verbs and in "subjunctivizing" forms (Bruner, 1986).

But it is a mistake to think of agency only as a general characteristic of autobiographical accounts. Its absence may also be selective. We know that girls experience their academic failures as due to their own inadequacies, their successes as due to good luck. (Boys experience their failures as bad luck, their successes as the result of competence.) Does this gender-linked downplaying of successes account as well for the historical eschewing of achievement tales in women's autobiographies (Smith, 1988)? Certainly cultural pressures can selectively alter the experience of Self as readily as biological ones. Indeed, it is precisely this matter that led me at the start to mention the transformation of agency into victimicy, a discussion of which would take us too far from our subject. I can only refer in passing to Kardiner and Ovesy's (1951) classic volume on this topic, and to two particularly insightful recent works, one by Patricia Williams (1991) on combining female gender, blackness, and the practice of law, and the other by Kristin Bumiller (1988) on the social construction of the victim in public law.

After our autobiographical subjects had finished their spontaneous self-accounts, we asked them some prepared questions to explore a num-

ber of issues that particularly interested us. One was devised to confront
them with dissonances in their lives: "As you look back, was there anything in your life that was really atypical or out of character for you?"
Indeed there was, and everybody could give an example or two – and
nearly all seemed to be able to explain them away with little difficulty.
Some few still kept the sensed anomaly alive. One 60-year-old who otherwise considered himself to be a generous man and was proud of being so
regarded by others, recalled an episode of refusing a small loan to a
friend who had just suffered a fire at home. Remorse was still alive. He
was still engaged in what Charles Taylor (1989) refers to as "radical reflection" about it. And in private we all do this in some degree.

Yet we were struck at the fluency with which most of our subjects "explained themselves" out of their malaise or their puzzlement concerning
their out-of-character acts. We typically invoke such notions as "rationalization" to account for such activity, but such terms are demeaning and
miss something crucial. John Austin (1970) once wrote a brilliant essay,
"A Plea for Excuses." His close analysis of the rhetoric of excuses could as
easily serve for the rhetoric of self-consistency in autobiography. Rhetoric,
indeed, is as pervasive a feature of Self construction as narrative itself,
and though we tend to dismiss it on moral grounds as mere "self-
justification," such dismissals fail to recognize to what degree the concept
of Self (and autobiography itself) is a form of apologia: an arraignment
of oneself against a set of normative standards.

We must return now to "turning points" in autobiography. Doubtless,
as Erik Erikson (1950) insists, some of them have a real biological and/or
cultural basis. But there are many more reported that seem to reflect
something quite different from the universal stages through which we
are said to pass. A few words are in order concerning these idiosyncratic
turning points that people so persistently report. What are they like?
They are vividly particular, even though they carry some affective or
moral message with them. Take some instances. The football coach tells
the high school kid to "get" the opposing end, get him out of the game.
The kid turns in his uniform the next day, revolted by "winner" morality.
He gives up the adolescent ideal of being an athlete, and becomes a
"brain" instead. Parenthetically, let me also tell you that the protagonist
of this account finally ends up a Vietnam War protester and a follower of
the Berrigan brothers and is now an academic. Or a stout young adolescent girl is infuriated that her father wants her to wear, as she puts it,
only "blacks and browns." She decides she'll have no more of it, and decks
herself out in the loudest colors she can get hold of – with her own sav-
ings. "That's when I realized I had to live my own life." In another turning point, a woman tells of living with an alcoholic for eight years. He
comes home at all hours, threatening to beat her and sometimes carrying

out the threat – but "once too often: I remember that night; that was enough." She leaves him.

Note first that these turning points, though they may be linked to things happening "outside," are finally attributed to a happening "inside" – a new belief, new courage, moral disgust, "having had enough." They are thickly agentive. Secondly, they ride into the story on a wave of episodic memory retrieval, rich in detail and color. They remind one of the tumbling return of forgotten episodes during recovery from traumatic amnesia (Cermak, 1984). A third feature of these turning points is that they usher in a new and intense line of activity: The outraged young football player takes himself into the library and reads avidly; the stout adolescent girl gets a new circle of friends; the escapee from the alcoholic's threats starts a career; and so on. A new deal lies beyond the turning point: Agency is not lost, but redirected and even redoubled. Finally, turning points are drenched in affect – certainly in the telling and presumably in the living.

It would be unseemly to detract from the "psychic reality" of turning points: They plainly feel real enough to those who recount them. Still, I want to offer the hypothesis that rather than regarding them simply as "true reports" about "what happened," we do better to consider them as preternaturally clear instances of narrative construction that have the function of helping the teller clarify his or her Self-concept. They are prototype narrative episodes whose construction results in increasing the realism and drama of the Self. In that sense, the narrative construction, whenever it actually happened, is as important as what is reported to have actually happened in the turning point episode. Turning points, in a word, construct emblems of narrative clarity in the teller's history of Self. Narrative, we know, imposes a particular structure on the "reality" that it depicts. Elsewhere, I have tried to characterize some of the features of narratively constructed "reality" (Bruner, 1991). The turning points recounted by our subjects faithfully fill the bill for most of these features: diachronicity, particularity, intentional state entailment, hermeneutic composability, a breach of canonicity, concrete referentiality, generativeness, normativeness, context sensitivity, and narrative accrual. They serve as generative "gists" for the life as a whole, and in this sense they are as much *tropes* as literal accounts of "what happened." Indeed, the little boat-caulking episode I drew from my own autobiography is a typical example of an episodic account turned into a trope.

Indeed, with literary power, these tropelike turning points get turned into the leitmotif of a life. One of our subjects in the study of spontaneous autobiography was a poet of considerable merit. Let me take him as an example of what I mean. In his late thirties, he starts his unusual account with the "story" of his birth. The attending physician slapped him on the back to get his breathing started, and purportedly broke three ribs. "You see, I was suffering from osteoporosis. But I should tell you that it's rather like the story of my life: people breaking my bones with the intention of doing me good." Though he never mentions the episode again, it has plainly become a leitmotif of his life account. We do not know exactly when this wry insight, this "internal turning point," first occurred to him – but certainly not at the time of happening! All we can infer is that it took shape shortly after he admitted to himself that he was homosexual. He then realized that "everybody" was engaging in the subtle and often not so subtle process of trying to talk him out of or seduce him out of his homosexuality, to recapture him for the "straight" world, whatever the consequences for him – slapping him on the back to get him to breathe, even if his bones were broken in the process.

In our culture, turning points are often cast as "second chances," but like Henry James's characters who experience adventures because they know the narrative adventure form, we experience them as new chances because we are brought up to think in this cheerful mode. But in another culture, they might as easily be framed as the working out of karma, as a gift from God, or even as an affliction of witchcraft. Another way of putting the matter is to note that the condensed turning point narratives are not only tropes but emblems of the genre in terms of which we construe our lives. Carol Feldman (1991) notes in her analysis of genres that they are both forms of thought and ways of using language for representation and communication. She is struck by the fact that oral genres, like Ilongot oratory or Wana *kivori* (political poems), also have a distinctly pragmatic function. They are meant for an occasion; what is said cannot be interpreted without appreciating the generic occasion of its delivery. That is to say, genres are also indexical in the linguistic sense. They presuppose a situational way of extracting meaning from discourse.

So it is with autobiography. Self-accounts are strikingly generic in this same sense. Our young footballer, for example, couches his autobiography in the classic terms of the *Bildungsroman*, the novel form that tells of how one achieves one's moral formation. It becomes increasingly difficult for him to see events in which he participates in any other way. He tells the story of meeting in Los Angeles an attractive young woman with whom he has an affair. One evening, lounging together in bed, she tries to talk him out of being so serious and working so hard. Next morning, before she is awake, he tiptoes off and takes a plane back East without so much as saying farewell to the California golden girl. There was to be no genre shift, no turning point. I used to think that turning points were like Kuhnian paradigm shifts. I doubt it very much now. I think, rather, they serve as idealization of a genre of narrative we have chosen for our lives. And by the same token, I'm inclined to think that when one's life story changes to meet the requirements of another interlocutor, the changes are variants within a genre rather than massive recastings. When they need massive recasting, I suspect, the teller is usually threatened by the kind of identity crisis made so well known by Erikson (1950). Perhaps psychoanalysts like Roy Schafer (1981) and Donald Spence (1982) are right in remarking that the task of the therapist then becomes rather like that of a "play doctor": to help the patient find a Self narrative that works for him or for her.

5

I have placed a great deal of emphasis on the role of narrative in structuring our conceptions of our lives and particularly our roles as agents in life. Let me close with a brief rationale for this emphasis – brief because I have recently tried to deal with the matter more extensively elsewhere (Bruner, 1990). As I argued there, the narrative mode is one of the few ways we have for organizing indefinitely long diachronic sequences involving the activities of ourselves, our fellows, and the symbolic world of culture.

I have even argued that early language acquisition cannot be fully explained without positing some underlying push toward narrative encoding. Even the case forms of most natural languages reflect the basic notions of agents acting intentionally toward goals in relation to others by the use of instruments in aspectual time and with the possibility of interfering circumstances. Although it is an oversimplification to say that narrative is the discourse mode that goes with our earliest specialization for living in groups governed by common cultural symbols, the evidence for some more sophisticated version of that position grows steadily. There are more and more primatologists who urge that the demands of living in complex groups marked by alliances whose success depends upon "reading" the intentions and stratagems of conspecifics constituted the major selective factor in the evolution of hominid intelligence (see, for example, Whiten, 1991). Even tool use, on this view, was a spinoff of the increase in intelligence that accompanied this social way of life, which would account for why the evolution of tools was so counterintuitively slow in our record of the emergence of *Homo*. When language emerged, it did so in a form compatible with conceptualizing and telling about human actions and intentions and their vicissitudes – the backbone of narrative discourse.

But I am not sure I want to rest the case on the evolutionary evidence, which, after all, is quite remote. I would be happier with a less ambitious version. I think that cultures are powerful systems for specifying possible ways of knowing, striving, feeling, and acting with respect to ourselves and others. Culture, through its store of narratives and its formulas for devising them, defines, as I remarked earlier, different ways not only of conceiving of our present states of being, but also our past and our future states. It is the premier source of plans for constructing our lives and our Selves. And its principal form (whatever its evolutionary origin) is the narrative. As David Polonoff (1987) remarked in a perceptive critique of the philosophical concept of personal identity, it is this persistence of narrativity that marks identity as much as any other conceptual feature of Self.

So to conclude, Self is a perpetually rewritten story. What we remember from the past is what is necessary to keep that story satisfactorily well formed. When new circumstances make the maintenance of that well-formedness sufficiently difficult, we undergo turning points that clarify or "debug" the narrative in an effort to achieve clearer meaning. Sometimes these changes or their prospect become so difficult that we even go to the doctor or priest for help. More often, the culture has a sufficiently rich store of prescriptions so that we can make out on our own. Another way of saying all this is to note that if the Self is a remembered self, the remembering reaches far back beyond our own birth, back to the cultural and language forms that specify the defining properties of a Self.

REFERENCES

Austin, J. L. (1970). A plea for excuses. In *Philosophical essays* (2nd ed., pp. 175–204). Oxford: Oxford University Press.
Bartlett, F. C. (1932). *Remembering*. Cambridge University Press.
Bruner, J. (1986). *Actual minds, possible worlds*. Cambridge, MA: Harvard University Press.
Bruner, J. (1990). *Acts of meaning*. Cambridge, MA: Harvard University Press.
Bruner, J. (1991, Autumn). The narrative construction of reality. *Critical Inquiry*, 1–21.
Bruner, J. (in press–a). The autobiographical process. In Robert Folkenflik (Ed.), *Essays on the poetics of self*. Stanford, CA: Stanford University Press.
Bruner, J. (in press–b). Two modes of thought. In G. Harman (Ed.), *Essays for George Miller*. Hillsdale, NJ: Erlbaum.
Bruner, J., & Feldman, C. (in press). Theories of mind and the problem of autism. In S. Baron-Cohen, H. Tager-Flusberg, & D. Cohen (Eds.), *Understanding other minds: The perspective from autism*. Cambridge University Press.
Bruner, J., & Weisser, S. (in preparation). *Autobiography and the construction of self*. Cambridge, MA: Harvard University Press.
Bumiller, Kristin. (1988). *The civil rights society: The social construction of victims*. Baltimore: Johns Hopkins University Press.
Burke, K. (1945). *The grammar of motives*. New York: Prentice-Hall.
Cermak, L. A. (1984). *Human memory and amnesia*. Hillsdale, NJ: Erlbaum.
Edelman, G. (1990). *The remembered present*. New York: Basic.

Erikson, E. (1950). *Childhood and society.* New York: Norton.

Feldman, C. (1991). Genres as mental models. In M. Ammaniti & D. Stern (Eds.), *Rappresentazioni e narrazioni.* Rome-Bari: Laterza.

Festinger, L. (1957). *A theory of cognitive dissonance.* Evanston, IL: Row Peterson.

Freud, S. (1950). The relation of the poet to daydreaming (1908). In E. Jones (Ed.), *Collected papers* (Vol. 4, pp. 173–183). London: Hogarth Press.

Goffman, E. (1959). *The presentation of self in everyday life.* Garden City, NY: Doubleday.

Griffin, D. W., & Ross, L. (1991). Subjective construal, social inference, and human understanding. *Advances in Experimental Social Psychology, 24,* 319–404.

Happe, F. G. E. (1991). The autobiographical writings of three Asperger syndrome adults: Problems of interpretation and implications for theory. In U. Frith (Ed.), *Autism and Asperger syndrome.* Cambridge University Press.

Kardiner, A., & Ovesy, L. (1951). *The mark of oppression: Explorations in the personality of the American Negro.* Cleveland: World.

Markus, H., & Kitayama, S. (1991). Culture and the self: Implications for cognition, emotion, and motivation. *Psychological Review, 98,* 224–253.

Markus, H., & Nurius, P. (1986). Possible selves. *American Psychologist, 41,* 954–969.

Mead, G. H. (1934). *Mind, self, and society.* Chicago: University of Chicago Press.

Polonoff, D. (1987). Self-deception. *Social Research, 54,* 53–62.

Propp, V. (1968). *Morphology of the folktale* (2nd ed.). Austin: University of Texas Press.

Schafer, R. (1981). Narration in the psychoanalytic dialogue. In W. J. T. Mitchell (Ed.), *On narrative.* Chicago: University of Chicago Press.

Smith, Sidonie. (1988). *A poetics of women's autobiography.* Bloomington: Indiana University Press.

Spence, D. (1982). *Narrative truth and historical truth: Meaning and interpretation in psychoanalysis.* New York: Norton.

Steele, C. (1988). The psychology of self-affirmation: Sustaining the integrity of the self. In L. Berkowitz (Ed.), *Advances in experimental social psychology* (Vol. 21, pp. 181–227). San Diego, CA: Academic Press.

Tajfel, H. (1978). Part 1 in H. Tajfel (Ed.), *Differentiation between social groups: Studies in the social psychology of intergroup relations.* European Monographs in Social Psychology, 14 (pp. 1–100). London: Academic Press.

Taylor, C. (1989). *Sources of the self: The making of modern identity.* Cambridge, MA: Harvard University Press.

Tomasello, M., Kruger, A. C., and Ratner, H. H. (1993). Cultural learning. *Behavioral and Brain Sciences, 16,* 495–552.

White, R. W. (1959). Motivation reconsidered: The concept of competence. *Psychological Review, 66,* 297–323.

Whiten, A. (Ed.). (1991). *Natural theories of mind: Evolution, simulation, and development of everyday mindreading.* Oxford: Basil Blackwell.

Williams, Patricia. (1991). *The alchemy of race and rights.* Cambridge, MA: Harvard University Press.

4

Composing protoselves through improvisation

CRAIG R. BARCLAY

This is a theoretical essay about cognitive, emotional, social, and cultural activities that work together to create remembered selves through autobiographical remembering. It is not an essay about an abstraction – *The Self*. Instead, it is about selves that are grounded in, but emerge through productive remembering and productive interacting in, everyday life (Barclay & Smith, 1992). Such remembered selves are part of our phenomenal experiences of the individual; they are often shared and formed in interpersonal relationships. Remembered selves serve contemporary adaptive purposes, deriving their meaning in the seemingly mundane activities of daily living. What becomes one's remembered self at any particular moment is a gestalt composed and objectified in constructed and reconstructed "personal" and generic memories (Brewer, 1986; Pillemer, 1990). These memories have acquired personal and cultural significance through socially structured activities and transactions between people in face-to-face encounters. On this view, a contemporary remembered self is not a collection of debris haphazardly gathered up from various mental compartments that presumably reflect the compartmentalization of modern life into family, career, or leisure activities. Like Grene (1993), I prefer to think of a remembered self as being inseparable from a "historical self" such that memories are not fleeting fragments of a past more forgotten than remembered, but recollections that are part of a perceived pattern to one's life.

The essay is in four main sections. A theoretical overview is presented first, along with my purpose and position regarding the nature of the remembered self. In the second section, I give my perspective on autobiographical remembering as currently conceived (Neisser, 1988a); questions regarding the origins and nature of autobiographical memories and remembered selves are addressed briefly; and a revised conceptualization of autobiographical memory is offered, followed by a summary discussion of possible relationships between autobiographical memory and self. In the third section, a theory of autobiographical remembering is elaborated, with particular emphasis on the social and affective functions of autobiographical remembering. The fourth section offers a process explanation of autobiographical remembering and self-composing, with a description of how *protoselves* may be created through improvisational acts that continuously form and reform a remembered self over time. The notion of protoselves is put forth as an alternative way of viewing the remembered self because it captures best what I think to be the dynamic and emergent qualities of autobiographical remembering and interpersonal relatedness – qualities that make the remembered self "real" and useful to the individual and social community.

Throughout, my remarks regarding the nature of the remembered self address three related issues. The first issue is the nature and origins of *personal significance* for certain kinds of memories, including episodic memories (Tulving, 1972), scripted memories (Nelson, 1986; Fivush, 1988), personal memories, generic personal memories, autobiographical facts, and self-schemata (Brewer, 1986). The second issue is the *functions* of autobiographical remembering, especially the intentional use of such recollections. And the third issue is the *relational and distributed nature* of remembered selves; that is, remembered selves in interactions with others and remembered selves as shared, collective knowledge of a person. The relational and distributed properties of remembered selves, reflecting cultural models of self, promote broad-based understanding of what is, in fact, remembered (manifest content) and the meaning (latent content) of those memories to the person and group.

1. Theoretical Overview

> Self, then, is not a static thing or a substance, but a configuring of personal events into an historical unity which includes not only what one has been but also anticipation of what one will be.
>
> Polkinghorne (1988), p. 150

> Everyday practical remembering is not just a matter of self-consciously remembering facts, but of sometimes 're-feeling' certain events, sometimes of being able to reorder by reshaping such feelings to imagine either new relations between well-known things, or completely new worlds. In such practical remembering, our remembering is, so to speak, 'embodied' within us as a part of who we are, rather than 'external' to us and dependent upon signs or representations.
>
> Shotter (1990), pp. 135–136

My purpose here is twofold: to offer an elaborated conceptualization of the remembered self as proposed by Neisser (1988a) and describe a process through which remembered selves are formed (Barclay & Hodges, 1990; Barclay & Smith, 1992). I argue that a unique remembered self does not exist, nor does a remembered self exist only as the current "text" of a life story or personal narrative. Unchanging uniqueness is not a defining feature of a remembered self because new experiences occur, memories of old experiences are reinterpreted, fitted to contemporary needs or become inaccessible and forgotten, and the contexts and purposes for remembering change over time. In addition, there may be experiences a person or culture cannot shape into canonical narrative forms, especially experiences associated with victimization (Langer, 1991). An individual's remembered self (selves) is thus marked by variability in content, structure, and interpretation. This is not to argue that a totally new remembered self emerges every time the person engages in autobiographical remembering. Such an extreme hermeneutic approach is rejected here because it denies the reality both of direct perception – namely, the co-perception of oneself in perceiving the world (J. Gibson, 1979/1986, p. 126; Neisser, 1990) – and of lived experience which is felt and remembered by oneself and related others.

Elaborating Neisser's views, I suggest that remembered selves may be formed through at least four related kinds of activities: affective-practical activity, instantiation of cultural models, the use of metaphor, and the use of canonical narrative forms. My position is that, from the phenomenal perspective of the individual, remembered selves are often extrapolations of embodied psychosocial and affective experiences – for example, reconstructing the self to justify an image of a comforting caregiver. These experiences can be relived and often visualized and felt, and at times experienced as "personal memories" (Brewer, 1986, pp. 30, 34; Brewer & Nakamura, 1984; Brewer & Pani, 1982; Salaman, 1970). Unlike an ecological (E. Gibson, 1993; Neisser, 1988a) or interpersonal self (Stern, 1990; Trevarthen, 1990), remembered selves are formed mostly in language and thought (semiotic systems), both of which are honed by cultural practices, habits, and rituals (practical activities) (Vygotsky, 1978). Remembered selves are, therefore, embedded in cultural models and explanatory systems (D'Andrade, 1990; Holland & Quinn, 1987; Linde, 1987; Nuckolls, 1990; Ogbu, 1990) that give background, shared meaning, and significance to an individual's particular memories.[1] Such cultural models can function at the individual level as idealized cognitive models (ICMs: Lakoff, 1986), thought of as ICMs projected from image schemata (Johnson, 1987) that have been internalized through social speech acts and dynamic activities (Vygotsky, 1978).

From a metaphorical perspective, a remembered self could be extrapolated from memories of my marriage if I used the metaphor "marriage is like a wheel" – one that spins a lot but also goes somewhere! The dynamic (and perhaps visual) image of the wheel anchors my attention and thoughts to its parts and movement. I can then imagine and reconstruct memories of my marriage that are metaphorically similar to those parts and movement. From those reconstructed memories I can extrapolate further until I meet some subjective criteria (e.g., a sense of closure, boredom, etc.) that indicate the recollection is complete. Furthermore, somewhat different remembered selves could be extrapolated if I had a roulette wheel instead of a spoked wagon wheel in mind because the parts and functions of these wheels are different: My embodied experiences with wheels would influence the likelihood of using one metaphor or another (Johnson, 1987; Lakoff, 1986, 1987; Lakoff & Johnson, 1980). An important implication of this view is that consistency in remembered selves over time is a function of the consistency with which we use the same metaphors for reconstruction.

A narrative perspective suggests that autobiographical recollections are momentary objectifications of a remembered self. Such selves are structured by familiar and culturally shared explanatory systems (Linde, 1987); namely, narrative forms, which serve as different types of generative models available to the individual at the time of remembering (Bruner, 1987, 1990). Narrative forms exist in the world (Carr, 1986; Gergen & Gergen, 1988), at least as social experiences and in cultural artifacts like books (fiction, nonfiction, biography, and autobiography), stories told, sung, or danced, movies, folklore, and theater. For instance, a particular narrative element (e.g., Macbeth's speech about life from Act 5, Scene 5), either imagined or spoken, can be taken from a larger narrative form (e.g., tragedy) and used to explore and shape one's own thoughts and feelings. Importantly, recent developmental work has shown that certain kinds of self-narratives may originate from temporally and socially organized scripts found in interactions between parents and children early in life (Fivush, 1991; Miller, Potts, Fung, Hoogstra, & Mintz, 1990; Nelson, 1989), and subsequently internalized by children as they develop social speech and language (Bakhurst, 1990; Vygotsky, 1978).

Narrative forms and conventionalized narrations (e.g., ballads, Wallace & Rubin, 1988), taken as cultural models for self-construction, can constitute important elements of an interpretative social context, that is, a framework that guides the composition of a remembered self. This context thus mediates comprehension, understanding, and memory for oneself and others by signaling the availability of a commonly known interpretative framework. Thus, shared (and probably unspoken) understandings regarding narrative structure – similar to Bartlett's (1923, 1932) notion of "organizing settings" in the world and in the mind – can function as culturally based psychological tools (see Bakhurst, 1990). The use of these tools is, in part, for the purpose of creating "narrative fit" in terms of adequacy (self-consistency, coherence, and comprehensiveness) and accuracy (Spence, 1982, p. 180) between the facts of one's life and meaningful interpretations of those facts for oneself and others.

Considering the remembered self in narrative terms, however, does not mean that a person creates (or can create) just any self-narrative any more than a person can fabricate "remembered" events that never occurred (except perhaps when there is a social contract between the rememberer and others that made-up events are being used for dramatic or poetic goals; Johnson & Raye, 1981). There are known and verifiable events in one's life to be accounted for at different times and for different reasons; and, for most individuals, there are needs to satisfy a sense of personal coherence and integrity, at least as these needs are understood in most Western cultures. Each of these constraints on possible self-narratives is limited even further by the more public negotiations associated with establishing and maintaining self-legitimacy and acceptance of one's self-narration by others who share a common culture.

In brief, my claims to this point are that remembered selves are constructed and reconstructed within certain contexts, especially through the use of narration. In composing a remembered self in narration, strands of "narrative truth" ("defined as the criterion we use to decide when a certain experience has been captured to our satisfaction; it depends on continuity and closure and the extent to which the fit of the pieces takes on an aesthetic finality," Spence, 1982, p. 31) seem to provide connecting fibers among real events remembered over time. Since the plots and themes constituting the interpretative networks of our daily lives are relatively stable or mutate only slowly, our remembered selves are experienced as stable or as changing only gradually unless our lives are punctuated by some transformational event(s), for example, loss of job, birth of child, divorce, war.

Remembered selves may be composed through a process of loosely constrained, but referent-based (e.g., by metaphors, feelings, images of specific events), *improvisation* akin to that found in time-based phenomena like conversations (Middleton & Edwards, 1990), music, theater, dance, and mime (Pressing, 1984). As with autobiographical remembering, all of these kinds of activities take place over relatively long (minutes, hours) time periods and are nested in social and physical contexts rich in information that supports performance. This process may be universal to the extent that constructive and reconstructive memory processes are used; and the forms that improvised selves take are influenced greatly by the individual's motives, intentions, beliefs, and attitudes at the time of remembering and interacting (Barclay, Petitto, Labrum, & Carter-Jessop, 1991; Bartlett, 1932; Handel, 1987; Markus, 1977, 1983; Ross, 1989).

Therefore, the content and resulting structure of improvisational activities should differ widely depending upon the content domain and culture within which the improvisation occurs. In each improvisational instance, though, knowledge, skill, emotion, intention, and audience (either real or imagined) collaborate to create and re-create remembered selves.

Remembered selves emerging in the activities of autobiographical remembering and interacting are embedded as well within a community of other selves (Halbwachs, 1925; Neisser, 1988b). The members of this community judge and validate, support and perpetrate the productive activities of self-composition for the purposes of producing and reproducing themselves and perhaps to maintain social peace.

2. The remembered self

> The extended [remembered] self is the self as it was in the past and we expect it to be in the future, known primarily on the basis of memory.
>
> Neisser (1988a), p. 13

In describing the remembered self, Neisser (1988a) assumes, as I and others have (e.g., Barclay, 1986, 1988; Baddeley, 1988; Bannister & Agnew, 1976; Brewer, 1986; Eder, Gerlach, & Perlmutter, 1987; Fivush, 1988), that (autobiographical) memories are the phenomenal reality of self as existing in the present and extending over time past and into the expected future. Neisser's (1988a) stated position is that "my extended self . . . can be thought of as a kind of cumulated total of such memories: the things I remember having done and the things I think of myself as doing regularly" (p. 14). He argues further that the remembered self "is based on [accessible] stored information" (p. 16). The strong form of this argument holds that *(autobiographical) memory = the remembered self.* Although I tend to agree with this argument in principle, it needs to be explicated in greater detail and broadened to include factors other than cognition.

One merit of the strong form of the argument is that it acknowledges a cognitive contribution to self, and offers an explanation of the remembered self deducible from our extensive knowledge of memory and memory processes (e.g., Rubin, 1986), and concepts of self derived from ego psychology. The argument, however, is inadequate for at least five reasons. First, there is simply too much information from a life (even a short one) for a remembered self to be remembered.

Second, the remembered self is not remembered in the sense of being largely retrieved from information stored in long-term memory. Memory is both the reconstruction of stored representations and an activity that people often do together (e.g., see Radley, 1990); therefore, there is no one self to be retrieved or remembered. Considering the remembered self as one kind of self-knowledge (Neisser, 1988a) highlights this problem even more, since such knowledge is unstable and is always being updated, interpreted, and reinterpreted as it is used in the commerce of everyday life. Put simply, memorial processes are centrally involved in the forming of self, but a *self* is not an entity (e.g., Eakin, 1985; Sartre, 1965, 1966) represented or located in memory that can be contacted and brought forth on important occasions.

Third, equating the remembered self with memory alone overemphasizes the cognitive contribution to self and underemphasizes the role of affect (Deci & Ryan, 1990; Stern, 1990). This differential emphasis may shadow important relationships between emotions and meanings which give certain recollections "personal significance" relative to that associated with other memories. Remembrances that become selves are pregnant with meanings: Meanings are bound together by the emotional life of individuals interconnected with the lives of others. The meanings and derived significance of such recollections are in flux as memories are used and reused for various purposes, as in emotional regulation of oneself and others. My view is that personally significant memories are those that carry meanings acquired in their adaptive (consequential) uses, mostly in relationships with others.

Fourth, important cultural, historical, and relational (e.g., joint remembering) aspects of remembering may be overlooked by specifying an identity relationship between memory and the remembered self. And fifth, Neisser's (1988a) notion of the remembered self is rooted in an as yet underspecified assumption about the nature of autobiographical memories as being memories for self-referenced information. As Brewer (1986) states, "Autobiographical memory is memory for information related to the self" (p. 26). This assumption implies that a self (as either a cognitive structure, motive, or essence) must be in place prior to and separate from the information being remembered. It may be that cognition, essence, and the remembered self develop in parallel instead of sequentially.

The logical problems associated with specifying self as irreducible beyond motives or essence are as daunting as the problems that arise by specifying self as a cognitive structure. Each set of claims assumes an existing referent; what distinguishes a motivational from a cognitive perspective on self is their respective (teleological) referent. My own ontological stance when considering the remembered self draws from perceptual, interpersonal, cognitive, and motivational theories of self. In brief, the *me*, as separate from the *it* and the *other*, is first known in and through the spontaneous activities of the whole organism. I view these activities as properties of all living systems; they need not imply human motives or be motivated in the sense of a psychological need for control or autonomy. Such needs seem to develop as infants interact with their environment and through relatedness with significant others, and depend in part on the cultural context of development. The *I,* as a self-legislating agent that willfully acts, is known in and through the uniquely human capabilities for, and activities associated with, imagination, reflection, and reason.

On this view, self, and the remembered self especially, is initially a consequence rather than a cause of activity, constructed originally via the direct perception of affordances and invariant structures in the (physical and social) world. The "present self" (Neisser, 1988a, p. 13) is specified by interaction with the environment by an organism that moves in that environment, both physically and affectively (E. Gibson, 1990; Loveland, 1990; Neisser, 1988a; Trevarthen, 1990). The remembered self, relative to the present self, is a later development; it is distinct from (but related to) the global vitality of living human organisms, and it is formed through the use of semiotic systems like language, which eventually mediate thought and social activities.

The relevance of this discussion for understanding how remembered selves are composed goes to the heart of my conception of what makes a memory autobiographical and the relationship between autobiographical remembering and self; specifically, the discussion raises the issue of *how* meaning is constructed in and by human activity. Determining how meaning is created in activity, in turn, leads to an alternative conception of autobiographical memory; specifically, an autobiographical memory is autobiographical because it has acquired "personal significance" through the allocation and appropriation of meaning. From the perspective of direct perception and the experience of the present self, the meaning of objects, events, and experiences is in the emergent information flow as the person and environment interact. What something means, be it physical or social (Loveland, 1990), is determined by what interactional (physical and emotional) activities it affords.

For instance, consider the case of the forming of attachments between primary caretakers and infants. The forms attachments take are determined both by patterns of relatedness established through primary intersubjectivity during infancy (Trevarthen, 1983) and by the needs of society's members to produce and reproduce themselves by conveying to children the meanings and uses of cultural symbols (e.g., Heath, 1990; Herdt, 1990). The activities associated with interpersonal relatedness involve mutuality in the control and regulation of attention, intention, and emotion. In this instance meaning is in social (re)productive activities which are activities that are inherently purposeful and oriented toward some goal, for example, becoming a community member with full rights and responsibilities, a person who shares cultural meanings with others.

One avenue for understanding how meaning is created is to consider

Obeyesekere's (1981) explanation of how *shared meanings* are acquired (see also Berger & Luckmann, 1966). Obeyesekere proposes an objectification–subjectification process whereby *objectification* is the process of making private feelings public (p. 77). These feelings are often expressed in public idioms like "I blew my stack" to express anger. Thus, personal feelings are objectified and made available for consumption by others. He proposes further that *subjectification* "is the process" of internalization whereby objectified feelings are assimilated by the person (p. 169).

The objectification–subjectification process is clearly transactional among members of a community. It is the process through which *cultural experts* (or ritual experts in many cases; Barth, 1987) objectify meaning in social activities (and objects) for others to participate in, consider, and subjectify. Accordingly, through subjectification, culture (e.g., in the sharing of narrative forms) is not only preserved but also created, as individuals continue to objectify their interpretations of what they have learned and remembered from others, and repeatedly objectify and subjectify those extended or new interpretations.

Presumably, children not only learn what to do from more capable others – for instance, parents and teachers who function as cultural experts in our society. They also learn and remember the meaning and associated personal significance of what they do through culturally and socially organized activities. Determining what is or is not meaningful and personally significant is marked initially by others and subsequently internalized and felt (subjectified) by the child. In short, meaning is in doing socially structured activities that are relevant at different times during the lifespan.

An alternative conception of autobiographical memory. Grounding the remembered self and, consequently, autobiographical memories in the ecological epistemology of Gibsonian direct perception, the social-interactional approach to development espoused by Trevarthen, Stern, and Vygotsky, and the notion of an ongoing process of objectification–subjectification of feeling in social contexts to create and transmit cultural meanings leads to an alternative conception of autobiographical memories. My view is that autobiographical memories arise from embodied experience via direct perceptual experiences (i.e., exteroceptive, proprioceptive, and kinesthetic) and interpersonal interactions with others, whose meaning and personal significance is marked by the (social) activities engaged in at the time of perception and in the process of reconstructive memory. The argument that autobiographical memories are linked to direct perception is a move around the teleological problems of either a strong cognitive or motivational account of self. In short, a memory is autobiographical because it carries meaning that is personalized through perceptual, language-based and sociocultural activities, and not because it is initially referenced to an ego-self.

To parallel the arguments made above, the remembered self is more a consequence than a cause of remembering, at least in the early phases of memory development and self-construction. The remembered self may be formed in personal and other kinds of autobiographical memories (Brewer, 1986; for memories that could be considered as basic-level personal prototypes, see Rosch, 1978; Rosch, Mervis, Gray, Johnson, & Boyes-Braem, 1976) once it is understood how certain memories become "personalized" through experience. It is only at this point that the remembered self can be thought of as influencing the perception and remembering of new information, as well as influencing selective judgments that some experiences and memories are self-relevant while others are not.

The relationships between autobiographical memory and self: The remembered self reconsidered.   Sartre wrote that "without the world, there is no selfness, no person; without selfness, without the person, there is no world" (1966, p. 157). From Sartre's theory of existence, it follows that a real world has consequences for humans who are ultimately responsible for their actions because their actions do not simply affect themselves alone, they affect all others as well (Sartre, 1965, pp. 63–73).

The relationship between autobiographical memory and self mirrors Sartre's insights. Autobiographical memories as the objectifications of selfness are rooted in the world since they derive from a directly perceived physical and social reality; the remembered self is then reconstructed in autobiographical memories that can impact the world. In this way, self eventually becomes both the consequence and cause of purposeful human activity. I suspect that when remembering for some purpose like emotional regulation or the establishment of friendships, many people extrapolate from an "island" of personal memories to a remembered self; one autobiographical recollection serving to illuminate yet others (Linton, 1986; Neisser, 1986; Salaman, 1970), eventually establishing an archipelago whose pattern and form reveals both the remembered self of the moment and the contours of the historical self.

The remembered self described above can serve many pragmatic and symbolic purposes for the individual and society. For instance, remembered selves in autobiographical memories can convey to children the character and meaning of family through the parents' telling their personal histories. Or, personal histories can be used to write the history of a particular time period and place (e.g., Thompson, 1988). The use of autobiographical memories for such purposes points to the social, relational, and distributed aspects of remembering as a collective activity, and by extension, the collective properties of remembered selves.

3. Autobiographical remembering

> The history of the study of memory is a tale of the search for a faculty, a quest for the way in which the mind-brain codes, stores and retrieves information. Only with the recent interest in language and in cultural aspects of thinking has there emerged the wider view of remembering as something people do together, reminding themselves of and commemorating experiences which they have jointly undertaken.
>
> Radley (1990), p. 46

How the theorist conceives the nature of self, memory in general, and autobiographical memory in particular, determines the kind of remembered self proposed. My purpose in this section is not to consider the nature of memory per se; instead, my concern is with how autobiographical memory is used in adaptive ways – in particular, in intrapsychic ways and in interpersonal relationships (Barclay & Hodges, 1990; Baddeley, 1988; Neisser, 1988b). Considering the adaptive functions of autobiographical memory, nevertheless, has implications for how we conceptualize memory as a human faculty.

My particular view of autobiographical remembering derives in part from Bartlett's (1932) (re)constructive theory of remembering and recent work on cultural models (e.g., Holland & Quinn, 1987; Stigler, Shweder, & Herdt, 1990) and collective remembering (Middleton & Edwards, 1990). For Bartlett, constructive and reconstructive remembering is both a social and mental activity organized around justifying feelings. Bartlett writes, "When a subject is being asked to remember, very often the first thing that emerges is something of the nature of attitude. The recall is then a construction, made largely on the basis of this attitude, and its general effect is that of a justification of the attitude" (p. 207). He argues further that this process not only serves social functions – for instance (citing Halbwachs's [1925, pp. 294–296] views), the role played by collective family memories and the constitution of social groups (see also Schwartz, 1990, for the role of collective remembering and the social practices of commemoratives); remembering is also shaped by practices associated with social institutions and practices. The influences of sociocultural practices and institutions are revealed by the "conventionalization" of memories (e.g., through the use of a particular canonical narrative form) as they are passed among people who share a common culture (pp. 268–280).

Considering autobiographical remembering as an activity for justifying feelings suggests that what is remembered is, at times, an emergent or manifestation of individual productive ([re]constructive) remembering and collective activities (co-[re]constructive) (Barclay & Smith, 1991).

At least four reasons can be cited to support the claim that many autobiographical recollections are emergents. First, there is growing evidence from the developmental and cognitive literature suggesting that autobiographical memories are used very often in interaction with others for identifiable purposes, thereby providing opportunities for new memories to be formed and old ones to be reshaped (e.g., Baddeley, 1988; Bruner, 1990; Fivush, 1991; Fivush & Fromhoff, 1988; Middleton & Edwards, 1990; Miller et al., 1990; Neisser, 1988b). Second, one's feelings (alone and in interpersonal relationships) ebb and flow over short and long time periods, thus requiring "on-line" fine tuning and occasionally major additions and revisions in the (re)construction of the past to adapt to a dynamic and somewhat uncertain present. Third, because remembering and interacting usually occur over time and not instantaneously, it is often difficult to anticipate with precision either what in fact will be remembered or the reactions of oneself and others to what is being remembered – a dynamic whose consequences can influence what is subsequently (re)constructed. And fourth, as autobiographical recollections are used to adapt to novel situations and variations in familiar contexts, they acquire new meanings and interpretations that may change how the past is recollected and what is subsequently remembered in the future.

If the line of reasoning developed thus far is correct and captures, at least descriptively, important aspects of how memories might be used in the world as well as some of the factors that influence those uses, then remembered selves composed through processes of productive autobiographical remembering and productive interacting are also emergent properties of such activities.

Functions of autobiographical remembering. An assumption central to my position is that autobiographical remembering and remembered selves serve adaptive purposes in everyday life. In particular, they function at individual, social, and cultural levels (see also Robinson & Swanson, 1990). At the individual level autobiographical memories can be used to maintain a sense of coherence (Allport, 1955; Barclay & Hodges, 1990; Epstein, 1973; see, however, Barclay, 1992; Langer, 1991) and associated mental health as currently understood within a culture. An inability to reconstruct autobiographical memories can be distressing and anxiety-provoking, and under certain circumstances indicates the effects of extreme stress. For example, functional retrograde amnesia (Schacter, Wang, Tulving, & Freedman, 1982) and neuropathology, such as organic retrograde amnesia as found in Alzheimer's disease, can be indicated. Individuals may also use autobiographical memories as a means of regulating their own feelings (e.g., as self-objects) and thoughts (Barclay & Smith, 1992; Smith & Barclay, 1990); as such, autobiographical remembering is a conscious strategy for controlling attention when coping with either anxiety or boredom or when maintaining a sense of well-being through reflection or meditation. In addition, autobiographical memories may be used imaginatively to explore possible selves (Markus, 1983) or the nature of other selves (Robinson & Swanson, 1990) and to relate one's personal memories to cultural events, as in "flashbulb memories" (Brown & Kulik, 1977; Neisser, 1982a).

Altogether, autobiographical memories serve emotional, cognitive, and imaginative intrapsychic functions, and in so doing, demonstrate how inseparable feeling and thinking are in the phenomenal world of the individual. It is hypothesized that the remembered self at this level is experienced phenomenally by the individual when autobiographical memories are being used for one or more of the functions outlined above. Since the person remembering is the same person for whom some particular recollection is being used, the wholeness of self may be experienced instantly: For example, a personal memory (figure) is experienced within the gestalt of the historical self (ground), thereby becoming a conscious token of self. The significance and meaning of such recollections are known and understood because of the symbiotic relationship between any single recollection and a person's awareness of the overall pattern of his or her life.

At the social level, autobiographical memories appear to be of special importance (the social and individual functions are obviously related) because they function to establish and maintain intimate interpersonal relationships (Barclay & Hodges, 1990; Halbwachs, 1925; Neisser, 1988b; Ross & Holmberg, 1990) through the mutual regulation of attention, feelings, and thoughts. Establishing and maintaining interpersonal relationships, such as parent–child and significant-other relationships, friendships, and companionships, are rooted in the social nature of being human, from infancy through the lifespan. Intimacies are sustained through shared intellectual and emotional experiences, interests, and meanings, common and co-constructed autobiographical memories, and, in general, joint personal histories. The relevance of the intimacy function of autobiographical remembering can be seen easily in cases of people, such as couples married for a long time, whose shared histories are interrupted or ended, as through long separation, divorce, or death. In such situations, the initial feelings of loneliness and emptiness (there are probably gender differences here, with males more likely to feel lonely and females to feel relieved) often result from the loss of the social relationship that was mutually structuring of attention and emotion, as well as from the loss of that part of the remembered self in common with the other (J. Broughton, personal communication). At the social level, autobiographical memories are experienced as being in relation with an other; at this level, the remembered self is perceived as a relational self inseparable from the other (Buber, 1958; Gergen & Gergen, 1988).

The possible functions of autobiographical remembering suggested here at the cultural level are speculative. To my knowledge there are few, if any, systematic data showing how autobiographical memories are used at this level, although it is apparent that such uses of autobiographical remembering occur frequently. Anecdotal observation suggests that cultural experts like teachers convey their interpretations of culture by reporting their own autobiographical memories in conversations with children or telling about their lives in relation to the lives of significant cultural figures and events. For example, veterans recall Pearl Harbor or D-Day, and ex–civil rights activists tell stories of marching with Martin Luther King, Jr., or meeting other historical figures personally. Often, memories are used as oral histories of particular times and places, although it is not clear to what extent these memories are autobiographical in the sense of carrying meaning for the individual remembering. In our culture, written autobiographies (and biographies) are widely available and represent cultural artifacts (Olney, 1980). These kinds of materials are also found in autobiographies written for children (e.g., Cleary, 1988), in children's storybooks (e.g., Paterson, 1977), and in school textbooks as character studies of historical figures. Novels for adolescents, such as those of Judy Blume (e.g., Blume, 1957), often recount the lives of characters struggling with existential problems similar to those being experienced by the reader. However, such products of culture are not necessarily spontaneous uses of autobiographical remembering as might be found in cultures with strong oral traditions, or in the everyday conversational remembering that forms much of the basis of interpersonal relationships and the remembered self.

Intriguing examples of how memories and (perhaps) autobiographical memories might be used to create and maintain culture are given in a collection of papers reported by Neisser (1982b). One well-known piece is that by Lord (1960/1982) on the use of themes, formulas, and songs by bards in Yugoslavia to convey epic tales. Although these stories may not be tied directly to the experiences of the bard or anyone else for that matter, the epic character and events portrayed may function as prototypes, offering objectified imagery that may be used by listeners to interpret and understand their own life experiences or cultural origin.

In another paper, D'Azevedo (1962/1982) reports on the "griots," elder oral historians among the Gola of the Liberian coast of West Africa who give presumably first-hand historical accounts or accounts of events and people that were told to them by former elders. Whether or not elders experienced remembered events directly seems unimportant as long as those listening believe that they have. In Gola society, a concept of the past plays a central role in daily life because orally conveyed knowledge about families and genealogies gives individuals a sense of their position and influence in society and connects them with ancestors who have "distinct personalities" and "who continue to concern themselves with the affairs of their living descendants" (p. 260). Thus, the past is preserved in a way that maintains the integrity of the family. Knowledge of the past is also important for the Gola because it suggests possible solutions to problems in the present, helps to propagate social practices and customs, and preserves the "thoughts and experiences of the ancestors" (p. 267).

In each of these examples individual and, at times, collective remembering results in the transmission and creation of culture. In the case of the Gola, when elders reconstruct history they provide an authenticated basis for constituting similar experiences in the uninformed because they themselves experienced the past either directly or indirectly. What is remembered is both autobiographical and cultural because of the individual and collective significance of history. In part, the remembered self at the cultural level is experienced and used at the time histories are told or when public forums are called to recount the past. In the latter instance, the remembered self is relational and distributed because of the social activities elders or other cultural experts engage in to maintain their social role in and with their communities.

Most generally, observing the uses of autobiographical remembering at the individual, social, and cultural levels will involve explicating *how* such recollections create, transform, and transmit knowledge in the context of cultural models; one possible general activity for doing so is suggested in the last section of this essay.

4. Composing protoselves through improvisation

> When we speak of a canvas of Picasso, we never say that it is arbitrary; we understand quite well that he was making himself what he is at the very time he was painting, that the ensemble of his work is embodied in his life.
>
> Sartre (1965), p. 55

Throughout this essay I have argued that autobiographical remembering is a productive activity associated with affect and interpersonal relationships, and an activity that is nested in the context of cultural models. Autobiographical remembering is of special importance because it is through autobiographical remembering that remembered selves are objectified in the present as memories of particular experiences. These experiences presumably reflect underlying patterns in a life that are recognizable to the individual and intimate community members with shared personal histories.

I now propose that autobiographical remembering is largely an improvisational act. Accordingly, the improvisational activities that are characteristic of autobiographical remembering – for example, ongoing justifications of fluctuating feelings in and between people – create *protoselves*, or remembered selves in the making. Protoselves coalesce as a contemporary remembered self as they are shaped and reshaped in memory and interaction, and as they gain legitimacy and become socially accepted by others who know us well. The notion of remembered selves in the making, therefore, captures best the qualitative and dynamic aspects associated with creating self-knowledge, and provides a summary description of the activities collaborating to form a remembered self in the present.

By definition, to improvise is "to compose, recite, or sing on the spur of the moment; to make, invent, or arrange offhand" (*Webster's Seventh New Collegiate Dictionary*, 1965, p. 421). Ostransky (1960), in discussing jazz, points out that there are two broad kinds of improvisation, "free and controlled" (p. 47). However, as Ostransky notes, all improvisations are more or less controlled, even so-called free improvisations, since, as Pressing (1984) argues, constraints can emerge at the time of actual performance through context effects or as physical limitations of the performer.

To show that an improvisation is controlled is to specify the contextualizing referential system within which the improvisation occurs. (Examples of such systems were discussed earlier as cultural models, metaphor, and narration.) Pressing (1984), in reference to improvisation in music, dance, and theater, argues that the notion of *referent* is central to improvisation where "the referent is an underlying formal scheme or guiding image specific to a given piece, used by the improviser to facilitate the generation and editing of improvised behavior" (p. 346).

Even though *referent* is used here largely in the sense of a mental representational system, it need not be so limited: Improvisational acts in most domains occur in social and cultural contexts that provide structure to activity beyond that given by the mental representational system. Put simply, the images, schemata, and frameworks forming the referential base guiding improvisation can have multiple source domains both within and outside the person.

Examples of referents external and internal to the performer are abundant in the arts. Historically, common referents for music include musical structures, motives, and mood; for dance, typical referents are music, kinetic or structural images, movement qualities, stories, and emotions; and for drama, social situations, stories, and emotions (Pressing, 1984, p. 347). Pressing argues that the great variety found in improvised behavior results from the large number of referential systems available for use within particular performance domains.

In my view, a similar situation exists when we improvise in autobiographical remembering. It is because of the variety of internal and external referential systems available and accessible to improvise from – for example, attitudes and feelings, metaphors, personal memories, meaningful objects in our immediate environment (Csikszentmihalyi & Rochberg-Halton, 1981), and others with whom we are interacting – that we can create variability in our autobiographical memories and, consequently, in our remembered selves. However, even with wide variability in objectified remembered selves, the improvised selves created are grounded in referent systems that have social, cultural, and historical significance, and which tend to remain relatively stable over a person's lifespan, except during times of personal or cultural upheaval.

It is noteworthy that improvisation is an *acquired skill*. Although improvising shares characteristics (e.g., generativity) with language and language development, it also requires practice and the acquisition of broad-based knowledge about a genre (e.g., music or dance) as well as domain-specific knowledge (e.g., jazz and traditional Japanese music, or modern dance and ballet; Pressing, 1984). The genre to be known when improvising protoselves is a cultural concept of *person*; the domain-specific knowledge is one's own personal history. Learning to improvise, like learning most other skills, is often done in relation with a more skilled and knowledgeable improviser, someone who offers guided practice in a fashion analogous to teaching within the zone of proximal development (Vygotsky, 1978), as in the Suzuki method for teaching violin or the mentoring of youth during adolescence. Furthermore, improvising involves feedback from what is produced as well as from others directly (e.g., a participating partner with shared responsibilities) or indirectly (an attentive audience) involved in the improvisation.

Conclusion

My position is that the self is not remembered because the self does not exist as something to be remembered. I make this claim for reasons derived from two basic commitments: The self is not an entity whose existence becomes separate from and controlling of the dynamics of perception, interpersonal relationships, and cognition; and remembering is an adaptive process through which the constructed and reconstructed past serves present psychosocial and cultural needs. I have argued that remembered selves are in the making at times when autobiographical memories are (re)constructed for purposes like maintaining intimate interpersonal relationships and regulating one's own emotions. Resulting protoselves are composed through a skilled process of improvisation such that what is created anew is referenced and firmly tied to the past – the declarative knowledge that certain events and lived experiences in fact happened even though those experiences cannot be remembered in the sense of veridical recall. These recollections are, nevertheless, innovatively adapted to present circumstances and legitimized through social consensus. Like other acts of objectification, improvisations yield protoselves constrained by a life lived and a life being lived and by evolving social agreements regarding the range of culturally acceptable selves.

ACKNOWLEDGMENTS

This essay was prepared while I was on sabbatical at Emory University. It was supported by the Emory Cognition Project and Mellon Colloquium on the Self. I am especially indebted to Ulric Neisser as a friend and colleague for sharing his wonderment and insights regarding self with me; and to Robyn Fivush and the students and faculty who participated in the Remembered Self seminar. I would also like to thank Charles W. Nuckolls for introducing me to the literature on cultural models in language, thought, and emotion, and to Robert McCauley and John Pani for commenting on an early version of this essay.

NOTE

1 Ogbu (1990) writes: "I define a cultural model as an understanding that a people have of their universe – social, physical, or both – as well as their understanding of their behavior in that universe. The cultural model of a population serves its members as a guide in their interpretations of events and elements within their universe; it also serves as a guide to their expectation and actions in that universe or environment. Furthermore, the cultural model underlies their folk theories or folk explanations of recurrent circumstances, events, and situations in various domains of life. . . . Members of a society or its segment develop their cultural model from collective historical experiences. . . . The cultural model has both instrumental and expressive dimensions. . . .

"Some students of cultural models focus on its cognitive organization – how cultural knowledge or the people's understanding of their universe is organized inside their head – and the relation of that organization to behaviors and actions (Holland & Quinn, 1987).

"My approach is different, I focus on the nature of cultural model as can be learned or constructed from what members of a population say (their 'talk') as well as from what they actually do (their 'behavior' or 'action'), rather than on how their cultural model or cultural knowledge is organized inside their head" (p. 523).

REFERENCES

Allport, G. W. (1955). *Becoming*. New Haven, CT: Yale University Press.

Baddeley, A. (1988). What the hell is it for? In M. M. Gruneberg, P. E. Morris, & R. N. Sykes (Eds.), *Practical aspects of memory: Current research and issues: Vol. 1. Memory in everyday life* (pp. 3–18). New York: Wiley.

Bakhurst, D. (1990). Social memory in Soviet thought. In D. Middleton & D. Edwards (Eds.), *Collective remembering* (pp. 203–226). London: Sage.

Bannister, D., & Agnew, J. (1976). The child's construing of self. In J. Cole (Ed.), *Nebraska symposium on motivation* (pp. 99–125). Lincoln, NE: University of Nebraska Press.

Barclay, C. R. (1986). Schematization of autobiographical memory. In D. C. Rubin (Ed.), *Autobiographical memory* (pp. 82–89). Cambridge University Press.

Barclay, C. R. (1988). Truth and accuracy in autobiographical memory. In M. M. Gruneberg, P. E. Morris, & R. N. Sykes (Eds.), *Practical aspects of memory: Current research and issues: Vol. 1. Memory in everyday life* (pp. 289–294). New York: Wiley.

Barclay, C. R. (1992). Remembering ourselves. In G. M. Davies & B. Logie (Eds.), *Memory in everyday life*. The Netherlands: North Holland Press.

Barclay, C. R., & Hodges, R. M. (1990). La composition de soi dans les souvenirs autobiographiques. *Psychologie Française, 35,* 59–65.

Barclay, C. R., Petitto, A., Labrum, A. H., & Carter-Jessop, L. (1991). Mood-related self-schemata and mood-congruity effects in autobiographical memory: A study of women with premenstrual syndrome. *Applied Cognitive Psychology, 5,* 461–481.

Barclay, C. R., & Smith, T. S. (1992). Autobiographical remembering: Creating personal culture. In M. A. Conway, D. C. Rubin, H. Spinnless, & W. Wageman (Eds.), *Theoretical perspectives on autobiographical memory* (pp. 75–98). The Netherlands: Kluwer.

Barclay, C. R., & Smith, T. S. (1993). Autobiographical remembering and self-composing. *International Journal of Personal Construct Psychology, 15,* 1–25.

Barth, F. (1987) *Cosmologies in the making: A generative approach to cultural variation in inner New Guinea*. Cambridge University Press.

Bartlett, F. C. (1923). *Psychology and primitive culture*. Cambridge University Press.

Bartlett, F. C. (1932). *Remembering: A study in experimental and social psychology*. Cambridge University Press.

Berger, P. L., & Luckmann, T. (1966). *The social construction of reality*. New York: Doubleday.

Blume, J. (1957). *Forever. . . .* New York: Pocket Books.

Brewer, W. F. (1986). What is autobiographical memory? In D. C. Rubin (Ed.), *Autobiographical memory* (pp. 25–49). Cambridge University Press.

Brewer, W. F., & Nakamura, G. V. (1984). The nature and functions of schemas. In R. S. Wyer & T. K. Srull (Eds.), *Handbook of social cognition* (Vol. 1, pp. 119–160). Hillsdale, NJ: Erlbaum.

Brewer, W. F., & Pani, J. R. (1982). *Personal memory, generic memory, and skill: An empirical study*. Paper presented at the 23rd annual meeting of the Psychonomic Society, Minneapolis, MN.

Brown, R., & Kulik, J. (1977). Flashbulb memories. *Cognition, 5,* 73–99.

Bruner, J. (1987). Life as narrative. *Social Research, 43,* 11–32.

Bruner, J. (1990). *Acts of meaning*. Cambridge, MA: Harvard University Press.

Buber, M. (1958). *I and thou*. New York: Macmillan.

Carr, D. (1986). *Time, narrative, and history*. Bloomington: Indiana University Press.

Cleary, B. (1988). *A girl from Yamhill: A memoir*. New Holland, CT: Yearling Books (Dell).

Csikszentmihalyi, M., & Rochberg-Halton, E. (1981). *The meaning of things*. Cambridge University Press.

D'Andrade, R. (1990). Some propositions about the relation between culture and human cognition. In J. W. Stigler, R. A. Shweder, & H. Gilbert (Eds.), *Cultural psychology: Essays on comparative human development* (pp. 65–129). Cambridge University Press.

D'Azevedo, W. L. (1982). Tribal history in Liberia. In U. Neisser (Ed.), *Memory observed: Remembering in natural contexts* (pp. 258–268). San Francisco: Freeman. (Original work published 1962)

Deci, E. L., & Ryan, R. M. (1990). A motivational approach to self: Integration in personality. In R. Dienstbier (Ed.), *Nebraska symposium on motivation* (Perspectives on motivation, Vol. 38, pp. 237–288). Lincoln: University of Nebraska Press.

Durkheim, E. (1954). *Elementary forms of the religious life*. London: Allen & Unwin.

Eakin, P. J. (1985). *Fictions in autobiography: Studies in the art of self-invention*. Princeton, NJ: Princeton University Press.

Eder, R. A., Gerlach, S. G., & Perlmutter, M. (1987). In search of children's selves: Development of the specific and general components of the self-concept. *Child Development, 58*, 1044–1050.

Epstein, S. (1973). The self-concept revisited: Or a theory of a theory. *American Psychologist, 28*, 404–416.

Fivush, R. (1988). The functions of event memory: Some comments on Nelson and Barsalou. In U. Neisser & E. Winograd (Eds.), *Remembering reconsidered: Ecological and traditional approaches to the study of memory* (pp. 277–282). Cambridge University Press.

Fivush, R. (1991). The social construction of personal narratives. *Merrill-Palmer Quarterly, 37*, 59–82.

Fivush, R., & Fromhoff, F. A. (1988). Style and structure in mother–child conversations about the past. *Discourse Processes, 11*, 337–355.

Gergen, K. J., & Gergen, M. M. (1988). Narrative and self as relationship. *Advances in Experimental Social Psychology, 21*, 17–56.

Gibson, E. J. (1993). *Ontogenesis of the perceived self*. In U. Neisser (Ed.), *The perceived self: Ecological and interpersonal sources of self-knowledge* (pp. 25–42). Cambridge University Press.

Gibson, J. J. (1990). *The sociological approach to visual perception*. Hillsdale, NJ: Erlbaum. (Original work published 1979)

Grene, M. (1993). *The primacy of the ecological self*. In U. Neisser (Ed.), *The perceived self: Ecological and interpersonal sources of self-knowledge* (pp. 112–117). Cambridge University Press.

Halbwachs, M. (1925). *Les cadres sociaux de la mémoire*. Paris: Alcan (Travaux de l'Année Sociologique).

Handel, A. (1987). Personal theories about the life-span development of one's self in autobiographical self-presentations of adults. *Human Development, 30*, 83–98.

Heath, S. B. (1990). The children of Trackton's children: Spoken and written language in social change. In J. W. Stigler, R. A. Shweder, & G. Herdt (Eds.),

Cultural psychology: Essays on comparative human development (pp. 496–519). Cambridge University Press.

Herdt, G. (1990). Sambia nosebleeding rites and male proximity to women. In J. W. Stigler, R. A. Shweder, & G. Herdt (Eds.), *Cultural psychology: Essays on comparative human development* (pp. 366–400). Cambridge University Press.

Holland, D., & Quinn, N. (Eds.). (1987). *Cultural models in language and thought.* Cambridge University Press.

Johnson, M. (1987). *The body in the mind: The bodily basis of meaning, imagination, and reason.* Chicago: University of Chicago Press.

Johnson, M. K., & Raye, C. L. (1981). Reality monitoring. *Psychological Review, 88,* 67–85.

Kohut, H. (1971). *The analysis of the self: A systematic approach to the psychoanalytic treatment of narcissistic personality disorders.* New York: International Universities Press.

Kohut, H. (1977). *The restoration of the self.* New York: International Universities Press.

Lakoff, G. (1986). *Women, fire and dangerous things: What categories reveal about the mind.* Chicago: University of Chicago Press.

Lakoff, G. (1987). Cognitive models and prototype theory. In U. Neisser (Ed.), *Concepts and conceptual development: Ecological and intellectual factors in categorization* (pp. 63–100). Cambridge University Press.

Lakoff, G., & Johnson, M. (1980). *Metaphors we live by.* Chicago: University of Chicago Press.

Langer, L. L. (1991). *Holocaust testimonies: The ruins of memory.* New Haven, CT: Yale University Press.

Linde, C. (1987). Explanatory systems in oral life stories. In D. Holland & N. Quinn (Eds.), *Cultural models in language and thought* (pp. 343–366). Cambridge University Press.

Linton, M. (1986). Ways of searching and the contents of memory. In D. C. Rubin (Ed.), *Autobiographical memory* (pp. 50–67). Cambridge University Press.

Loevinger, J. (1976). *Ego development.* San Francisco: Jossey-Bass.

Lord, A. (1982). Oral poetry in Yugoslavia. In U. Neisser (Ed.), *Memory observed: Remembering in natural contexts* (pp. 243–257). San Francisco: Freeman. (Original work published 1960)

Loveland, K. (1990). *Autism, affordances and the self.* Paper presented at the Emory Cognition Project Conference on the Interpersonal Self, Emory University, Atlanta, GA.

Lowenthal, D. (1985). *The past in a foreign country.* Cambridge University Press.

Markus, H. (1977). Self-schemata and processing information about the self. *Journal of Personality and Social Psychology, 35,* 63–78.

Markus, H. (1983). Self-knowledge: An expanded view. *Journal of Personality, 51,* 543–565.

Middleton, D., & Edwards, D. (Eds.). (1990). *Collective remembering.* London: Sage.

Miller, P. J., Potts, R., Fung, H., Hoogstra, L., & Mintz, J. (1990). Narrative practices and the social construction of self in childhood. *American Ethnologist, 17,* 292–311.

Neisser, U. (1982a). Snapshots or benchmarks? In U. Neisser (Ed.), *Memory observed: Remembering in natural contexts* (pp. 43–48). San Francisco: Freeman.

Neisser, U. (Ed.). (1982b). *Memory observed: Remembering in natural contexts.* San Francisco: Freeman.

Neisser, U. (1986). Nested structure in autobiographical memory. In D. C. Rubin (Ed.), *Autobiographical memory* (pp. 71–81). Cambridge University Press.

Neisser, U. (1988a). Five kinds of self-knowledge. *Philosophical Psychology, 1,* 35–59. (Emory Cognition Project Rep. No. 14, Department of Psychology, Emory University, Atlanta, GA.)

Neisser, U. (1988b). Time present and time past. In M. M. Gruneberg, P. E. Morris, & R. N. Sykes (Eds.), *Practical aspects of memory: Current research and issues: Vol. 2. Clinical and educational implications,* pp. 545–560. New York: Wiley.

Neisser, U. (1990). *Modes of perception and forms of knowledge.* Paper presented at the Japanese Psychological Association, Tokyo, Japan.

Nelson, K. (1986). *Event knowledge: Structure and function in development.* Hillsdale, NJ: Erlbaum.

Nelson, K. (1989). Monologue as representation of real-life experience. In K. Nelson (Ed.), *Narratives from the crib* (pp. 27–72). Cambridge, MA: Harvard University Press.

Nuckolls, C. W. (1990). *Cultural models in language, thought, and emotion.* Department of Anthropology (Anthropology 597), Emory University, Atlanta, GA.

Obeysekere, G. (1981). *Medusa's hair: An essay on personal symbols and religious experience.* Chicago: University of Chicago Press.

Ogbu, J. U. (1990). Cultural model, identity, and literacy. In J. W. Stigler, R. A. Shweder, & G. Herdt (Eds.), *Cultural psychology: Essays on comparative human development* (pp. 520–541). Cambridge University Press.

Olney, J. (1980). *Autobiography: Essays theoretical and critical.* Princeton, NJ: Princeton University Press.

Ostransky, L. (1960). *The anatomy of jazz.* Westport, CT: Greenwood.

Paterson, K. (1977). *Bridge to terabithia.* New York: Harper & Row.

Piaget, J. (1952). *The origins of intelligence in children.* New York: International Universities Press.

Pillemer, D. B. (1990). *Remembering personal circumstances: A functional analysis.* Paper presented at the Emory Cognition Project Conference on Flashbulb Memories, Emory University, Atlanta, GA.

Polkinghorne, D. (1988). *Narrative knowing and the human sciences.* Albany, NY: SUNY Press.

Pressing, J. (1984). Cognitive processes in improvisation. In W. R. Crozier & A. J. Chapman (Eds.), *Cognitive processes in the perception of art* (pp. 345–363). North Holland: Elsevier Science Publishers.

Radley, A. (1990). Artefacts, memory and a sense of the past. In D. Middleton & D. Edwards (Eds.), *Collective remembering* (pp. 46–59). London: Sage.

Robinson, J. A., & Swanson, K. L. (1990). Autobiographical memory: The next phase. *Applied Cognitive Psychology, 4,* 321–335.

Rosch, E. (1978). Principles of categorization. In E. Rosch & B. B. Lloyd (Eds.), *Cognition and categorization* (pp. 27–48). Hillsdale, NJ: Erlbaum.

Rosch, E., Mervis, C. B., Gray, W. D., Johnson, D. M., & Boyes-Braem, P. (1976). Basic objects in natural categories. *Cognitive Psychology, 8,* 225–238.

Ross, M. (1989). Relation of implicit theories to the construction of personal histories. *Psychological Review, 96,* 341–357.

Ross, M., & Holmberg, D. (1990). Recounting the past: Gender differences in the recall of events in the history of a close relationship. In M. P. Zanna & J. M. Olson (Eds.), *Self-inference processes* (Vol. 6: The Ontario Symposium, pp. 135–152). Hillsdale, NJ: Erlbaum.

Rubin, D. C. (Ed.). (1986). *Autobiographical memory.* Cambridge University Press.

Ryan, R. M. (1991). The nature of the self in autonomy and relatedness. In G. R. Goethals & J. Strauss (Eds.), *Multidisciplinary perspectives on the self.* New York: Springer-Verlag.

Salaman, E. (1970). *A collection of moments: A study of involuntary memories.* London: Longman.

Sartre, J.-P. (1965). *Essays in existentialism.* Secaucus, NJ: Citadel Press.

Sartre, J.-P. (1966). *Being and nothingness.* New York: Pocket Books.

Schacter, D. L., Wang, P. L., Tulving, E., & Freedman, M. (1982). Functional retrograde amnesia: A quantitative case study. *Neuropsychologia, 20,* 523–532.

Schank, R., & Abelson, R. P. (1977). *Scripts, plans, goals, and understanding.* Hillsdale, NJ: Erlbaum.

Schwartz, B. (1990). The reconstruction of Abraham Lincoln. In D. Middleton & D. Edwards (Eds.), *Collective Remembering.* London: Sage.

Shotter, J. (1990). The social construction of remembering and forgetting. In D. Middleton & D. Edwards (Eds.), *Collective remembering* (pp. 120–139). London: Sage.

Smith, T. S., & Barclay, C. R. (1990). *Memory and interaction: Emotional regulation through joint reconstruction of autobiographical knowledge.* Unpublished manuscript, University of Rochester, Rochester, NY.

Spence, D. P. (1982). *Narrative truth and historical truth: Meaning and interpretation in psychoanalysis.* New York: Norton.

Spence, D. P. (1988). Passive remembering. In U. Neisser & E. Winograd (Eds.), *Remembering reconsidered: Ecological and traditional approaches to the study of memory* (pp. 311–325). Cambridge University Press.

Stern, D. N. (1990). *The role of feelings for an interpersonal self.* Paper presented at the Emory Cognition Project Conference on the Interpersonal Self, Emory University, Atlanta, GA.

Stigler, J. W., Shweder, R. A., & Herdt, G. (Eds.). (1990). *Cultural psychology: Essays on comparative human development.* Cambridge University Press.

Thompson, P. (1988). *The voice of the past: Oral history.* New York: Oxford University Press.

Trevarthen, C. (1983). Emotions in infancy: Regulators of contacts and relationships with persons. In K. Scherer & P. Ekman (Eds.), *Approaches to emotion* (pp. 129–157). Hillsdale, NJ: Erlbaum.

Trevarthen, C. (1990). *The self born in intersubjectivity: Dyadic states of mind and communication before language.* Paper presented at the Emory Cognition Project Conference on the Interpersonal Self, Emory University, Atlanta, GA.

Tulving, E. (1972). Episodic and semantic memory. In E. Tulving & W. Donaldson (Eds.), *Organization of memory* (pp. 381–403). New York: Academic Press.

Vygotsky, L. (1978). *Mind in society.* Cambridge, MA: Harvard University Press.

Wallace, W. T., & Rubin, D. C. (1988). "The Wreck of the Old 97": A real event remembered in song. In U. Neisser & E. Winograd (Eds.), *Remembering reconsidered: Ecological and traditional approaches to the study of memory* (pp. 283–310). Cambridge University Press.

Webster's seventh new collegiate dictionary. (1965). Springfield, MA: Merriam.

5

Mind, text, and society: Self-memory in social context

KENNETH J. GERGEN

We may begin by contrasting two personal recollections. The first is from the autobiography of the Harvard philosopher W. V. O. Quine. Consider Quine's description of the "romance" that preceded his second marriage:

Ensign Marjorie Boynton, ultimately Lieutenant, had been a Wave in my office in Washington and had waxed in my esteem. When I left, she was put in charge of the office in its continuing project of organizing the files for posterity. Now she was out of the Navy and counseling in Ruth Jean Eisenbud's summer camp for children in Wayne County, Pennsylvania. I drove there to see her in August. I visited her on subsequent occasions in New York, where she had taken a job, and we went to Greenwich Village for dancing, Mexican music, or Dixieland. It became clear that we would marry when circumstances permitted. (1985, p. 195)

Although but a fragment of the work, this account is sufficient to reveal the contours of a particular orientation to self-remembrance. Note that each sentence contains "factual" information: names, places, dates, and activities. The sentences are short and rhetorically unadorned; the tone is flat and neutral. As it appears, autobiography for Quine is a matter of retrieving from memory the most accurate possible record of events as they actually occurred. The mind, then, serves as a repository for one's knowledge of the world, and the challenge to the autobiographer is, insofar as possible, to assay its knowledge of the past – unbiased by rhetoric or passion. In Quine's words, the aim is to "tell the truth; not the whole truth, which would tax everyone's patience, but to tell nothing but the truth" insofar as the memory and its various aids will allow.

Quine's view of self-remembrance represents what can more generally be viewed as a *psychological essentialism*. For the psychological essentialist, memory is fundamentally a mental process, or more formally, the mental capacity of retaining and reviving impressions, or of recalling or recognizing previous experiences. Although psychological essentialism is embodied within the common folklore – or Western ethnopsychology – its most sophisticated adherents are to be found in experimental psychology. From Ebbinghaus's 19th-century explorations through contemporary experiments on information storage and retrieval, the common presumption is that memory is a self-contained process within the mind (or more technically the brain). With respect to processes of memory, psychological essentialism has typically been coupled with a *universalist assumption*. Because psychological processes are necessarily biological processes, and the biology of the human species is roughly similar around the globe and across recorded history, then experimental study should reveal the universal characteristics of memory processes. Thus, typical discussions of memory in psychology seminars emphasize sensory registers, short- and long-term memory, retrieval processes, and memory disorders without respect to history or culture. They are simply autonomous processes inherent in the individual organism.

It is enlightening, however, to contrast Quine's account with a passage from Roland Barthes's exposition of self. The title of Barthes's "autobiography" is simply *Roland Barthes*, which title at once drives a wedge between the life as lived and his task as an author of representing this life. To accentuate the disparity between the ongoing factuality of life and the process of representation, Barthes often writes in the third person – not as "I" who lived this life but as a distant "he" who writes. The volume itself is composed of a series of disconnected fragments, treating such disparate topics as arrogance, proper names, Eros and the theater, forgeries, and so on. The following passage both illustrates the work and reveals Barthes's conception of the remembered self:

I delight continuously, endlessly, in writing as in a perpetual production, in an unconditional dispersion, in an energy of seduction which no legal defense of the subject I fling upon the page can any longer halt. . . . Writing is that *play* by which I turn around as well as I can in a narrow place: I am wedged in, I struggle between the hysteria necessary to write and the image-repertoire, which oversees, controls, purifies, banalizes, codifies, corrects, imposes the focus (and the vision) of a social communication . . . the closer I come to the work, the deeper I descend into writing; I approach its unendurable depth; a desert is revealed.

We find here no attempt to turn the mirror of the mind back upon itself, to report on its residues of factual information. Rather, we confront an acutely critical self-consciousness of the very idea of accurate memory. To engage in autobiography, for Barthes, is to enter a process of writing (a "perpetual production" with strongly seductive properties). Yet the joys of the process are simultaneously frustrated by the limitations of the art form of autobiography itself – which oversees, controls, purifies, banalizes, and codifies that which is written. For Barthes, the writing of life as a unified whole, as a story of a single individual unfolding in an orderly way over time, is to engage in an illusionary nostalgia. Barthes writes "without . . . ever knowing whether it is about my past or my present that I am speaking." The past cannot be recovered, and his patchwork autobiography stands as the very negation of the possibility of recovery. "I . . . rewrite myself," he says, "at a distance, a great distance – here and now."

More generally, Barthes replaces the psychological essentialism manifest in Quine's work with a *textual essentialism*. From the textual point of view, the remembered self is a literary achievement. Selves are preeminently textual constructions, with autobiography forming a literary genre subject to the historically shifting conventions unique to this genre. Thus, as it is proposed, the very idea of an autobiography (a story of the self) is a cultural byproduct. To put it squarely, self-remembrances are achieved by the skilled use of narrative figuration, a rhetoric of an objective past, and the judicious use of the first person as the subject or object of the various sentences making up the text ("I" now am reporting on a "me" of the past). In contrast to psychological essentialism, textual essentialism is a relative newcomer to Western thought. However, its recent contributions are enormous and wide-ranging. Included is not only the work of semiologists such as Barthes, Eco, and Todorov, but as well literary analysts of narrative (Rimmon-Kenan, 1983; Hume, 1984), historians of autobiography (Eakin, 1985), rhetoricians (Simons, 1989), and philosophers of history (Lindenberger, 1975; White, 1978).

It is also important to realize that these two orientations to the remembered self – the psychological and the textual – are mutually annihilating. That is, when either perspective is fully extended, the other is either forced to a marginal position or obliterated altogether. For the psychological essentialist, written or spoken language is primarily a vehicle for conveying the outcomes of the fundamental processes operating within the person. The psychologist is not so much interested in the markings on paper or the sound utterances that an individual makes in the presence of others, as the cognitive (and possibly biological) processes that give rise to these as communicative signals. Such markings or sounds are interesting only to the extent that they furnish indicators or cues regarding the nature of the internal processes. Thus, in Mandler's (1978) research on story schemata, or Schank and Abelson's (1977) exploration of scripts, people's public actions (their "texts") are of secondary importance to the cognitive processes responsible for such actions.

In contrast, for the textual essentialist, the very idea of psychological processes lying behind and giving rise to texts is placed in jeopardy. The texts of memory (such as those of autobiography) are not fashioned and formed by an authorial impulse somewhere in the brain (although brain processes may be necessary to moving the pen across paper); rather, what can be said about one's past and how it can be made intelligible are fashioned by the rhetorical conventions of the time. "Personal memories" are not thus distinctly personal. Instead, they exist in a state of intertextuality, borrowing and bending and replying to the cultural conventions of writing about the personal past. Barthes writes elsewhere (1977) of the "death of the author," or the demise of the traditional assumption of the individual author as an originary power, the source of knowledge from which the account springs forth. Barthes is joined in this challenge to the individualistic assumptions of the Western tradition by Michel Foucault (1979). The latter has questioned the sociopolitical implications of the presumption of individual authorship. "The coming into being of the notion of 'author' constitutes the privileged moment of *individualization* in the history of ideas, knowledge, literature, philosophy, and the sciences" (p. 101). On what grounds, it is asked, can one claim to author a work when its entire intelligibility is dependent upon one's drawing from the common repository of available language? Can one speak outside the existing dialogues of the culture and still be heard? Why then do we so honor (or scorn) the mind of the individual author, when we are all responsible for the product? In effect, to write or speak of "my memories" is subverted as an ontological claim and revealed as a sociopolitical act.

For the most part, the psychological and textual essentialists have little contact with each other. Save for a few bold and curious theorists (such as Jerome Bruner and Ulric Neisser), psychological essentialists tend to vegetate within the laboratories of the behavioral sciences, while the textualists graze in the open ranges of the humanities. However, it is my hope in the present essay to open the gates ever so slightly so that all the *fauves* may come out to play. The vehicle of invitation will largely take the form of provocation. For it is my major aim in the present paper to articulate a third alternative to comprehending self-memory, that of *social constructionism*. As I will elaborate, this orientation attempts to establish memories of the self within forms of relational practice. Or, in terms of the preceding discussion, it seeks to replace both mind and text with processes of social interdependence. Such a position is first invited because of deep-seated problems inhering in both the major traditions at hand. As I hope to make clear, a constructionist view not only avoids certain of these problems, but opens up new lines of inquiry. Further, it is a perspective that utilizes and integrates certain of the substantive gains made within the conflicting traditions. I will attempt first to demonstrate the advantages of a constructionist position through a discussion of rules for accounting for one's personal past. We can then turn to the lived narratives of self-remembrance.

Troubled traditions

Both the psychological and textual traditions have furnished a rich and sophisticated body of thought concerning memories of the self. Scholarly work continues to thrive within each domain, and indeed without the enthusiasm surrounding this work I suspect the present volume would not have materialized. Yet, when considered in broader context, each of these orientations suffers from substantial shortcomings. These limitations are sufficiently important that the active pursuit of alternatives is much to be desired. I shall first treat the problems of psychological essentialism, and then turn attention to the problematics of textual essentialism. In the former case, I shall confine discussion to three critical issues.

The dualistic premise

At the outset, it is important to realize that the concept of memory as a psychological process depends for its intelligibility on a network of preliminary assumptions – for example, that persons are bounded entities who possess cognitions, motives, plans, and so on. Without a commitment to this forestructure of assumptions, theories of personal memory would lapse into unintelligibility. Two aspects of this assumptive network are worthy of special attention. First, the concept of memory is lodged within the tradition of Western dualist epistemology. The issue of memory largely gains its importance from the more general belief in individual minds as separate from (and independent of) the surrounding world, and the companionate assumption that the mind is capable of registering, recording, and deliberating about the nature of that world. It is primarily when one believes in the mind as the locus of knowledge, and knowledge as essential for effective action, that matters of memory and forgetting become critical. For in the degree that the records of the mind cease to be accurate representations of the world as it is (or was), the individual's capacity for survival is threatened.

Yet, the dualistic view of knowledge has come under increasingly sharp attack within recent years, and at least within the philosophic sphere, many feel that the burden of intelligibility now rests with its defenders. Included within these critiques are not only the traditional plagues of an unjustified metaphysics, the failure to account for how knowledge can be built up from experience (including the problem of inductivism), but as well a pinpointing of problems in justifying a priori conceptual schemata (top-down processing), accounting for the relation of mind to action, and the infinite regress of mental explanations.[1] It is thus that Richard Rorty proposes in *Philosophy and the Mirror of Nature*:

To think of knowledge which presents a "problem," and about which we ought to have a "theory," is a product of viewing knowledge as an assemblage of representations – a view of knowledge which . . . was a product of the seventeenth century. The moral to be drawn is that if this way of thinking of knowledge is optional, then so is [the problem of knowledge]. (p. 7)

For present purposes, the drama of this passage is rendered more complete by substituting "memory" for the more inclusive concept of "knowledge."

For many scholars these same assumptions of the individual, knowing and remembering mind are also bearers of a problematic ideology. To believe that individual rational process serves as the originary source of action is simultaneously to champion a form of self-contained individualism.[2] It is to view individuals as fundamentally separate, isolated, and ultimately self-serving. Does this view of human action, critics ask, not foster forms of social life (e.g., competitive, hierarchical) that are inimical to the ultimate survival of the species? If, as Rorty says, the present conception of individual knowledge is optional, can we not locate alternative ways of conceptualizing human action that would serve more promising ends? Most centrally, can we reconceptualize what we have traditionally taken as processes of personal memory in ways that would be more beneficial to the common good?

The paradox of memory

While psychological essentialism is thrown into question indirectly by attacks on dualism, there are additional enigmas inhering in the assumption of personal memory itself. As Shotter (1990) points out, it is Wittgenstein's later work that most threatens the adequacy of the traditional view of memory. Wittgenstein (1963) proceeds by asking questions for which the commonly shared assumptions of the culture offer no credible answers, and for which the lack of answers challenges the very grounds of the question. How, asks Wittgenstein, does an individual asked to fetch a red flower from the meadow manage to obey the request? "How is he to know what sort of flower to bring, as I have only given him a word? Now the answer one might suggest first is that he went to look for a red flower carrying a red image in his mind," presumably an image furnished from memory, "and compared it with the flowers to see which of them had the color of the image" (p. 3). Such a process would be similar, Wittgenstein points out, to the individual having a chart of colored squares, and, in order to know whether he saw a red flower, having to compare it against the entries on the chart. Such an image seems absurd. Rather, proposes Wittgenstein, "We go, look about us, walk up to a flower and pick it, without comparing it to anything." Or, he asks, if requested to "imagine a red patch," must you first "imagine a red patch to serve you as the pattern for the red patch you were ordered to imagine?" (p. 3). Again such a conclusion stretches the borders of credulity. Thus the questions thrust the concept of memory as a process of accessing images into question.

Let us press such questioning to the point of paradox. Consider first the concept of forgetting. I announce, "I knew the name of my stuffed bear when I was 3, but now I have forgotten it." Yet, how is it that I can remember that I knew the name? Would I not have to possess instances of using the name – calling the bear, talking about the bear to my mother, and so on – in order to know that I knew it? Yet, if my memory did contain such instances, then the name of the bear must be present in mind, and if present, then clearly I have not forgotten. In order to know that I forgot it, I would have to know what it is that I forgot; but if I know what I forgot, then it must be present in memory. To put it more generally, the concept of forgetting, by traditional standards, requires that one possess some criterion for recognizing that one has forgotten. By definition such a criterion must include the recollection of once having the object in mind; yet to know one had the object in mind simultaneously means that the object has not been forgotten.

A similar paradox haunts the traditional view of remembering. In scanning the interior of the mind to see if one can remember, how is one to distinguish between a true and a false memory? If asked to recall the name of my neighbors when I was aged 9, and various names (e.g., the Rodnicks, the Clarks, the Roberts) come to mind, how can I recognize which are correct in order to report, "Now I remember my neighbors' names"? Presumably I am using some standards or criteria for making such judgments, or I would have no means of reaching a conclusion. Yet, if I do possess such criteria – of the kind that enable me to say, "Yes, the Rodnicks and the Clarks lived close by, but not the Roberts," then I must have known this before embarking on the exploration of memory. I must have known what I was looking for, or I would not have been able to identify it when it passed in review. Yet, if I knew what I was looking for, then there would have been no reason for the memorial review. If I know the answer, then there is no reason for memory to be set in motion.

The hermeneutic impasse

The problems inherent in the dualistic metaphysics essential to the psychological view of memory, along with the conceptual incoherence of the view itself, are formidable. However, they are no less substantial than those inhering in the task of scientific judgments about memory processes. For the psychological essentialist, acquiring knowledge of memory through direct observation proves impossible. There is no means by which the scientific investigator can directly observe memory in motion. Thus, propositions about processes of memory must rest for their validity on behavioral inference. The investigator must observe the subject's behavior, make inferences from linguistic expressions, and so on. However,

as direct observation is replaced by inference, so does the scientific investigation of memory confront the age-old challenges of hermeneutic theory: justifying conclusions about the unknown based on evidence of the
known. Although hermeneutic scholars have for centuries labored over
the problem of justifying textual interpretations, no viable solution has
yet been located. And, as a substantial body of theory now demonstrates,
there is no logical means of deriving conclusions about internal processes
from observations of exterior behavior (of moving logically from a text
to the writer's intention or private meaning). As Hans Georg Gadamer
(1975) and a host of reader-response theorists (Suleiman & Crossman,
1980) point out, to "read" human action requires a forestructure of understanding, or in terms of our preceding discussion, a set of preliminary
assumptions. In particular, one must presume a priori that there are certain kinds of "interior events" or processes, and that these events are systematically related to specific sets of behaviors. Once such presumptions
are in place, then one can "read" the interior. However, the presumptions
themselves are without empirical justification.

To apply this line of reasoning to the case of memory, it may be proposed that there is no means by which empirical study can reveal the
nature of memory processes until one presumes that (1) there are such
processes, and (2) they are systematically tied to or expressed in certain
designated actions. Yet, these presumptions are without empirical warrant; their credibility is derived largely from the shared conventions of
the culture (and more specifically, Western culture). The empirically arbitrary nature of our inferences about memory can be demonstrated in two
ways. The first is to ask how we distinguish actions that are specifically
indicative of a *remembrance* as opposed to some other mental phenomenon – that we know we are correctly identifying memory and not processes of hope, desire, or need, for example. If I announce that "Smith's
conference presentation was outstanding," I appear to be offering a
memory. Yet, to utter these words I must have, by common standards,
been exercising my conceptual abilities, been motivated to speak, anticipated the intelligibility of my words, recognized an emotional state, intended to be understood, and so on. Thus, in what sense are my words
transparent indicators of memory? Indeed, they might reasonably furnish insight into a wide number of other psychological states and processes. If any of these processes were subtracted from my repertoire, I
would scarcely be able to furnish such a report. How, then, are we to
extricate "memory" from the array? Or, if I am taught that the first psychological laboratory was established in 1879, and am unable to furnish
this answer when later tested, how can it be determined that my memory
has failed me? Is it not possible that I never really learned the fact, my
motivation to remember was inoperative, I was not aware that 1879 was

correct when it flashed through consciousness, or that I repressed the entire matter? How are we to distinguish among all the possible candidates?

The hermeneutics of identifying memories from actions becomes more acute when we ask why certain actions are precluded as indicators of memory. On what grounds do we conclude that memory is *not* revealed in a given action? We do not generally view the act of walking as a revelation of memory, congratulating ourselves with each successful step. Yet, if pressed, is it not sensible that with each movement of one leg forward, I must then remember to move the other leg in the same direction? And if by chance I am walking to work, must I not remember at every moment of my journey where it is that I work? If I periodically forget the destination of my walk should I not require professional help? Nor do we generally view acts of reading as indicators of memory. Yet, how could reading proceed if one were not continuously attempting to remember the meaning of words, the preceding text, and indeed what it is to carry out an act of reading? We do not typically credit rising from the bed in the morning as an indicator of memory, but would we ever do so if we could not recall how to accomplish the act, and why it is essential to do so? Are there *any* actions (save the spontaneous movements of the infant) that are not indicators of memory? And if all actions are expressions of memory, and simultaneously indicators of numerous other conditions (motives, plans, schemata, etc.), then how are we to draw definitive conclusions about the nature of memory in particular? The hermeneutic puzzle remains unsolved,[3] and we face the possibility that scientific conclusions about memory largely owe their rhetorical power to existing folk myths about the mind.

The textual alternative

These three problems – the shaky network of preliminary assumptions, the paradox of explanation, and the impasse of interpretation – all give reason for substantial pause. What can psychological essentialism offer in the longer march toward understanding? How can we justifiably sustain a view of the remembered self lodged within this tradition? At this point one might be strongly inclined toward a textual orientation to personal memory. From the textual perspective, the dualistic epistemology is abandoned at the outset, and with it the complex problems of mental representation, paradox, and interpretation. Indeed, in many respects I find myself strongly moved in this direction. And, as the present essay will make more fully clear, considerations of narrative form and rhetorical technique open a fascinating vista of research and theory into the remembered self.

At the same time, textual essentialism itself harbors a number of difficulties, at least one of which represents a substantial deficit for the social scientist. From the textualist perspective, the personal remembrance is an exercise in discourse; it is simply to put in motion the textual conventions of the time. On the scholarly level, this is to reduce the study of self-memory to textual analysis. That which is to be understood is a textual production, and the tools of literary analysis become the favored means of rendering description and explanation. Thus, for example, once the genre of a given production has been identified, the tropes tabulated, the semiotic structure elucidated, and the intertextual history clarified, there is little left to say. Analytic description serves as an end in itself, or at its most distressing, as the production of yet another text, an entry into an array of signifiers in an endless process of intersignification. More specifically, this is to say that literary essentialism extracts the act of remembrance (the text) from its social context. It removes from analysis the actor and the array of relationships in which he/she participates. It is to strip the remembrance from the context of its production and reception. From a strict literary standpoint, there are no persons, relationships, or cultures; there are only texts that create the sense of these realities. Analysis becomes narrow and parochial.

Must an appreciation of the textual orientation necessarily preclude considerations of personal relatedness? If one begins with text is there no means of escape, no way of understanding how we proceed that is not itself a product of textuality? Such a conclusion seems both pessimistic and unwarranted – even on textualist grounds. For the textual purist, self-remembrances don't refer to actual events; words are not mimetic – rather, they gain their meaning from their function within the text, and in this case, within the genre of texts that make up what we can say when asked to recount our personal past. Yet, is this deconstruction of the referent ("my actual life as lived") not premised on the assumption that analysis is itself referential, that there is a text with certain properties and features that may be elucidated through careful scrutiny? Is textual analysis not describing and explaining something *outside* itself? The jaded analyst can respond in the negative to these questions, asserting that textual analyses are themselves self-referential, only playing out a genre of critical writing. However, such an answer cannot be sustained. For if words within a text are self-referential, then some form of referentiality is presumed after all. And if there is reference within a text, there is no principled reason to suppose that referentiality does not pertain across texts (the latter presumption borne out in the literary analysis of intertextuality). Yet, if there is referentiality across texts, then we can scarcely stop short of the conclusion that referentiality may be established between words and that which we take to be the remainder of the world. Indeed, without the presumption that there is a "remainder" that is outside of text, the concept of text would itself cease to be meaningful. If there is truly "nothing outside of text," then the concept of text stands empty of significance.

As we find, when its supporting assumptions are unfolded, textual essentialism cannot remain viable as an insulated enterprise. The possibility of reference beyond text becomes virtually inescapable. Further, there is much to be gained both intellectually and practically by expanding analysis to include not only text but context. Further, if we may presume that texts operate as means of linking persons – writers and readers, speakers and listeners – then the favored context of concern is the social one. We are drawn to inquiry concerning the role of textuality in ongoing relationships. To press the matter to conclusion, we may view texts as but a byproduct of a more fundamental process of social interchange.

A social constructionist view of the remembered self

In brief surmise, both the orientations just described leave the analyst roving the confines of a dictionary – the one of mind and the other of text. For the psychological essentialist the task is complete when the necessary psychological processes are explained; for the textual essentialist there is little outside the pleasures of the text. How are we to escape the constraints posed by these competing positions? In my view there is a means of doing so, one that opens new avenues of inquiry while simultaneously retaining certain features of these venerable traditions. To appreciate these potentials, it is necessary to assay the conditions under which issues of self-memory take place. How is it that we come to be occupied with questions of self-memory, either within everyday life or in the scholarly disciplines? I do not believe the psychological essentialist can answer the question. There is nothing about the inchoate flux of what we call internal experience that demands or requires the predicate *memory* (nor for that matter the concept of *I*). There is no viable means of inducing our psychological vocabulary from raw introspections. In effect, there is nothing about the internal workings of the individual that suggests or demands that we inquire into people's remembrances of self. Nor, for the textualist, is there any means of determining how questions of self-memory acquire importance within the culture, why we presume people have memory, and why reports of a personal past are significant. Such issues are simply outside the textual realm.

I submit that the conditions under which issues of self-memory become focal are either directly (or indirectly) social in character. They occur within such processes as conversing about the past, answering questions about personal history, justifying actions, entertaining one's children, setting the record straight, demonstrating how certain tasks were accomplished or goals obtained, or documenting events for the public record. Further, by Western conventions most expressions of what we call self-memory take place in language – an inherently social medium. If W. V. O. Quine entitles his autobiography *The Time of My Life,* we do not complain when he furnishes us with 500 pages of writing. And, without immersion in social interchange it would indeed be impossible to act so that it would properly count as remembering. If asked what I did last night, I cannot report on the displacement of my feet from one instant in time to the next. Even if the report were accurate by common standards it would not properly constitute a memory. To speak on such occasions of "events" such as "working," "dining," and "reading" requires an immersion in cultural practices; to "do memory" is essentially to engage in a cultural practice. Instances of self-memory, then, take place within and are shaped by social process.

It is also by virtue of social process that the concept of self-remembrance becomes meaningful. If memories were private psychological events, my announcement that I was going to tell you "what I remember" would be indecipherable. There is no means by which you could ascertain the psychological referent in question, by which you could identify something within your own sensorium to which the term *memory* corresponded. If I use the term *memory* under the same conditions as you would speak of your *wishes,* there is no means by which we could negotiate a correction (and indeed, who in such a situation would be subject to correction?). Nor can texts in themselves determine the meaning of their constituent elements – the meaning, in this case, of terms such as remembrance. The sounds and markings that come to constitute language possess no meanings within themselves. Rather, to employ the terms of reader response theory, the meaning of a text is importantly dependent on what readers are willing to assign it. Or more succinctly, meaning is generated within relationships – by virtue of the coordinated actions among persons. When I speak, my words are nonsense until you grant them meaning, and the meaning you assign to them falls fallow until I, in turn, grant it significance.

In broader terms this is to argue that accounts of memory gain their meaning through their usage, not within the mind nor within the text, but within social relationships. In effect, memory is a "social institution" (Shotter, 1990). The concepts of "memory" and "forgetting" as psychological processes are byproducts of Western dialogue, and the ways in which such concepts function in everyday life (and in science) are prescribed by culturally specific conventions of conduct. This *social constructionist* view of memory shares much with the Durkheimian tradition in sociology, and most specifically the work of Durkheim's student, Maurice

Halbwachs (1951/1980). It is also consistent with some of Bartlett's classic work. As Bartlett put it, "social organization gives a persistent framework into which all detailed recall must fit, and it very powerfully influences both the manner and matter of recall" (1932, p. 296). The view is further informed by much recent work in the sociology of knowledge and in ethnomethodology (see especially Coulter, 1985).

Particularly important inroads into a uniquely social view of memory have been made by investigators into what is now called *social* (Nerone & Wartella, 1989) or *communal* memory (Middleton & Edwards, 1990). To illustrate, Edwards and Middleton (1988) demonstrate how children are taught within families what constitutes an appropriate "memory" of family events. As children are shown photographs of family outings, rituals, and the like, they are often asked to identify and narrate. If they lack words, parents will supply them; if they fail to furnish the sanctioned report of memory, they will be corrected. Or they may be informed outright how to identify and assign meanings to the photographs and how they should feel about these past experiences. Such inquiry also demonstrates that as adults discuss their past experiences together, they use a variety of conversational devices for generating mutually acceptable accounts of "what happened." They use tags that invite ratification by others ("didn't he?"), build on each other's reports so as to generate narrative continuity, request each other to fill out particulars, or lend affirmation to others' accounts ("yes, I remember that"). The past, then, is molded from conversations, and to "remember oneself" cannot then be extricated from the agreements reached within relationships. To report on one's memories is not so much a matter of consulting mental images as it is engaging in a sanctioned form of telling.

In the remainder of this essay I wish to elaborate further on two aspects of a constructionist view of the remembered self. First I want to explore more fully the relationship between textualism and constructionism. More specifically, my focus is on ways in which textualist analyses can be linked to constructionist concerns for outcomes of mutual benefit. This discussion will center on the narratives of personal memory. Second, by way of amplifying the constructionist perspective, I wish to cement these narrative explorations more fully to the social context. The central concern in this case is the social praxiology of self-memory.

The boundaries of self-narrative

From a constructionist perspective, we are scarcely free to report on our past lives in any way we wish. We are importantly constrained by cultural rules for self-accounting. Prominent among these conventions are rules derived from our history of folktales, parables, myths, and legends – in effect, our narrative heritage. If you ask me how it is that I came to be interested in self-remembrance, and I respond with, "Eyes, hair, movement, desire, One Fifth Avenue, rain, fear, ennui in an automobile, warmth, the river . . . ," chances are you wouldn't be content. You may not doubt that these are my mental images of the moment, but this account is insufficient as a report on memory. You might, of course, attribute my reply to playfulness or an inappropriate poetic impulse; and if especially interested, you might say to yourself, "Ah, One Fifth Avenue, boredom, fear . . . therein hangs the real tale of origins." And it is precisely this suspicion that portends the requirements for a proper remembrance. For whatever the past might have been, its present rendering must be poured into the mold set by the cultural rules of narrative.

The rules of narrative have been matters of lively interest for literary theorists (Kermode, 1967; Martin, 1986), semiologists (Young, 1982; Rimmon-Kenan, 1983), philosophers of history (Mink, 1970; White, 1973), and many others concerned with the nature of human intelligibility. Drawing from this work, Mary Gergen and I (Gergen & Gergen, 1988) have attempted to distill critical ingredients of the well-formed narrative. In present terms, what are the rules for constructing one's personal past? Briefly, the following rules appear to apply over a broad range of conditions:

Valued endpoint.   As proposed above, accounts of personal history are embedded within ongoing social processes. They function so as to sustain or alter relational patterns in various ways. This functional aspect of personal memory is manifested in the pervasive tendency to build such memories around some valued condition or state – a goal failed or accomplished, a condition prized or reputed, an outcome embraced or eschewed. Thus, if I asked you about the history of your professional life, you would probably not tell me about the styles of shoes worn over the years, changes in office furnishings, or amount of time spent gazing out the office window – all surely part of professional life. Chances are your memories would be built around intellectual hopes, desires for improving some aspect of cultural life, or goals within the structure of the profession – all sanctioned endpoints for a proper professional life. Another way of putting it is that intelligible narratives are often organized around "a point," with established value within the culture, and this point both gives the story its direction and implies its termination.

Selection of related events.   Once a valued endpoint has been established, it will largely determine the subsequent contents of the personal memory. The events that constitute the story of one's past will be related to the endpoint – either hastening or thwarting its achievement. Thus, if you are telling me how it is that you came to break some new intellectual ground, chances are you will not inform me of your restaurant choices, musical tastes, or sexual habits of the time – unless these are specifically related to the endpoint of the intellectual achievement. These might constitute amusing digressions, but digressions nevertheless. Indeed, that which gives biography much of its drama is its capacity to demonstrate how events outside the strictly professional realm impinged on or brought about endpoints in the lives of the protagonists. We learn in Richard Graves's (1991) volume on his uncle Robert's life how the brilliant and wily Laura Riding influenced the poetry of Robert Graves, or in Ray Monk's *Ludwig Wittgenstein: The Duty of Genius,* how Wittgenstein's inclinations toward self-persecution were related to his philosophical writings. The interesting biographer broadens the network of factors relevant to various life accomplishments, and thereby furnishes future *auto*-biographers additional criteria for a "discerning memory."

Temporal ordering of events.   In the works of both Proust and Joyce we learn that conscious experience is temporally inchoate. For these writers, personal experience does not unfold in a linear temporal ordering; rather, an experience at a given moment may trigger an image of what we now (perhaps mistakenly?) feel is time past, or time future, or perhaps a fantasied time. Any given experience may also incorporate events from the past, or from the imagination, creating difficulties in determining precisely whether present experience is indeed "of the present." In effect, they suggest, our consciousness of self over time is not correspondent with clock time. Yet, the modernist literary view of aleatory consciousness is little reflected in common accounts of self-memory. For common convention requires that self-memory operates like a movie camera set before the self: Events unfold in a linear, clock-time sequence. Telling the story of one's professional life requires that one begin at a point far removed in time – "the beginning" – and relate events as they occurred sequentially. Quine thus begins his autobiography at his birth, and each chapter follows chronologically upon the preceding. To proceed as does Barthes, with single incidents cut away from clock time, fails to count as proper memory. Rather, it smacks of artifice, a rhetorical maneuver.

Causal linkages.   Quine's autobiography recounts a five-day conference in the lodge of Windsor Castle in which the intellectual exchange was so undisciplined and boring, the food so bad, and the conviviality so lacking that he departed unceremoniously before the conference was terminated. Such an account seems a genuine recollection, just the way it happened. However, it does so in large measure because of the causal linkages used to connect the events. The quality of the intellectual exchange, the food, and the social life *caused* the early departure. Yet, as Kant convincingly demonstrated, causality is not a fact of nature, open to observation, but an interpretive commitment. We cannot derive the concept of causality from nature, but given the concept we can "see" it everywhere. More specifically, we may say, the concept of cause is a textual or rhetorical device for generating acceptable accounts of the relation among otherwise isolated events. If Quine had simply described a ponderous conversation, a poor meal, an uncongenial sherry hour, and his departure on the fourth day of the conference, the remembrance would lack a critical ingredient. We would find it sparse and understated. This is hardly to propose that all events within a narrative must be causally linked in order for intelligibility to be achieved. There are numerous exceptions even within fully elaborated memoirs. Events are often added for atmosphere, or to lend power to the account. However, a self-narrative without any causal linkages among events would generally strike us as the product of an inferior memory.

Demarcation signs. In his autobiographical work *W: Or the Memory of Childhood*, Georges Perec recounts the history of his early years in Nazi Germany. Yet, as the tale unfolds, Perec admits that he cannot discern the difference between true memory and his imaginative re-creations of the past. Further, the reader finds, alternating chapters describe an island society where sport is king, athletic competition is the primary way of life, winners are given enormous privileges, and losers mocked or even executed. Is Perec attempting to tell us of his childhood in these chapters, but now in allegory? And if this is so, are we to conclude that the "truthful" chapters are fantasied and the fabricated chapters the emotionally accurate ones? The reader is left in a state of tantalizing doubt. It is in this very doubt that we locate the ingredients of an additional rule of self-memory. Proper remembrance must be demarcated in some way, set off as "memories of the self." A statement such as "I lost my virginity at the age of 16" would in itself appear to be a statement of fact rather than a report of a memory. If preceded by the metastatement "I remember that birthday because . . . ," or another's question, "Do you remember when you lost your virginity?" the same statement now constitutes a self-remembrance. Demarcation signs are thus used to indicate when various accounts figure as reports on self-memory.[4]

These five rules for remembering the self are scarcely universal, and their demands may vary over time and from one relationship to another. However, if one's memory is to be trusted by others, the conventions may be essential. A study by Bennett and Feldman (1981) on the construction of courtroom reality illustrates the importance of this conclusion. Research participants were exposed to 47 testimonies that were either genuine attempts at recounting the past or fabricated stories. It was found that the participants were unable to detect a difference between the two kinds of accounts. Subsequent analysis attempted to differentiate between the cues used by the participants to distinguish true memory from fabrication. Here it was revealed that stories judged to be true were primarily those conforming to the rules of the well-formed narrative. The accounts that were believed were those containing more events related to the endpoint of the stories and a greater number of causal linkages among events. Memorial accounts thus achieve their intelligibility – and thus their legitimacy – from the cultural conventions of telling.

Personal memory as a relational resource

A certain irony pervades the analysis thus far. Traditionally, memory is viewed as a private act of the individual, and remembrance of the self as an intimately personal event. To say, "But I have my memories," is to lay claim to an inner resource of lifetime sustenance. Yet, as we have seen, that which counts as legitimate memory of the self is not a set of random images scattered over personal consciousness, but a culturally fashioned production. To remember oneself is to join in a public ritual. Are there limits to this conclusion?

If the rules of narrative and its employment are strongly encumbering, what remains of the personal memory that is strictly personal? Perhaps the *facts* of one's previous life are the primary refuge for individual autobiography. In an earlier study with Mary Gergen (Gergen & Gergen, 1988), we asked adolescents to write about their earlier years. As we found, many students adopted the same narrative form: Their earliest years had been very happy ones, but their fortunes turned during early adolescence. In one form or another, they were on the skids. However, in their most recent years they were beginning to rebound. They were striving toward positive goals. There was considerable similarity in the narrative form of the accounts, but the events that formed the high points of the life stories were quite diverse. If life stories are unique to their owners, perhaps it is to be attributed to this realm of content.

Yet, if we consult recent annals in the social studies of science, even this conclusion is found wanting. Traditional science has been lodged within a form of realist philosophy stressing a close relationship between the language of scientific description and the realm of observation. From this perspective scientific description should accommodate itself to our most assiduous estimates of the world as it is. Proper description should operate as a map of the existing terrain; the signifiers should accurately reflect the signified. In contrast, much work in the social studies of science extends the Saussurian project of breaking the link between signifier and

signified. As it is argued, the objects of science do not determine or require any particular description. Rather, social processes (largely within
the scientific community) direct the course of description. Thus, when
scientists gaze at their experimental findings, the data do not "speak for
themselves." Rather, the scientist typically considers how his/her peers
would interpret the data; what interpretation would be agreeable to his/
her peers, generate the greatest interest, be acceptable to the prestigious
journals, encourage grant support, and so on.[5]

And so it may be argued in the case of memory. In the process of
translating the everyday world into language, its every feature will be
prefigured by the character of this language. To divide the world into
"present versus past events," "I versus you," "males versus females," and
so on, is to participate in a historical tradition. To be asked in court to
"report the whole truth and nothing but the truth" is thus not a request
for a mirror of the past. Rather, the demand is for a report that takes the
form customary and congenial to the common conventions used by those
within the courtroom settings. To describe a murder most foul in terms
of shifting color patterns, the movements of bodies through time and
space (including angle and velocity of movement), or atomic composition
would not be a proper memory, but an irritating obfuscation.[6]

In summary, we may view personal remembrance not as an intimate
portrayal of one's uniquely configured interior, but as a deployment of a
public resource. The discursive traditions of one's culture supply a wide
variety of memorial devices. As if selecting from the wardrobe of a reper-
tory theater company, one may locate narrative forms and factual tropes
from the Elizabethan period, the roaring 20s, or the avant garde. To be
sure, the precise combination of costuming may vary from one actor to
the other, but in the end it is all theater. And unless it is theater, it will not
be recognizable as self-remembrance at all.

Scenarios and narration as social practice

Thus far I have tried to develop the rationale for a social constructionist
account of self-remembrance, to explore prevailing rules for narrative
accounts of the personal past, and to demonstrate the extent to which
such accounts reproduce cultural traditions. Yet, this analysis still lacks a
critical ingredient, in particular one demonstrating the difference between a constructionist and a textualist orientation to self-memory. Although painted in constructionist hues, there is little about the preceding
to which a textualist could not also subscribe. Jeff Coulter (1985) locates
this ingredient in his statement, "The primary thrust of the social constructionist analysis is to articulate the *praxiological* (i.e. practical-action-
based) character of the mental" (p. 130). Thus, while the preceding analy-

sis has been social in its emphasis, what remains is to demonstrate the ways in which memorial episodes are embedded within broader social patterns. My argument is that memories of the self are not "events in themselves," either psychological registerings or textual renderings. Rather, self-remembrance gains its intelligibility as "an event" only within the confines of cultural interchange. Or, to extend Wittgenstein's metaphor, memories of the self acquire this status by virtue of their function within the language games of the culture. A critical focus for the constructionist, then, is to elucidate the cultural life forms in which the doing of self-memory plays a role, and to explore the functions of such accounts within these practices.

I shall not undertake a full review of work that contributes to such understanding. The praxiological emphasis does play a role in the previously cited work of Edwards and Middleton (1988) on the construction of memory within the family. Similarly, it is featured in Schwartz's (1990) treatment of the way various generations have reconstructed the identity of Abraham Lincoln, and Schudson's (1990) discussion of the social construction of Ronald Reagan's popularity. Shotter (1990) opens discussion on the practical use of memorial accounts by arguing that "our ways of speaking become central, because . . . the primary function of our speech is to 'give shape' to and to co-ordinate diverse social action. We speak in order to create, maintain, reproduce and transform certain modes of social and societal relationships" (p. 121). In an earlier work with Mary Gergen (Gergen & Gergen, 1987), we have discussed the use of narratives for cementing bonds within close relationships. Mary Gergen (1992) has also discussed masculine-versus-feminine forms of autobiography as they sustain various ideological and mythical forms within the culture.

In the present context I wish to extend the scope of these various endeavors in but a single direction. Most constructionist analyses to date have concluded with a discussion of the various ends possibly served by solidifying certain positions on the past (e.g., "what happened," "what I did," "what you did"). Much less attention has been given to the broader pattern of interchange in which the constitution of memory and forgetting occurs. To appreciate the possibility of placing self-memory within the broader patterns of interdependence, first consider the case of emotion.

In our earlier work on emotion (Gergen & Gergen, 1988), we attempted to demonstrate how emotional expressions are embedded within and also derive their significance from their placement in relational sequences. To illustrate, one cannot express emotional depression at just any time or place. There are complex cultural conventions that tell us of the conditions under which depression is warranted (e.g., it is plausible to become depressed upon the loss of a job opportunity but not typically at the loss of a handkerchief). Further, once depression has been expressed, there are conventional requirements governing possible responses. One may respond to depression with sympathy, advice, or a redefinition of the situation, but not with a lecture on statistics. And, once an acceptable response has been expressed, the original actor is once again limited in terms of possible responses (e.g., if sympathy is offered, the actor may be appreciative or doubting, but not enthusiastically joyful). In this sense, depression is not the result of a physical state wending its causal way toward the exterior of the body, but a move within a culturally choreographed dance – or more congenial to the present analysis, a *lived narrative*. In our previous work we have termed these lived narratives *relational scenarios*.

In the present context, let us consider how memory and forgetting are also integers within relational scenarios of extended duration. The doing of memory, no less than emotion, is a move within a more extended interpersonal dance. It is to the more extended choreography that I wish to draw present attention. The more general challenge in this case is to locate and elucidate the kinds of relational scenarios in which reports on memory or forgetting play a critical role. How is it, in particular, that remembrances of the self fit within the more extended patterns of cultural interchange? What roles do they serve in this respect? In what ways are relationships dependent on just such reports? I cannot lay out a full range of patterns at this juncture, nor am I prepared to formulate a general view of the functions of the remembered self in social life. Only now do we reach the juncture where such relational conceptualizations of traditional psychological processes can be formulated. Rather, the attempt at present is simply to open a space for such analyses. An illustrative sketch is offered.

At least one important function that self-remembrances play in social life is that of establishing and sustaining a particular identity within relationships. As Coulter (1985) has cogently argued, memories and forgettings operate as means of establishing oneself in a relationship as a particular kind of person, with particular privileges and duties. Memories and forgetting, in his terms, "are morally ordered phenomena" (p. 132). To illustrate, consider *scenarios of doubted identity*, that is, exchanges in which the self-definition of one of the participants has yet to be established or has been challenged. Such scenarios occur in wide-ranging contexts, from the formalized setting of the job interview to the informal processes of courting, repairing breaches in trust, and establishing credit for one's actions. In all cases such scenarios typically begin with an *identity probe*, that is, some form of inquiry (in the form of a query or an invitation) on the part of Person A into the identity of Person B. The identity probe is used to determine, for example, what kind of person (e.g., what potentials, traits, intentions) is applying for this job, asking me out, breaking a promise, and so on. Although there are means of evading such probes, the conventional response within the scenario is an *identity offering*. The job applicant speaks of her qualifications, the suitor talks of his travel interests, the delinquent declares that she is trustworthy after all. If A accepts the offering, the scenario may be terminated. The job interview may be ended, the suitor rejected, or the relationship of trust resumed. However, there is a second and frequent option to be employed at this juncture, namely an *authenticity challenge*. Person A may cast doubt on the identity offering. Why does the job applicant believe she has these qualifications, are the suitor's interests in travel anything more than trivial, and are the delinquent's claims of trustworthiness simply a means of escaping punishment?

It is precisely at this point that *personal remembrance* becomes a legitimate option. Person B may properly introduce memories of a personal past. The job applicant may recall how she succeeded at various challenges over the years, the suitor may recall the joys of Barcelona and Marrakech, and the delinquent may recall the many times she was available when needed. Realize that these personal remembrances could, in principle, be introduced at any moment into the interchange. There is nothing that would physically prohibit one from speaking of past successes, early travel experiences, and so on. However, to do so before this point in the scenario would be either nonsensical or suspect. (To speak suddenly and spontaneously of the couscous in Marrakech, or to recall one's trustworthiness before it is placed in question would border on unintelligibility.) Further, if one does not engage in personal remembrance at this juncture there are only a limited number of alternative options available to meet the authenticity challenge (e.g., to furnish records or references). Failing to make any of these moves would essentially abort the scenario (and possibly the relationship). And finally, if the person is to remain legitimate, these remembrances should be functionally geared to the challenge at hand. The job applicant cannot recall the Gaudis of Barcelona, the suitor cannot speak of his devotion to another, and the delinquent cannot muse about her job capabilities. In effect, personal remembrance is delimited to a specific moment within the scenario, it is virtually encumbent upon the person to furnish such remembrances at this point, and the rules for its content are highly circumscribed.

For purposes of illustration, the rough contours of the scenario of doubted identity are outlined in Table 5.1. As we have seen, the scenario can be completed prior to the insertion of a personal remembrance. However, once the remembrance has occurred, the recipient's actions are also guided by the conventions of the dance. Person A may *accept* the account as supporting the purported identity of the individual, in which

Table 5.1. *Scenario of doubted identity*

Person A	Person B
Identity probe	Identity offering
Authenticity challenge	Personal remembrance
Acceptance	(Scenario end)
or	
Rejection	Memory authentication

case the scenario may again be terminated. However, if the remembrance is *challenged*, B is required to make an additional move. For example, he/ she may offer a more elaborated account of the past, or appeal to third-party knowledgeables. Again, without some implicit form of acceptance on A's part, the scenario remains incomplete. We find, then, that self-remembrance is not a mental picture operating causally to produce verbal likeness, or a text without context. Rather, to remember a self is a socially functional action embedded within a form of relationship. Without the relational scenario in which it occurs, self-remembrance lapses into unintelligibility.

It is the relational scenario that, at last, enables us to gain proper purchase on the problem of accuracy in self-remembrance. The problem of accuracy cannot be solved from the standpoint of the psychological essentialist. Problems of dualist metaphysics insure the intractability of the problem. For the textual essentialist there simply is no problem of accuracy. However, from the constructionist standpoint what we view as "accurate memory" can properly be understood as a communal byproduct. To appreciate the point, consider first a scenario form in which persons come to agree on how states of affairs are to be called. In the classic *naming game*, for example, the mother teaches the child that a given illustration in a book is called a "monkey." Consider a second scenario, a *recognition game*, in which persons come to agree that a state of affairs has recurred. For example, the mother and the child come to agree that the creature before them in the zoo is "the same" as the configuration in the child's book. With these rituals in place, the stage is set for the mother to ask the child the name of the creature. This may be viewed as a *memory game*, with certain local rules of success and failure. Success is achieved, in the mother's terms, only if the child furnishes the same word used in viewing the book. It is success in playing this game that we tend to index as "accurate memory." However, for the constructionist, a complete account of "accurate memory" can be furnished in this case without recourse to mental or physiological discourse. Accurate memory of the self would thus depend on the social context in which the game was being played. An accurate memory of one's past for one group would constitute a failed memory in the presence of others.

Psychology and self-memory revisited

At the beginning of this essay I outlined two major approaches to the study of self-memory, the psychological and the textual. I went on to demonstrate problems inhering in both of these projects, and proceeded to develop a social constructionist alternative. As we found, this alternative was able both to incorporate and to extend many of the contributions of the textual tradition. However, this still leaves open the question of psychological research into processes of memory. Is there any means of linking this work to the constructionist? At the outset, it should be clear that the constructionist account is inimical to traditional research on memory. As sketched above, the constructionist raises difficult questions concerning the grounds for the psychological study of memory – its roots in a dualist metaphysics, its internal ironies, its lack of hermeneutic justification, and its individualist ideology. For the constructionist, memory as a *phenomenon in nature* (and more specifically "in the head") is deontologized. For the constructionist, there is a *cultural discourse* (currently intelligible forms of conversation) on memory. We speak at length of our memories and our forgettings. But this discourse is not ostensively grounded in the sense of referring to an inner event. There is no mental object to which terms of memory and forgetting are semantically related. Rather, for the constructionist, this discourse is embedded within ongoing relationships, and gains its meaning and importance from its use in these interchanges.

Yet, the psychologist may aptly reply, a constructionist analysis seems to deny that *anything* is going on in the head of the actor. Persons are able to recount events long removed in time, and to do so in ways that can be publicly verifiable. Persons are little able to account for their childhoods, but they recount their recent pasts in vivid detail. Without the capacity to "carry the past with us" in some fashion, existence would indeed be short-lived. These facts simply demand some form of explanation, and it is this explanation that psychology seeks to provide. In reply, the constructionist does not wish to deny that "something is going on" in the individual's brain when he/she remembers or fails to engage in activities that we call remembering. However, the major question is whether the bodily occurrences taking place when one speaks of "my childhood," for example, necessitate a concept of memory as a distinctly psychological process. Why must we presume that my ability to furnish you with the name on my birth certificate raises questions of a *psychological* nature, or questions to which psychological research must necessarily provide an answer? Why, for example, is the question not more likely one of physiology, or, given the material nature of the body, of physics? And, given strong arguments against the possibility of reducing the folk language of personal memory to physiology or physics, why does a social account of these activities not suffice? We are willing to accept social accounts of people's manners, styles of dress, and forms of religion. Why is a similar form of explanation not sufficient as well for people's accounts of their personal past?

From the constructionist standpoint, a social explanation is indeed to be favored – borrowing none of the conceptual, ideological, and hermeneutic problems of a dualist metaphysics. However, is this to say that there is *no* place for the kinds of experimental explorations that have been the hallmarks of psychology as a science? I don't think so. From a constructionist standpoint the aim of the sciences should not be that of abandoning all languages save that of the constructionist. If language is inherently a social phenomenon, and the language of personal memory is useful for carrying on relationships, then it ill behooves the scholar to opt for obliterating the language. Given the contribution of psychologists to the common language, and the use of experimental research to enrich this language (e.g., demonstrating differences between types of memory), a certain amount of research is useful. However, the aim of such research would not be that of providing truth warrants for theoretical propositions, but of vivifying or illustrating the concepts in question.[7]

Yet, I think there is finally a more efficient and effective use to be made of experimental research in the domain of self-memory, one that plays a congenial counterpoint to the constructionist view outlined here. From the present standpoint, carrying out acts we index as personal memory is essentially a form of social skill; one *performs* personal memory, as it were, as an effective participant in the culture. In this light, empirical research on personal memory can demonstrate people's capacities for social participation; it not only can reveal what people are apt to say or do under the social conditions of the research itself, but can also indicate possible limits of action. Thus, it may be useful to identify conditions under which people can or cannot identify faces to which they were exposed, repeat actions once mastered, and make socially agreeable reports of incidents in the past. Findings such as these may help in fostering acceptable courtroom testimony, good study habits, or athletic proficiency; they may also aid in the treatment of amnesia or other cases where skills have been lost. However, in my view, such research should ideally be geared to practical contexts within the culture – answering questions arising within the legal, educational, or medical profession, for example. To use the results primarily as a means of validating a contextually abstracted theory of psychological memory is to squander their potential.

And, from the present standpoint, such practical pursuits may be greatly enhanced by taking into account the social embeddedness of the various performances.

NOTES

1 For a classic philosophic account of such problems see Ryle (1949); for a critique relevant to current cognitive theory see Gergen (1989).
2 For a critique of the sociocultural implications of self-contained individualism see Bellah (1985) and Sampson (1977).
3 For amplification of the hermeneutic dilemma see Gergen (1988).
4 This convention, like the preceding, is more honored in certain occasions than others. Indeed, professional writers often make serious attempts to "break the rules." For example, in his autobiographical work *Resident Alien*, Clark Blaise intentionally attempts to blur the boundary between a factual and fictional memory, and in doing so suggests that the idiosyncratic and fanciful account may carry more "truth about self" than the so-called objective account.
5 For elaboration see Latour (1987) and Knorr-Cetina (1981).
6 In the debate in autobiographical memory (see Rubin's 1986 volume) between those favoring *copy* theories of memory as opposed to *reconstructive* accounts, social constructionism clearly favors the latter. However, constructionism adds an important dimension to the argument by holding that the initial account of reality is itself constructed. Autobiographical memory is not initially a transparent copy of reality that is later reconstructed. Rather, the initial account one makes of reality is itself conducted within a system of social conventions, and later accounts may change with varying sociodiscursive conditions.
7 See Gergen (in press) for amplification.

REFERENCES

Baldwin, C. (1977). *One to one*. New York: Evans.
Barthes, R. (1977). *Roland Barthes* (R. Howard, Trans.). New York: Hill and Wang.
Bartlett, F. C. (1932). *Remembering as a study in social psychology*. Cambridge University Press.
Bellah, R. N. (1985). *Habits of the heart*. Berkeley: University of California Press.
Bennett, W., & Feldman, M. (1981). *Reconstructing reality in the courtroom*. New Brunswick, NJ; Rutgers University Press.
Blaise, C. (1986). *Resident alien*. Markham, Ontario: Penguin.
Bromley, R. (1988). *Lost narratives*. New York: Routledge.
Bruner, J. (1986). *Actual minds, possible worlds*. Cambridge, MA: Harvard University Press.
Connerton, P. (1989). *How societies remember*. Cambridge University Press.
Coulter, J. (1985). Two concepts of the mental. In K. J. Gergen & K. E. Davis (Eds.), *The social construction of the person*. New York: Springer-Verlag.
Derrida, J. (1974). *Of grammatology*. Baltimore: Johns Hopkins University Press.

Eakin, P. J. (1985). *Fictions in autobiography: Studies in the art of self invention.* Princeton: Princeton University Press.

Edwards, D., & Middleton, D. (1988). Conversational remembering and family relationships: How children learn to remember. *Journal of Social and Personal Relationships, 5,* 3–25.

Foucault, M. (1979). *Discipline and punish.* New York: Random House.

Gadamer, H. G. (1975). *Truth and method.* New York: Seabury.

Gergen, K. J. (1988). If persons are texts. In S. Messer, L. Sass, & R. Woolfolk (Eds.), *Hermeneutics and psychological theory* (pp. 28–51). New Brunswick, NJ: Rutgers University Press.

Gergen, K. J. (1989). Social psychology and the wrong revolution. *European Journal of Social Psychology, 19,* 463–484.

Gergen, K. J. (in press). *Realities and relationships.* Chicago: University of Chicago Press.

Gergen, K. J., & Gergen, M. M. (1987). Narratives of relationship. In P. McGhee, D. Clarke, & R. Burnett (Eds.), *Accounting for relationships* (pp. 269–288). London: Methuen.

Gergen, K. J., & Gergen, M. M. (1988). Narrative and the self as relationship. In L. Berkowitz (Ed.), *Advances in experimental social psychology* (Vol. 21). New York: Academic Press.

Gergen, M. M. (1992). Life stories: Pieces of a dream. In G. C. Rosenwald & R. L. Ochberg (Eds.), *Storied lives: The cultural politics of self-understanding.* New Haven: Yale University Press.

Graves, R. (1991). *The years with Laura, 1926–40,* New York; Viking.

Halbwachs, M. (1980). *The collective memory.* New York: Harper & Row. (Original work published 1951).

Hume, K. (1984). *Fantasy and mimesis.* London: Methuen.

Kermode, F. (1967). *The sense of an ending.* New York: Oxford University Press.

Knorr-Cetina, K. D. (1981). *Manufacture of knowledge: An essay on the constructivist and contextual nature of science.* Oxford: Pergamon Press.

Latour, B. (1987). *Science in action.* Cambridge, MA: Harvard University Press.

Lindenberger, H. (1975). *Historical drama.* Chicago: University of Chicago Press.

Mandler, J. M. (1978). A code in the node: The use of story schema in retrieval. *Discourse Processes, 1,* 14–35.

Martin, W. (1986). *Recent theories of narrative.* Ithaca, NY: Cornell University Press.

Middleton, D., & Edwards, D. (1990). *Collective remembering.* London: Sage.

Mink, L. (1970). History and fiction as modes of comprehension. *Literary History, 1,* 541–558.

Monk, R. (1990). *Ludwig Wittgenstein: The duty of genius.* London: Cape.

Nerone, J., and Wartella, E. (1989). Introduction to special issue on "social memory." *Communication, 11,* 86–88.

Quine, W. V. O. (1985). *The time of my life: An autobiography.* Cambridge, MA: MIT Press.

Rimmon-Kenan, S. (1983). *Narrative fiction: Contemporary poetics.* London: Methuen.

Roediger, H., III. (1990). Implicit memory: Retention without remembering. *American Psychologist, 45,* 1043–1057.

Rorty, R. (1979). *Philosophy and the mirror of nature.* Princeton, NJ: Princeton University Press.

Rubin, D. (Ed.) (1986). *Autobiographical memory.* Cambridge University Press.

Ryle, G. (1949). *The concept of mind.* London: Hutchinson.

Sampson, E. E. (1977). Psychology and the American ideal. *Journal of Personality and Social Psychology, 35,* 767–782.

Schank, R., & Abelson, R. (1977). *Scripts, plans, goals, and understanding.* Hillsdale, NJ; Erlbaum.

Schudson, M. (1990). Ronald Reagan misremembered. In D. Middleton & D. Edwards (Eds.), *Collective remembering.* London: Sage.

Schwartz, B. (1990). The reconstruction of Abraham Lincoln. In D. Middleton & D. Edwards (Eds.), *Collective remembering.* London: Sage.

Shotter, J. (1990). The social construction of remembering and forgetting. In D. Middleton & D. Edwards (Eds.), *Collective remembering.* London: Sage.

Simons, H. (Ed.). (1989). *The rhetorical turn.* Chicago: University of Chicago Press.

Suleiman, S. R., & Crossman, I. (Eds.). (1980). *The reader in the text.* Princeton, NJ: Princeton University Press.

White, H. (1973). *Metahistory: The historical imagination in nineteenth-century Europe.* Baltimore: Johns Hopkins University Press.

White, H. (1978). *Topics of discourse.* Baltimore: Johns Hopkins University Press.

Wittgenstein, L. (1963). *Philosophical investigations.* New York: Macmillan.

Young, K. (1982). Frame and boundary in the phenomenology of narrative. *Semiotica, 41,* 277–315.

6

Personal identity and autobiographical recall

GREG J. NEIMEYER AND APRIL E. METZLER

Many years ago an unmanageable adolescent by the name of Samuel Clemens took leave of what he described as his "stupid, know-nothin'" father. Several years later, when the famous American humorist had returned home as a young adult after weathering the world on his own for a while, Mark Twain was, again in his own words, "astonished to find out how much the old man had learned in those few years." Episodes such as this stand not only as amusing testaments to predictable developmental trajectories, but also as subtle reminders that autobiographical memories necessarily follow personal pathways, pathways constituted in the very act of self-construction. Even as we forge notions of our "selves," we shape and frame the nature of our later recollections. Our identities and memories are two sides of the same coin (Greenwald & Banaji, 1989).

This paper addresses the constructive and reconstructive aspects of autobiographical memory broadly, placing particular emphasis on the interdependence between memory recall and the continuously evolving self. It follows Robinson's (1976) definition of an autobiographical memory as a personal "record of discrete experiences arising from a person's participation in acts or situations which were to some degree localized in time and place" (p. 578). The central features of this definition are shared by other, more recent descriptions, such as Neisser's (1988, p. 361) characterization of autobiographical memory as "the form of memory in which the events of one's life comprise the significant memoria" (cf. Brewer's 1986 definition of personal memory).

By way of foreshadowing, we would like first to underscore some assumptions associated with a constructivist approach to memory and to develop the claim that autobiographical memory is better understood as a process of personal reconstruction than one of faithful reconstitution. Because this reconstruction is embedded within the broader developmental context of the evolving self, processes of self-construction are inextricably linked to autobiographical memory recall, and much of this essay will be devoted to illustrating this. In particular, we will be arguing that the process of personal identity development carries important implications for memory recall, implications concerning both the availability and the utility of personal recollections. More specifically, personal identity provides both structure and stricture to autobiographical memory recall, with different styles of identity development differentially enabling and disabling the recollection of memories that are central to the self. Operating as alternative forms of personal science, various styles of identity formation may support memories that bolster or bombard cherished self-images, and they may be differentially responsive to the impact of these recollections. By detailing recent efforts to test this notion, we hope to support the conceptualization of personal identity and memory processes as twin facets of the self (see Greenwald, 1981) and highlight the contingency of each upon the other in the developmental process of self-construction.

Construction and recollection

Mahoney (1988, 1991) has traced the historical origins of constructivist thinking and has identified the Italian philosopher Giambattista Vico (1668–1744) as an important progenitor of contemporary conceptualizations. Vico's (1725/1948) discussion of memory in his *New Science* may represent one of the earliest constructivist accounts in this regard as well. In this work Vico distinguished among three different aspects of memory: memory as memory itself (*memoria*), memory as imagination (*fantasia*), and memory as invention (*ingegno*).

The first of these underscores the power of memory to recall things that are not currently present; to render things here that are not here, and in this way to materialize in the present the specter of what is properly regarded as part of the past. Memory as *memoria* highlights the mind's ability to transport to the present that which has already transpired.

Memory as *fantasia*, by contrast, illustrates the fact that reconstruction begins at the instant of perception. For Vico there is no pictorial realism. Objects cannot be apprehended in themselves. Rather, they are reordered in personal, human terms, and their recollection necessarily reflects this primordial reconstruction. Memory as fantasy, then, emphasizes the contingency of recollection upon interpretation, and highlights the fact that autobiographical recall is not the literal reproduction of psychologically embalmed events, but rather is, in the apt phrase of Frederic Bartlett (1932), "far more decisively an affair of construction."

And lastly, memory as invention highlights the additional contribution to meaning that is made in the very act of recollection. "The world of human meaning is a totality," writes Verene (1981) in his interpretation of Vico, "in which any act of meaning leads to and is part of a total system of meaning" (p. 105). Therefore, recollection is provisory upon the shifting network of meanings into which it is translated. As Reiser, Black, and Kalamarides (1986) have noted, "Remembering an experience involves reunderstanding that experience" (p. 119). This facet of memory as invention, then, underscores the fact that recollection is, ontologically speaking, wholly contingent upon comprehension, and developmental shifts in comprehension would therefore necessarily influence autobiographical recollection (see Fitzgerald, 1986; Fivush, 1988; Nelson, 1988).

Each of these features of memory, its capacity to bring to the present that which is past, its translation of events into personal terms, and its contingency upon shifting tides of self-construction, are features now receiving attention within constructivist accounts of autobiographical memory recall. For example, after decades of profound slumbering beneath the Ebbinghaus blanket of research, investigators are increasingly drawn toward the ecological study of memory and toward the interplay between personality and memory processes (Barclay, 1986; Barclay & DeCooke, 1988; Barclay, Hodges, & Smith, 1990; Barclay & Subramaniam, 1987; Barclay & Wellman, 1986; Brewer, 1988; Fitzgerald, 1986; Greenwald & Banaji, 1989; Kihlstrom, 1981; Ross, McFarland, & Fletcher, 1981; see Banaji & Crowder, 1989, for a dissenting opinion).

Central to these efforts has been concern with the role of current self-constructions in personal recollections. Beginning with Bartlett (1932) and continuing through the contemporary efforts of multiple researchers (Barclay, 1986; Barclay & DeCooke, 1988; Barclay, Hodges, & Smith, 1990; Barclay & Wellman, 1986; Barsalou, 1988; Bower & Gilligan, 1979; Brewer 1986, 1988; Kihlstrom, 1981; Linton, 1986; Neimeyer & Rareshide, 1991; Neisser, 1981; Neisser & Winograd, 1988; Ross et al., 1981; Ross & McFarland, 1988), this work broadly argues that autobiographical recollections are sustained and transformed within personal frameworks of meaning. As Linton's (1986) intensive longitudinal efforts have documented, personal "memories are not random excreta, but both guide and are shaped by our hierarchically organized knowledge structures" (p. 65).

George Kelly (1955) gave form to these structures in his personal construct psychology. Arguing that individuals operate as personal scientists, he proposed that we develop increasingly comprehensive networks of meaning composed of myriad bipolar constructs (e.g., introverted vs. extroverted) that serve to channelize anticipation and recollection. Directed toward progressively more viable understandings of the self and experience, these networks are understood as idiographic (Individuality Corollary) and hierarchically organized (Organization Corollary) templates of meaning that undergo continuous revision as a function of their validation or invalidation through contact with perceived events (Experience Corollary). Indeed, much of Kelly's (1955) early insights can be viewed as a prophetic preface to contemporary themes emerging within the autobiographical literature. Foremost among these is the delicate interplay between personal and memory processes, where one's biography can be understood as "a present structure which is documented by selected memories of the past and is in part a viewing screen upon which the events of the past seem to have form and consequence" (Kelly, 1955, p. 989).

Personal science and personal memories

Kelly's (1955) characterization of the individual as a personal scientist resonates well within the contemporary constructivist climate in psychology. Presaging later theories of self-development (e.g., Berzonsky, 1990; Epstein, 1973; Greenwald, 1980), Kelly likened the individual's quest for meaning to the programmatic efforts of the research scientist. Like the scientist, the individual is directed toward an increasingly viable and comprehensive understanding of experience through a process of continual confirmation and disconfirmation of anticipations. And, like the more formal scientific offspring, the personal scientist is guided by implicit theories. Einstein's recognition that "it is the theory which decides what we can observe" (Heisenberg, 1972, p. 77) is as applicable in this regard to the individual's naive inquiry as it is to the more disciplined investigations of full-fledged scientists. As an example, the widespread operation of confirmation bias has served to document the powerful pull toward the conservation of a belief system, a bias that is as evident among professional scientists (see Kuhn, 1970; Lakatos, 1970) as it is among their nonprofessional counterparts (Greenwald, 1975; Snyder, 1981; Snyder & Swann, 1978; Neimeyer, Prichard, Berzonsky, & Metzler, 1991). Biases such as these are less the product of misguided inquiry or deliberate design than they are the natural consequences of the organization of self-knowledge; efforts to elaborate the self necessarily embrace core aspects of one's current self, aspects that support the preservation of viable self-structures even while they direct attendant elaboration (Guidano, 1991). In this regard, memory serves a potent instrumental function, designed not merely to preserve a perished past, but also to utilize it in the service of the present and future selves.

Our own recent work has been directed at exploring the interface between personality and memory processes by demonstrating the impact of identity development on autobiographical recall. Central to this work has been the conceptualization of identity development as reflecting different styles of personal science, a formulation that follows from the early work of Erikson (1956, 1959, 1968) and its more recent extensions (Marcia, 1966; Berzonsky, 1989, 1990; Neimeyer et al., 1991). In his original conceptualization, Erikson recognized identity formation as the critical task of adolescence and imbued it with constructive and psychosocial implications. "Identity formation," wrote Erikson (1968, p. 159), "begins where the usefulness of identification ends. It arises from the selective repudiation and assimilation of childhood identifications, and their absorption in a new configuration."

In his extension of this work, Marcia (1966) attempted to reify two prominent processes in Erikson's (1956) account of identity formation, *commitment* and *exploration*, and in so doing he provided a major impetus to what has become a longstanding research literature. Commitment refers to the degree to which an individual has achieved stable values and beliefs within important domains in life (interpersonal, ideological, etc.), whereas exploration refers to the person's active degree of crisis in seeking and defining these identity commitments. According to this perspective, the primary task of adolescence is to forge a stable sense of ego commitments that provide integration and continuity to the self, rather than generating a sense of uncertainty and confusion.

Four different identity statuses can develop according to Marcia's (1966) paradigm, *Diffusion, Foreclosure, Moratorium,* and *Achievement,* and each reflects the presence or absence of exploration and commitment. *Diffuse* individuals lack stable identity commitments as well as any active process of exploration aimed at achieving them. In contrast, *Foreclosed* individuals have negotiated the resolution of firm self-commitments, but have done so by prematurely co-opting available (often parental) value systems. As a result, their strong commitments occur in the absence of any active self-exploration or identity crisis. *Moratorium* individuals, on the other hand, are actively involved in the struggle to explore alternative beliefs, but have yet to attain firm identity commitments. Finally, *Achieved* individuals have settled on a stable system of commitments after an active and prolonged period of identity exploration.

A sustained body of literature now supports the utility of this status paradigm for studying individual differences in identity development (see Archer, 1989; Berzonsky, 1990; Marcia, 1980; Waterman, 1982), and has demonstrated theoretically consistent differences among the four statuses. Foreclosures, for instance, have been found to be relatively intolerant of ambiguity and more authoritarian (Marcia, 1966; Schenkel & Marcia, 1972; Waterman & Waterman, 1974) and narrow (Berzonsky & Neimeyer, 1988; Berzonsky, Rice, & Neimeyer, 1990) in their belief systems. The validity of the status designations is further supported by their predictable differences along measures of confirmity (Adams, Ryan, Hoffman, Dobson, & Neilsen, 1985), social anxiety (Schenkel & Marcia, 1972), and locus of control (Adams & Shea, 1979), as well as several other interpersonal (Donovan, 1975; Podd, Marcia, & Rubin, 1970) and cognitive measures (Berzonsky et al., 1990; Leiper, 1981; Tzuriel & Klein, 1977).

In his recent extension of Marcia's conceptualization, Berzonsky (1988, 1989, 1990) has advanced a conceptualization of these four identity sta-tuses as representing three different styles of conducting personal science. An *information orientation* is characteristic of both Achieved and Moratorium individuals since both are marked by active efforts to seek, process, and utilize self-relevant information prior to developing firm personal beliefs or commitments. In contrast, a *normative orientation* to personal science is more apt to reflect reliance on available prescriptions and standards of significant referent groups. Like Marcia's (1966) Foreclosed identity status, normative-oriented personal scientists place a premium on conservation of existing beliefs, preferring to cordon off core aspects of their identities in order to protect them from potential disconfirmation. Lastly, a *diffuse orientation* is associated with heightened attention to situational demand. Lacking significant self-structure, diffuse-oriented individuals experience largely external control, with behavior and beliefs being determined primarily by immediate consequences and contextual demands rather than being directed by internal commitments and convictions (see Berzonsky, 1988, 1989, 1990; Berzonsky & Sullivan, 1990).

The major premise of our recent work (Neimeyer & Rareshide, 1991) has been that, because each of these identity styles represents a characteristically different approach to the processing and assimilation of self-relevant information, these differences should be reflected in autobiographical memory recall in at least three ways. The first way concerns differences in the overall *number* of memories available to an individual. Because the availability of autobiographical memories depends, in part, upon the existence of a firm identity structure, we would expect identity style to influence the quantity of personal recollections available to the individual. Secondly, this availability should be qualified by the *nature* of the recollection. In general, memories that support and confirm existing self-constructions should be more readily available than those that disconfirm self-perceptions, with this effect itself being qualified by the individual's characteristic identity style. And finally, the *response* of the individual to recollections that confirm or disconfirm current self-views should also vary as a function of identity style. For example, information-oriented and normative-oriented individuals should respond very differently to identity-discrepant recollections. The former might actively embrace and assimilate discrepant information into evolving self-images, whereas the latter might jettison the discrepant recollections, dismissing their information value in an effort to preserve extant self-constructions. These three sets of predictions follow from differences outlined in the current literatures on autobiographical recall and personal identity, and are detailed below.

Personal structure, style, and recall

Like other constructivist thinkers, Kelly (1955) appreciated the delicate interplay between contemporary identity and personal recollections, stipulating that "in order for an experience to be remembered or perceived clearly it must be supported within a system of constructs" (p. 471). The central role of self-schemata in autobiographical recall is now clearly evident, and much of the work in personal memory stands as empirical testament to this effect. Markus's early finding that individuals who are "schematic" for a particular dimension recall more memories consistent with these schemata than do "aschematic" individuals (Markus, 1977; Markus & Sentis, 1980), for example, is consistent with this notion, as is the substantial empirical literature that follows from other contemporary research programs (Barclay, 1986; Barclay & DeCooke, 1988; Barclay, Hodges & Smith, 1990; Barclay & Subramaniam, 1987; Barclay & Wellman, 1986).

Among the most persuasive programs of research along these lines is the contemporary work of Barclay and his colleagues. The gist of this work suggests that we do recall events that are related to important self schemata, but that these memories are largely reconstructions aimed at preserving the essential integrity of existing self-structures, often at the expense of any fidelity to the "facts." Most autobiographical memories are, in Barclay's (1986, p. 97) apt phrase, largely "true but inaccurate" in the sense that "truth in autobiographical memory is preserved as one conveys the meaning of life events through plausible reconstructions of those events" (Barclay, 1988, p. 293, see also Neisser, 1981). This plausibility is bounded, at least in part, by the person's self views, images of the self that can be likened to perimeter scaffolding that supports and constrains interior reconstruction. At least in ambiguous instances permitting inferential leeway, autobiographical recollections are moulded by what Brewer (1986) has termed generic personal memories, and by personal convictions about how one might typically experience a given event (Barclay, 1986; Barclay & DeCooke, 1988). These generic personal memories are personal compositions, cumulative constructions of repeated experiences, the kind of memories that Neisser (1981) has dubbed *repisodic* because they appear as constructive amalgams of repeated episodic memories. As Barclay (1988) has noted, when details fade sufficiently and we have a difficult time reproducing what Spence (1982) has termed *historical* truth, we gravitate instead toward preserving what he termed its *narrative* truth. This narrative truth may serve the general integrity of the past and the present by preserving the gist of an event while at the same time supporting the perceived continuity and coherence of the self (Barclay, 1988; Barclay et al., 1990; Barclay & Subramaniam, 1987).

Work such as this stands testament to Bartlett's (1932) early recognition that "the past is being continually re-made, reconstructed in the interests of the present" (p. 309). By highlighting the transactional relationship between self and memory processes, these contemporary efforts illustrate how each simultaneously enables and constrains the other (see Barsalou, 1988; Greenwald, 1980; Robinson, 1986). According to the current reasoning, however, the nature of this transactional relationship should vary as a function of an individual's identity style. The memory recall of information-oriented individuals, for example, should reflect a relatively balanced record of experiences that are consistent and inconsistent with currently held beliefs about the self. Analogous to the "equal opportunity" (Snyder, 1981) approach of more objective hypothesis testers, information-oriented identity styles should actively generate a more balanced array of confirmatory and disconfirmatory personal memories (see Neimeyer et al., 1991).

By way of contrast, the normative-oriented identity style should demonstrate the most lopsidedly confirmatory approach to autobiographical memory recall, generating disproportionately more memories that are consistent with contemporary self-constructions and correspondingly fewer that jeopardize those constructions. Consistent with findings linking them with a higher fear of negative evaluation and lower levels of openness to experience (see Berzonsky, 1990), normative-oriented individuals would be expected instead to cordon off cherished self-perceptions, rendering them impervious to invalidation. One reflection of this protectionist stance might well be their relative inability to generate disconfirmatory memories, memories that threaten the validity of current self-constructions.

Diffuse-oriented individuals, on the other hand, neither possess firm identity commitments to protect, nor engage in an active process dedicated to developing them. Therefore, although we would expect them to generate the lowest overall levels of autobiographical recall (owing to their absence of firm identity structure), we would not necessarily anticipate that they would be lopsidedly confirmatory in relation to their memory recall. More likely, they would be responsive to the situational demands of the given context, generating memories according to the perceived objectives or rewards of the specific task.

The impact of autobiographical recollections

Finally, considerable work has been directed at investigating the impact of autobiographical recall on subsequent self-perceptions. Entire therapeutic interventions have been developed and implemented on the assumption that positive benefits accrue from the incorporation of autobiographical recollections into such procedures as life review (Butler, 1963) or reminiscence therapy (Ebersole, 1978). Here, as Hyland and Ackerman (1988, p. 35) note, "Reminiscence is conceptualized simply as memory for personal experiences from one's past," and for this reason, "might have much in common with other memory processes, in particular, autobiographical memory." The intended impact of such procedures varies widely, of course, often targeting cognitive (Hyland & Ackerman, 1988), affective (Perotta & Meacham, 1981–1982), or interpersonal (Goldwasser, Auerbach, & Harkins, 1987) change. The effects of such recollection can be widely variable, ranging from the adaptive maintenance of self-esteem to the exacerbation of negative emotion that accompanies rumination (see Poulton & Strassberg, 1986).

One promising line of research that addresses the impact of personal recollections on contemporary self-constructions is the recent work of Ross and his colleagues. Ross and Conway (1988), for example, have adduced evidence in support of the position that the recollection of events consistent with a newly formed belief enhances an individual's commitment to that belief. In contrast to control groups, individuals who engaged in recalling events that supported their newly acquired beliefs indicated (a) stronger expectations to behave in line with these beliefs, (b) increased resistance to counterattitudinal attacks on their beliefs, and (c) a tendency to selectively recall arguments that supported their newly acquired convictions. In explaining this effect, Ross and Conway (1988) noted that "a review of past actions appears to validate the attitudes," giving rise to "a form of self-fulfilling prophecy: Attitudes alter recall, which, in turn, inappropriately bolsters a person's commitment to those attitudes" (p. 129). If the reasoning advanced in this paper is viable then we might expect individual differences in this propensity toward self-fulfilling prophesy. In this and other similar biases, we should see more robust efforts at self-preservation among normative-oriented individuals, with correspondingly less bias among diffuse- and information-oriented individuals.

To clarify these predictions, consider that autobiographical recollections can be viewed broadly along dimensions of valence (positive or negative) and perceived self-consistency (confirmatory or disconfirmatory). Recollection could then be regarded as either confirming or disconfirming a positive or a negative self-image. Therapeutic as well as dysfunctional analogs of these conditions are readily available in the clinical literature (Berghorn & Schafer, 1986–1987). The adaptive advantages of directing individuals to recall positive, self-enhancing experiences that disconfirm negative self-schemata have been stressed by certain schools of cognitive therapy, for example, as have the constructive applications of self-enhancing recollections in reminiscence therapy (Poulton & Strassberg, 1986). Likewise, the maladaptive impact associated with selective attention to negative events that disconfirm positive self-features occupies a prominent target of intervention in many cognitive therapies, as does the excessive preoccupation with ruminations that catalog one's shortcomings (see Poulton & Strassberg, 1986).

The impact of autobiographical recollections that confirm or disconfirm positive or negative self-perceptions should vary directly with identity style. As Berzonsky (1990, p. 155) has noted, "These orientations encompass the mechanisms by which self-relevant information . . . is processed, structured, utilized, and revised." Information-oriented individuals, actively searching for and assimilating self-relevant information, should be the most responsive to contemporary self-reconstruction in this regard, a prediction consistent with their greater flexibility, cognitive liberality (see McCrae & Costa, 1985), and openness to experience (Berzonsky, 1990; Berzonsky & Sullivan, 1990). When directed to recall instances that challenge existing self-perceptions, information-oriented individuals should be maximally receptive to incorporating this image-discrepant information into their self-views.

Diffuse-oriented individuals, lacking firm internal commitments to rely upon, should be similarly responsive to change, but for different reasons. Without internal moorings to secure self-perceptions, diffuse-oriented individuals would be expected to drift in the direction of the image-discrepant recall, but without firmly anchoring on the new self-constructions. Externally oriented and subject to immediate contextual exigencies and reinforcements, the self-constructions of diffuse individuals would be expected to ebb and flow with immediate environmental influences.

The least responsive to self-change based on autobiographical recall should be normative-oriented individuals. Firmly committed to self-perceptions that were arrived at without exploration or circumspection, these foreclosed identity types are the least open to experience (Berzonsky, 1989; Berzonsky & Sullivan, 1990) and would be expected to fortify preexisting beliefs, even in the face of contradictory evidence. "When it comes to 'hard core' areas of the self such as values," note Berzonsky and Sullivan (1990, p. 7), "a normative style might lead individuals to defensively close themselves off from specific information or experiences that might induce dissonance."

In sum, identity and memory processes have long been linked. Characteristic features of identity style, therefore, should carry implications regarding the nature of the transactional relationship between current self-constructions and autobiographical recollections. Identity orientations marked by an openness to redefinition and a quest for information should vary in predictable ways from those marked either by the defensive preservation of existing self-constructions or the general absence of such constructions. Autobiographical recall should generally be facilitated by more firmly committed identity structures, but the availability of such recollections should be qualified by the nature of the memory's self-consistency (consistent or inconsistent) and valence (positive or negative). Information-oriented identity styles should be maximally receptive to generating a more balanced record of memories in this regard, whereas normative-oriented styles should be marked by more pronounced confirmation bias. In addition to memory generation effects, the identity styles should also be differentially responsive to self-reconstruction as a function of memory recall. The self-perceptions of diffuse-oriented individuals should swing widely with the nature of the memories recalled, in contrast to the more judicious incorporation of self-discrepant as well as self-consistent information by information-oriented individuals. Normative-oriented individuals should be least responsive to self-change, particularly when confronted with image-discrepant, negative recollections.

Methods

Subjects

In an effort to test these predictions concerning the relationship between identity style and autobiographical recall, we pretested a large sample ($N = 880$) of college undergraduates (median age = 19 years) on the revised version of the Extended Objective Measure of Ego Identity Status (EOM-EIS; Bennion & Adams, 1986). This instrument represents the most recent revision of the most widely used objective measure of identity status in the current literature. Beginning with the pioneering efforts of Adams, Shea, and Fitch (1979), the continuing development of this 64-item paper-and-pencil questionnaire has been directed toward improving the reliability and validity of the status designations based on Marcia's (1966) earlier interview procedure, while at the same time offering the advantages of large-group administration and objective assessment. A review of 14 studies in which the EOM-EIS was administered (Adams, Bennion, & Huh, 1989) indicated that the four status subscales have adequate internal consistency (median alpha coefficient = .66) and test-retest stability (median correlation = .76). Data attesting to the predictive and construct validity of the measure have been collected in 40 studies (see Adams et al., 1989). Although some studies have reported sex differences on particular subscales (e.g., Grotevant & Adams, 1984), most have not (e.g., Abraham, 1983; Adams et al., 1979; Adams et al., 1985; Bennion & Adams, 1986; Berzonsky et al., 1990), and recent reviews have noted the absence of any systematic sex differences in the development of identity status (Adams et al., 1989; Waterman, 1985). See Adams et al. (1989) for a comprehensive review of reliability and validity of the instrument.

The instrument was administered in group settings to participants who volunteered to take part in "a study of personal attitudes" in exchange for experimental credit in their undergraduate psychology classes. On the basis of their EOM-EIS scale scores, subjects were classified as to their identity status using the criteria specified by Adams et al. (1979, p. 227) for designating pure identity types. Pure types are individuals whose identity status scores fall more than one standard deviation above the sample mean along one and only one of the four status subscales (Achievement, Moratorium, Foreclosure, or Diffusion). Subjects failing to meet these criteria included the transitional types (with two or more status subscores falling more than a standard deviation above the sample means) or undifferentiated types (with no subscores falling more than a standard deviation above any of the four means). These subjects were excluded from the analysis. Based on these classification criteria, 216 subjects were identified as pure identity status types and participated in this study (62 Achieved; 50 Moratorium; 50 Foreclosed; 54 Diffuse). A chi-square analysis confirmed that gender was randomly distributed across the various conditions of the study (see Design, below).

Design and procedure

Each of the 216 subjects was contacted and scheduled for an individual session, during which the subject completed a computer-interactive memory recall procedure designed by Landy (1986) and revised by Reese and Metzler (1989; see below). The purposes of the computer-interactive procedure were fourfold. First, it was designed to determine important and self-relevant constructs (schemata) for each person individually. Second, it was designed to assess participants' self-perceptions along these dimensions. Third, it systematically elicited memory recall related to these dimensions. And fourth, it assessed subsequent self-perceptions along these dimensions in order to provide a measure of perceived self-change as a function of autobiographical recall. A synopsis of this paradigm and its development is followed by a more detailed account of each of these four steps.

Paradigm and development. In designing the overall paradigm we were interested in developing a procedure that facilitated the systematic recall of autobiographical memories, defined as "discrete experiences arising from a person's participation in acts or situations which were to some degree localized in time and place" (Robinson, 1976, p. 578; see Brewer's

1986 description of *personal memories*). Because we were interested in assessing the availability of real-life memories related to the various identity styles, as well as the impact of those recollections on subsequent self-perceptions, we needed a system that simultaneously provided for ecological validity and experimental control. Facing a similar conundrum, Robinson (1976, p. 579) observed, "What is needed is a research paradigm which combines . . . the open-endedness of anecdotal inquiry and the controlled quantitative comparisons inherent in experimentation." Like Robinson (1976) we found that Sir Francis Galton's (1879) chronometric studies of word association and memory provided a means of marrying these methods. Specifically, following Crovitz & Shiffman (1974), we utilized the word cue method of eliciting memories, since, as Robinson (1976) noted: "This simple task has the cardinal advantage of eliciting discrete memories pertaining to a wide variety of life experiences which span a large portion of a person's life. If the conditions for eliciting such recollections are suitably controlled . . . we should be able to probe autobiographical memory in a systematic and objective manner" (p. 580).

Because the overall availability (and latency) of recall is clearly related to the kind of words used as memory cues (Robinson, 1976), the word cues were controlled along several critical dimensions. First, because personality traits (e.g., *dependent – independent; outgoing – shy; cooperative – stubborn*) should be most closely linked to personal memories, all word cues were limited to personality characteristics. Second, since we were interested in varying the valence of the memories recalled (positive or negative), we wanted to develop word cues that were differentially valenced, but still highly meaningful. To do this we consulted Anderson's (1968) original list of 555 personality traits. From this list we selected a set of 28 highly meaningful, positive traits (i.e., meaningfulness ratings ranging from 3.58 to 3.86, $M = 3.72$ on a 4-point scale) that had associated antonyms that were similarly salient (ranging from 3.60 to 3.86, $M = 3.72$). While equally meaningful, the positive word cues were rated as considerably more favorable (likableness ratings ranging from 4.12 to 5.54, $M = 4.69$) than were the negative antonyms (ratings ranging from 0.43 to 2.63, $M = 1.53$). Because even minor deviations in word cues or word cue instructions can produce widely variable results (see Brewer, 1986; Robinson, 1976), considerable effort was exerted to assure that the characteristics were clear, commonly recognizable, highly meaningful, and carefully controlled for the level of imagery that they evoked (Gargus, 1990).

Given the development of the stimulus set of word cues, we also needed to embed these cues into a procedure that would enable us to (a) determine for each individual a subset of particularly "schematic" dimensions (i.e., characteristics that were highly self-descriptive and self-relevant), (b) identify the nature of each person's self-perceptions along each of these dimensions prior to autobiographical recall, (c) systematically control the presentation of these characteristics as memory cues, varying their valence (positive, negative) and self-consistency (consistent, inconsistent) according to the design of the study (see below), and (d) reassess self-perceptions as a measure of self-change. Each of these features is detailed in the three procedural steps listed below.

Step 1: Prerecall ratings. Subjects were called into the lab individually and seated in front of a personal computer. Instructions for this and all subsequent steps were provided by the computer. The experimenter remained in the room at a distance from the subject in order to appear available if needed, but unobtrusive (i.e., positioned so that he/she could not see the monitor screen or the subject's responses). Subjects were given an orientation to the keyboard and to the positioning of the six numerical keys (1–6) and the "enter" key that would be used throughout the study. They then practiced keystrokes on cue from instructions appearing on the screen until they achieved equal response latency (within 500 milliseconds) for all keys. The actual procedure for Step 1 then began and consisted of two tasks: ratings of construct importance and self-descriptiveness.

The first task was to rate the importance of the 28 bipolar constructs (e.g., *trustworthy* vs. *untrustworthy*) according to "how important you believe it is in forming an impression of a person." Presentation of these bipolar dimensions, appearing on the screen one at a time, was randomized. The initial three pairs functioned solely to orient subjects to the task. These practice pairs (*ambitious–lazy; forgiving–unforgiving; conformist–nonconformist*) were not included in the analyses. Each construct pair remained on the screen until the subject pressed a rating key indicating its perceived importance, at which point the computer recorded the rating and presented the next construct pair.

The next part of this prerecall stage instructed subjects to rate themselves along a set of 50 individual traits, "according to the degree that you privately believe that the trait describes you," using a 6-point scale ranging from 1 (not me) to 6 (like me). The 50 traits were the individual characteristics of the 25 bipolar constructs used in the preceding task. For example, in the earlier task they were asked to rate how important it was to them to know whether someone was *tidy* or *untidy* in forming an impression of the individual. In this task they were presented with these two characteristics (*tidy* and *untidy*) separately (randomized among the other 48 characteristics) and asked to rate how self-descriptive each was, again using a six-point scale.

When this task was completed the computer had stored ratings of construct importance for each subject along all 25 bipolar constructs, and self-descriptiveness ratings along all 50 individual characteristics. These two features, construct importance and self-descriptiveness, were used to identify four trait words for each individual that would then be used as memory cues in the subsequent procedure. To determine these characteristics, the computer was programmed first to select as memory cues only those bipolar constructs rated as "most important" by an individual (i.e., rated a 6 on the 1–6 scale). If fewer than four constructs received a rating of 6 for a given individual, then the computer selected randomly from among the next most highly rated traits (i.e., those given a rating of 5). Because all constructs used as memory cues in this study were selected on the basis of their importance to the individual, we designated these as *superordinate schemata* (see Metzler & Neimeyer, 1988, for a comparison of this with other means of determining superordination).

Beyond assuring that all memories would be recalled in relation to superordinate schemata, we also wanted to be able to manipulate the valence (positive or negative) and the self-consistency (consistent or inconsistent) of the memories to the individual. To do this the computer was programmed to sort positive from negative features and then to sort separately according to self-descriptiveness ratings. Positive (e.g., *generous*) and negative (e.g., *stingy*) features that received high self-descriptiveness ratings (i.e., 5 or 6) were considered to be self-consistent, and those that received low self-descriptiveness ratings (i.e., 1 or 2) were considered to be self-inconsistent. We further reasoned that self-consistent memories would operate to confirm or validate existing self-perceptions, whereas self-inconsistent memories would disconfirm or invalidate contemporary self-constructions.

For each individual, then, the computer calculated a set of four memory cues: positive cues that validated self-perceptions (positive/validate), positive cues that invalidated self-perceptions (positive/invalidate), negative cues that validated current self-perceptions (negative/validate), and negative cues that invalidated current self-perceptions (negative/invalidate).

Positive/validate. Subjects assigned to this condition were presented with four memory recall cues that were positive and consistent with their own self-ratings on this trait. For example, subjects who viewed the trait *generous* as highly self-descriptive (i.e., a rating of 5 or 6) would be asked to recall autobiographical memories in which they exemplified the cue word *generous*, according to the instructions below (see Step 2). The memories recalled would be positive and would validate currently positive self-perceptions.

Positive/invalidate. Subjects assigned to this condition were presented with four memory recall cues that were positive but inconsistent with their own self-ratings on this trait. For example, subjects who viewed the trait *generous* as not self-descriptive (i.e., a rating of 1 or 2), would be asked to recall autobiographical memories in which they exemplified the cue word *generous*. The memories recalled would therefore be positive but would invalidate currently negative self-perceptions.

Negative/validate. Subjects assigned to this condition were presented with memory recall cues that were negative and consistent with their own self-ratings on this trait. For example, subjects who viewed the trait *stingy* as highly self-descriptive (i.e., a rating of a 5 or 6) would be asked to recall autobiographical memories in which they exemplified the cue word *stingy*. The memories recalled would therefore be negative and would validate currently negative self-perceptions.

Negative/invalidate. Subjects assigned to this condition were presented with memory recall cues that were negative and inconsistent with their own self-ratings on this feature. For example, subjects who viewed the trait *stingy* as not self-descriptive (i.e., a rating of 1 or 2) would be asked to recall autobiographical memories in which they exemplified the cue word *stingy*. The memories recalled would therefore be negative and would invalidate currently positive self-perceptions.

Step 2: Memory recall. Step 2 consisted of the memory recall task itself. The recall paradigm utilized an adaptation of the Crovitz and Schiffman (1974) technique that was itself derived from the early work of Galton (1879). Since minor modifications of the method can significantly influence the nature of the memories recalled (see Franklin & Holding, 1977; Karis, 1979; Robinson, 1976; and Brewer's 1986 discussion of the issue), explicit recall guidelines were presented on the computer screen. Following Brewer's (1986) outline for eliciting *personal memories*, we wanted to reduce the recollection of fleeting visual impressions, generic personal memories, and autobiographical facts that would likely be elicited by open-ended recall, so the following specific memory recall instructions were provided:

A trait will be presented on the screen. Your task is to attempt to recall specific incidents in your life when you exemplified or demonstrated that particular trait. Press the red (Enter) key each time you recall an incident. Please note the following guidelines:
    (a)   You yourself must have exemplified the trait.
    (b)   The incident may have occurred quite recently or many years ago.
    (c)   You must be able to recall something that makes the incident a distinct

memory. If the same type of incident happened more than once, press the key for each incident only if you can recall something that makes you certain that the other incident happened on a different occasion.

(d) It doesn't matter if anyone else would agree with you as to whether a particular memory "counts" – your opinion is all that matters.

(e) Press the red key as soon as you recall a memory, but not before.

(f) It is important that you keep trying to recall incidents during the allotted time. A total of 4 traits will be presented. The computer is programmed to give you 2 minutes per trait and a 30-second rest period between traits. You will know when the time is up because a "Stop" message will appear all over the screen.

Subjects were also given a secondary task. They were instructed to jot down no more than a word or so about each memory (after pressing the key) so that "you yourself can identify the incident later for the purpose of answering an objective, standardized question about the incident after the memory task is over." It was emphasized that they would not be asked to disclose the content of their memories and that "no one will ever see your notes – you will discard them or take them with you when you leave." Following the memory recall procedure, subjects were asked to use these notes to recall the approximate date of each memory. This procedure enhances the validity of recall without jeopardizing confidentiality, and it has been the subject of promising validity studies in its own right (see Robinson, 1976).

Each participant was assigned randomly to one and only one of the four conditions detailed above (positive/validate; positive/invalidate; negative/validate; negative/invalidate) and instructed in a stepwise fashion through the completion of the recall procedure. Two dependent measures were derived from this memory recall phase: total number of memories recalled and average latency of recall. For each subject the number of memories recalled across the four memory cues was calculated and designated as total memories. Latency of recall was determined by calculating the mean response time (in $1/10$-second units) for each subject across all memories elicited in response to the four cues. These two measures, total memories and latency of recall, were two of the three dependent measures used in this study. The third measure, an index of perceived self-change, was derived from the final step of the overall procedure.

Step 3: Perceived self-change. Directly following the memory recall procedure subjects were again presented with all 50 of the traits, one at a time, and again asked to rate the self-descriptiveness of each. The traits were presented in randomized order and the four target dimensions were therefore embedded randomly among the other 46 characteristics in the stimulus set of words. The self-descriptiveness ratings at this postmemory recall period served as the third dependent variable and was designated as an index of perceived self-change.

Results and discussion

· In order to test predictions concerning the impact of identity style on autobiographical memory recall and perceived self-change, data were analyzed by way of a $3 \times 2 \times 2$ between-subjects factorial design. The first factor referred to the three levels of identity style (information-oriented, normative-oriented, diffuse-oriented). The second factor referred to the two levels of memory valence (positive, negative). And the third factor reflected the two levels of memory self-consistency (validate, invalidate). Analyses of variance were conducted along each of the three dependent variables: (1) total number of memories, (2) latency of recall, and (3) perceived self-change.

Total memories recalled

The first ANOVA tested the relationship between identity style and the total number of memories recalled. Main effects were found for valence, $F(1, 215) = 23.91, p < .0001$, and for identity style, $F(2, 215) = 3.45, p > .03$, but these were qualified by a three-way interaction between valence, identity style, and validation, $F(2, 215) = 3.39, p < .03$.

The two main effects reflected the fact that, overall, subjects recalled more positive memories ($M = 18.0$) than negative memories ($M = 10.4$), and that memory recall varied as predicted according to identity style. The highest numbers of autobiographical memories were reported by information-oriented individuals ($M = 15.7$), followed by normative-oriented ($M = 13.2$) and diffuse-oriented ($M = 12.0$) individuals.

These effects were qualified, however, by the three-way interaction. As Figure 6.1 indicates, the three different identity styles reported significantly different patterns of recollections across the four recall conditions. When presented with a positive memory cue that validated self-perceptions (positive/validate), information-oriented individuals reported appreciably more autobiographical memories ($M = 21.7$) than did normative-oriented ($M = 14.5$) or diffuse-oriented ($M = 10.0$) participants. This pattern supports predictions concerning the general quest for self-relevant information on the part of information-oriented personal scientists, as well as the relative dearth of autobiographical recollections associated with identity styles marked by an absence of identity commitments or firm self-structure (see Barclay, 1986; Neimeyer & Rareshide, 1991).

Relatively little difference, by contrast, emerged under the positive/

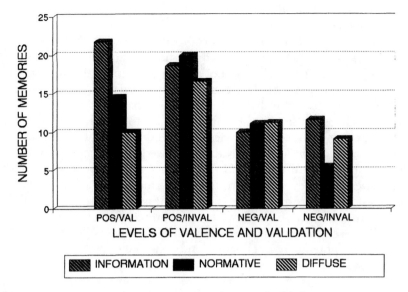

Figure 6.1. Number of memories by identity style, valence, and validation

invalidate condition. When subjects were asked to recall positive memories that were *inconsistent* with current self-perceptions, there was a tendency for normative-oriented individuals to recall slightly more memories ($M = 19.9$) than information-oriented ($M = 18.6$) or diffuse-oriented ($M = 16.6$) subjects, but these differences were relatively modest.

Less difference still was associated with the negative/validate condition, where all three identity styles showed consistently lower levels of memory recall for negative events that validated negative self-perceptions (information-oriented, $M = 10.0$; normative-oriented, $M = 11.1$; diffuse-oriented, $M = 11.2$).

And finally, under the negative/invalidate condition, differences among the identity styles again emerged. Asked to recall negative events that invalidated positive self-perceptions, information-oriented individuals showed the greatest ability to generate such instances ($M = 11.6$), whereas normative-oriented individuals generated the fewest ($M = 5.5$). The diffuse-oriented identity style was intermediate in this regard ($M = 9.1$). This pattern of findings supports the relatively greater receptivity of information-oriented individuals to negative identity-discrepant information. It also supports other research noting the greater difficulty that more normative-oriented individuals have in resolving discrepant and conflicting information (see Read, Adams, & Dobson, 1984; Slugoski, Marcia, & Koopman, 1984), and data indicating their tendency toward constriction and withdrawal under ego-threatening conditions (Waterman & Waterman, 1974).

Looking across the four memory recall conditions, these data invite some intriguing speculation worthy of further attention. For example, contrary to predictions, it does not appear that normative-oriented individuals engage in markedly greater confirmatory memory recall than do information-oriented individuals. Indeed, there is remarkably little discrepancy between levels of confirmatory and disconfirmatory memory recall for any of the identity styles. Across conditions of memory valence the information-oriented individuals showed little discrepancy between the number of confirmatory ($M = 16.4$) and disconfirmatory ($M = 15.1$) memories that they generated, and the same is true of the normative-oriented (confirmatory, $M = 12.7$; disconfirmatory, $M = 13.6$) and the diffuse-oriented (confirmatory, $M = 10.0$; disconfirmatory, $M = 13.1$).

If, however, the data are examined in relation to self-enhancement effects, some potentially interesting tendencies emerge. Self-enhancement in this study would be defined by the tendency to generate relatively greater numbers of positive than negative memories, regardless of their consistency with self-perceptions. Viewed from this perspective, both the information- and normative-oriented individuals appeared to engage in greater self-enhancement than did diffuse-oriented individuals. In this regard the information-oriented individuals generated significantly more positive ($M = 20.1$) than negative ($M = 11.2$) memories, as did the normative-oriented subjects (positive $M = 17.2$; negative, $M = 8.8$). Only the diffuse-oriented identity style was marked by a more equal balance of positive ($M = 11.2$) and negative ($M = 10.3$) memories recalled. One possible interpretation of this effect concerns the endemic function of identity development to preserve a favorable sense of self. In this regard such biases may be viewed as "indicating that ego's cognitive biases are pervasive and characteristic of normal personalities . . . as manifestations of an effectively functioning organization of knowledge" (Greenwald, 1980, p. 603).

Latency of memory recall

Viewed as a second indicator of the accessibility of autobiographical memories, data concerning the mean latency of recall were arrayed and analyzed according to the $3 \times 2 \times 2$ factorial design. Results indicated a significant main effect for valence, $F(1, 215) = 13.86, p < .001$; a tendency toward a main effect for identity style, $F(2, 215) = 2.43, p < .09$; a two-way interaction between valence and validation, $F(1, 215) = 4.32, p < .04$; and a three-way interaction between valence, validation, and identity style, $F(2, 215) = 3.47, p < .03$.

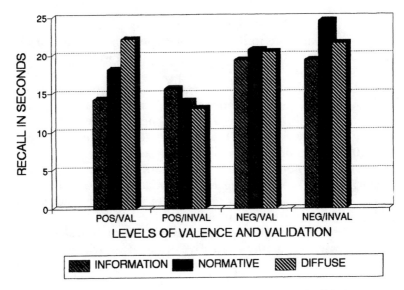

Figure 6.2. Mean latency of memory recall by identity style, valence, and validation

The main effects indicated that positive memories were recalled more quickly (latency, $M = 15.6$) than negative memories (latency, $M = 20.0$), and that information-oriented individuals tended to recall memories more quickly (latency, $M = 16.7$) than either normative-oriented (latency, $M = 18.9$) or diffuse-oriented (latency, $M = 18.9$) subjects.

The two-way interaction indicated that when memories recalled were negative, the latency of recall was unaffected by whether they were consistent ($M = 19.9$) or inconsistent ($M = 20.0$) with subjects' self-perceptions. Under positive memory recall conditions, however, self-inconsistent memories were recalled more quickly ($M = 14.6$) than were self-consistent ($M = 16.7$) memories. These effects were qualified by the significant three-way interaction.

As depicted in Figure 6.2, latency of recall results generally conformed to the pattern noted earlier regarding the total number of memories recalled. Under the positive/validate condition, memories were recalled most quickly by the information-oriented individuals (latency, $M = 14.2$), followed by the normative-oriented (latency, $M = 18.1$) and diffuse-oriented (latency, $M = 22.1$) individuals, respectively.

Again, relatively little difference was noted in the latency of memory recall under the positive/invalidate condition. When asked to recall positive memories that were inconsistent with self-perceptions, latency of recall was in the predicted direction, but not significantly different for the information-oriented (M = 15.6), normative-oriented (M = 14.0), and diffuse-oriented (M = 13.0) individuals.

The same was true under the negative/validate condition. Although generally longer latency to recall was associated with this condition than with the previous (positive/invalidate) one, the three identity styles showed no significant differences among themselves in recall latency. When asked to recall negative memories that validate existing self-perceptions, information-oriented (latency, M = 19.3), normative-oriented (latency, M = 20.7), and diffuse-oriented individuals (latency, M = 20.4) responded similarly.

And finally, when asked to recall negative memories that invalidated existing self-perceptions (negative/invalidate), the pattern of data again reflected the relative reluctance of the normative-oriented individuals to engage in ego-threatening invalidation. Here the slowest response time for recalling negative memories that jeopardize current self-constructions was demonstrated by the normative-oriented individuals (latency, M = 24.3), and the quickest response time was associated with the information-oriented individuals (latency, M = 19.3). The diffuse-oriented identity style was intermediate in this regard (latency, M = 21.5).

Unlike the data regarding the total number of memories recalled, the latency of recall data do not support the differential operation of either a confirmation bias or a self-enhancement bias among the three identity styles. Regarding the confirmation bias, virtually no difference in latency of recall between validating and invalidating memories was noted for either the information-oriented (validating memories, M = 16.7; invalidating memories, M = 16.8) or the normative-oriented individuals (validating, M = 19.4; invalidating, M = 18.4). Only the diffuse-oriented individuals showed a tendency toward differential latencies, and that favored the quicker recall of invalidating (M = 16.9) over validating (M = 21.0) memories.

Differential self-enhancement effects among the three identity styles were similarly insubstantial. Across the board, shorter recall latency was noted for positive than for negative autobiographical memories, and this appeared consistently for the information-oriented (positive, M = 15.0; negative, M = 18.6), normative-oriented (positive, M = 16.0; negative, M = 22.2), and diffuse-oriented (positive, M = 16.5; negative, M = 20.9) identity styles.

Perceived self-change

The final analyses addressed the relative degrees of perceived self-change among the three identity styles following the autobiographical recall procedure. Because the two validational conditions (positive/validate, negative/validate) involved subjects in generating memories associated with what they had already described as highly self-descriptive characteristics (i.e., rated as 5 or 6 on the 6-point scale), these conditions were subject to a ceiling effect, and for that reason could not be used in the analyses. Conditions of invalidation (positive/invalidate, negative/invalidate), however, reflected memory recall along dimensions that were initially low in self-descriptiveness (i.e., rated as 1 or 2 on the 6-point scale), and for that reason could be subject to modification if disconfirmed. In other words, these originally non-self-descriptive characteristics might become more self-descriptive as a function of reviewing memories illustrating their applicability to the self.

Changes under the positive/invalidate condition would reflect the individual's willingness to attribute greater self-descriptiveness to the four positive memory cues following the recollection of positive, self-inconsistent memories. More simply, this would reflect the individual's willingness to relinquish negative self-constructions. So, for example, an individual may initially view *generous, tolerant, cooperative*, and *punctual* as low in self-descriptiveness. Following the recall of positive memories exemplifying these features (positive/invalidate), however, the dimensions may become more self-descriptive, and we expected that this would be differentially true for the three different identity styles.

Likewise, changes under the negative/invalidate condition would reflect the individual's willingness to attribute greater self-descriptiveness to the four negative memory cues following the recollection of negative, self-inconsistent memories. This would reflect the individual's willingness to relinquish positive self-constructions. So, for example, an individual may initially view *stingy, intolerant, stubborn*, and *unpunctual* as low in self-descriptiveness. Following the recall of memories exemplifying these features (negative/invalidate), however, the dimensions may become more self-descriptive, and we expected that this perceived self-change would be differentially true for the three different identity styles.

Results of a 3 (identity styles) $\times$ 2 (memory valence) ANOVA, using postmemory self-perceptions along the four targeted memory cues, generally supported predictions. Main effects were found for valence, $F(1, 106) = 789.5$, $p < .0001$; and identity style, $F(2, 106)$, $p < .03$; but the interaction failed to reach significance.

The nature of the main effects demonstrated that, following self-discrepant autobiographical memory recall, subjects viewed the positive traits as significantly more self-descriptive ($M = 20.2$) than they did the negative traits ($M = 7.7$), and that the highest levels of self-descriptiveness were reported by diffuse-oriented individuals ($M = 15.1$), followed by the information-oriented ($M = 13.9$) and normative-oriented ($M = 12.9$) individuals, respectively.

The overall pattern of these findings suggests that a review of self-discrepant memory recall can modify self-perceptions. As predicted, the greatest reconstruction appears to occur among those identity styles marked by an absence of firm self-commitments (diffuse-oriented individuals), and the least perceived change occurs in relation to the normative-oriented identity style. This finding is consistent with the findings of Berzonsky and Sullivan (1990), who concluded from their factor-analytic study of identity styles that "norm-oriented individuals may cordon off a core of the self from potential threats of invalidation" (p. 14). It is also consistent with the broader literature that documents (a) the role that firm self-commitments play in how information is processed (Swann & Read, 1981) and in whether memory is distorted (Greenwald, 1980), and (b) the extent to which beliefs persevere in the face of contradictory evidence. According to this reasoning, highly committed identity styles may be less amenable to potential disconfirmation of firmly held self-perceptions, preferring instead to adhere to previous personal convictions.

Summary

Although constructivist conceptualizations of memory processes have a long history (Vico, 1725/1948; see Mahoney, 1988, 1991), empirical studies of reconstructive recall have a more recent vintage (see Robinson, 1976, 1986), and only recently have begun to coalesce into durable, programmatic inquiries into the relationship between personal and memory processes. Certainly Bartlett's (1932) contributions were seminal in this regard, and these have been rewarded by a recent renaissance of interest in allied areas of autobiographical recall (Rubin, 1986; Neisser, 1982; Neisser & Winograd, 1988).

Central to these efforts has been a renewed interest in the relationship between personality and memory in general, as well as in the specific transformations in recall that may accompany personal change and reconstruction (Barclay, 1986, 1988; Barclay & DeCooke, 1988; Barclay & Smith, in press; Barclay & Subramaniam, 1987; Brewer, 1986; Kihlstrom, 1981; Markus, 1977; Markus & Sentis, 1980; Ross et al., 1981). Our own recent efforts have followed from the recognition of personal identity and personal memory as interdependent processes, efforts that are broadly consistent with a conceptualization of the self as a personal scientist (Kelly, 1955) or personal historian (Greenwald, 1980) whose efforts are directed toward the evolution and preservation of a meaningful sense of self. Bartlett (1932, p. 309) argued that "the past is being continually re-made, reconstructed in the interests of the present," and a growing literature provides support for the sometimes heavy hand that it plays in performing what Ross and McFarland (1988) aptly characterized as its role as "revisionist historian with respect to . . . personal memories" (p. 310).

As evidence of the self's role in the reconstruction, fabrication, and revision of its history continues to mount, the importance of addressing the function or purpose of such efforts continues to draw attention as well. Consistent with other accounts (Epstein, 1973; Greenwald, 1980), we regard the preservation of a meaningful sense of self-identity as an important factor in this reconstructive process (see Kelly, 1955; Guidano, 1991), and we admit the likelihood that there are important differences in identity development that may carry implications for autobiographical recall.

Berzonsky's (1988, 1989, 1990) conceptualization of identity style emphasizes the differential processes associated with information-oriented, normative-oriented, and diffuse-oriented personal scientists, and it has provided the scaffolding for our own most recent work. As relatively objective processors, information-oriented individuals actively seek self-relevant information and willingly embrace and assimilate viable reconstructions of the self. Concerning contemporary self-images, information-oriented individuals would be "skeptical and tentative about their (hypothetical) self-constructions, responsive to environmental feedback, and willing to test and revise self-constructs in light of contradictory evidence" (Berzonsky, 1990, p. 177). In contrast, normative-oriented individuals, who have arrived at current identity commitments in the absence of personal exploration or crisis, are primarily geared toward the preservation of existing self-constructions. Having foreclosed prematurely on readily available, externally provided self-images, they operate as dogmatic scientists who rely on assimilative processes such as rationalization and confirmation-biased searches in testing images of themselves. And finally, diffuse-oriented individuals are characterized as "ad hoc" self-theorists who continually engage in ephemeral accommodative changes in response to the vagaries of immediate contextual demand (see Berzonsky, 1988, 1990).

These broad-based differences in personal identity should carry implications for the nature of the transaction that occurs between self-constructions and recollections. Accordingly, the number of autobiographical memories recalled, the latency of that memory recall, and the impact of that recall on subsequent self-perceptions, all varied with the style of identity development that the individual brings to bear in forging a sense of self.

Overall, information-oriented individuals generated the greatest number of autobiographical recollections and, as predicted, diffuse individuals generated the fewest. More importantly, this recall varied across conditions, with information-oriented individuals showing the highest recollection among the three identity styles for memories that supported positive self-perceptions, as well as the greatest ability to generate memories that threatened those self-perceptions. This latter effect is particularly compelling in light of the fact that the number of negative, self-discrepant memories generated by the information-oriented individuals more than doubled that of the normative-oriented subjects (see Figure 6.1) whose predisposition is toward the preservation of central self-images. A general self-enhancement effect was also evident, particularly among information- and normative-oriented individuals, the latter being the most inclined of the three identity styles to generate invalidating memories when it benefited them (under the positive/invalidate condition) and the least inclined when it threatened them (under the negative/invalidate condition).

This general picture of autobiographical recall as influenced by differences in personal identity styles is strengthened by considering the impact of that memory recall on subsequent self-perceptions. Consistent with their accommodative orientation to situational contexts, diffuse-oriented individuals showed the greatest changes in self-perceptions following the recall of memories that were inconsistent with positive and negative self-images. As expected, normative-oriented individuals showed the least change, again underscoring their preference for assimilation over personal revision or accommodation (see Berzonsky, 1988, 1989, 1990).

As research such as this continues to turn toward understanding the emergence of the self and its relationship to autobiographical memories, it brings with it renewed appreciation for the original constructive aspects of memory outlined by Vico (1725/1948) more than two and a half centuries ago. Autobiographical recollections do, indeed, enable us to bring to the present that which is past (*memoria*), but never the thing itself, only its reconstructed image in personal terms (*fantasia*), and always in the context of our continuously evolving systems of self-constructions (*ingegno*). In this way it is clear that constructive cognition spans the entire spectrum of the self, from the furthest reaches of our future anticipations and back as well into the deepest recesses of our recollections.

REFERENCES

Abraham, K. G. (1983). The relation between identity status and locus of control among high school students. *Journal of Early Adolescence, 3,* 257–264.
Adams, G. R., Bennion, L., & Huh, K. (1989). *Objective measure of ego identity status: A reference manual* (2nd ed.). Logan, UT: Utah State University.

Adams, G. R., Ryan, J. H., Hoffman, J. J., Dobson, W. R., & Neilsen, E. C. (1985). Ego identity status, conformity behavior, and personality in late adolescence. *Journal of Personality and Social Psychology, 407,* 1091–1104.

Adams, G. R., & Shea, J. (1979). The relationship between identity status, locus of control, and ego development. *Journal of Youth and Adolescence, 8,* 81–89.

Adams, G. R., Shea, J., & Fitch, S. (1979). Toward the development of an objective assessment of ego-identity status. *Journal of Youth and Adolescence, 8,* 223–237.

Anderson, N. H. (1968). Likableness ratings of 555 personality trait words. *Journal of Personality and Social Psychology, 9,* 272–279.

Archer, S. C. (1989). Gender differences in identity development: Issues of process, domain, and timing. *Journal of Adolescence, 12,* 117–138.

Banaji, M. R., & Crowder, R. G. (1989). The bankruptcy of everyday memory. *American Psychologist, 44,* 1185–1193.

Barclay, C. R. (1986). Schematization of autobiographical memory. In D. C. Rubin (Ed.), *Autobiographical memory* (pp. 82–99). Cambridge University Press.

Barclay, C. R. (1988). *Construction et fonctionnemente de l'identité.* Paper developed for the social psychology section of the Society of French and Italian psychologists, Aix-en-Provence, France.

Barclay, C. R., & DeCooke, A. (1988). Ordinary everyday memories: Some of the things of which selves are made. In U. Neisser & E. Winograd (Eds.), *Remembering reconsidered: Ecological and traditional approaches to the study of memory* (pp. 91–125). Cambridge University Press.

Barclay, C. R., Hodges, R. M., & Smith, A. L. (1990). *Authenticity and accuracy: Self-schemata and the vicissitudes of autobiographical memories.* Unpublished manuscript.

Barclay, C. R., & Smith, T. S. (in press). Autobiographical remembering and self-composing. *International Journal of Personal Construct Psychology.*

Barclay, C. R., & Subramaniam, G. (1987). Autobiographical memories and self-schemata. *Applied Cognitive Psychology, 1,* 169–182.

Barclay, C. R., & Wellman, H. M. (1986). Accuracies and inaccuracies in autobiographical memories. *Journal of Memory and Language, 25,* 93–103.

Barsalou, L. W. (1988). The content and organization of autobiographical memories. In U. Neisser & E. Winograd (Eds.), *Remembering reconsidered: Ecological and traditional approaches to the study of memory* (pp. 91–125). Cambridge University Press.

Bartlett, F. C. (1932). *Remembering: A study in experimental and social psychology.* Cambridge University Press.

Bennion, L. D., & Adams, G. R. (1986). A revision of the extended version of the objective measure of ego identity status: An identity instrument for use with late adolescents. *Journal of Adolescent Research, 1,* 183–198.

Berghorn, F. J., & Schafer, D. E. (1986–1987). Reminiscence intervention in nursing homes: What and who changes? *International Journal of Aging and Human Development, 24,* 113–127.

Berzonsky, M. D. (1988). Self-theorists, identity status, and social cognition. In D. K. Lapsley & F. C. Power (Eds.), *Self, ego and identity: Integrative approaches* (pp. 243–262). New York: Springer-Verlag.

Berzonsky, M. D. (1989). The self as a theorist: Individual differences in identity formation. *International Journal of Personal Construct Psychology, 2,* 363–376; *4,* 363–376.

Berzonsky, M. D. (1990). Self-construction over the life span: A process perspective on identity formation. In G. J. Neimeyer & R. A. Neimeyer (Eds.), *Advances in personal construct psychology* (pp. 155–186). Greenwich, CT: JAI Press.

Berzonsky, M. D., & Neimeyer, G. J. (1988). Identity status and personal construct systems. *Journal of Adolescence, 11*, 195–204.

Berzonsky, M. D., Rice, K. G., & Neimeyer, G. J. (1990). Identity status and self-construct systems: Process X structure interactions. *Journal of Adolescence, 13*, 251–263.

Berzonsky, M. D., & Sullivan, C. (1990). *Social-cognitive aspects of identity style: Need for cognition, experiential openness, and introspection.* Unpublished manuscript.

Bower, G. H., & Gilligan, S. G. (1979). Remembering information related to one's self. *Journal of Research in Personality, 13*, 420–432.

Brewer, W. F. (1986). What is autobiographical memory? In D. C. Rubin (Ed.), *Autobiographical memory.* Cambridge University Press.

Brewer, W. F. (1988). Memory for randomly sampled autobiographical events. In U. Neisser & E. Winograd (Eds.), *Remembering reconsidered: Ecological and traditional approaches to the study of memory* (pp. 21–90). Cambridge University Press.

Butler, R. N. (1963). The life review: An interpretation of reminiscence in the aged. *Psychiatry, 26*, 65–73.

Crovitz, H. F., & Schiffman, H. (1974). Frequency of episodic memories as a function of their age. *Bulletin of the Psychonomic Society, 4*, 517–518.

Donovan, J. M. (1975). Identity status and interpersonal style. *Journal of Youth and Adolescence, 4*, 37–55.

Ebersole, P. P. (1978). A theoretical approach to the use of reminiscence. In I. M. Burnside (Ed.), *Working with the elderly: Group process and techniques.* Boston: Duxbury Press.

Epstein, S. (1973). The self-concept revisited or a theory of a theory. *American Psychologist, 28*, 404–416.

Erikson, E. H. (1956). The problem of ego identity. *Journal of the American Psychological Association, 4*, 56–121.

Erikson, E. H. (1959). *Identity and the life cycle.* New York: International Universities Press.

Erikson, E. H. (1968). *Identity, youth, and crisis.* New York: Norton.

Fitzgerald, J. M. (1986). Autobiographical memory: A developmental perspective. In D. C. Rubin (Ed.), *Autobiographical memory.* Cambridge University Press.

Fivush, R. (1988). The functions of event memory: Some comments on Nelson and Barsalou. In U. Neisser & E. Winograd (Eds.), *Remembering reconsidered: Ecological and traditional approaches to the study of memory* (pp. 277–282). Cambridge University Press.

Franklin, H. C., & Holding, D. H. (1977). Personal memories at different ages. *Quarterly Journal of Experimental Psychology, 29*, 527–532.

Galton, F. (1879). Psychometric facts. *Nineteenth Century, 5*, 425–433.

Gargus, T. (1990). The impact of imagery on autobiographical recall. Unpublished Senior Honors Thesis, University of Florida, Gainesville, FL.

Goldwasser, A. N., Auerbach, S. M., & Harkins, S. W. (1987). Cognitive, affective, and behavioral effects of reminiscence group therapy on demented elderly. *International Journal of Aging and Human Development, 25*, 209–222.

Greenwald, A. G. (1975). Consequences of prejudice against the null hypothesis. *Psychological Bulletin, 82*, 1–20.

Greenwald, A. G. (1980). The totalitarian ego: Fabrication and revision of personal history. *Journal of Personality and Social Psychology, 35*, 603–618.

Greenwald, A. G. (1981). Self and memory. In G. H. Bower (Ed.), *The psychology of learning and motivation* (Vol. 15, pp. 202–236). New York: Academic Press.

Greenwald, A. G., & Banaji, M. R. (1989). The self as a memory system: Powerful but ordinary. *Journal of Personality and Social Psychology, 57,* 41–54.

Grotevant, H. D., & Adams, G. R. (1984). Development of an objective measure to assess ego identity in adolescence: Validity and replication. *Journal of Youth and Adolescence, 11,* 33–47.

Guidano, V. F. (1991). *The self in process.* New York: Guilford.

Heisenberg, W. (1972). *Physics and beyond.* New York: Harper Torchbooks.

Hyland, D. T., & Akerman, A. M. (1988). Reminiscence and autobiographical memory in the study of the personal past. *Journal of Gerontology, 43,* 35–39.

Karis, G. D. (1979, September). *Individual differences in autobiographical memory.* Paper presented at the meeting of the American Psychological Association, New York.

Kelly, G. A. (1955). *The psychology of personal constructs.* New York: Norton.

Kihlstrom, J. F. (1981). On personality and memory. In N. Cantor & J. F. Kihlstrom (Eds.), *Personality, cognition and social interaction.* Hillsdale, NJ: Erlbaum.

Koriat, A., Lichtenstein, S., & Fischhoff, B. (1980). Reasons for confidence. *Journal of Experimental Psychology: Human Learning and Memory, 6,* 107–118.

Kuhn, T. (1970). *Structure of scientific revolutions* (2nd ed.). Chicago: University of Chicago Press.

Lakatos, I. (1970). Falsification and the methodology of scientific research programmes. In I. Lakatos & A. Musgrave (Eds.), *Criticism and the growth of knowledge.* Cambridge University Press.

Landy, C. R. (1986). *Memory retrieval latency and quantity as a function of objective self-awareness and self-schemata.* Unpublished doctoral dissertation, University of Florida, Gainesville, FL.

Leiper, R. N. (1981). *The relationship of cognitive development structures to the formation of ego identity in young men.* Unpublished doctoral dissertation, Simon Fraser University, Burnaby, British Columbia.

Linton, M. (1986). Ways of searching and the contents of memory. In D. C. Rubin (Ed.), *Autobiographical memory.* Cambridge University Press.

Mahoney, M. J. (1988). Constructive metatheory: 1. Basic features and historical foundations. *International Journal of Personal Construct Psychology, 1,* 1–36.

Mahoney, M. J. (1991). *Human change processes: The scientific foundations of psychotherapy.* New York: Basic.

Marcia, J. E. (1966). Development and validation of ego identity status. *Journal of Personal and Social Psychology, 3,* 551–558.

Marcia, J. E. (1980). Identity in adolescence. In J. Adelson (Ed.), *Handbook of adolescent psychology.* New York: Wiley.

Markus, H. (1977). Self-schemata and processing information about the self. *Journal of Personality and Social Psychology, 35,* 63–78.

Markus, H., & Sentis, K. (1980). The self in social information processing. In J. Suls (Ed.), *Social psychological perspectives on the self* (pp. 41–70). Hillsdale, NJ: Erlbaum.

McCrae, R. R., & Costa, P. T., Jr. (1985). Openness to experience. In R. Hogan & W. H. Jones (Eds.), *Perspectives in personality* (Vol. 1). Greenwich, CT: JAI Press.

Metzler, A. E., & Neimeyer, G. J. (1988). Vocational hierarchies: How do we count the ways? *International Journal of Personal Construct Psychology, 3,* 205–218.

Neimeyer, G. J., Prichard, S., Berzonsky, M. D., & Metzler, A. E. (1991). Vocational hypothesis testing: The role of occupational relevance and identity orientation. *Journal of Vocational Behavior, 38,* 318–332.

Neimeyer, G. J., & Rareshide, M. (1991). Personal memories and personal identity: The impact of ego identity development on autobiographical memory recall. *Journal of Personality and Social Psychology, 60,* 562–569.

Neisser, U. (1981). John Dean's memory: A case study. *Cognition, 9,* 1–22.

Neisser, U. (1982). Snapshots or benchmarks? In U. Neisser (Ed.), *Memory observed: Remembering in natural contexts* (pp. 43–48). San Francisco: Freeman.

Neisser, U. (1988). What is ordinary memory the memory of? In U. Neisser & E. Winograd (Eds.), *Remembering reconsidered: Ecological and traditional approaches to the study of memory* (pp. 356–373). Cambridge University Press.

Neisser, U., & Winograd, E. (Eds.). (1988). *Remembering reconsidered: Ecological and traditional approaches to the study of memory.* Cambridge University Press.

Nelson, K. (1988). The ontogeny of memory for real events. In U. Neisser & E. Winograd (Eds.), *Remembering reconsidered: Ecological and traditional approaches to the study of memory* (pp. 244–276). Cambridge University Press.

Perotta, P., & Meacham, J. A. (1981–1982). Can a reminiscing intervention alter depression and self-esteem? *International Journal of Aging and Human Development, 14,* 23–30.

Podd, M. H., Marcia, J. E., & Rubin, B. M. (1970). The effects of ego identity and partner perception on a prisoner's dilemma game. *Journal of Personality and Social Psychology, 82,* 117–126.

Poulton, J. L., & Strassberg, D. S. (1986). The therapeutic use of reminiscence. *International Journal of Group Psychotherapy, 36,* 381–398.

Read, D., Adams, G. R., & Dobson, W. R. (1984). Ego identity, personality, and social influence style. *Journal of Personality and Social Psychology, 46,* 169–177.

Reese, D., & Metzler, A. E. (1989). *The Ratimer program for autobiographical recall.* University of Florida, Gainesville, FL.

Reiser, B. J., Black, J. B., & Kalamarides, P. (1986). Strategic memory search processes. In D. C. Rubin (Ed.), *Autobiographical memory* (p. 119). Cambridge University Press.

Robinson, J. A. (1976). Sampling autobiography. *Cognitive Psychology, 8,* 598–595.

Robinson, J. A. (1986). Temporal reference systems and autobiographical memory. In D. C. Rubin (Ed.), *Autobiographical memory* (pp. 159–188). Cambridge University Press.

Rogers, T. B. (1980). A model of the self as an aspect of the human information processing system. In N. Cantor & J. F. Kihlstrom (Eds.), *Personality, cognition and social interaction* (pp. 193–214). Hillsdale, NJ: Erlbaum.

Ross, M., & Conway, M. (1988). Remembering one's own past: The construction of personal histories. In R. M. Sorrentino & E. T. Higgins (Eds.), *Handbook of motivation and cognition: Foundations of social behavior* (pp. 122–144). New York: Guilford.

Ross, M., & McFarland, C. (1988). Constructing the past: Biases in personal memories. In Bar-Tal & A. Kruglanski (Eds.), *The social psychology of knowledge* (pp. 299–314). Cambridge University Press.

Ross, M., McFarland, C., & Fletcher, G. J. O. (1981). The effect of attitude on the recall of personal histories. *Journal of Personality and Social Psychology, 40,* 4, 627–634.

Rubin, D. C. (1986). Introduction. In D. C. Rubin (Ed.), *Autobiographical memory.* Cambridge University Press.

Schenkel, S., & Marcia, J. E. (1972). Attitudes towards premarital intercourse in determining ego identity status in college women. *Journal of Personality, 40,* 472–482.

Slugoski, B. R., Marcia, J. E., & Koopman, R. F. (1984). Cognitive and social interactional characteristics of ego identity status in college males. *Journal of Personality and Social Psychology, 47*, 646–661.

Snyder, M. (1981). Seek, and ye shall find: Testing hypotheses about other people. In E. T. Higgins, C. P. Hermann & M. P. Zanna (Eds.), *Social cognition: The Ontario Symposium* (Vol. 1, pp. 277–303). Hillsdale, NJ: Erlbaum.

Snyder, M., & Swann, W. B., Jr. (1978). Hypothesis testing in social interaction. *Journal of Personality and Social Psychology, 36*, 1202–1212.

Snyder, M., & Uranowitz, S. W. (1978). Reconstructing the past: Some cognitive consequences of person perception. *Journal of Personality and Social Psychology, 36*, 941–950.

Spence, D. P. (1982). *Narrative truth and historical truth.* New York: Norton.

Swann, W. B., Jr., & Read, S. J. (1981). Self-verification processes: How we sustain our self-conceptions. *Journal of Experimental Social Psychology, 17*, 351–372.

Tzuriel, D., & Klein, M. M. (1977). Ego identity: Effect of ethnocentrism, ethnic identification, and cognitive complexity in Israeli, Oriental, and Western Ethnic groups. *Psychological Reports, 40*, 1099–1110.

Verene, D. P. (1981). *Vico's science of imagination.* Ithaca, NY: Cornell University Press.

Vico, G. (1948). *The new science* (T. G. Bergin & M. H. Fisch, Trans.). Ithaca, NY: Cornell University Press. (Original work published 1725)

Waterman, A. S. (1982). Identity development from adolescence to adulthood: An extension of theory and a review of research. *Developmental Psychology, 10*, 387–392.

Waterman, A. S. (1985). Identity in the context of adolescent psychology. In A. S. Waterman (Ed.), *Identity in adolescence: Processes and contents. New directions in child development* (No. 30) (pp. 5–24). San Francisco: Jossey-Bass.

Waterman, A. S., & Waterman, C. K. (1974). Ego identity status and decision style. *Journal of Youth and Adolescence, 3*, 1–6.

7

Constructing narrative, emotion, and self in parent–child conversations about the past

ROBYN FIVUSH

We are all the authors of our own autobiographies. We all tell stories about our past experiences both to ourselves and to others. These stories serve many different functions, such as entertainment, interpersonal bonding, and moral lessons. But one of the most important functions they serve is self-definitional. The stories of our lives tell us and our listeners something about who we are (Brewer, 1986; Fivush, 1988; Miller, Potts, Fung, Hoogstra, & Mintz, 1990; Neisser, 1988). Moreover, life stories seem to conform to canonical narratives, at least in Western cultures (Bruner, 1987; Labov, 1982; Spence, 1982). Canonical narratives give a particular form and meaning to our lives. Specifically, narratives provide a linear and often causal structure to life events. Good narratives are not simple chains of actions following an arbitrary temporal order; narratives are emotionally meaningful, causally connected sequences of actions that provide both temporal and evaluative cohesion to life events. Particular events become important parts of our life story because they provide some meaningful information about who we are, and the narrative forms for representing and recounting these events provide a particular structure for understanding and conveying this meaning. Moreover, as I will argue later, it is the evaluative and emotional aspects of life stories that link these experiences to the continuously developing sense of self.

In this chapter, I examine ways in which personal experiences come to be represented in conventionalized narrative and evaluative forms from a developmental perspective. The guiding assumption of the argument is that young children are socialized to represent their experiences in particular ways through participating in adult-guided conversations about the past. By examining the ways in which adults structure conversations about the past with their young children, we can begin to explore how children come to represent and understand their own experiences. Before turning to a more detailed discussion of the data, however, the theoretical framework will be more fully explicated.

Theoretical framework

The idea that the structure of personal narratives is constructed in social interaction stems from a dialectical approach to development first outlined by Vygotsky (1978; see also Wertsch, 1985). Vygotsky argued that each culture provides individuals with the "tools" necessary for becoming a competent member of that culture. Tools are conceptualized broadly as culturally appropriate forms and strategies for performing activities and tasks. Moreover, the cultural tools available influence individual development at two levels, the macro level and the micro level. At the macro level, by placing individuals in particular kinds of situations and valuing particular kinds of activities, the culture provides the individual with information about the kinds of activities that are important to engage in and perform (e.g., Cole, 1985; Rogoff, 1990). For example, in Western cultures, children are placed in formal schooling situations early in development and are expected to perform specific kinds of decontextualized activities such as reading and writing. Simply by the way the child's life is structured around schooling, the message is conveyed that these are important and valued activities in the culture.

But individuals actually learn culturally appropriate skills in more micro-level settings. According to Vygotsky, all skills develop first in social interaction and are later internalized by the individual. Essentially, the adult (or any more competent societal member) engages the child (or less competent societal member) in a task and supports the child's performance by providing the necessary structure for accomplishing the task goal. In so doing, the adult is displaying the necessary skills for accomplishing the task. At this point, it is the adult who is performing the task and the child is merely attending. With increasing experience with the task, the child comes to take over more and more of the component skills but is still somewhat dependent on the adult to provide the overall guiding structure. Now, the adult and child are accomplishing the task goal together, but the child is not yet able to perform the entire task alone. Finally, all of the component skills and the overall structure of the task are internalized and the child no longer needs the adult to support the performance; the child is able to accomplish the task alone (see Paris, Newman, & Jacobs, 1985, for a discussion of Vygotskian theory in relation to memory development).

In the domain of autobiographical memory, the task can be conceptualized as learning to recount the past in more coherent, conventionalized ways. By participating in adult-guided conversations about their past experiences, children are learning the culturally appropriate narrative forms for recounting the past. Moreover, to the extent that children are expected to engage in such conversations, they will be learning that talking about their past experiences with others is an important and valuable activity.

One further tenet of Vygotsky's theory is essential for the argument. It is postulated that the tools that cultures provide for individuals are both externally and internally directed. The skills that individuals learn are used to regulate their activities and performances in the world, but they are also internalized and used to regulate inner activities. Again, in the domain of autobiographical memory, it can be argued that the narrative forms that children are learning to organize their recounting of past experiences are also used for organizing their internal representations of past experiences. Thus as children become better and better able to tell a coherent personal narrative, it is assumed that they are also better and better able to represent their experiences in narratively coherent ways (see Eisenberg, 1985, for similar arguments).

Recent research supports at least the broad outlines of this kind of developmental progression. Even very young children engage in conversations about their past experiences. In fact, children begin talking about the past almost as soon as they begin talking at all (Eisenberg, 1985; Hudson, 1990; Miller & Sperry, 1988; Nelson, 1988). However, at this early period, at about 18 months of age, it is the adult who provides the structure and content of the recall. Essentially, the adult tells the child what occurred and the child responds by confirming or repeating the information provided. For example, the adult might ask, "Remember last Halloween?" and the child responds, "Yeah," and the adult continues, "And we cut up that pumpkin?" and the child responds, "Pumpkin," and so on. Quite soon, however, children begin participating to a greater extent. They provide unique information about the event under discussion and may even begin to initiate such conversations. By about 2 ½ to 3 years of age, children are actively engaged in co-constructing their past experiences in conversations with adults. And by the end of the preschool years, children are able to give a relatively coherent narrative account of their past experiences independent of adult guidance (e.g., Hudson & Shapiro, 1991; Peterson & McCabe, 1983).

This developmental pattern conforms to a Vygotskian progression; a task that the child can initially accomplish only with adult guidance comes to be accomplished independently. However, if the Vygotskian account is correct, then it is also expected that the particular ways in which the adult–child interaction is accomplished are important. That is, it is assumed that the child is learning the specific skills and the specific values that are being displayed in the interaction. Thus, in order to examine how children are learning to organize and understand their own past experiences, it becomes imperative to examine the specific kinds of narrative and evaluative structures adults are displaying during these early parent–child conversations. Further, in examining parent–child conversations about the past, we must also consider what parents are communicating to their children about the functions of sharing the past with others.

Narrative structure in parent–child conversations about the past

Over the past few years, my students and I have been examining parent–child conversations about the past. In particular, we have been investigating the ways in which parents structure conversations about past events with their young preschool children and how the narrative forms modeled in these early conversations might influence children's developing abilities to recount their past, and more speculatively, how these forms might influence the ways in which children come to think about their past and themselves (Fivush & Fromhoff, 1988; Fivush & Reese, 1992; Reese & Fivush, 1993). Children in our studies range from about 2 ½ years old to about 3 ½ years old. We have studied this age range because this is the period during which children are beginning to be able to participate competently in conversations about past events (Eisenberg, 1985; Hudson, 1990; Sachs, 1983). Our basic approach involves visiting the family in their home and asking the parent to engage the child in discussion of several specific experiences that the parent and child experienced together over the past few months. Virtually all of the parents in our studies find our instructions easy to follow; the vast majority report that they often engage in conversation with their child about the past in daily interaction. In fact, in other research in which more spontaneous parent–child conversations about past events have been assessed, conversations about past events have been found to be universal and frequent (e.g., McCabe & Peterson, 1991; Miller, chap. 8 of this volume). After the task is explained to the parents, the parent and child sit together comfortably with a tape recorder. The research assistant either leaves the room or sits out of view. Thus parents are free to select which events to discuss with their child and they are also free to determine the length of the conversations.

It should be noted at the outset that all of the parents in our research are drawn from a white middle-class population. Because we know that language and parent–child interaction varies with racial and economic status (see, e.g., Heath, 1983; Hoff-Ginsburg, 1991), we decided it would be best to restrict our sample to one group and to examine variations in parental behavior within this group. Of course, this limits the generalizations we can make. I will return to this issue briefly at the end of the chapter.

One of the most striking things in listening to these parent–child conversations is that parents talked about the past in very different ways. Some parents engaged in long conversations about past events, provided a great deal of background and contextual information for their child, and generally encouraged their child to share in retelling the experience. For example, here is a mother discussing a car trip to the grandparents' house with her 32-month-old daughter (*M* stands for Mother and *C* for Child):

> M: Remember when Mommy and Daddy and Sam [baby brother] went in the car for a long time and we went to Memaw's house?
> C: (nods head yes)
> M: Yeah. What did we see when we were in the car? Remember Daddy was showing you outside the car. What was it?
> C: I don't know
> M: Do you remember we saw some mountains and we went to that old house, and what did we do? We took off our shoes and we walked on the rocks. What did we do? What was there?
> C: I don't know
> M: Mommy and Noel [the child] took off our shoes and walked in the water.
> C: (nods head yes)
> M: Yeah, was that fun?

As you can see, this mother is actively engaged in constructing a story about this experience with her daughter. When the child indicates a willingness to continue the conversation by taking an appropriate conversational turn even though not providing any memory information, the mother provides additional information about the event under discussion and encourages the child to continue to participate. The child did eventually recall some information about this event, but that is really not the point. Rather what seems to be happening here is that in encouraging her child's participation, this mother essentially tells the story about what happened. And notice that it is a fully elaborated, highly detailed telling. We see this again in the following example of a father discussing a trip to the mountains with his 40-month-old daughter (*F* stands for Father and *C:* for Child):

> F: We went on a trail up into that woods, do you remember that?
> C: Yeah
> F: And there were all those roots in the ground, on the trail, that you had to watch out for.
> C: Uh huh
> F: Do you remember what happened to you?
> C: What?

F: With those roots?
C: What?
F: When you were running?
C: Wha . . .
F: What?
C: Umm, [unintelligible] fall down on 'em.
F: You did fall down, didn't you? You got your foot caught in one and went plop. Fell right down in the sand. Did it hurt?

Again, we have a situation where the child is not recalling much information, but the father continues to tell more and more of the story with each conversational turn. And when the child does recall some information, which just happens to be the climax of the narrative, the father immediately confirms this information and then provides a summary statement of the climax ending with an evaluation.

We labeled this style of interaction *elaborative*. Elaborative parents engaged in long conversations about past events with their children, and they provided rich and embellished information about the events under discussion. Moreover, even when their children were not recalling any information, elaborative parents continued to provide more and more information about the event, essentially telling a coherent story about what happened. In contrast to this style, some parents engaged in short, directive conversations. They tended to provide very little information about the event, but rather cajoled their child to remember by simply repeating the same questions over and over. Again, an example of a mother and her 34-month-old son illustrates:

M: Do you remember last Christmas?
C: Last Christmas
M: What did you get for Christmas? Do you remember?
C: What?
M: You can't remember anything. How about a dump truck. Do you remember the dump truck?
C: Yeah
M: What else did you get?
C: What did I get
M: Do you remember going to the circus?

This mother asks her child again and again for recall. When the child indicates a willingness to continue the conversation by taking his conversational turn but not recalling any information, the mother provides the requested information, and then asks another repetitive question. Finally, when the child still doesn't recall, instead of providing additional information about the event under discussion, the mother changes topic. We see a similar pattern in the following example of a mother talking about a trip to Florida with her 40-month-old son:

M: How did we get to Florida, do you remember?
C: Yes
M: How did we get there? What did we do? You remember?
C: Yeah
M: You want to sit here in my lap?
C: No
M: Oh, OK. Remember when we went to Florida, how did we get
    there. We went in the . . .
C: The ocean.
M: Well, be-, when we got to Florida we went in the ocean, that's
    right. But how did we get to Florida?

Again, the mother repeatedly questions the child about how they got to Florida, but provides no additional information. Even when the child recalls some information about the trip, the mother does not accept it or incorporate it into the conversation because it is not the information that she is looking for. Rather, she simply repeats her previous question. Notice especially in these conversations that there is no context, no description, no elaboration of the event; in effect, there is no story. We labeled this interactional style *repetitive*. Repetitive parents engaged in short conversations about past events with their children; they asked few and redundant questions and provided little embellishment or detail about what happened.

Although all parents show some elements of both styles, it was the case that each parent could be easily characterized as using a more elaborative or a more repetitive style. Moreover, several other researchers, using somewhat different methodologies and somewhat different age groups, have also found two very similar maternal styles for talking about the past (Engel, 1986; Hudson, 1990; McCabe & Peterson, 1991). Thus there is converging evidence that parents talk about the past in different ways with their preschool children, and these differences can be characterized along a dimension of repetitiveness to elaborativeness.

Additional analyses of our transcripts confirmed several important differences between elaborative and repetitive parents. First, as already discussed, elaborative parents have longer conversations about the past than do repetitive parents. Related to this, elaborative parents are more likely to keep questioning their child about an event when their child indicates a willingness to continue even though not recalling any new information. And in continuing to question their children, elaborative parents ask additional questions that incorporate new information about the event, whereas repetitive parents tend to repeat the same question over and over. What this means is that elaborative parents provide more unique units of information about the event under discussion than do repetitive parents. And, interestingly, elaborative parents provide more descriptive information, in the form of adjectives, adverbs, and other modifiers, than do repetitive parents. For example, one elaborative mother, in discussing a trip to a farm with her child, said, "We saw a big fat old pig living in the mud, and what else did we see? . . . Didn't you see some animals in the barn, in that big barn? What animals did you see in the barn?" Another elaborative mother talking about a trip to a petting zoo asked her child, "There were a bunch of animals there. And do you remember there was a real mean one. What kind of animal was that that almost bit you? . . . Do you remember that mean old animal?"

Descriptive information serves at least two functions: First, it provides the necessary information to distinguish this one experience from all other experiences, thus providing distinctive memory cues. But it also provides information about why this event is interesting or important to remember in the first place. By highlighting the distinctive aspects of this particular object or activity, elaborative parents are providing their children with information about what makes this event special. By talking a great deal about the past, by asking their children many questions and providing rich descriptive accounts of past events, elaborative parents are implicitly teaching their child that the past is interesting and worthwhile to talk about.

A most intriguing and unexpected finding emerged from this research. Both mothers and fathers were significantly more likely to use an elaborative style when talking about the past with daughters than with sons (Reese & Fivush, 1993). Conversations with girls are longer than conversations with boys, parents ask more questions, and they include more information in each additional question with girls than with boys. Related to this, girls recalled significantly more information about past events than did boys. Of course, there is a problem of interpretation here. Are parents more elaborative with daughters because their daughters are recalling more or are girls recalling more because their parents are more elaborative? Certain structural aspects of the conversations suggest that it is not simply the child's ability to participate in the conversation that leads to a more elaborative style. First of all, the girls and boys in this research were at comparable language levels, as determined by syntactical measures such as mean length of utterance. So it is not the case that girls are recalling more because they are linguistically more sophisticated than boys. Second, girls were not simply more willing than boys to sit still and participate in these conversations. Children of both genders were equally likely to change topic, make off-task comments and not respond to parental questions at all. Further, parents showed the greatest differences in style when their children were engaged in the conversation but not recalling any new information. In this situation, elaborative parents were significantly more likely to pursue these conversations than were repetitive parents. By asking more and more questions and providing more and more information with each question, elaborative parents are providing more memory cues for their children. By providing so much information about the event under discussion, elaborative parents may be making it easier for their children to access their own memories of the event. Thus, although the child's ability must play some role in eliciting particular kinds of parental interactions, these findings suggest that parental style is not a simple reaction to the child's conversational aptitudes. Rather, parents seem to choose to talk more about the past and talk in more embellished ways about the past with their daughters than with their sons.

Why might this be so? In thinking about this question, we need to consider why parents talk about the past with their young children at all. Elaborative parents seem to genuinely enjoy talking about the past with their children. They are interested in sharing past experiences and are interested in what their children have to contribute to these shared memories. In this way, elaborative parents are teaching their children that the past is interesting and important to talk about and share with others.

Of course, stories about the past can be important for many reasons. Perhaps they are amusing or frightening or fun. But, as argued earlier, personal narratives are also self-defining. What are parents teaching their young children about themselves in these conversations? One way to examine this question is to take a closer look at the kind of evaluative and descriptive information that parents are providing. Elaborative parents provide more information about the child's emotional reactions and responses than do repetitive parents. And by extension, parents are talking more about past emotions with daughters than with sons (Fivush, 1989; Kuebli & Fivush, 1992). Talking about the child's emotional reactions and states seems a critical part of relating past experience to self-concept. It is one's emotional reaction to an event that at least partly defines what this event means to the self, and, in turn, informs the self about what kinds of events are important because they cause happiness, anger, sadness, or some other feeling. Elaborative parents are not just implicitly teaching their children that the past is interesting and worthwhile to talk about; they may also be teaching their child why particular past events are important to the self. The way in which emotions are discussed in early parent–child conversations about past events, then, may provide crucial information for how children are learning to think about their past and themselves.

Emotional content of parent–child conversations about the past

That parents were more elaborative in conversations about the past with daughters than sons was unexpected, but that they talked more about emotions with daughters than with sons was not as surprising. Previous research has demonstrated that mothers talk more about emotions with girls than with boys, and that girls begin talking about emotions more than boys do as early as 24 months of age (Beeghly, Bretherton, & Mervis, 1986; Bretherton, Fritz, Zahn-Waxler, & Ridgeway, 1986; Dunn, Bretherton, & Munn, 1987). However, there is a critical difference between previous findings and the findings reported here. In previous research, talk about emotions was often about ongoing emotions; that is, about what the child was feeling right now. In our research, parents were talking about a past emotional state. This differs in fundamental ways from talking about ongoing emotions. Most important, in our situations, children had to recall both the past event and their emotional reaction. Because children were not directly experiencing the emotion, it is possible that they were better able to reflect on and interpret the past emotional experiences (see Dunn, Brown & Beardsall, 1991, for related arguments). This may be an important situation in which emotions are socialized; parents and children discuss what emotions are appropriate and how to deal with particular emotions in a situation in which the child is able to cognitively reflect on and possibly internalize these lessons.

Second, emotional reactions to past events help provide an evaluative framework for the past. Emotions are a critical link between what happened in the past and what that event means for the self. Emotions associated with past events provide information both about what kinds of events cause particular kinds of emotional experiences – for example, what kinds of events cause sadness or anger – and also about what kind of emotional being one is – for example, I am a person who is sad a lot, or I am a person who angers easily. By focusing more on daughters' emotional reactions to past events than sons', parents may be providing daughters with more information about the personal meanings of the past.

The obtained gender difference in emotional language was provocative. But in order to more fully understand what was happening in these conversations, it seemed essential to examine the ways in which emotions were discussed in more detail. However, because parents were not explicitly asked to talk about emotional content with their children in these studies, many parents did not discuss emotions at all, or only discussed a few emotional states. Therefore, a more structured interview method, in which parents were explicitly asked to talk about the emotional content of past events with their child, seemed desirable (Fivush, 1991a). Since mothers and fathers showed similar patterns of emotional language in the previous research, only mothers participated in this study, for purely practical reasons. Mothers were initially told that we were interested in how much children could remember about particular kinds of emotional events, and were asked to discuss four different past events during which

Table 7.1. Mean number of emotion words used by mothers and children across events

| | Type of emotion word | | |
	Positive	Negative	Total
Mothers			
To girls	10.80	19.40	30.20
To boys	8.20	17.27	25.47
Mean	9.50	18.33	
Children			
Girls	1.53	4.27	5.80
Boys	1.33	3.33	4.66
Mean	1.43	3.80	

their child experienced happiness, anger, sadness, and fear. These four emotions were chosen because these are the emotions most often discussed in the more spontaneous conversations. I was particularly interested in the ways in which mothers would talk about the child's experience of each of these emotions, and whether this would differ as a function of the child's gender. Thirty mothers and their 32–35-month-old children participated; half of the children were female and half were male.

The first question concerned the number and type of emotion words that mothers and children used in these conversations. As can be seen on Table 7.1, mothers used more negative emotion words – words like *scared, angry,* and *sad* – than positive emotion words – words like *happy, like,* and *fun* – with both boys and girls, but they used about the same number of emotion words overall with children of both genders. Children showed the same pattern. Both boys and girls used more negative than positive emotion words. But children used few emotion words overall, and because these numbers were so small, analyses focused on maternal language. Because mothers were explicitly asked to talk about three negative emotional events – sadness, anger, and fear – and only one positive emotional event, it is not surprising that they used more negative emotional words overall. A more interesting question concerns the way in which these different emotions were talked about. All conversational utterances focusing on emotions were identified and coded into categories. Inspection of the frequencies revealed that the majority of mothers' utterances fell into one of two categories: (1) attributions, in which the mother attributes an emotional state or reaction to the child (for example, "You were scared, weren't you?" or "Were you angry?"); and (2) explanations, in

Table 7.2. Mean number and type of mothers' conversational utterances about emotions for each event type

	Event type			
	Sad	Angry	Scared	Happy
To girls				
Attributions	4.73	2.27	4.73	3.00
Explanations	10.27	4.60	9.60	2.73
To boys				
Attributions	3.40	3.73	5.33	2.67
Explanations	5.80	7.27	10.13	3.20

which the utterance focuses on the cause or consequence of an emotional state or reaction (for example, "Did that loud noise scare you?" or "What did Aaron do that made you so angry?"). The mean number of attributions and explanations made by mothers is shown in Table 7.2 for each type of emotional event.

Overall, mothers gave more explanations about sadness, anger, and fear than attributions, but there was no difference between explanations and attributions for the happy event. In general, then, mothers focus on explaining the causes and consequences of negative emotions with their young children. However, it is also the case that mothers were talking more about sadness overall and they were emphasizing explanations of sadness more with daughters than with sons. In contrast, they were talking more about anger with sons than with daughters.

A closer look at the conversations indicated that mothers and children often engaged in a three-utterance sequence when discussing emotions. The mother would make an attribution or explanation, which the child would confirm, and then the mother would reconfirm, as shown in these examples:

 M: Were you scared?
 C: Yeah
 M: Yeah, I had never seen you so scared.

And:

 M: Did he bite you?
 C: Yes
 M: Yes, he did, he bit you on the chin.

Note that mothers could reconfirm the child's confirmation of either an attribution or an explanation. Reconfirmations of attributions function to accept a particular emotional response, whereas reconfirmations

Table 7.3. *Mean number of reconfirmations by mother for each event type following children's confirmations of attributions or explanations*

	Event type			
	Sad	Angry	Scared	Happy
To girls				
After child has				
confirmed attribution	0.87	0.33	0.13	0.47
After child has				
confirmed explanation	1.87	0.47	1.60	0.67
To boys				
After child has				
confirmed attribution	0.33	0.60	0.47	0.33
After child has				
confirmed explanation	1.47	1.40	1.73	0.27

of explanations function to confirm that specific kinds of objects or situations are likely to cause particular emotions. As shown in Table 7.3, mothers were more likely to reconfirm explanations than attributions for the three negative events. But they were also more likely to reconfirm attributions and explanations of anger with sons than daughters, suggesting that anger is, at least implicitly, more acceptable for boys than for girls.

In reading through the conversations, it also became apparent that mothers would often provide some kind of resolution about the emotional experience. For example, in discussing scary events, mothers would often end the conversations by reassuring the child that there was nothing to be scared of. All conversations containing a resolution were identified. Only about half of the conversations contained any resolution at all, but for those conversations that did end with a resolution, some interesting patterns emerged.

Of all the emotional events, fearful events were most likely to end with a resolution. Sixty-three percent of the conversations about fearful events ended with a resolution, and of these, 94% involved an adult comforting or reassuring the child. For example, in this excerpt, a mother talks about a time when her daughter's friend scared her by threatening her:

> *M:* You came downstairs crying
> *C:* Yeah
> *M:* Why were you crying?
> *C:* Cause Trent said he was gonna kill me
> *M:* Were you scared?
> *C:* Yeah
> *M:* Very scared?
> *C:* Yes
> *M:* What do you do when you're scared?

C: [unintelligible]
M: But did you cry?
C: No
M: Yes you did. But then we talked about it, right, and you were
OK.

In this conversation, as soon as the mother and daughter concur that
the daughter was scared of her friend, the mother immediately mentions
what they did to allay the child's fear, and reassures the child that everything is OK. By resolving fearful events in this way, mothers seem to be
reassuring their children that the world is a relatively safe place and that
adults are havens of comfort and security.

For sadness, 46% of the conversations with daughters ended with a
resolution, and of these, 86% were again an adult comforting or reassuring the child. In this excerpt, the mother and daughter are discussing a
physical injury that made the daughter sad:

M: What happened to your finger?
C: I pinched it
M: You pinched it. Oh boy, I bet that really made you feel sad
C: Yeah . . . it hurts
M: Yeah, it did hurt. A pinched finger is no fun . . . But who came
in and made you feel better?
C: Daddy!

Again we see the mother resolving the child's emotional turmoil by recalling how her father comforted her and made everything OK. Again,
adults are portrayed as safe havens. In this way, daughters are getting
the message that they should not necessarily try to resolve sad and fearful
emotions by themselves, but that they should seek out adults for help
and reassurance. With sons, only 14% of the conversations about sadness
ended with a resolution at all, and only one conversation involved adult
reassurance. Thus mothers are not providing the same kind of interpersonal setting for emotions with sons. The message to sons is that sadness
is not an emotion that needs to be resolved, or at least does not need to
be resolved through seeking out another person.

For anger, two types of resolutions emerged and they differentiated
by gender. With daughters, mothers most often tried to reestablish the
relationship that had been damaged by the anger; 57% of conversations
about anger with daughters ending in a resolution were of this type. For
example, in this excerpt the mother and daughter are talking about what
happened when the daughter's friend took away all of her toys during a
play session:

M: Did you play with Niklaus a little bit yesterday?
C: Yeah
M: Did he make you angry?
C: Yeah

M: What did he do?
C: . . . He took away my toys
M: Yeah, what toys did he take away?
C: My elephant
M: . . . What else did Niklaus do?
C: He played with me
M: Umhmm, was that fun when he played with you?
C: Yeah
M: Yeah, he only made you mad when he took away (the elephant)
C: Yeah

Here we see that after concurring that the child was angry, the mother changes the emotional tone of the conversation and asks if the child had fun. She ends the conversation by establishing that the daughter and Niklaus are good friends despite the transgression of the day before. With daughters, then, the relationship with the transgressor is more important than the transgression. Resolution involves reestablishing a harmonious relationship.

With sons, in contrast, resolution of anger most often involved some form of retaliation; 86% of conversations with sons about anger containing a resolution involved retaliation. It is important to emphasize that the retaliatory act was always initiated by the child but in every case it was accepted by the mother. Here is an example of a mother and son discussing what happened when another child bit him:

M: Who bites (you)?
C: Uh, ummm, Johnny bites me
M: Yeah and what do you think when Johnny bites you?
C: That I will shoot him
M: You're gonna shoot him?
C: (nods yes)
M: When he bites you?
C: Yes
M: Yeah, where did he bite you ?
C: He bite me on the cheek
M: That's right, he did
C: Yeah and [unintelligible] I got a gun, I'm gonna shoot him
M: You're gonna shoot Johnny?
C: Yeah and Johnny's got in my gun
M: Oh, OK

Here we see that the child mentions retaliation, which the mother accepts. In this way boys are learning that it is appropriate to act on anger. No attempt was made by mothers to reestablish a harmonious relationship with the transgressor in conversations about anger with sons. Again, it must be stressed that it was the child who brought up the retaliatory response. It is not clear why boys bring up retaliation and girls do not; perhaps this depends on earlier socialization. Whatever the reason, however, it is intriguing that as early as 2 ½ to 3 years of age, there are already gender differences in the discussion, interpretation, and evaluation of girls' and boys' experience of anger.

There was one excerpt in the entire corpus of data in which the mother brought up retaliation and it was with a daughter. It is an extremely interesting interchange:

M: When Jason bit you, did it make you angry?
C: (nods yes)
M: Did you hit him?
C: (shakes head no)
M: Did you try to bite him back?
C: No.
M: No, 'cause you're a sweet little girl.

In this conversation, the mother does, in fact, bring up possible retaliatory responses, which her daughter negates, and the mother ends the conversation by praising this behavior in terms of the kind of person her daughter is – a sweet little girl.

These results suggest that the ways in which mothers deal with their child's emotions may be very different with daughters and sons. A final aspect of the data to be considered concerns the type of events the mothers talked about for each emotion. Remember that in this task, the mother was asked to select four different past events during which her child experienced happiness, anger, sadness, and fear. What kinds of events did mothers choose to illustrate each of these emotional experiences?

Consideration of the transcripts suggested that mothers placed emotional conversations in one of two frameworks, a social-relational framework and an autonomous framework. In a social-relational framework, emotions were clearly and explicitly linked to other people, either as causes of the emotion (being sad because someone else was sick; being angry because someone hit you) or as regulators of the emotion (as in the examples of adult reassurance discussed above). In an autonomous framework, no mention was made of other people; emotions were caused by objects or events in the environment and impacted on the individual child (being sad because you lost a toy; being happy at receiving a present). The number of events placed in a social-relational or an autonomous framework for each type of emotion is shown in Figure 7.1 for girls and boys. The pattern suggests that mothers focus more on social-relational situations when discussing emotions with their daughters than with their sons. All four of the target events were caused by other people: Others' discomfort or death causes sadness, others' aggression causes anger, people's actions can be scary, and playing with friends causes happiness. For boys, only anger is caused by others. Sadness for boys is

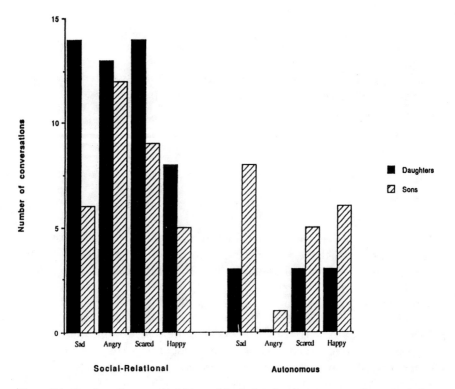

Figure 7.1. Number of events placed in social-relational and autonomous frameworks for boys and for girls for each emotional event type

caused by not getting one's own way and fear is caused by noises and animals. Even for happy events, where the most common theme was family or school outings, the focus of the conversation was on the activities that occurred rather than on the people who were present.

Together, the results of this study suggest that mothers are talking in very different ways about emotional experience with daughters and sons. In particular, these differences emerge when talking about sadness and anger. With daughters, mothers emphasize sadness, they emphasize explanations of sadness, and they are concerned with reassuring and comforting their daughters about feeling sad. With sons, mothers emphasize anger, they accept anger as an appropriate emotional reaction, and they even accept retaliation as an appropriate response. With daughters, in contrast, anger is most often resolved by reestablishing the damaged relationship. Moreover, emotions are generally placed in a more interactional framework with girls and a more individual framework with boys.

These findings seem related to some recent theoretical proposals by Nancy Chodorow (1978) and Carol Gilligan (1982). They have argued that females are socialized to be relational whereas males are socialized to be individualistic. Without going into too much detail, the basic argument follows a psychoanalytic theme, such that girls never have to separate completely from their mother, and therefore remain emotionally related to the mother and to others by extension. Females, then, define themselves in terms of their emotional attachments to others. Their self-concept depends on their emotional and social relatedness. Boys, on the other hand, must give up the mother as a love object; in order to do this, they must sever their emotional ties and deny their own feminine attributes. Their self-concept is based on being separate and individuated from others. I don't necessarily agree with the psychoanalytical interpretation, but the mother–child conversations about past emotions certainly support the idea that girls are being socialized to be relational whereas boys are being socialized to be individual.

A final word needs to be said about interpreting these findings. There is a tendency when thinking about these data to conclude that girls are being socialized in potentially harmful ways. That is, they are being socialized out of feeling anger and toward feeling responsible for others' emotional states. This may be partly true. But they are also being socialized to understand that anger does not mean the dissolution of a relationship and that communities are responsible for the well-being of their members. Similarly, whereas boys are being socialized into accepting anger as a reasonable emotional response in certain situations, which might seem healthy, the only skill they are learning for dealing with anger is retaliation. Thus, rather than placing absolute values on these socialization patterns, it would be more productive to think about the positive and negative aspects that both boys and girls are learning in these interactions.

Narrative, emotion, and the remembered self

How do the findings on gender differences in the discussion of past emotions relate to the findings about elaborative and repetitive interaction styles presented earlier and what does it tell us about the remembered self? Across the research discussed in this essay, we are seeing a pattern that indicates that females are being socialized into being more concerned about the past and about emotional aspects of the past. Parents talk more about the past with girls than with boys, talk in more richly elaborated and embellished ways about the past, and, in spontaneous conversations, talk more about past emotions. Most interesting, talk about past events and emotions seems to be embedded in a more social interactional framework for girls than for boys. Through these conversations, girls are being taught that relationships are important and that they should be responsive to the emotional experiences of others. After all, it is other people who cause one's own emotional states. Girls are also responsible to some extent for others' distress. One of the most common causes of sadness for girls in these conversations is other people being sick and dying. Even when others' behavior induces anger, girls are being taught that anger and retaliation are not acceptable responses, but rather one should work to reestablish a positive relationship. In this way, girls are establishing a remembered self that is embedded in a social network, and more specifically, a network in which they feel responsible for keeping others happy. Further, because young girls are participating in richly embellished, emotionally laden conversations about the past, we can speculate that females will come to have more narratively and emotionally elaborated structures for recounting and representing their past experiences. Thus their remembered selves will be rich, detailed, and interpersonally oriented.

Boys, in contrast, are learning a very different structure for their remembered selves. The past is not talked about as much nor as richly. Other people's emotions are not emphasized. One's own emotional reactions are more self-contained and individual. The remembered self is not a social self to the same extent as it is for girls. Through participating in these kinds of interactions about past events, boys' remembered selves will be spare, limited in emotional tone, and autonomously oriented. In fact, there is some research with adults demonstrating that, for females, personal memories are more detailed (Ross & Holmberg, 1990) and more emotionally saturated (Davis, 1991) than they are for males. What we are seeing in the early adult-guided conversations about past experiences discussed here are the early beginnings of what may come to be enduring individual differences in the remembered past and the relationships between past experiences and self-understanding and self-evaluation.

Of course we need to be extremely cautious in interpreting these results for several reasons. First, as with all empirically demonstrated gender differences, there is a great deal of variability within each gender group as well as variability between the groups. Clearly, gender is not the only factor contributing to differences in parental style. Second, whereas differences in parental interaction seem to be well documented, there is little evidence yet as to how these differences influence children's developing understanding of narrative and their selves. What evidence does exist suggests that, indeed, children are learning specific narrative and evaluative devices through participating in these conversations (Fivush, 1991b; McCabe & Peterson, 1991), but more longitudinal research is necessary.

Further, we need to extend the research to other cultural groups. Research now being conducted by Miller and her colleagues indicates that the role of narratives and evaluation in narratives are very different in different economic and racial groups in the United States (Miller et al., 1990; and chap. 8 of this volume). It would be extremely informative to examine the ways in which different subcultural groups discuss past experiences with their children. Do parents in other subcultural groups show these same stylistic variations in the way they talk about past events and past emotions?

Finally, we need to examine the role of the child in these early conversations more closely. In this essay, I have focused almost exclusively on parental styles of interaction, and have only touched upon children's contributions to these conversations. Are parents showing more elaborative styles of interaction with children who for some reason are more interested in or more able to talk about the past? Are differences in the way in which past emotions are talked about partly dependent on gender differences in the experience of emotions? Future research needs to look more closely at exactly what children are contributing to these conversations and how children's contributions influence what adults do.

Still, the research conducted so far indicates that parents talk in different ways about past events and past emotions with sons and with daughters. Some of the differences are quite startling and some are quite subtle. But these differences exist, and in all probability have a profound influence on the way in which children come to understand and evaluate their past and themselves.

ACKNOWLEDGMENTS

Parts of this research were supported by a grant from the Spencer Foundation. I would especially like to thank Elaine Reese, Janet Kuebli, Catherine Haden, Liza Dondonan, Naomi Singer, and Winifred Diggs for their work in collecting, transcribing, and analyzing the data.

REFERENCES

Beeghly, M., Bretherton, I., & Mervis, C. (1986). Mothers' internal state language to toddlers. *British Journal of Developmental Psychology*, 4, 247–261.

Bretherton, I., Fritz, J., Zahn-Waxler, C., & Ridgeway, D. (1986). Learning to talk about emotions: A functionalist perspective. *Child Development*, 55, 529–548.

Brewer, W. F. (1986). What is autobiographical memory? In D. C. Rubin (Ed.), *Autobiographical memory* (pp. 24–49). Cambridge University Press.

Bruner, J. (1987). Life as narrative. *Social Research*, 54, 11–32.

Chodorow, N. (1978). *The reproduction of mothering.* Berkeley: University of California Press.

Cole, M. (1985). The zone of proximal development: Where culture and cogni-

156   R. FIVUSH

tion create each other. In J. V. (Wertsch (Ed.), *Culture, communication and cognition* (pp. 146–161). Cambridge University Press.

Davis, P. J. (1991, July). *Gender differences in autobiographical memory.* Paper presented at the NATO Advanced Research Conference on Theoretical Perspectives on Autobiographical Memory, Grange, England.

Dunn, J., Bretherton, I., & Munn, P. (1987). Conversations about feeling states between mothers and their young children. *Developmental Psychology, 23,* 132–39.

Dunn, J., Brown, J., & Beardsall, L. (1991). Family talk about feeling states and children's later understanding of others' emotions. *Developmental Psychology, 27,* 448–455.

Eisenberg, A. R. (1985). Learning to describe past experience in conversation. *Discourse Processes, 8,* 177–204.

Engel, S. (1986, April). The role of mother–child interaction in autobiographical recall. In J. A. Hudson (Chair), *Learning to talk about the past.* Symposium conducted at the Southeastern Conference on Human Development, Nashville, TN.

Fivush, R. (1988). The functions of event memory. In U. Neisser & E. Winograd (Eds.), *Remembering reconsidered: Ecological and traditional approaches to the study of memory* (pp. 277–282). Cambridge University Press.

Fivush, R. (1989). Exploring sex differences in the emotional content of mother–child conversations about the past. *Sex Roles, 20,* 675–691.

Fivush, R. (1991a). Gender and emotion in mother–child conversations about the past. *Journal of Narrative and Life History, 1,* 325–341.

Fivush, R. (1991b). The social construction of personal narratives. *Merrill-Palmer Quarterly, 37,* 59–82.

Fivush, R., & Fromhoff, F. A. (1988). Style and structure in mother–child conversations about the past. *Discourse Processes, 11,* 337–355.

Fivush, R., & Reese, E. (1992). The social construction of autobiographical memory. In M. A. Conway, D. C. Rubin, H. Spinnler, & W. Wagenaar (Eds.), *Theoretical perspectives on autobiographical memory* (pp. 1–28). The Netherlands: Kluwer.

Gilligan, C. (1982). *In a different voice.* Cambridge, MA: Harvard University Press.

Heath, S. B. (1983). *Ways with words: Language, life and work in communities and classrooms.* Cambridge University Press.

Hoff-Ginsburg, E. (1991). Mother–child conversation in different social classes and communicative settings. *Child Development, 62,* 782–796.

Hudson, J. A. (1990). The emergence of autobiographic memory in mother–child conversation. In R. Fivush & J. A. Hudson (Eds.), *Knowing and remembering in young children* (pp. 166–196). Cambridge University Press.

Hudson, J. A., & Shapiro, L. (1991). Effects of task and topic on children's narratives. In A. McCabe & C. Peterson (Eds.), *New directions in developing narrative structure* (pp. 89–136). Hillsdale, NJ: Erlbaum.

Kuebli, J., & Fivush, R. (1992). *Gender differences in parent–child conversations about past emotions. Sex Roles, 27,* 683–698.

Labov, U. (1982). Speech actions and reactions in personal narrative. In D. Tannen (Ed.), *Analyzing discourse: Text and talk* (pp. 219–247). Washington, DC: Georgetown University Press.

McCabe, A., & Peterson, C. (1991). Getting the story: A longitudinal study of parental styles in eliciting narratives and developing narrative skill. In

A. McCabe & C. Peterson (Eds.), *Developing narrative structure* (pp. 217–253). Hillsdale, NJ: Erlbaum.

Miller, P. J. (1994). Narrative practices: Their role in socialization and self-construction. Chapter 8 of this volume.

Miller, P. J., Potts, R., Fung, H., Hoogstra, L., & Mintz, J. (1990). Narrative practices and the social construction of self in childhood. *American Ethnologist, 17*(2), 292–311.

Miller, P. J., & Sperry, L. L. (1988). Early talk about the past: The origins of conversational stories of personal experience. *Journal of Child Language, 15,* 292–315.

Neisser, U. (1988). Five kinds of self-knowledge. *Philosophical Psychology, 1,* 35–59.

Nelson, K. (1988). The ontogeny of memory for real world events. In U. Neisser & E. Winograd (Eds.), *Remembering reconsidered: Ecological and traditional approaches to memory* (pp. 277–282). Cambridge University Press.

Paris, S. G., Newman, R. S., & Jacobs, J. E. (1985). Social contexts and functions of children's remembering. In C. J. Brainerd & M. Pressley (Eds.), *The cognitive side of memory development* (pp. 81–115). New York: Springer-Verlag.

Peterson, C., & McCabe, A. (1983). *Developmental psycholinguistics: Three ways of looking at a child's narrative.* New York: Plenum.

Reese, E., & Fivush, R. (1993). *Parental styles for talking about the past. Developmental Psychology, 29,* 596–606.

Rogoff, B. (1990). *Apprenticeship in thinking.* New York: Oxford University Press.

Ross. M., & Holmberg, D. (1990). Recounting the past: Gender differences in the recall of events in the history of a close relationship. In M. P. Zanna & J. M. Olson (Eds.), *The Ontario Symposium: Vol. 6. Self-inference processes* (pp. 135–152). Hillsdale, NJ: Erlbaum.

Sachs, J. (1983). Talking about the there and then: The emergence of displaced reference in parent–child discourse. In K. E. Nelson (Ed.), *Children's langauge* (Vol. 4, pp. 1–27). New York: Gardner Press.

Spence, D. (1982). *Narrative truth and historical truth.* New York: Norton.

Vygotsky, L. S. (1978). *Mind in society: The development of higher psychological processes.* Cambridge, MA: Harvard University Press.

Wertsch, J. (1985). *Vygotsky and the social formation of mind.* Cambridge, MA: Harvard University Press.

8

Narrative practices: Their role in socialization and self-construction

PEGGY J. MILLER

The use of narrative as a socializing tool is most apparent when myths or traditional tales, embodying the collective wisdom of a people, are told in a deliberate attempt to edify or enlighten. Among the Western Apache, for example, stories about the early history of the group are directed at transgressors on the belief that they will be moved to reflect upon and correct their misconduct (Basso, 1984). In such cases narrative serves overtly as a "culture-preserving instrument" (Sapir, 1933/1949). Group stories function not only to maintain community values among their members but also to instill those values in the young (Gates, 1989). In some cultures, telling stories about the mythic origins or history of the group is even institutionalized as part of the formal preparation for adult roles and responsibilities (Herdt, 1981). Thus, the socializing power of sacred and traditional narrative is widely recognized. More than 60 years ago Malinowski (1926/1984) wrote,

Myth fulfills in primitive culture an indispensable function: it expresses, en-hances, and codifies belief; it safeguards and enforces morality; it vouches for the efficiency of ritual and contains practical rules for the guidance of man. Myth is thus a vital ingredient of human civilization; it is not an idle tale but a hard-worked active force. (p. 199)

The present essay focuses on a type of narrative that has received less attention with respect to its socializing potential, namely the informal, mundane, and often pervasive narrative accounts that people give of their personal experiences. The verbal activity of telling other people about events that have happened to oneself may well be a cultural univer-sal: Versions of this type of storytelling occur in diverse cultural traditions within the United States and around the world (Miller & Moore, 1989). On first impression, personal stories may seem like idle tales: They are told by ordinary people in the course of their everyday activities. They are not associated with religious rituals nor restricted to venerable elders. They do not evoke godly or heroic deeds but re-create events from the humble autobiographies of those near at hand. Nevertheless, stories of

158

personal experience are not idle tales. A basic premise of this essay is that they too are a hard-worked active force. I shall argue that even when personal stories are told informally and without didactic intent, even when they are not addressed directly to the young, they play a powerful role in childhood socialization and are especially consequential for self-construction.

This view of personal storytelling rests on two related assumptions about ordinary talk: (1) that it is a pervasive, orderly, and culturally organized feature of social life in every culture (Goodwin, 1982; Gumperz & Hymes, 1972; Hymes, 1967; Sacks, 1965–1971/1984); and (2) that it is a major, if not the major, mechanism of socialization (Ochs & Schieffelin, 1984; Miller & Sperry, 1988b; Sapir, 1933/1949; Schieffelin & Ochs, 1986; Vygotsky, 1978, 1934/1987). Research on language socialization (Heath, 1983; Ochs, 1988; Schieffelin, 1990; Miller, 1986; Miller & Sperry, 1987; Watson-Gegeo & Gegeo, 1986) and moral development (Much & Shweder, 1978; Shweder & Much, 1987) has shown that the flow of social and moral messages is relentless in the myriad small encounters of everyday life. Although there are general properties of language – propositionality, representational capability, and indexicality – that make it an effective purveyor of meanings (Miller & Hoogstra, in press), little is known as yet about the socializing implications of particular, culturally constituted species of talk. Yet any model of socialization that takes language seriously as a socializing medium has to grapple with this problem.

Socialization through discourse

All models of socialization involve at minimum three terms: an institution, a member of that institution, and a novice. If early childhood socialization is the issue, the minimal terms are the family as institution, the caregiver, and the child. Deterministic models portray socialization as the simple transmission of norms and values from caregiver to child. Such models cannot account for how people create, sustain, and change the society in which they live (Wentworth, 1980), nor can they accommodate a basic insight of modern developmental psychology, namely that children, even infants, are actively engaged in constructing and negotiating meaning. Interactionistic models of socialization are an advance in these respects, in that they envision the process of socialization to be negotiated and the outcomes to be variable. They admit to the psychological complexity of the child and acknowledge the child's contributions to his or her own socialization.

The model that I advocate is not only an interactionist model but a discourse model. It attempts to incorporate talk in a principled way, and, hence, it has not three but four minimal terms: an institution, a novice, a member, and a type of discourse. According to this model, institutions are organized so as to bring novice and member together recurrently for particular activities that are mediated by particular forms of discourse, which lead to particular social and psychological consequences for the novice. This kind of model has been applied to a variety of socializing institutions, each of which is associated with specialized forms of discourse. The best known of these is Vygotskian theory (Vygotsky, 1978, 1934/1987; Wertsch, 1985), which ties the acquisition of scientific concepts to the specialized discourse associated with the institution of formal schooling. Another application is to the institution of psychoanalysis, where the patient's development of the self-analytic function is linked to the specialized discourse of psychoanalytic treatment (Nye, 1988).

As applied to the family, the institution in which early socialization occurs, the model posits that young children are socialized into systems of meaning through recurring interactions with family members, these interactions being mediated by particular types of discourse. This model shares with Rogoff (in press) an emphasis on the interrelated contributions that caregiver(s) and child make to the child's socialization through their mutual participation in semiotically mediated routine practices. According to this model, the social and psychological consequences for the child of routine participation in socializing practices depend on how messages are packaged in discourse. Attention is thereby directed to recurring forms of discourse that mediate child–caregiver interactions. One such type of discourse is personal storytelling.

This model suggests that there are a number of consequences for the child of habitual participation in personal storytelling. One consequence is the acquisition of narrative skills. Another, and the one most germane to the topic at hand, is self-construction. Now, there are obviously many sorts of discourse that occur in families, and there is a sense in which self-construction is implicated in each. Why single out personal storytelling? The rationale, developed more fully elsewhere (Miller, Potts, Fung, Hoogstra, & Mintz, 1990), is that the stories that people tell about remembered experiences from their own lives provide an important, indeed a privileged, site for the social construction of self.

In capsule form, the argument is that there are four affinities between narrative and the self that especially apply to personal storytelling. First is the temporal affinity: Because both the experiences of the self and the events in a story are organized with respect to time, narrative is especially well suited to representing self-continuity (Ricoeur, 1984). Second is the affinity for representing human action: Narrative generates understanding of human action by replicating linguistically the process by which understanding is achieved (Gergen, 1986). Third is the evaluative affinity: Stories, like selves, are inherently evaluative. Because stories of personal experience are expressed from a personal perspective, they are replete with explicit and implicit messages about the narrator-protagonist (Goffman, 1974; Labov & Waletsky, 1967). Fourth is the conversational affinity: Self-expressive messages are entailed in every social encounter, and when the encounter involves informal talk, self-expression is accomplished largely through "replayings" of personal experience (Goffman, 1974). Because these various affinities between narrative and self converge in a narrative genre that is a probable cultural universal, they provide a rationale for treating stories of personal experience as a privileged site for the social construction of self.

Locating personal storytelling within a discourse model of socialization and self-construction raises several questions, all of which revolve around the notion of practice. Is personal storytelling routinely practiced in everyday family life? If so, what forms does it take? Or more to the point, how is it practiced with reference to young children? What are the implications of these practices for self-construction in early childhood? As it turned out, these questions are particularly apt as applied to South Baltimore.

Personal storytelling in South Baltimore

I first got interested in personal storytelling when I was doing research on early language socialization in South Baltimore, an urban, working-class community whose residents are descended from people of German, Polish, Irish, Italian, and Appalachian origin (Miller, 1982). The children I studied were 2-year-old girls of unmarried mothers. Family income and educational level were low, and the children were growing up in extended families. Although I had not gone to South Baltimore to study storytelling, it soon became clear that stories of personal experience were a major form of adult talk, occurring profusely in everyday conversation. I was impressed, as I listened, not only by the ubiquity of these stories but by the vigor and skill with which they were told. Men and women alike were accomplished practitioners, capable at times of inspired performances.

As a woman studying children and child rearing, I spent more time with women and heard more stories and more intimate stories from them. I was not surprised to learn that pregnancy and childbirth were a favorite narrative topic among women. In the following excerpted example, the narrator recounts experiences that occurred more than two years earlier.

Example 1

I'm telling you I was huge. Had to start wearing maternity clothes when I was two months. And I think I gained forty-two pounds with her. . . . And I guess when I was about seven months, I was so huge that they thought I was expecting twins. So they told me that when I went into delivery, if I started having complications, like I said, they'd send me down for X-rays. But when the X-rays came, there was one. But I could put two grocery bags on my stomach when I finally went into the ninth month with her. . . . The only thing that got big on me was like my stomach. I didn't gain it anywhere else. I mean, my legs stayed real small and my hips. And like, I mean I'm not little but I'm not that big-built. And I went up to like a forty-four in a bra. The straps were cuttin into my shoulders and my bust was so huge, I was bent backwards trying to hold myself up. And people would just look at me and start laughin. My brother-in-law said to me, "My God," he says, "Where are you carrying that baby at, your belly or your bust? You're terrible lookin."

When a listener laughed and commented, "So, what did you do the last couple of months? You must have sorta sat around," the narrator replied, "Well, no, I moved furniture," leading smoothly into another story and yet another, all culminating in the story of the birth itself.

Example 2
He [the Cesarean specialist] said, "I know what you're lookin for." I said, "Yeah." He said, "Yeah," he said, "It's a little girl." I said, "You sure?" He said, "Yes, I wouldn't lie to you." So he felt my stomach and he said, "It's a little girl." When they delivered her, the nurse turned around and she said, "Oh, you got a little black-headed girl." He said, "See, I didn't disappoint you, did I?"

While stories of pregnancy and childbirth occurred in everyday conversation, they were obligatory at baby showers, an all-female ritual event. On these occasions mothers and grandmothers reveled in evoking experiences that occurred years or even decades earlier to an audience who had heard the tales many times before. Apparently, the assumption of the maternal role remained a lasting touchstone of female identity.

However, there were many other facets of self that these women projected in their stories. Or perhaps a better way to put it is that the maternal self was one of many narrated selves. Also prominent was the tough, angry, clever, assertive self.

Example 3
Oh my God, I suffered for three whole hours and I yelled at him. I says, "Now I'm mad," and I don't cuss that much, and I says, "You get the hell out of here and don't you ever come back. I'm suffering and you don't even give a shit. . . ."

Example 4
And my boss come by the other day and wanted me to work it. And I said, "I'm not doing it." . . . I tell you why he wanted me to work: Because the floor lady is going on vacation that week. The sprayer is going on vacation that week. Dorothy's going on vacation that week. She's the stacker in there. And I'm goin that week. And that's four of us out in one week and that's gonna kill him because Mildred's been missing a lot of time. . . . I'm not running it. I told him. I said, "There's no way, Al." I said, "Na-uh." I said, "You asked who wanted to take their

vacation first so Mildred took hers cause I told her she could." I said, "but there's no way I'm gonna give up my week's vacation," I said "because I'm gonna tell you," I said, "I really worked hard this year for that."

Example 5
Even when we, I got free lunch, you know? We went through the cafeteria. And the group in the table would all stand up and say, "You got free lunch tickets" (teasing singsong intonation), you know, and they start, all of em around the room start doin, hittin the tables and everythin. And I would stand up and I says, "Well, well, you all think you're really teasin somebody. At least I know I'm agettin somethin free and youse ain't. Hahaha, what do you think of that?" And they shut their mouths, boy. They did. And the, and the ladies behind the, would, that give the food out, they just laughin their tails off back there. They say, "Did you hear that little girl, she stood up there." And I sit down and I says, "You see, I'm gonna enjoy my free lunch." I was eatin, boy, eatin. And I says, "I even got fifteen cents to buy me a fudge bar" (laughs). They come in there with baloney sand-wiches in them bags. I'd say, "you can eat that stale baloney. I'm gettin jello on the side of my plate."

Example 6
I was walkin on Charles Street – and the girl happens to be my girlfriend now. She big and fat, boy. She could sit on me and flatten me out, but I stuck up to her. Her name was Janie. And she hung with the bad people too, boy. And she says, "Look at the big-nosed B-I-T-C-H." And I turned around and I says, 'Uh, you talkin to me? I SAID, ARE YOU TALKING TO ME?" I says, "Well, you fat slob you, I put you in a skillet and strip you down to normal size, if you mess with me."

In each of these stories the narrator created an interpersonal drama around a self-protagonist who was bold, quick-witted, feisty, and protec-tive of her rights and her dignity. Our research on the socialization of anger and aggression revealed that these personal qualities were highly valued by women in South Baltimore and figured prominently in their theories of child rearing (Miller, 1986; Miller & Sperry, 1987, 1988b).

But there is another feature of these stories that deserves comment, namely that they are strikingly effective tellings. The last two stories, in particular, are highly "performed" in the Hymes (1975) and Bauman (1986) sense, drawing attention to the storyteller's narrative skill and to the communicative act itself. Note the strategic selection of narrative top-ics and the artful deployment of repetition, parallel constructions, taboo words, original metaphors, shifting rhythms, modulation of volume, and so on. Note that these stories, like Bauman's Texas stories, are built around a replayed conversational exchange: There is a shift from re-counting the past event (in the past tense) to reenacting the past conver-sational exchange in the here-and-now (in the historical present tense), culminating in a "punch line" rendered in direct quotation. These vari-ous artistic effects function not only to convey the point or significance of the story but to create in the audience an appreciation of the performance and the performer. The self as narrator – the inhabited self as distinguished from the represented self-protagonist – is thereby affirmed.

To summarize, from this initial work in South Baltimore I learned that personal storytelling was habitually and avidly practiced by adults in this community and that it was a rich source of patterned messages about who the narrator is or claims to be. This led me to wonder about the developmental implications of growing up in an environment in which people are constantly telling stories about themselves. And it led me to wonder about how South Baltimore compared to other, culturally different communities with respect to personal storytelling and self-construction. Since then my students and I have done several studies in South Baltimore and elsewhere that speak to these questions.

Personal storytelling practices

One goal of this work has been to develop a clearer, more adequate conception of the fourth term in the model, namely personal storytelling itself. The approach that we have taken is to treat stories not as disembodied texts – as I have in working the preceding examples rhetorically into this text – but as integrated performances, embedded in their immediate contexts of use (Miller & Moore, 1989). That stories are situated communications, reflecting the particulars of the circumstances in which they occur, is a theme uniting many recent sociolinguistic, anthropological, and folkloric accounts of narrative (Bauman, 1984, 1986; Bauman & Briggs, 1990; Hymes, 1975; Kirshenblatt-Gimblett, 1975; Robinson, 1981; Polanyi 1985). This idea is not new; it is traceable to such theorists of language and social life as Jakobson, Malinowski, and Sapir. When stories are approached in this way what usually comes to mind are such matters as the time, location, and occasion of the telling, the nature of the speech event in which the story is embedded, and the characteristics of narrator and interlocutor. An important but rarely explored implication of this perspective is the possibility that the narrative event includes young children. To put this another way, if our concern is with the use of narrative to socialize the young, we need to ask how personal storytelling is *practiced* with reference to children in different communities. (This may seem like an obvious question, but until recently, neither of the obviously relevant literatures has had much to say about it. Developmental psychologists have studied narrative but not in terms of the narrative environments that children inhabit. Anthropologists have studied the practice of storytelling but not in terms of how children are involved.)

The notion of narrative practices forefronts the particularity and the situatedness of personal storytelling, the fact that stories defined in particular ways are told for particular purposes in particular contexts of use.

Personal storytelling is not monolithic, just as literacy is not monolithic (Scribner & Cole, 1981). Narrative practices are the set of situated, socially conducted narrative activities that are meaningful within a specific culture and that bear a family resemblance to one another in their discourse form. In addition, the notion of practice carries with it the requirement of recurrence or habitualness. Demonstrating the recurrent nature of the practice in the contexts of the child's everyday life is an important step in establishing claims about its social and cognitive consequences.

In further defining narrative practices for comparative purposes, it has been necessary to make an analytic distinction between two sets of parameters: (1) the particular version of personal storytelling that prevails in a given culture – that is, the indigenous, genre-defining properties of personal storytelling; and (2) the ways in which children are exposed to or included in narrative events – that is, indigenous participant structures. By keeping these two issues separate, we do not prejudge whether children are permitted the same forms of narrative participation prescribed for adults, nor do we prejudge the particular configurations of child exposure and genre-defining characteristics that occur cross-culturally.

There are a whole host of parameters along which the genre itself can vary cross-culturally. For example, what are the norms of reportability in different communities? Are narrators required to stick close to the literal truth, as in the white working-class community in the Piedmont Carolinas described by Heath (1983), or is there considerable latitude for fictional embellishment, as in the black working-class community she described? How do stories function to structure the immediate discourse? Does the didactic function take precedence over the entertainment function, as we suspect it does for Chinese stories (Miller, Fung, & Mintz, 1991)? What kinds of verbal and nonverbal techniques are used to evaluate or convey the point of the story (Watson, 1973; Rosaldo, 1986)? Is the discourse structured around a single topic (topic-centered) or around a series of associated topics (episodic) (Michaels, 1991)? Is the interactive style of the narration unilateral, so that responsibility for telling the tale lies with the narrator? Or does it resemble the highly negotiated style of Athabaskan performance described by Scollon and Scollon (1981), in which the audience, in effect, tells the story?

Although these parameters of variation are crucial in delineating implications for the construction of selves cross-culturally, I will focus instead on participant structures because far less is known about this issue. In the sections that follow, findings from the South Baltimore study will be reviewed. These findings indicate that young children from South Baltimore are included in personal storytelling in three ways: Stories are told *around* them as co-present others, *about* them as ratified participants, and *with* them as co-narrators. Findings and examples from a new study of personal storytelling in culturally diverse children will also be cited. This study was designed to investigate the role that personal storytelling plays in the socialization of young children from five different cultural groups (low-income African-American, middle-class African-American, working-class white, middle-class white in Chicago, and middle-class Chinese in Taipei, Taiwan).

Telling stories around the child

The primary way in which stories of personal experience were available to young children in South Baltimore was through stories told around them by adults and older children. That is, a story of personal experi-ence – a temporally ordered and evaluated account of a past event in which the narrator portrayed himself or herself as a protagonist – was addressed to another person in the presence of the child. Transcripts of 40 hours of video-recorded home observations in four families were examined for tellings of this sort (Miller & Moore, 1989). These tapes were made for the purpose of studying child language, and neither the researcher nor the families knew then that narrative would become a focus of inquiry. Stories around the child occurred in 38 of the 40 sam-ples, at an overall average rate at 8.5 per hour. Average rates per hour for the individual families were 4.4 (with a range of 0–11), 5.3 (with a range of 4–9), 9.8 (with a range of 3–24), and 12.8 (with a range of 2–15).

I recently returned to South Baltimore and made a recording of the women and children from one of these families under conditions in which they were "primed" to tell stories. On this occasion three genera-tions of women were present for a cookout on the back porch. Also pres-ent were three of their children, aged 1, 7, and 10 years; the researcher, whom the family has known for more than a decade; and two female radio producers who were preparing a program on storytelling. The ex-pressed purpose of the visit was to make a recording of the stories told by a family of skilled storytellers. Under these conditions, stories occurred at an average rate of nearly 40 per hour in a four-hour sample.

Note that stories told around the child are generated only by a certain kind of social configuration, namely one that includes at least two per-sons, narrator and listener, in addition to the child. Child-rearing con-figurations that isolate the mother–child dyad obviously do not permit this type of participant structure. This means that if the model of social-ization through storytelling is to produce meaningful generalizations it cannot be restricted to dyadic or scaffolded interactions but must accom-modate multiparty constellations.

From the standpoint of self-construction, these findings suggest that children from South Baltimore inhabited a verbal environment that afforded many opportunities for listening to stories addressed to other persons, stories in which the narrator – the child's mother or grandmother or aunt or cousin – projected a particular kind of self-protagonist. These significant others repeatedly conveyed, in effect, "This is who I am: These are the experiences I've had with my mother, my sister, my boyfriend, my boss, the doctor at the clinic, a stranger on the street." There is no evidence that these stories were told deliberately *for* children, nor did they appear to be censored on behalf of children (Miller & Moore, 1989). Nonetheless, they constituted a steadily available and constantly updated resource about the most important people in the child's life.

If it is the case that self-understanding develops hand in hand with understanding of others – more about this issue later – then these stories could be quite important in the self-construction of children, for they provide the child with expanded access to the experiences of significant others. A child who has achieved a minimal ability to comprehend oral stories and who is inclined to listen, can gain access to a whole host of previously inaccessible experiences about other people. These include temporally inaccessible experiences (such as those that happened before the child was born), spatially inaccessible experiences (such as those that occurred in places from which the child is excluded), and affectively/cognitively inaccessible experiences (such as bewildering experiences that the child has witnessed).

Determining what children actually take from these overheard stories is, of course, an analytically separable and methodologically challenging issue. The most that can be claimed at this point is that at times young children made relevant verbal responses to stories told around them, produced appropriate generalizations from such stories to new situations, and created detailed and affectively charged retellings of their own (Miller, 1989). For example, the most complex story in the South Baltimore corpus of young children's stories was traceable, according to maternal report, to an adult story about choking that the child had overheard some days earlier. The child, aged 32 months, produced a highly animated version of the story, complete with gestural enactment and facial miming. She inserted the story deftly into the conversation, supplied orienting information as to the time and place of the choking, and added an explicit moral about the dangers of "eating beer." What is remarkable about this performance is not only its sophistication as a narrative but the child's affective involvement in the telling. Apparently, the overheard story had left a strong impression. An interesting related phenomenon is what we have called story appropriation, in which the child retells someone else's story but casts himself or herself as protagonist (Miller et al., 1990). Story appropriation bears further investigation as a self-constructive process by which the child takes claims about another person and converts them into claims about the self.

Telling stories about the child

A related narrative practice in South Baltimore that is relevant to self-construction was the telling of stories about the child. This participant structure may be thought of as a variant of telling stories around the child in that a caregiver told the story to another person in the child's presence. That is, again the social configuration required at least two persons, narrator and listener, in addition to the child. The difference is that the child herself was cast as protagonist. We analyzed the complete corpus ($N =$ 66) of naturally occurring stories that mothers told about the child. These stories made up roughly one-quarter of the total corpus of mother stories around the child and occurred at an average rate of 1.7 per hour across the four mothers during the 40 hours of observation. Means per mother were 1.4, 0.67, 2.9, and 1.7 per hour.

Elsewhere we have analyzed several levels of self-relevant meanings entailed in these stories (Miller et al., 1990). At the level of content, for example, narrators conveyed particular images of the child-protagonist in action, images that recurred across stories and across children. The children were portrayed as active, spirited, mischievous; as speaking up or talking back; as "mouthy," feisty, and sharp. The mothers, thus, created child-protagonists who resembled the self-protagonists in their stories of their own experiences.

In addition, stories about the child conveyed messages about the significance and organization of the child's experiences. By consistently telling stories about some experiences rather than others, caregivers conveyed which ones were reportable. By creating a particular rendition of the experience, they showed what the component events were, how the events were related, and what was important about them. In the following example, told in the presence of 23-month-old Amy and her 5-year-old cousin Kris, Amy's mother related to the researcher an event in which Amy made a clever, assertive retort.

Example 7
(Participants: A = Amy; K = Kris; M = Amy's mother, Marlene; R = researcher. Setting: A's home. Video-recorded. A is sitting on her mother's lap.)
M to R:
> Johnny [A's stepfather] told her the other night, he says to her, "Isn't your mother a creep?"
> (A reaches for and grabs stuffed pig, gazes at M.)

A to M: Mar! Mar!
M to R:
> And he kept tellin' her all these things and she says, "Na huh." She says, "You are, Daddy. You're the creep."

> R: (laughs)
> M: That's what she told him. He like to come off that chair.
>   (*A* slides onto sofa next to *M*.)
> *A to M:* Mar [unintelligible]
> *M to A:* Yeah.
> *A to M:* Yeah (shifts gaze downward)
> M: Yeah, he says, "Tell your mother she's a creep." And finally she's just sittin' there takin it and takin it and he said, "Tell her, tell your mother she's a creep." That's when she said, "Nuh uh, Daddy." She said, "You're the creep."
>   (*A* turns attention to *M*'s pocketbook.)

In this example the narrator starts with Johnny's repeated efforts to goad Amy into calling her mother a "creep." Amy responds to this provocation by calling Johnny a "creep." The narrator organizes both the initial account of the event and its recycling around a reported conversational exchange of a particular sort: an insult–return insult sequence. Moreover, she singles out Amy's retort for comment ("That's what she told him"), thereby highlighting it further. She thus structures her narration to establish Amy's quick-thinking assertiveness as the "point" of the story. The event is represented more fully than this, however. In her account the mother links Johnny's insult and the child's retort through Amy's subjective experience of "takin it," that is, of enduring repeated offenses that finally impel her to act. As she describes it, the event ends with Johnny's astonished reaction to Amy's retort, "He like to come off that chair."

Stories of this sort are important because they provide models for interpreting the child's response, connecting it to someone else's prior actions, to the child's own subjective experience, and to its interpersonal consequences. They personalize for the child the culture's interpretive strategies by applying them to the child's own experiences.

Moreover, children are responsive to these stories. We found that by the age of 2½ years children from South Baltimore made relevant verbal contributions to 33% of these stories. They were four times more likely to make relevant verbal contributions to stories in which their mothers portrayed them as protagonists, compared with mothers' stories in which the child did not appear as a protagonist (see Miller et al., 1990). This contrast existed despite the fact that stories involving child protagonists were on average shorter than stories involving other protagonists. The children's greater verbal engagement in stories about themselves seemed to reflect, in part, a different participant structure: The mothers were more likely to tell such stories in a way that included the child as "ratified" participant (Goffman, 1981). Thus, it is probable that both the inherent interest value for the child of a story about herself as well as the higher rate of the mother's invitations to participate contributed to the children's responsiveness to stories in which they were cast as protagonists.

To summarize, we identified in South Baltimore two participant structures – telling stories around the child and telling stories about the child – that meet the requirement of recurrence, that is, both occurred repeatedly in everyday family contexts. These personal storytelling practices are plausibly relevant to self-construction in that they provide the child with a series of enacted interpersonal dramas in which the most important people in her life – the people with whom she most closely identifies – represent themselves and the child herself as particular kinds of actors. By the age of 2½ years the children in these families were already making significant verbal contributions to stories about the self. They contributed much less to stories told around them about other people but, at times, responded relevantly to such stories, retold them, and even appropriated others' stories as their own. In addition, field notes and audio and video recordings from our study of culturally diverse children indicate that telling stories around the child and telling stories about the child occur regularly not only in South Baltimore but in Taipei and in various communities in Chicago (low-income African-American, middle-class African-American, working-class white, and middle-class white in Chicago).

Telling stories with the child

There is a third way in which children were included in personal storytelling in South Baltimore, namely as collaborators or co-narrators of their own experiences.[1] In this participant structure the child was, by definition, a contributor to the story. In a study tracing the very early acquisition of personal storytelling we found that by the time the five children were 2½ years old, co-narrated personal storytelling occurred at an average rate of 2.2 per hour in everyday conversation (Miller & Sperry, 1988a). The narrations reflected variation in linguistic sophistication among the younger children.

Having established that co-narrating personal experience was a recurrent phenomenon for these culturally diverse children, we asked a series of basic questions about the relational self or what Bruner (1990) has recently called the distributed self. There is a curious disjuncture between theory and research on children's self-development. On the one hand, there is the pervasive acceptance by developmental theorists that understandings of self and other develop interdependently; yet, as Dunn (1988) has pointed out, empirical work on early self-development has tended not to examine self in relation to other. Empirical studies of self-development have tended to rely on units of analysis – utterance-level propositions or lexical items – that often preclude an analysis of self in relation to other. Arguing that a discourse unit – in this case co-narrated personal storytelling – is a more appropriate unit of analysis for studying the relational self, we examined the corpus of co-narrations to see what they revealed about self in relation to other.

In the majority of co-narrated stories both overall and for the individual children, the child related personal experiences in which other persons took part. Although both the younger children and the older children created self-protagonists whose experiences were interpersonal, the proportion of interpersonal stories was even higher among the older children than among the younger children. The findings for the co-narrators (mothers, fathers, siblings) were similar. That is, the stories were co-constructed so as to locate the child within a social world. Moreover, the represented social world was primarily a familial one: The majority of actors invoked by child and co-narrators were mothers, fathers, siblings, grandparents, and other family members. Not surprisingly, however, there was a large increase with age in the children's references to peers and others, reflecting the expanding social network and preschool/kindergarten experience of the 5-year-olds.

Further analysis of the specific ways in which self and other were linked in these co-narrations revealed that the same small set of relations accounted for the majority of the data for both age groups. These were "joint activity/experience," in which the self-protagonist was portrayed as simply sharing an activity or experience with another person; "other benefits the self," in which another person liked or benefited the self-protagonist; and "social comparison," in which the self-protagonist was compared with another person in the past event. A fourth category – "self apart from other" – emerged only in the older children. This code was applied when the child explicitly said that he or she was not with another person, did not share an activity or experience with another person, or did some activity "all by myself."[2] This category deserves more study for possible cultural differentiation between the Chinese and American groups (see Markus & Kitayama, 1991).

Finally, there is one additional finding worth noting. We found that the social comparison category was highly specific in its range of application: It was used to define self in relation to other children. Not only did the majority of social comparisons occur when a sibling or peer participated in the co-narration but the focal child was overwhelmingly compared with siblings or peers in the recounted event. A link is thereby established between the event of narration (who participated in the co-narration) and the narrated event (what was talked about).

In sum, these findings suggest that this participant structure occurs not only in families from South Baltimore but in culturally diverse families. These jointly created accounts of the young child's experience define and redefine self in relation to other in the past event while also reflecting the here-and-now social circumstances of the telling.

Implications for socialization and self-construction

This brief review of the ways in which personal storytelling is practiced in the everyday home environments of young children suggests several conclusions and implications for the discourse model of socialization and self-construction presented earlier. We have identified three different but related personal storytelling practices of plausible relevance to self-construction. We have established that all three occur regularly in South Baltimore and in several other culturally different communities. And we have shown that by the age of 2½ years children are participating in these various narrative practices.

In addition, the analysis of co-narrated personal storytelling revealed that the narrated self is a relational self and that there are particular self–other linkages that children and their co-narrators create, some of which probably apply to culturally diverse children and some of which are probably culture-specific. We suspect that a comparable analysis of telling stories around the child and telling stories about the child would further strengthen the claim that selves as represented in narrative are relational selves. Further, we maintain that the relational nature of selves is revealed not only at the level of the narrated event – how the self-protagonist is represented in the past event – but at the level of the event of narration. Narrative practices are social practices: The narrated self is constructed with and responsive to other people. The child's experiences – even his or her subjective experiences – are subject to selection, interpretation, challenge, and elaboration by others (Miller et al., 1990; Snow, 1990). The version of the self-protagonist that gets created (e.g., whether or not he or she is compared to a peer in the past event) depends on particulars of the co-narration (e.g., whether a peer participates in the telling).

Moreover, the distribution of storytelling rights – the fact, for example, that mothers have rights to tell stories about their children's experiences – further reveals the distributed nature of the narrated self (Miller et al., 1990). Personal storytelling is socially expansive: Narrators not only create interpersonal dramas around events purportedly experienced by the self but they create stories of vicarious experience, borrowing, under specifiable conversational conditions, narratable events from persons with whom they are associated. Our corpus of adult stories includes, for example, stories in which the narrator's sister threw a pot of boiling water at her abusive husband, the narrator's young child uttered a clever, assertive, and silencing retort to a teasing adult, and the narrator's co-workers were threatened at gunpoint by the owners of the car that they were trying to repossess. At times, narrators of vicarious experience make explicit their identification with the story protagonist. For example, after recounting how the neighbor down the block beat his wife with a lead pipe, a mother from South Baltimore said, "I'm afraid I'd a had picked up somethin, the nearest thing that was to me and slammed him in the head with it before he'd a gotten me real good." Contrary to Labov and Waletsky (1967), stories of vicarious experience are often as highly evaluated as stories of personal experience, suggesting that it is impossible to draw a sharp distinction between stories of personal experience and stories of vicarious experience.

These insights concerning the relational self, in conjunction with the finding that personal storytelling practices occurred regularly in everyday family contexts, suggest that personal storytelling is an important means by which young children, together with family members, experience and reexperience self in relation to other. They suggest that a comprehensive account of self-development would have to be much more dynamic than has previously been envisioned: It would have to take into account not only the child's moment-by-moment interpersonal encounters but his or her participation in iterative narrations of those encounters (which are themselves embedded in moment-by-moment interpersonal encounters). Once children are able to narrate their experiences (during the third year of life), a qualitative transformation occurs in the self-constructive process, for now practical understanding of self is subject to revision and reconstruction (Stern, 1989). The repeated interaction of original experiences, memory and encoding of experiences, and exchanges of messages about experiences – during a period of rapid socio-cognitive development – is likely to be far more complex than former theories of self-development have posited.

The dynamic nature of self-construction follows not only from the recurrent nature of narrative practices but from their inherent variability. This is most apparent when a narrator spontaneously retells a particular story. Occasionally, we have captured on our audio or video recordings two or more tellings of a single story within the same observation session.

For example, a 2½-year-old child from Daly Park, a working-class white community in Chicago, produced three versions of what happened when he went sledding. In the first version William's contribution was limited to "Sledding! I hold on! (excited) . . . I hold on to sled." In the second version, after he had said, "I go sled. I go on," his mother selected for him the important incident in the story: "Tell Lisa what happened to your face. Who did that?" To this William replied, "I felled on you – . I cut mine." The mother proceeded to elaborate what happened: William and his older brother Eddie went on the sled together, William got smashed by Eddie, William then went down on the sled by himself and had fun.

In the third version William not only structured the telling around the mishap that his mother had highlighted in the second telling but supplied several evaluative details about the mishap and its consequences, details not mentioned by co-narrators in previous versions and not prompted or modeled by co-narrators in the current narration: "I – I didn't hurt my face. [He] did, Eddie – and Eddie said I am fraidy cat. [She] was supposed catch me, um – . . . . I didn't get catched." Note here William's skillful deployment of evaluative devices, including negative constructions, quoted speech, and affect words (see Labov & Waletsky, 1967; Labov, 1972; Miller & Sperry, 1988a for discussion of evaluative devices). Later in the third co-narration the mother added that William had been scared, which he vigorously denied. These several tellings thus show a microgenetic progression toward a more sophisticated and autonomous performance on the part of the child: from a brief contribution to the first telling; to an expression of the point of the story, prompted and modeled by the co-narrating mother, in the second telling; to an independently provided elaboration of the point of the story, detailing the ramifications of the mishap for the self-protagonist and emphatically asserting William's own perspective on the event, in the third telling.

It would be a mistake, however, to see retellings as functioning only or primarily in the service of creating more mature performances. Sometimes children seem to retell stories as a means of gaining relief from or resolution to intrapsychological problems (Miller, Hoogstra, Mintz, Fung, & Williams, in press). By replaying or reenacting for the self some troubling experience from the past, children seem to come to an acceptance of or reintegration of past experience (Bruner & Lucariello, 1989). For example, a 2½-year-old from West Side, a low-income African-American community in Chicago, told three versions of being frightened of a movie. In the first instance, Monique represented a scared self-protagonist who fled from the scene: "I was scared. And I wanted – and wanted – and I wanted to go downstairs. . . . And I was keepin runnin downstairs." In the second telling, the self-protagonist was still scared but found solace in her parents: "I – I keep runnin upstairs, Daddy. And I and I wanted *you*. . . . And I wanted *you* [mother] too." Monique then went to her mother and hugged and kissed her. In the third version, she said: "I was keep runnin upstairs and I was scared of that movie. . . . Then I wanted – then I wanted to go back downstairs. . . . Then I wasn't scared no more." There are two notable innovations in this final version: The self-protagonist is explicitly represented as no longer being scared, and the conjunction *then* is used to connect temporally ordered actions. There is a progression, across the tellings, toward both affective resolution and coherence.

Eventually many of these retold stories will be forgotten, whereas others will find a place in the individual's lasting repertoire of personal stories. Even for the latter, those stories that become an individual's personal canon, no two tellings are ever identical. The circumstances of the telling are always different, the meaning of the narrated event is always getting recalibrated relative to the narrator's vision of the present and the future. For example, one mother from South Baltimore told repeatedly and with bitterness the story of her troubles in school, culminating in her expulsion from the eighth grade. As her daughter approached school age, the mother added a new conclusion to her story: "And that's why I hope she [the daughter] don't have trouble in school." An experience that had occurred eight years before became meaningful in a new way within the context of her worries about her daughter's future.

This brings us to the issue of memory. When approached via personal storytelling, remembering emerges as a process that occurs in the service of something else. Events are not remembered for the sake of remembering but for the sake of creating tellable stories about the self. In South Baltimore, Daly Park, and West Side, where traditions of highly performed oral narrative flourish, speakers do not seem to define personal storytelling as a memory task. They infrequently use *remember* or related terms when telling or introducing stories and they rarely revise their accounts in the interest of accuracy. To do so would destroy the integrity of the story as an artistic performance. In extreme cases, as in the Yucatec ritual described by Hanks (1984), the individual may be unable to remember the relevant material outside the ritual context.

In addition, remembering in the service of personal storytelling is inherently evaluative. A neutral story about the self is virtually inconceivable. Even the earliest protonarratives produced by 2–2½-year-olds in South Baltimore were evaluated accounts (Miller & Sperry, 1988a). The narrating or inhabited self always takes some stance toward the self-protagonist. This raises the question of how autobiographical remembering is organized for children whose family life is permeated by highly performed personal storytelling. Is it organized around narratable events? Is the dramatic heart of the story – the quoted conversational exchange – most likely to be remembered?

And, finally, remembering in the service of personal storytelling is dynamic and reconstructive in the Bartlett (1932) sense. The reconstructive work is, however, socially distributed. Remembered details are selected for their perceived effect on an audience, for their fit or challenge to a co-narrator's contribution. Thus, personal stories are not idle tales, whether the process at issue is self-construction or remembering. Selves, like cultures, are not so much preserved in stories as they are created, reworked, and revised through participation in everyday narrative practices that are embedded in and responsive to shifting interpersonal conditions. Memories of self and other provide a constantly updated resource that narrators exploit in projecting tellable and interpretable selves.

ACKNOWLEDGMENT

Preparation for this essay was supported by a grant from the Spencer Foundation.

NOTES

1 A co-narration was defined as an interactive episode of talk involving two or more child utterances, addressed to an interlocutor, describing a particular past event or class of past events in which the child portrayed himself or herself as a protagonist.
2 Note that "self apart from other" was one way in which self and other were linked within interpersonal stories. In representing herself as apart from or independent of another person, the child mentioned the other, thereby invoking an interpersonal frame of reference. This contrasts with noninterpersonal stories (of which there were few), in which the child reported an experience in which no other person was mentioned.

REFERENCES

Bartlett, F. C. (1932). *Remembering.* Cambridge University Press.
Basso, K. H. (1984). Stalking with stories: Names, places, and moral narratives among the Western Apache. In E. M. Bruner & S. Plattner (Eds.), *Text, play, and story: The construction and reconstruction of self and society* (pp. 19–55). Washington, DC: American Ethnological Society.
Bauman, R. (1984). *Disclaimers of performance.* Paper presented at the annual meeting of the American Anthropological Association, Denver, CO.
Bauman, R. (1986). *Story, performance, and event: Contextual studies of oral narrative.* Cambridge University Press.
Bauman, R., & Briggs, C. L. (1990). Poetics and performance as critical perspectives on language and social life. *Annual Review of Anthropology, 19,* 59–88.
Bruner, J. (1990). *Acts of meaning.* Cambridge, MA: Harvard University Press.
Bruner, J., & Lucariello, J. (1989). Monologue as narrative recreation of the world. In K. Nelson (Ed.), *Narratives from the crib* (pp. 73–97). Cambridge, MA: Harvard University Press.
Dunn, J. (1988). *The beginnings of social understanding.* Cambridge, MA: Harvard University Press.
Gates, H. L., Jr. (1989). Introduction. In L. Gross & M. E. Barnes (Eds.), *Talk that talk: An anthology of African-American story-telling.* New York: Simon & Schuster.

Gergen, K. J. (1986, October). *Understanding, narration and the cultural construction of self.* Paper presented at the Chicago Symposia on Culture and Human Development, Chicago.

Goffman, E. (1974). The frame analysis of talk. In *Frame analysis: An essay on the organization of experience* (pp. 496–559). Cambridge, MA: Harvard University Press.

Goffman, E. (1981). *Forms of talk.* Philadelphia: University of Pennsylvania Press.

Goodwin, M. H. (1982). Instigating: Storytelling as social process. *American Ethnologist, 9,* 799–819.

Gumperz, J. J., & Hymes, D. (1972). *Directions in sociolinguistics: The ethnography of communication.* New York: Holt, Rinehart & Winston.

Hanks, W. (1984). Sanctification, structure, and experience in a Yucatec ritual event. *Journal of American Folklore, 97,* 384.

Heath, S. B. (1983). *Ways with words: Language, life and work in communities and classrooms.* Cambridge University Press.

Herdt, G. H. (1981). *Guardians of the flutes: Idioms of masculinity.* New York: McGraw-Hill.

Hymes, D. (1967). Models of the interaction of language and social setting. *Journal of Social Issues, 23,* 8–28.

Hymes, D. (1975). Breakthrough into performance. In D. Ben-Amos & K. S. Goldstein (Eds.), *Folklore: Performance and communication* (pp. 11–74). The Hague: Mouton.

Kirshenblatt-Gimblett, B. (1975). A parable in context: A social interactional analysis of story-telling performance. In D. Ben-Amos & K. S. Goldstein (Eds.), *Folklore: Performance and communication* (pp. 105–30). The Hague: Mouton.

Labov, W. (1972). *Language in the inner city.* Philadelphia: University of Pennsylvania Press.

Labov, W., & Waletsky, J. (1967). Narrative analysis: Oral versions of personal experience. In J. Helm (Ed.), *Essays in the verbal and visual arts* (pp. 12–44). Seattle: University of Washington Press.

Malinowski, B. (1984). The role of myth in life. In A. Dundes (Ed.), *Sacred narrative* (pp. 193–206). Berkeley: University of California Press. (Original work published 1926)

Markus, H., & Kitayama, S. (1991). Culture and the self: Implications for cognition, emotion, and motivation. *Psychological Review, 98,* 224–253.

Michaels, S. (1991). The dismantling of narrative. In A. McCabe & C. Peterson (Eds.), *New directions in developing narrative structure* (pp. 303–351). Norwood, NJ: Ablex.

Miller, P. J. (1982). *Amy, Wendy, and Beth: Learning language in South Baltimore.* Austin: University of Texas Press.

Miller, P. J. (1986). Teasing as language socialization and verbal play in a white, working-class community. In B. B. Schieffelin & E. Ochs (Eds.), *Language socialization across cultures* (pp. 199–212). Cambridge University Press.

Miller, P. J. (1989). *Socialization through narrative.* Paper presented at the meeting of the Society for Psychological Anthropology, San Diego, CA.

Miller, P. J., Fung, H., & Mintz, J. (1991, October). *Creating children's selves in relational contexts: A comparison of American and Chinese narrative practices.* Paper presented at the biennial meeting of the Society for Psychological Anthropology, Chicago.

Miller, P. J., & Hoogstra, L. (in press). Language as tool in the socialization and apprehension of cultural meanings. In T. Schwartz, G. White, & C. Lutz (Eds.), *New directions in psychological anthropology.* Cambridge University Press.

Miller, P. J., Hoogstra, L., Mintz, J., Fung, H., & Williams, K. (in press). Troubles in the garden and how they get resolved: The history of a story in one child's life. In C. A. Nelson (Ed.), *The Minnesota Symposia on Child Psychology* (Vol. 26). Minneapolis: University of Minnesota Press.

Miller, P. J., Mintz, J., Hoogstra, L., Fung, H., & Potts, R. (1992). The narrated self: Young children's construction of self in relation to others in conversational stories of personal experience. *Merill-Palmer Quarterly, 38,* 45–67.

Miller, P. J., & Moore, B. (1989). Narrative conjunctions of caregiver and child: A comparative perspective on socialization through stories. *Ethos, 17,* 43–64.

Miller, P. J., Potts, R., Fung, H., Hoogstra, L., & Mintz, J. (1990). Narrative practices and the social construction of self in childhood. *American Ethnologist 17,* 292–311.

Miller, P. J., & Sperry, L. (1987). The socialization of anger and aggression. *Merrill-Palmer Quarterly, 33,* 1–31.

Miller, P. J., & Sperry, L. (1988a). Early talk about the past: The origins of conversational stories of personal experience. *Journal of Child Language, 15,* 293–315.

Miller, P. J., & Sperry, L. (1988b). The socialization and acquisition of emotional meanings, with special reference to language: A reply to Saarni. *Merrill-Palmer Quarterly, 34,* 217–222.

Much, N., & Shweder, A. (1978) Speaking of rules: The analysis of culture in the breach. In W. Damon (Ed.), *Moral development: New directions for child development* (pp. 19–39). San Francisco: Jossey-Bass.

Nye, C. H. (1988). *Psychoanalytic narratives: The formulation of meaning.* Unpublished doctoral dissertation, Department of Behavioral Sciences, University of Chicago.

Ochs, E. (1988). *Culture and language development: Language acquisition and language socialization in a Samoan village.* Cambridge University Press.

Ochs, E., & Schieffelin, B. B. (1984). Language acquisition and socialization: Three developmental stories and their implications. In R. A. Shweder & R. A. LeVine (Eds.), *Culture theory: Essays on mind, self, and emotion* (pp. 276–320). Cambridge University Press.

Polanyi, L. (1985). *Telling the American story.* Norwood, NJ: Ablex.

Ricoeur, P. (1984). *Time and narrative* (Vol. 1) (K. McLaughlin & D. Pellauer, Trans.). Chicago: University of Chicago Press.

Robinson, J. A. (1981). Personal narratives reconsidered. *Journal of American Folklore, 94,* 58–85.

Rogoff, B. (in press). The joint socialization of development by young children and adults. In M. Lewis & S. Feinman (Eds.), *Social influences and behavior.* New York: Plenum.

Rosaldo, R. (1986). Ilongot hunting as story and experience. In V. Turner & E. Bruner (Eds.), *The anthropology of experience* (pp. 97–138). Champaign: University of Illinois Press.

Sacks, H. (1984). Notes on methodology. In J. M. Atkinson and J. Heritage (Eds.), *Structures of social action* (pp. 21–27). Cambridge University Press. (Original work published 1965–1971)

Sapir, E. (1949). Language. In D. G. Mandelbaum (Ed.), *Selected writings of Edward Sapir in language, culture, and personality* (pp. 7–32). Berkeley: University of California Press. (Original work published 1933)

Schieffelin, B. B. (1990). *The give and take of everyday life: Language socialization of Kaluli children.* Cambridge University Press.
Schieffelin, B. B., & Ochs, E. (1986). Language socialization. *Annual Review of Anthropology, 15,* 163–246.
Scollon, R., & Scollon, S. B. K. (1981). *Narrative, literacy and face in interethnic communication.* Norwood, NJ: Ablex.
Scribner, S., & Cole, M. (1981). *The psychology of literacy.* Cambridge, MA: Harvard University Press.
Shweder, R. A., & Much, N. C. (1987) Determination of meaning: Discourse and moral socialization. In W. Kurtines & J. Gewirtz (Eds.), *Moral development through social interaction* (pp. 197–244). New York: Wiley.
Snow, C. E. (1990). Building memories: The ontogeny of autobiography. In D. Cicchetti and M. Beeghly (Eds.), *The self in transition: Infancy to childhood* (pp. 213–242). Chicago: University of Chicago Press.
Stern, D. N. (1989). Crib monologues from a psychoanalytic perspective. In K. Nelson (Ed.), *Narratives from the crib* (pp. 309–319). Cambridge, MA: Harvard University Press.
Vygotsky, L. (1978). *Mind in society.* Cambridge, MA: Harvard University Press.
Vygotsky, L. (1987). *Thinking and speech* (N. Minick, Trans.). New York: Plenum. (Original work published 1934)
Watson, K. A. (1973). A rhetorical and sociolinguistic model for the analysis of narrative. *American Anthropologist, 75,* 243–264.
Watson-Gegeo, K. A., & Gegeo, D. W. (1986). Calling-out and repeating routines in Kwara'ae children's language socialization. In B. B. Schieffelin & E. Ochs (Eds.), *Language socialization across cultures* (pp. 17–59). Cambridge University Press.
Wentworth, W. M. (1980). *Context and understanding.* New York: Elsevier.
Wertsch, J. V. (1985). *Vygotsky and the social formation of mind.* Cambridge, MA: Harvard University Press.

9

Comments on children's
self-narratives

REBECCA A. EDER

This discussion is based on the assumption that a consideration of the emotional basis of self-understanding will lead to a better appreciation of the role of personal narratives in self-construction. Recently, there has been a great deal of attention paid to the role of emotionality in personality and self-concept development. For example, Watson and Clark (in press) have delineated the emotional core of extroversion in adults. Emde (1983) and Stern (1985) have suggested that early affective experiences form a core around which children organize their representations of themselves and their world. Eder and Mangelsdorf (in press) suggest that this underlying emotionality is a complex construct that is derived from the interaction between infant temperament, parental personality, and the infant–caregiver attachment relationship.

Emotionality is distinct from emotion and affect in several ways. First, it describes nonspecific affects (e.g., the presence or absence of positive affects), as opposed to the specific affects (e.g., anger, fear, sadness) that are usually called "emotion." Second, emotionality is relatively long-term and is thus distinct from affect, which is often associated with short-term mood fluctuations. Third, the terms *emotion* and *affect* usually describe states, whereas emotionality is viewed as a trait.

Emotionality is often conceived of as a somewhat primitive feeling of self that can exist prior to the ability to assign linguistic labels to one's feelings (e.g., Tellegen, 1985; Watson & Clark, in press). In fact, Stern (1985) has suggested that the ability to describe these early feelings of self may radically alter the nature of self-knowledge. One function of the self-concept is to explain (and perhaps rationalize) one's emotionality. Hence, one's construction of personally significant events is related to – but not isomorphic with – one's emotional experience of the event. For example, a child who describes him- or herself as "cautious," might actually *feel* fearful. Thus, the emotional basis of the self-concept is directly experienced but seldom directly stated (Eder & Mangelsdorf, in press; Stern, 1985).

Emotionality and young children's self-concepts

Given the hypothesized early origins of emotionality, it is not surprising that children and adults reveal certain organizing constructs in common (e.g., issues of self-acceptance are relevant to everyone) but on which they may differ (e.g., some people may feel more accepted than others). Recent research has shown that even 3-year-olds possess such psychological conceptions of themselves. For example, I developed a new method of testing 3- to 8-year-old children's self-concepts in which children were presented, in a random order, with pairs of statements representing the high and low endpoints of 10 common psychological dimensions (e.g., achievement, aggression, well-being). It was assumed that if children selected these statements in a nonrandom (i.e., strategic) manner, they must be referring to an underlying psychological concept. In these tests even 3-year-olds demonstrated psychological self-understanding. Moreover, substantial individual differences were found and these were relatively stable over a one-month retest (Eder, 1990).

Children's responses on my measure appeared to be organized based on the emotionality common to particular items. Children who stated, for example, that they climbed high things and went down slides head-first were also more likely to state that they hit people, were naughty, and were upset compared with children who stated that they did not engage in these behaviors. Taken together, these items describe the extent to which children feel in control in the face of actual or anticipated distress. Elsewhere, I have suggested that these self-reports do not necessarily reflect children's memories of actual behaviors, but rather are revealing of their emotional experience of past events (Eder & Mangelsdorf, in press).

The role of personal narratives in the development of young children's self-concepts

Recently, developmentalists have begun to explore the role of narrative practices in early self-concept development. For example, Fivush has highlighted the role of parent–child conversations about the past in the development of young children's self-conceptions (Fivush, chap. 7 of this volume). Miller and her colleagues have described the part that personal storytelling plays in self-construction in early childhood (Miller, chap. 8 of this volume; Miller, Potts, Fung, Hoogstra, Mintz, 1990). These researchers have stressed the affinity between the narrative and the self-concept, in that both are based on memories for personally significant events, both are causally and temporally ordered, and both are evaluative (i.e., emotional).

An examination of the role of narrative practices in the emergence of the self-concept is a natural extension of earlier work in which investigators suggested that parental storytelling and parent–child conversations play a major role in the socialization of conversational style, in talk about emotion, and in sex-role development. For example, parental narratives have been reported to play an important role in the socialization of anger and aggression (Miller & Sperry, 1987). Furthermore, such a direction is consistent with the notion that a person's self-concept is best viewed as a story with oneself as the central character (e.g., Gergen, 1977; McAdams, 1988; Thorne, 1988).

Empirical research has yet to address the relation between the content of personal narratives and the content of children's self-conceptions. In particular, how can we predict the emotional content of children's self-concepts from listening to parents' personal storytelling? How is coherence across different narratives achieved? How do children get from hearing particular narratives to forming general representations of their autobiographical memories (e.g., "I usually play with my friends in school") and to becoming aware of their personality traits and characteristics (e.g., "I am an affiliative person")?

I explore these issues in the remainder of this discussion by focusing on the possible functions of adults' and children's personal storytelling for the development of self-understanding. I examine three types of personal narratives: (1) stories told around children, (2) stories told about children, and (3) stories told by children. To anticipate, I will propose that even when the *features* (i.e., structure) of different types of narratives are similar, the *function* of these narratives for young children's emergent self-concept may diverge based on the underlying emotionality. I highlight three functions of personal storytelling: self-construction, self-regulation, and self-presentation.

Stories told around children. How do the stories that other people tell when children are present impact on children's emotionality? Miller (chap. 8 of this volume) suggests that when children overhear personal narratives, they are gaining access to previously inaccessible experiences and information. One type of previously inaccessible information that is especially relevant to emotionality is other people's view of the world. For example, mothers from South Baltimore in Miller's sample portray their world – probably quite accurately – as a dangerous place. Learning how important others view the world must have a substantial impact on children's own perception of and feeling about their world. Hence, personal narratives can play an important role in the development of children's feelings about the world and their place in it. In this way, personal narratives told in the presence of children can contribute to individual differences in emotionality, regardless of whether the narrative is told about the child or involves other people.

Stories told about children. Stories told about a child in his or her presence often reflect the narrator's attitude toward the child and/or his or her actions. For example, Miller (chap. 8 of this volume) reports a story told by a mother in South Baltimore in which the mother's boyfriend tries to provoke Amy, a 23-month-old girl, into calling her mother a creep. Instead, the child tells the boyfriend, "You're the creep." The mother proudly states, "That's what she told him." Through this story, the mother conveys her attitude that her child is bold, feisty, and spirited. Miller suggests that the mother's attitude reflects the value that is placed on self-assertion and self-defense in this community.

This story also illustrates several points that are relevant to individual differences in emotionality. First, stories told about children are presumably prompted (or constrained) by the child's behaviors. That is, the child's own actions, in part, triggered her mother's story. It is likely that Amy is an energetic and rambunctious girl and that this story would not be told (in the same way) about a child who is sluggish. Hence stories told about the child are influenced by individual differences in their behavioral dispositions.

Second, these stories reflect individual differences in the *teller's* feelings and attitudes. Whereas this mother values assertiveness in her daughter, a different mother might tell a story in which the same behavior is depicted as disrespectful and ill-mannered. Hence, the narrator's character depiction reflects individual differences in both the child's behavior *and* the teller's attitudes. Put another way, these stories reflect preexisting individual differences in the child's and the adult's emotionality.

Third, the content of personal narratives is constrained by cultural roles (e.g., Miller et al., 1990). For example, Fivush (chap. 7 of this volume) has indicated that parents give different emotion labels to similar behaviors in boys and girls and differentially accept, explain, reconfirm, and resolve emotions recalled by boys versus girls. She speculates that this may lead to gender differences in emotional experience and self-concept.

Finally, such narratives must be influenced by the child's own self-concept. For example, Fivush (1990, Example 1) reports a conversation between a mother and son in which the mother asks, "Does it make you sad when mommy and daddy tell you you can't do something?" and the child answers, "No, you make me mad." Hence, children do not simply have their attitudes toward themselves handed down by their parents; they negotiate with their parents to arrive at a shared account of who they are (see also Dunn, 1988).

In sum, it is likely that the stories that others tell around children or about children in their presence contribute to their emotionality by providing replayings of particular emotional experiences. Children who consistently hear stories about danger, even when only perceived by others, may begin to feel that their world is a dangerous place. When children hear evaluative stories about their own actions, they may begin to experience and reexperience themselves as "worthy," "unworthy," "feisty," "wimpy," and so on. In addition, several factors (e.g., behavioral dispositions, gender roles) prompt or constrain the types of stories that are told and their subsequent impact on the content of children's self-understanding.

How do personal narratives contribute to children's representations of personally significant events (i.e., their *extended self*) and to their beliefs about themselves (i.e., their *conceptual self*)? Malatesta and Wilson (1988) contend that the on-line response of parents to an infant's state (e.g., "You're feeling cranky today, aren't you," p. 94) is a central factor in the emergence of self-awareness. Whereas this explanation accounts for children's awareness of their basic emotional states, it cannot elucidate how children develop a sense of continuity in their emotional experience across time. Further, it is difficult to imagine how an appreciation of one's nonspecific emotions (e.g., badness, worthiness) can emerge from parents' contingent responses to basic emotional states (e.g., anger, fear).

Personal narratives told about children must contribute to the emergence of self-understanding by providing characterizations of the child that go beyond the basic emotional states to depictions of complex actions and nonspecific affects. In addition, personal narratives are not on-line characterizations of the current event, but rather are, by definition, removed from the current context. In being thus "disentangled from the current situation," personal narratives are informative of autobiographical memory (Neisser, 1988, p. 47). In sum, personal narratives told by others in the presence of children play a key role in the emergence of individual differences in emotionality and in how emotional experience is represented in their *extended* and *conceptual selves*.

Children's own personal storytelling. Investigators have noted the similarities in the structure of young children's and adults' personal narratives (e.g., Peterson & McCabe, 1991). Investigators have also suggested that children's own personal storytelling serves a similar function to adults' narratives about children by being implicated in self-construction. For example, Wolf (1990) suggests that the different roles that children take during play is informative of children's understanding of the multiplicity of the self.

The idea that children's own personal narratives play a pivotal role in self-construction seems problematic if we consider the function of children's personal storytelling. Children's personal storytelling serves two primary functions. First, it is involved in the self-regulation of affect (Barclay, chap. 4 of this volume; Miller, chap. 8 of this volume). For example, Miller describes how children replay and change stories to resolve intrapsychic conflict. Second, children's stories about themselves reveal what the child chooses to disclose about his or her self and as such are informative of self-presentation (Goffman, 1959). Given that my work has focused on self-presentational issues, I underscore the self-presentational function of children's personal narratives.

Personal storytelling involves the deliberate control of expressive behaviors. It has an analogue in nonverbal expressive behaviors in which display rules of emotional expression are deliberately used for self-presentational purposes. For example, children who wish to appear as grateful – even when receiving an undesirable gift – mask their disappointment by smiling. Like personal storytelling, display rules are thought to be learned in social interaction and are considered a result of socialization (for a review see Cole, 1985). The display rules used (e.g., masking vs. exaggerating negative emotions) have been found to differ among individuals, males and females, age groups, contexts, and cultures (e.g., DePaulo, 1991). Hence we might expect that the amount and type of personal storytelling in which children engage would also vary as a function of these variables.

Developmental differences. DePaulo (1991) contends that in order to care about conveying certain impressions, one's self-system must be sufficiently sophisticated to desire certain identities and to actively try to claim these identities during social interactions. Hence, she believes that the emergence of self-presentation occurs at a later time than self-concept development. If this is the case, then children's personal storytelling is the *result* of self-construction rather than a mechanism for self-construction.

The relation between the development of one's self-concept and one's self-presentational goals raises some interesting questions for studying children's personal storytelling. Many researchers have demonstrated substantial developmental changes in children's self-concept, especially between 3 and 8 years of age and during adolescence (e.g., Damon & Hart, 1982; Eder, 1989). Of interest is whether the content of children's personal narratives changes to reflect these developmental changes. For example, do children tell more interpersonal stories at one point in time and more intrapersonal stories at other developmental periods as a function of their self-concerns?

Individual differences. Individuals who have a high concern about positive self-presentation presumably would engage in more personal storytelling than children who are less concerned with positive self-presentation. In support of this idea, individual differences in children's ability to deliberately control their nonverbal emotional expressions are associated with teachers' ratings of children's concern about positive self-presentation. That is, children who are rated by their teachers as being highly concerned about positive self-presentation are more nonverbally expressive in social situations (e.g., when interacting with an experimenter in the lab) and are better at posing emotional expressions than children who are rated as less concerned about positive self-presentation (Eder, Edwards, & Jones, 1992).

What is the relation between children's emotionality and their self-presentation? Kim Harkins and I have recently found that 5-year-olds who are concerned with positive self-presentation (rated by their teachers) score lower in *self-acceptance via affiliation* on my self-report measure than children less concerned about self-presentation. These results indicate that children's emotionality results in a concern with self-presentation that affects their deliberate control of expressive behaviors. Children who feel anxious in social settings are more concerned with self-presentation and more expressive in social situations. It is interesting to speculate whether these children would also be more likely to engage in personal storytelling in social situations.

What is the relation between children's self-concept and the content of their personal narratives? That is, can the emotional content of children's personal stories be predicted from measures of their self-concept? Knowing the emotionality inherent in one's self-concept should enable us to make predictions about the types of stories that children relate about themselves. In support of this idea, Norah Feeny and I have recently found that 3- to 8-year-old children who score high on well-being on my measure provide more spontaneous stories during the interview about empathy, affiliation, and the absence of negative feelings, and fewer stories involving negative consequences, than children who score low on well-being. Those who agreed with high-stress reaction items produced personal narratives involving negative emotions and adverse consequences. Children who score high on achievement provide more narratives about competition; and those who score high on affiliation are more likely to mention interpersonal contexts than low scorers.

Cross-cultural differences. Given that the amount and type of concern about self-presentation vary from one culture to another, many researchers have reported cross-cultural differences in the control of nonverbal expressive behaviors for the purpose of self-presentation (for a review see DePaulo, 1991). Similarly, the content of adults' personal storytelling around children differs across different cultures as a function of the culture's or subculture's values (e.g., Miller et al., 1990). If children's personal stories reflect their self-presentational goals, then we would anticipate substantial cross-cultural diversity in the frequency and content of personal narratives.

Gender differences. Researchers have also consistently reported gender differences in the type of display rules used by males and females. These differences are thought to be due to different self-presentational goals resulting from sex-role socialization. For example, by school age, boys tend to inhibit affect expression to a greater extent than girls, perhaps to convey the impression that they are not emotional (e.g., Cole, 1985). Current research suggests that the amount and type of personal storytelling would show a similar pattern of results. Investigators find that 2-year-old girls tend to use more emotion terms than boys in their conversations (Dunn et al., 1987); parents of girls are more likely to show an elaborative narrative style and these girls subsequently recall more information about past events than boys (Fivush, this volume).

Familial differences. Families play a central role in the socialization of nonverbal expressiveness. For example, Halberstadt (1991) finds substantial congruence within families and differences among families in the degree and type of nonverbal expressiveness. Hence, we might expect to see a similar pattern in children's and their parents' personal storytelling. Some support for this comes from work demonstrating that parental conversational style is predictive of children's narrative style (e.g., Dunn et al., 1991; Fivush, 1991). Of interest is whether such differences can be predicted from knowing the level of a family's concern with positive self-presentation.

Context effects. If personal storytelling serves a self-presentational function, then we would expect that it should be more likely to occur in those contexts in which self-presentation is especially warranted (e.g., when meeting new people). We might anticipate, for example, that children employ more personal storytelling at the beginning rather than the end of the school year. In addition, the content of such storytelling should change as children become more familiar with each other.

Conclusion

Adult narratives involving children are thought to be frequent, pervasive, and thus a major socialization mechanism across different cultures (e.g., Fivush, chap. 7 of this volume; Miller, chap. 8 this volume). In contrast, the frequency and type of children's personal narratives will likely vary as a function of individual and group differences in self-presentational goals. Further, researchers have reported a substantial degree of congruence between parents' stories and their values (e.g., parents who value self-assertiveness tell positive stories with feisty protagonists), whereas we expect a certain degree of discontinuity between children's self-conceptions and their personal narratives due to self-presentational goals. Socially undesirable aspects of one's self-concept, for example, may be omitted from one's self-narratives. Hence, despite the fact that many of the *features* of children's and adults' narratives are similar, the *functions* of these narratives in regard to self-construction differ substantially based on the underlying emotionality.

In sum, a consideration of the emotional basis of self-understanding will result in the most complete account of differences among individual self-concepts as well as coherence within a given child's self-concept. Thus, apprehending the emotional basis of the emergent self-concept will also enable investigators to uncover the relation between personal narrative practices and the development of the self-concept in young children. In this volume, Fivush and Miller have provided a compelling case for the need for developmentalists to examine this relation empirically.

ACKNOWLEDGMENTS

This essay was written when the author was a visiting faculty member at the Department of Human Development, Bryn Mawr College, Bryn Mawr, Pennsylvania. I would like to thank Norah Feeny, Kim Harkins, Joan Manhardt, and Mary Rourke, whose thoughtful perspectives contributed a great deal. Thanks also to Lila Braine for her helpful comments on an earlier draft.

REFERENCES

Barclay, C. R. (1994). Composing protoselves through improvisation. Chapter 4 of this volume.

Cole, P. M. (1985). Display rules and the socialization of affective displays. In G. Zivin (Ed.), *The development of expressive behavior* (pp. 269–290). New York: Academic Press.

Damon, W., & Hart, D. (1982). The development of self-understanding from infancy through adolescence. *Child Development, 53*, 841–864.

DePaulo, B. M. (1991). Non-verbal behavior and self-presentation: A developmental perspective. In R. S. Feldman & B. Rime (Eds.), *Fundamentals of nonverbal behavior* (pp. 351–400). Cambridge University Press.

Dunn, J. (1988). *The beginnings of social understanding.* Cambridge, MA: Harvard University Press.

Dunn, J., Bretherton, I., & Munn, P. (1987). Conversations about feeling states between mothers and their young children. *Developmental Psychology, 23,* 132–139.

Dunn, J., Brown, J., Slomkowski, C., Telsa, C., & Youngblade, L. (1991). Young children's understanding of other people's feelings and beliefs: Individual differences and their antecedents. *Child Development, 62,* 1352–1366.

Eder, R. A. (1989). The emergent personologist; The structure and content of 3 ½-, 5 ½-, and 7 ½-year-olds' concepts of themselves and other persons. *Child Development, 60,* 1218–1228.

Eder, R. A. (1990). Uncovering children's psychological selves: Individual and developmental differences. *Child Development, 61,* 849–863.

Eder, R. A., Edwards, L., & Jones, M. (1992). *Preschool and college students' self-presentational goals and abilities: Individual and developmental differences in display rules.* Manuscript submitted for publication.

Eder, R. A., & Mangelsdorf, S. C. (in press). The emotional basis of early personality development: Implications for the emergent self-concept. In S. Briggs, R. Hogan, & W. Jones (Eds.), *Handbook of personality psychology.* Orlando, FL: Academic Press.

Emde, R. N. (1983). The prerepresentational self and its affective core. *Psychoanalytic Study of the Child, 38,* 165–192.

Fivush, R. (1990, August). *Self, gender, and emotion in parent–child conversations about the past.* Paper presented at the annual meetings of the American Psychological Association, Boston, MA.

Fivush, R. (1991). The social construction of personal narratives. *Merrill-Palmer Quarterly, 37,* 59–82.

Fivush, R. (1994). Constructing narrative, emotion, and self in parent–child conversations about the past. Chapter 7 of this volume.

Gergen, K. J. (1977). The social construction of self-knowledge. In T. Mischel (Ed.), *The self: Psychological and philosophical issues* (pp. 139–169). Oxford: Basil Blackwell.

Goffman, E. (1959). *The presentation of self in everyday life.* New York: Doubleday.

Halberstadt, A. G. (1991). Family socialization of emotional expression and nonverbal communication styles and skills. *Journal of Personality and Social Psychology, 51,* 827–836.

Malatesta, C. Z., & Wilson, A. (1988). Emotion cognition interaction in personality development: A discrete emotions functionalist analysis. *British Journal of Social Psychology, 27,* 91–112.

McAdams, D. P. (1988). The development of a narrative identity. In D. M. Buss & N. Cantor (Eds.), *Personality psychology: Recent trends and emerging directions* (pp. 160–174). New York: Springer-Verlag.

Miller, P. J. (1994). Narrative practices: Their role in socialization and self-construction. Chapter 8 of this volume.

Miller, P. J., Mintz, J., Hoogstra, L., Fung, H., & Potts, R. (in press). The narrated self: Young children's construction of self in relation to others in conversational stories of personal experience. *Merrill-Palmer Quarterly.*

Miller, P. J., Potts, R., Fung, H., Hoogstra, L., & Mintz, J. (1990). Narrative practices and the social construction of self in childhood. *American Ethologist, 17,* 292–311.

Miller, P. J., & Sperry, L. L. (1987). The socialization of anger and aggression. *Merrill-Palmer Quarterly, 33,* 1–31.

Neisser, U. (1988). Five kinds of self-knowledge. *Philosophical Psychology, 1,* 35–59.

Peterson, C., & McCabe, A. (1991) Linking children's connective use and narrative macrostructure. In A. McCabe & C. Peterson (Eds.), *Developing narrative structure* (pp. 217–253). Hillsdale, NJ: Erlbaum.

Stern, D. N. (1985). *The interpersonal world of the infant: A view from psychoanalysis and developmental psychology.* New York: Basic.

Tellegen, A. (1985). Structures of mood and personality and their relevance to assessing anxiety with an emphasis on self-report. In A. H. Tuma & J. D. Maser (Eds.), *Anxiety and the anxiety disorders* (pp. 681–706). Hillsdale, NJ: Erlbaum.

Thorne, A. (1988). Conditional patterns, transference, and the coherence of personality across time. In D. M. Buss & N. Cantor (Eds.), *Personality psychology: Recent trends and emerging directions* (pp. 149–159). New York: Springer-Verlag.

Watson, D., & Clark, L. A. (in press). Extraversion and its positive emotional core. In S. Briggs, R. Hogan, & W. Jones (Eds.), *Handbook of personality psychology.* Orlando, FL: Academic Press.

Wolf, D. P. (1990). Being of several minds: Voices and versions of the self in early childhood. In D. Cicchetti & M. Beeghly (Eds.), *The self in transition: Infancy to childhood* (pp. 183–211). Chicago: University of Chicago Press.

10

Is memory self-serving?

WILLEM A. WAGENAAR

In the preparation of this volume the question was put to me whether forgetting in autobiographical memory is of a self-serving nature; whether the forgetting and remembering of events from one's own life serve the selfish goal of preserving a positive self-image. Suggestions of that kind were made by Greenwald (1980) and of course before by a large number of clinical psychologists. Ross (1989) contested this view, arguing that what looks like a preservation of self-esteem may in reality be only a preservation of consistency. But even that would be an instance of selfish forgetting. Is there any empirical evidence that autobiographical memories are tainted by such phenomena?

While reflecting upon this question, it occurred to me that the relationship between autobiographical memory and the self can be rather complex. Autobiographical memory is a loose term, ill founded in psychological theory. It refers to a type of experiment in which questions about one's personal life are asked; it definitely does not refer to a specific sort of memory store or mechanism. The self or selves, on the other hand, refer to highly abstract concepts, not to a specific type of experiment. Although it is true that the existence and maintenance of these concepts rely on memory, it is not obvious that the memory of concepts has anything to do with autobiographical memory. It is possible that there is no relationship between autobiographical memory and the remembered self, one being defined by an experimental method, the other being a rather broad and abstract concept. Before we can further investigate the issue of selfish remembering we must theorize a little about the possible role that personal experiences play in the updating of concepts, and how this may affect memory.

The five selves, if we follow the distinction made by Neisser in 1988, are abstract concepts, not unlike such notions as "food," or "friendly animals." What constitutes edible food, and which animals can be considered to be friendly, need to be updated on the basis of personal experiences; but the notions are not personal experiences themselves. In the same manner the selves are supposed to develop on the basis of personal experience. Sometimes this experience is largely the same for all people, as in the case of the ecological self. Sometimes it is vastly different, as in the case of the conceptual self. We must assume that people with different life experiences will develop different conceptual selves through a process of *updating*. This view is supported by Markus and Nurius (1986), who said that "self-knowledge . . . is the most vulnerable and responsive to change in the environment" (p. 956). The role of autobiographical memory is probably most pronounced when we consider the conceptual self, and not the other four selves, such as the ecological and interpersonal selves. If there is any effect of selfish updating and selfish forgetting, the process of updating the conceptual self is the most likely candidate.

The process of concept updating on the basis of experience and the fate of memories after the updating have been little studied as such. For ecological reasons one should postulate two widely differing mechanisms, which I will call *slow* and *fast updating*. In the slow updating process single experiences have little effect. The concepts are more or less stationary: Oranges are orange, and Georgia is a Southern state. Concepts that are changed through slow updating should have been tested thoroughly before they were stored, because if they are wrong, it will take a long time to correct them. When new conditions render the old concepts useless, there is a long and painful period in which the old concepts exert their detrimental influence. Many problems with new machines or new work procedures stem from the fact that the old ways are changed by means of slow updating processes. A nice recent example is the sudden creation of a united Germany: People refer quite often to "East Germany . . . uh . . . I mean . . . the new states." East Germany is not a concept that is changed from one day to the next. In the fast updating process immediate updating is possible, but it is used for such fleeting information as where my car is parked today.

The advantage of having two different updating processes is obvious. When I have learned that lions are dangerous animals, an encounter with one friendly lion (as in Alphonse Daudet's *Tartarin de Tarascon*) should not remove my basic distrust of lions. The danger of lions should be updated according to the slow process. When I meet a lion around the corner of our street, which is usually a perfectly safe place, the safety of that place should be updated immediately. Safety is therefore updated according to the fast process. Adapting the concept of danger immediately on the basis of new information is unwise; likewise is the failure to update the sense of safety on the basis of danger encountered only once.

Memory plays a dual role in these updating processes. The newly updated concept *must* be stored in memory. And the experiences that caused the updating *may* be stored in memory. The relationship between these dual roles is different for the slow and fast processes. In the fast process one may suppose that the updated concept is identical to the remembered event; that the notion of the safety of the street around the corner is nothing else but the immediate recall of the lion I saw there. Thus the fast updating process might create the sort of phenomena described by Tulving as "episodic memory." Fast updating removes any discrepancy between the new experience and what was stored before. The situation is different for the slow updating process. When the concept is marginally adapted on the basis of incoming information there will generally remain a discrepancy between the concept and the new information. Thus, even if the adapted concept is remembered perfectly, it is still problematic what happens to the discrepant event. Is it forgotten once it has played its role? If it is stored in memory, how can we prevent it from affecting the concept again, every time it is rehearsed? The disastrous result may be that after having remembered Tartarin's friendly lion 10 times, the effect is the same as meeting with 10 different friendly lions.

It seems that there are in principle three solutions to this problem. One is that the memory of the events that gave rise to the updating is *suppressed*. The second solution is that the discrepant memory is stored together with the rule but tagged as an exception, signaling that it was already used for adaptation of the corresponding concept. Unlike confirming events, the exception is always recalled together with the rule, because rules can only be applied safely when the exceptions are remembered. I will call this procedure *storing the exception*. The obvious effect of storing the exception rather than the cases that confirm the rule is that exceptions are more accessible than ordinary cases. Thus the effect of exception tagging will be that the discrepant events appear to be remembered better. The third solution is that not only is the concept (slightly) adapted, but also the memory of the event is made to match the concept. Festinger's notion of resolving cognitive dissonance would describe such a process. I call this third solution *concept-driven adaptation*. Suppression will remove the friendly lion from memory; storing the exception makes it likely that the one exceptional friendly lion is remembered together with the general rule saying that lions are dangerous; concept-driven adaptation will transform the friendly lion into a rather dangerous animal. Thus the slow updating process may lead to three different effects on the recall of discrepant events: increased forgetting, enhanced recall, and concept-driven adaptation.

The suggestion that maintenance of the conceptual self could promote selfish forgetting seems to be based on the expectation that the conceptual self is updated according to the slow process. Events that promote adaptation will have small effects, and will therefore remain in conflict with the conceptual self. The memory of these events will be suppressed, tagged as an exception, or transformed to match the concept.

The study of autobiographical memory provides a means of detecting the traces of the slow updating processes. Assuming that the conceptual self paints a picture of oneself that is somewhere between an utter villain and a saint, the events that would give rise to adaptations are those that are more villainous than one would expect of oneself, or more sainted. The question is whether memory of such extremely bad or good behavior is suppressed, enhanced, or distorted. However, the obvious problem is that one needs a number of controls. It is quite possible that one's good behaviors are classified as pleasant memories, and remembered better along with all other pleasant memories. In that case the enhanced recall would not signify the operation of a specific updating of the conceptual self. Hence we must compare two types of events of the same degree of pleasantness or unpleasantness. In the first type our role was either very good or very bad; in the second type we played only a neutral role. Later on I will give some examples. This then describes the design of the experiment that will be reported: Events in the life of one subject are recorded, which were experienced as very unpleasant or very pleasant. There are events in which the subject played a very good or very bad role, and events in which others or nobody played such a role. After variable time intervals recall of these events is measured. The question is, What happened to the recall of experimental items, as compared to the control items? Was it suppressed, enhanced, or distorted?

The material used in this study comes from an experiment in which I was my own subject. Parts of this material were published in Wagenaar (1986, 1988). The method was first used by Marigold Linton (1975, 1978) in her classic studies on autobiographical memory. In principle the method consists of recording events from one's own life. At the time of recording a number of judgments are made and recorded; in my study these judgments were related to the saliency of the recorded event, the emotional involvement, the pleasantness, and the likelihood of later recall. After elapsed time some cues are presented to the subject, to see whether they elicit a memory of the events. The cues used by Linton were the dates of the events. I used four types of cues: *who, what, where,* and *when;* singly or in combinations. My study revealed, among other things, that very unpleasant events were less well reproduced than very pleasant events (see Table 10.1).

These data are suggestive of a self-serving recall of autobiographical events, but that conclusion would be ill founded. First, it is not known what role I played in the very unpleasant and very pleasant events. If I played a neutral role in both the pleasant and the unpleasant events, it is not obvious that the differential effect on recall is self-serving. Second, it is not possible to conclude whether unpleasant memories are suppressed or pleasant memories are enhanced. Comparison to the neutral set sug-

Table 10.1. The pleasantness effect (from Wagenaar, 1986)

Pleasantness of event	% Correctly recalled	Number of events
Very unpleasant	34	47
Unpleasant	38	204
Neutral	36	600
Pleasant	43	679
Very pleasant	53	73

gests the latter, which does not point to a self-serving suppression of unpleasant memories. But this comparison to the neutral set is somewhat difficult because necessary control data are lacking. It can be expected that both very unpleasant and very pleasant events are highly salient; for that reason both categories should be remembered better than the neutral events. Hence the data in Table 10.1 may mean that pleasant events are just remembered better because they are more salient, whereas the memory of unpleasant events is suppressed. That interpretation would indeed suggest some self-serving forgetting. The most important aspect of the data in Table 10.1 is that there were 47 + 73 events that were classified as either very unpleasant or very pleasant. The present essay discusses further what, with respect to the issue of selfish updating, can be concluded from the recall of these 120 events.

Method

Recording. A recording sheet used in the experiment is presented in Figure 10.1. The recorded event was described by *who, what, where,* and *when* aspects. The diagram to the left of the four aspects describes in which order the retrieval cues would later be presented. In the example, the first retrieval attempt was based on the cue "Leonardo da Vinci." The second attempt was cued by *who* and *when:* "Leonardo da Vinci and Saturday, September 10, 1983." The third attempt was based on three cues: *who, what,* and *when.* Only the *where* information needed to be recalled. Thus each reproduction contained three attempts per event, leading to a maximum of six correct responses.

In the open cells of the matrix I noted the subjective probability that I would recall the required information on the basis of the available cues.

The second half of the recording sheet contains a scaling on three dimensions: saliency, emotional involvement, and pleasantness.

At the bottom of the sheet a *critical detail* was recorded. These were selected such that a retrieval of the event would almost guarantee the recall of the detail.

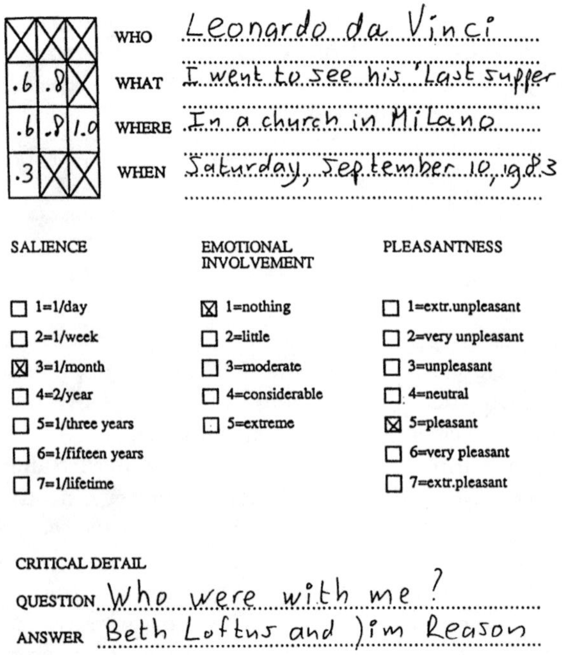

WHO *Leonardo da Vinci*

WHAT *I went to see his 'Last supper'*

WHERE *In a church in Milano*

WHEN *Saturday, September 10, 1983*

(grid with values .6 .8 / .6 .8 1.0 / .3)

SALIENCE

☐ 1=1/day
☐ 2=1/week
☒ 3=1/month
☐ 4=2/year
☐ 5=1/three years
☐ 6=1/fifteen years
☐ 7=1/lifetime

EMOTIONAL
INVOLVEMENT

☒ 1=nothing
☐ 2=little
☐ 3=moderate
☐ 4=considerable
☐ 5=extreme

PLEASANTNESS

☐ 1=extr.unpleasant
☐ 2=very unpleasant
☐ 3=unpleasant
☐ 4=neutral
☒ 5=pleasant
☐ 6=very pleasant
☐ 7=extr.pleasant

CRITICAL DETAIL

QUESTION *Who were with me ?*

ANSWER *Beth Loftus and Jim Reason*

Figure 10.1. The recording sheet.

Events were selected at the end of each day, between September 21, 1979, and September 20, 1983. Every year 400 events were recorded, which means that usually 1 event per day was selected, and sometimes 2. The most remarkable event that occurred on a day was selected. The total corpus consisted of 1,605 events.

Recall. Each event was recalled only once, after the end of the recording, between September 21, 1983, and September 21, 1984. Cues were presented by means of small *recall booklets*, prepared by my assistant, Mrs. Joke Fokkens. Her involvement was essential, because the transference to recall booklets solved the problem of handwriting, paper, or ink giving any indication of time period. However, the inclusion of a transcription stage made it impossible to include highly personal events that would have embarrassed my assistant. There were no passionate kisses, as mentioned by Linton. I will discuss later to what extent this can have influenced the results.

There were 24 different recall orders (for instance, first *who* alone; then *who+ when;* then *who* + *when* + *where*), which were not equally difficult. For instance, starting with *when* only was extremely difficult; starting with *what* was relatively easy. All recall orders were used with the same frequency (1,605 divided by 24) in the main experiment, but for the 120 most unpleasant and most pleasant events the even distribution was not warranted.

Subject. I myself was the only subject.

Results

Self-related and other-related events. Events in which I myself played the good or the bad role will be called *self-related.* The others will be called *other-related* events; this does not mean that others played a particularly good or bad role in them. Here are some examples.

Very unpleasant, self-related (n = 11): I complain in a rather impolite manner to a lady who parked her car on the sidewalk in front of our house; it appears that she is an invalid with a special permit, who was visiting the neighbors.

Very unpleasant, other-related (n = 36): The daughter of a close colleague dies from cancer; I go to her funeral.

Very pleasant, self-related (n = 14): I have a big success with a magic lantern show at the International Convention of the Magic Lantern Society, in London.

Very pleasant, other-related (n = 59): I dine with Maya Bar-Hillel and Gideon Keren on the Margareten Island in Budapest, and we laugh ourselves almost to death.

First it should be noted that the proportion of self-related and other-related events was the same for the unpleasant and pleasant categories (chi-square = 0.25, $df = 1$). This does not mean that I have been equally selective because it is not known how many self-related pleasant and unpleasant events occurred in the population. It is possible that the pleasant self-related events in the corpus exhausted the population, while only a small proportion of the unpleasant self-related events were reported. Thus the selection of events may have been self-serving or just the opposite. But it cannot be argued that the results to be reported were caused by unequal proportions of self-related events in the unpleasant and pleasant categories.

The recall of events is measured by the percentage of correctly reproduced responses, out of the possible seven per event (six cued aspects

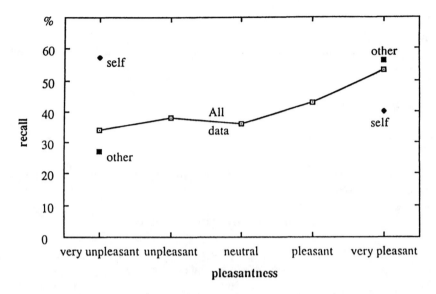

Figure 10.2. Recall (percent) as a function of pleasantness ratings, separated at the extremes into self-related and other-related events

plus one critical detail). The results are presented in Figure 10.2. The upshot is clear: The condition that should be most conducive to self-servance, unpleasant self-related events, produced the *highest* recall score. For the unpleasant condition the difference between self-related and other-related events was significant (median test, chi-square = 6.41, df = 1). For the pleasant condition there was no significant difference between self-related and other-related events (median test, chi-square = 1.42, df = 1). Before interpreting this result as an indication that exceptions to a rule are especially well remembered, it is necessary to exclude a number of other interpretations.

Different retention periods. The retention periods in the four conditions were not significantly different, as is revealed in Table 10.2. On the basis of these data it can be concluded that the results cannot be attributed to differences in retention time.

Different cuing orders. Some of the 24 cuing orders were easy, some were difficult. It is possible that the unequal sampling from these 24 orders caused the observed differences. This is checked by computing the mean expected recall, based on the average per cuing order, weighted by how often these orders occurred in the four conditions. The result is shown in Table 10.3. The data in Table 10.3 do not support the notion that the

Table 10.2. *Comparison of the retention periods in the four experimental conditions*

	Retention period (days)	
Condition	Mean	*SD*
Unpleasant		
Self-related	1,091	408
Other-related	1,121	447
Pleasant		
Self-related	873	424
Other-related	1,102	407

Table 10.3. *Prediction of mean scores in the four experimental conditions, based on the cuing orders used in each condition*

Condition	Mean expected recall
Unpleasant	
Self-related	34%
Other-related	38%
Pleasant	
Self-related	35%
Other-related	40%

Table 10.4. *Mean saliency scores in the four experimental conditions*

Condition	Mean saliency (max = 7)
Unpleasant	
Self-related	3.2
Other-related	2.7
Pleasant	
Self-related	2.9
Other-related	2.7

results shown in Figure 10.2 are caused by an unbalanced sampling from the 24 cuing orders.

Different saliency. The saliency, judged at the time of recording, is shown in Table 10.4. The differences between the two scores for unpleasant events were nonsignificant (median test, chi-square = 0.68, $df = 1$), and

Table 10.5. *The recall of highly unpleasant events, analyzed by aspects*

Remembered aspect	Self-related	Other-related
Who	75% ($n = 20$)	32% ($n = 44$)
What	58% ($n = 19$)	22% ($n = 63$)
Where	57% ($n = 14$)	37% ($n = 57$)
When	15% ($n = 26$)	6% ($n = 52$)
Critical detail	73% ($n = 11$)	44% ($n = 36$)

so were the two scores for pleasant events (median test, chi-square = 0.02, $df = 1$). Thus the effects shown in Figure 10.2 are also not caused by a difference with respect to saliency.

Differential effects on aspects. It appears that the effect of the self-related versus other-related distinction on the recall of unpleasant events is not easily dismissed as an artifact. Self-related highly unpleasant events are better remembered than other-related highly unpleasant events. The notion that storage of the exception is responsible for this effect implies that the improved accessibility must be the same for all aspects, *who, what, where,* and *when.* This is checked in Table 10.5. Overall, in the unpleasant condition, self-related events were remembered twice as well as other-related events. The same ratio applied to all separate aspects. It cannot be said that one particular aspect is responsible for the effect.

Memory distortions. When incorrect responses were given, it was possible that these incorrect memories constituted intrusions of less offending memories in the case of unpleasant events, or more flattering memories in the case of pleasant events. Storing the exceptions implies that such concept-driven adaptations do not occur. The strongest effects are expected for the *what* aspect; the analysis of *what* errors is presented in Table 10.6. It shows that most of the errors were failures to retrieve anything at all. Only 18 out of 126 incorrectly answered *what* questions were retrievals of a different event. It never happened that unpleasant self-related events were retrieved as other-related events. Unpleasant other-related events were twice retrieved as the wrong other-related events, and twice retrieved as neutral (not unpleasant) events. Pleasant self-related events were twice retrieved as different but equally pleasant self-related events, and twice as neutral (not especially pleasant) events. Pleasant other-related events were 10 times retrieved as neutral events. Thus, although the number of wrong retrievals was really small, we may still conclude that memory was not distorted in a self-serving manner.

Table 10.6. Errors in remembering "what"

Condition	No response	Same pleasantness, self-related	Same pleasantness, other-related	Neutral pleasantness
		Wrong event retrieved		
Unpleasant				
Self-related	8	—	—	—
Other-related	45	—	2	2
Pleasant				
Self-related	15	2	—	2
Other-related	40	—	—	10

Table 10.7. Mean predictions of retrievability made during recording

Condition	Predicted recall	
	Mean	*SD*
Unpleasant		
Self-related	57%	23%
Other-related	37%	27%
Pleasant		
Self-related	45%	35%
Other-related	54%	28%

Predictions. The predictions of retrievability made at the time of recording showed the same effect as demonstrated in Figure 10.2. This can be seen in Table 10.7. The difference between the two predictions for unpleasant events was significant (median test, chi-square = 8.22, $df =$ 1). For pleasant events the difference was not significant (median test, chi-square = 0.84, $df =$ 1). This effect of predictability means that the better retrievability is inherent in the event descriptions, and recognizable.

Discussion

I assume that my self-image, as retained in the conceptual self, is much better than what transpires from the very unpleasant self-related events. Hence these events are exceptions to the rule. The rather good recall of highly unpleasant self-related events, then, appears to confirm that updating of the conceptual self is accompanied by storing the exceptions, not by suppression or distortion of discrepant memories. The overall effect of remembering unpleasant events less well than pleasant events, displayed in Table 10.1, is even totally absent for self-related events. Thus there is not a semblance of self-servance. However, the results of remembering very pleasant events are not fully in accordance with this conclusion. Exception tagging would imply that very pleasant self-related events would also be remembered better than other-related events, because these flattering events should be exceptions. It should be admitted that in the very pleasant condition no significant difference between self-related and other-related events was found, but there is definitely a strong suggestion that the self-related events are at least not remembered worse. Thus it might be that my conceptual self was positioned quite close to the self-related events that were judged as very pleasant. This explains the interaction between the pleasant – unpleasant and self – other dimensions: I expect that others (or nature) will behave badly against me; when they do it fits the existing structure and no special emphasis is placed upon such an event. I do not expect that others (or nature) will provide me with extremely pleasant events; if they do, it does not fit the existing structure, and I will store these events as exceptions. If one wants to be nasty, one can say that the results portray me as a rather unpleasant person: self-assured about my own virtues and rather distrustful of others. Here the disadvantage of only having one subject becomes obvious. Even when I myself have conserved an extremely optimistic conceptual self, it should be possible to find others who think of themselves in a less favorable manner. Also it might have helped to record more extreme pleasant events, such as Linton's "passionate kisses."

There should be no confusion between rarity of an event and the degree to which an event fits an existing concept. Table 10.4 illustrates that all four conditions of events had the same (judged) frequency of occurrence. But within the same frequency category, some events may fit existing structures, while others do not. The deviating events are exceptional in the sense of not fitting the concept, not in the sense of being rare.

One hypothesis about how storing the exception might come about supposes that at the time of their occurrence some events receive more attention than others. There may be a "there is a lesson in this" mechanism that caused me to analyze the unpleasant self-related events more deeply than others. The effect would be that, even without any special tagging function or extra rehearsal, such events become more accessible in memory through increased depth of processing. Again, the extra attention for such events does not signify a self-serving forgetting; rather it illustrates the intensity with which the conceptual self attempts to come to grips with reality. This explanation is supported by the prediction results, which confirm that at the time of recording I already *knew* which events would be better remembered.

The model of storing what is exceptional in an autobiographical event dates back as far as Bartlett's "schema + correction" (Bartlett, 1932).

Since then Schank and Abelson (1977) proposed that story episodes are remembered by representing them in terms of fixed *scripts*, and additional atypical details not predicted by the script. Later Reiser and his associates demonstrated that autobiographical events are retained in memory by relating them to fixed *knowledge structures* that were active during the original experience (Reiser, Black, & Abelson, 1985). Each event is encoded by the way in which it fits the structure or deviates from it. These models, however, do not take into account that knowledge structures should be *updatable*, and that single experiences are the vehicle for accomplishing this. Thus, there is an extra reason to encode experiences in terms of their deviation from fixed structures. There is also a reason to remember them in that way when the updating process is of the slow type, because only through accumulation of deviating experiences can one reach the conclusion that the structures must be adapted.

A totally different explanation, which cannot be ruled out altogether, is that unpleasant self-related events have more sequellae in actual life. This means that life is organized in such a way that we are confronted with the consequences of what we did wrong, more often than with consequences of other negative experiences. This would cause more rehearsal for these events, and hence a better recall. But still, even if that explanation were true, it is implied that self-protecting mechanisms like suppression or concept-driven distortion do not compensate for this effect.

Storing the exception differs from the two other mechanisms in that it is highly adaptive. Suppression and distortion of memories after usage in the updating process is obviously not very efficient, because it means loss of information that may be quite useful later. Storing the exception is probably also efficient. It is like learning the grammar of a foreign language: Learning general rules plus lists of exceptions is more efficient than either learning all instances or learning rules only. Thus autobiographical memory serves the updating of the conceptual self in a highly adaptive and efficient manner, and makes us optimally equipped to deal with the singularities of everyday life.

ACKNOWLEDGMENT

This essay was prepared while the author was at the Netherlands Institute for Advanced Study (NIAS) in Wassenaar, the Netherlands.

REFERENCES

Bartlett, F. C. (1932). *Remembering: A study in experimental and social psychology.* Cambridge University Press.

Greenwald, A. G. (1980). The totalitarian ego: Fabrication and revision of personal history. *American Psychologist, 35,* 603–618.

Linton, M. (1975). Memory for real-world events. In D. A. Norman & D. E. Rumelhart (Eds.), *Explorations in cognition* (chap. 14). San Francisco: Academic Press.

Linton, M. (1978). Real world memory after six years: An in vivo study of very long term memory. In M. M. Gruneberg, P. E. Morris, & R. N. Sykes (Eds.), *Practical aspects of memory* (pp. 69–76). Orlando, FL: Academic Press.

Markus, H., & Nurius, P. (1986). Possible selves. *American Psychologist, 41,* 954–969.

Neisser, U. (1988). Five kinds of self-knowledge. *Philosophical Psychology, 1,* 35–59.

Reiser, B. J., Black, J. B., & Abelson, R. P. (1985). Knowledge structures in the organization and retrieval of autobiographical memories. *Cognitive Psychology, 17,* 89–137.

Ross, M. (1989). Relation of implicit theories to the construction of personal histories. *Psychological Review, 96,* 341–357.

Schank, R. C., & Abelson, R. P. (1977). *Scripts, plans, goals, and understanding.* Hillsdale, NJ: Erlbaum.

Wagenaar, W. A. (1986). My memory: A study of autobiographical memory over six years. *Cognitive Psychology, 18,* 225–252.

Wagenaar, W. A. (1988). People and places in my memory: A study on cue specificity and retrieval from autobiographical memory. In M. M. Gruneberg, P. E. Morris, & R. N. Sykes (Eds.), *Practical aspects of memory: Current research and issues* (pp. 228–233). New York: Wiley.

11

Creative remembering

MICHAEL ROSS AND ROGER BUEHLER

Research on nonliterate societies reveals striking examples of "amnesia": Prior events or beliefs that contradict current ideas and values are either erased from the collective memory or altered so as to be consistent with present understandings (Goody & Watt, 1968; Henige, 1980; Ong, 1982; Packard, 1980). For example, when the British arrived in Ghana in the early part of this century, they found that the state of Gonja was divided into seven territories, each ruled by its own chief (Goody & Watt, 1968). When British authorities asked them to explain their system, the Gonja revealed that the founder of their state, Ndewura Jakpa, had fathered seven sons. Jakpa divided the land so that each son ruled one territory. The British preserved this account of the history of Gonja in their written records. Shortly after the British arrived, two of the seven states in Gonja disappeared as a result of changes in boundaries. Sixty years later, oral historians again recorded the myths of state. In the updated version, Ndewura Jakpa begot only five sons; the Gonja made no mention of the founders of the two territories that had vanished from the scene. Oral historians have observed similar instances of forgetting or altering inconvenient aspects of the past in many other nonliterate societies (Goody & Watt, 1968).

In literate societies, individuals also revise history, especially in response to changing knowledge and political regimes (Greenwald, 1980). People interpret the past in terms of the present and therefore "every generation rewrites its history" (Mead, 1929/1964, p. 351). Because the earlier records are often preserved, people may notice differences between current and previous accounts of the past (Goody & Watt, 1968; Ong, 1982). Writing promotes an awareness of change and inconsistency. By comparison, inhabitants of oral societies are less likely to detect disparities across time; furthermore, their awareness of inconsistency is probably temporary.

In the present chapter, we analyze individuals' recollections of their own pasts. We suggest that individuals in Western cultures exhibit these characteristics of oral tradition to a certain degree while constructing and authenticating their own personal memories. To be sure, documentary records – photographs, letters, birth certificates, and so forth – act to constrain people's accounts. Nonetheless, an individual's history resides primarily within the memory of that person, and the recollections of those with whom he or she comes in contact. Moreover, people typically convey their remembrances orally; it is largely the elite who write their life stories or attract the attention of biographers.

In drawing this analogy, we acknowledge significant differences between historical studies of oral traditions and psychological research on personal recall. Historians of nonliterate cultures trace recollections of the same episodes across generations or social groups within a society. The episodes are often crucial to the history of that culture and may have transpired prior to the lifetimes of the informants. In contrast, psychologists concentrate on people's recall of their own pasts. We suggest, however, that both lines of investigation indicate that individuals may alter their accounts of the past, bringing history in line with current exigencies.

Our chapter proceeds as follows. To begin, we review constructivist analyses of memory and supporting psychological research. We next examine the impact of people's goals on the content and form of their recollections. Our discussion highlights the role of remembering in social discourse. We then note that people are not always delving into their pasts. Indeed, individuals may sometimes ignore or even suppress the past. We detail some of the causes and consequences of people's efforts to turn away from their histories. Next, we note that people tend to express confidence in their own recollections even when their recall differs markedly from that of other rememberers. In order to understand people's faith in their own memories, we discuss the criteria that they may use to evaluate the accuracy of recollections. Finally, we suggest that remembrances may be affected by outside sources and discuss the influence of the media on people's collective memories.

Constructing the past

Our analysis of recall falls within the general framework of constructivist approaches to memory. Constructivist theorists assume that recollections change as people revise the past to satisfy their present concerns and reflect their current knowledge (e.g., Bartlett, 1932; Greenwald, 1980; Loftus & Loftus, 1980; Ross, 1989). The psychologist Frederick Bartlett and the philosopher George Herbert Mead are two of the more influential 20th-century advocates of the constructivist approach. Bartlett (1932) noted that "the description of memories as 'fixed and lifeless' is merely an unpleasant fiction" (p. 311). Mead (1932) was even more forceful: "We speak of the past as final and irrevocable. There is nothing that is less so . . . the past (or some meaningful structure of the past) is as hypothetical as the future" (p. 12). Other writers have also presumed that long-term recall is a constructive process, rather than a straightforward retrieval of stored events. For instance, in an article entitled "Marriage and the Construction of Reality," Berger and Kellner (1964) suggested that marriage prompts spouses to reinterpret their pasts. As they create a joint history in ongoing conversation, husbands and wives alter their views and memories of previous relationships.

Constructivist accounts of memory have not gone unchallenged. In response to a survey conducted by Loftus and Loftus, most psychologists and nonpsychologists reported believing that people store everything they learn permanently in memory, but that the information is not always readily accessible (Loftus & Loftus, 1980). According to this outlook, people can retrieve information from memory in the form in which they initially encoded it (Alba & Hasher, 1983; Loftus & Loftus, 1980). There is research evidence to support this position: The traces of past events stored in memory are richer and more detailed than constructivist theorists such as Mead and Bartlett implied (Alba & Hasher, 1983).

We adopt the middle-of-the-road view (as perhaps befits a couple of Canadians) that memory may be detailed and that recall may be constructive. In proposing a constructivist account of recall, we do not argue that recall is necessarily an illusion or a confabulation. We accept the premise that recollections can contain detailed representations of events (Alba & Hasher, 1983). Recall is constructive, we suggest, in that people's current beliefs, knowledge, and perspectives can influence which episodes they retrieve from memory and how they interpret that information (Bartlett, 1932; Cantor & Mischel, 1977; Hastie, 1981; Hirt, 1990; Loftus, Miller, & Burns, 1978; Markus, 1977; Mead, 1929/1964; Ross, 1989; Rothbart, 1981; Schank & Abelson, 1977; Taylor & Crocker, 1981). People's present beliefs can also direct their guesses about the past; individuals may fill in gaps in their memories using their beliefs as guides (Bellezza & Bower, 1981). In sum, recall can involve the selective retrieval of stored events, the judicious interpretation of the meaning and causes of those events, and inferences about what might or must have occurred. Rememberers may supplement, change, or omit details as they construct pasts that adequately reflect their current knowledge.

Research by Anderson and Pichert (1978) neatly demonstrates the effects of people's current perspective on their recall of a story. Experimental participants read a description of a house and its furnishings from the point of view of either a potential burglar or a home buyer. After a short delay, participants wrote as much of the exact story as they could remember. Relative to participants adopting the perspective of a burglar, individuals with the home buyer orientation recalled more items pertinent to home buyers (e.g., a leaky roof) and fewer items relevant to thieves (e.g., a rare coin collection). Interestingly, Anderson and Pichert then shifted the participants' orientations without having them read the passage again. Former home buyers adopted the perspective of a burglar, and vice versa. Participants then wrote as much as they could recall of the entire passage for a second time. In comparison to their earlier reports, participants now recalled additional items relevant to their new perspective and fewer items pertinent to their first orientation. Anderson and Pichert's findings are extremely reliable. The present authors have replicated their results repeatedly in seminars over the years.

A theory of personal recall

Anderson and Pichert examined recall of a rather meaningless story after a short period of time. However, people's long-term recall of their own pasts reveals a similar impact of current perspective. Our examination of autobiographical memory begins with a consideration of how people construct their past standing on a personal attribute such as a feeling, behavior, or trait. Ross (1989) proposed an analysis of personal recall based on the premise that individuals possess implicit theories about the stability of their own attributes. Implicit theories incorporate specific beliefs regarding the inherent stability of an attribute, as well as general principles concerning the conditions likely to promote change. Ross assumed that, within a culture, individuals share many implicit theories. For example, people in our culture seem to suppose that an adult's attitude toward an ethnic group will normally remain stable over time, but might change under certain circumstances, such as increased exposure to that group (Ross, 1989). A theory of this sort is implicit in that people typically do not learn it through formal education and they may rarely discuss it.

Ross (1989) posited that individuals often invoke implicit theories to construct their past standing on a personal attribute. To demonstrate the role of implicit theories, we ask you to answer the question: What was your attitude toward abortion five years ago? Most people probably find it difficult to retrieve a past attitude directly from memory. Ross proposed that people will answer such questions by means of a two-step process. They begin by noting their current attitude toward abortion. The present serves as a benchmark because it is generally more salient and available than a person's earlier standing on an attribute. Construction of an earlier attitude therefore consists in large part of characterizing the past as different from, or similar to, the present. To determine their attitude toward abortion five years ago, people might ask themselves: Is there any reason to suppose that I felt differently than I do now? Because adults normally assume that their beliefs are consistent over time (Ross, 1989), most people should answer the abortion query by asserting that their earlier attitude was virtually identical to their current position. Typically, they would be able to corroborate their inference by selectively recalling instances of past behavior that are congruent with their presumed earlier belief.

Ross (1989) reviewed a large number of investigations that provided support for his analysis. For example, several researchers demonstrated that people who had recently evidenced a change in attitudes exaggerated the consistency between their former and present opinions. In one of these studies, participants described how they had recalled their earlier attitudes. Many individuals reported that they had inferred their earlier attitudes from their current opinions, assuming that their attitudes were stable over time. Like inhabitants of nonliterate societies, these experimental participants had no written annals that could alert them to the discrepancy between their present attitudes and their earlier positions.

People's implicit theories can predict change as well as stability; consequently, individuals may sometimes exaggerate the difference between the past and the present. Researchers have examined the implications of implicit theories of change in several contexts. Conway and Ross (1984) asked individuals to evaluate their study skills before participating in a study skills program. Although participants expected to improve their skills (and grades), their program, like other study skills courses, was ineffective. At the conclusion of the program, participants were asked to recall their original ratings of their study skills. They remembered their preprogram ratings as being worse than they had initially reported. In contrast, control subjects, who had not received the program, demonstrated no systematic bias in recall. The biased recollections of participants would support their theory that the program improved their skills. More generally, a tendency to revise the past in order to claim personal improvement may explain why many individuals report that they benefit from ineffective pop therapies and self-improvement programs (Conway & Ross, 1984).

McFarland and her associates have demonstrated that individuals revise their memories in other contexts on the basis of apparently erroneous theories of change. After reviewing the research literature on the menstrual cycle, McFarland, Ross, and DeCourville (1989) concluded that many women hold theories of the menstrual period that exaggerate its effects on their physical and psychological well-being. Why do women fail to alter their beliefs on the basis of their personal experiences? McFarland and her colleagues suggested a possible answer to this question: Perhaps women inadvertently bias their recall in a way that corroborates their theories of menstrual distress. McFarland and her associates conducted a diary study that offered support for their hypothesis. When not menstruating, women engaged in theory-guided retrieval that led them to overestimate the difference between their present level of well-being and their status during their last period. For example, although their mean levels of depression did not differ systematically across the menstrual cycle, women recalled being more depressed during their last period than they had reported being at the time or than they now were. More recently, McFarland, Ross, and Giltrow (1992) found that older people tend to exaggerate the degree to which they have changed since middle age on characteristics such as leadership ability, intelligence, shyness, physical health, and happiness. McFarland et al. provided evidence that such exaggeration was due, in part, to theory-guided recall. Older people invoke implicit theories of aging as they try to recall their middle-aged selves, theories that predict greater change than seems to occur.

This research on theory-guided recall does not necessarily indicate that biased recollections are more common than accurate recollections, or that people's theories are generally false. Research conducted on autobiographical recall in other contexts has revealed that people's recollections can be fairly accurate, at least for the gist of past experiences (e.g., Neisser, 1982). In the studies that we have described, researchers chose to study recall in domains in which they had good reason to suppose that people's theories were misleading. Researchers adopted this strategy in order to demonstrate that individuals may use implicit theories to construct their past standing on personal attributes.

It is also important to emphasize that researchers obtained biases in recall even though their experimental instructions typically included strong demands for accuracy. In all of these studies, researchers asked participants to recall their pasts as precisely as they could. Moreover, participants were often informed that the experimenter would evaluate the validity of their recall by comparing it to their initial reports. The findings suggest that theories may lead people astray even when individuals strive to recall their pasts accurately.

To this point, we have argued that individuals may construct their pasts, in part, on the basis of culturally shared, implicit theories. We have discussed people's theories about the stability of attributes and consequently their recall of their past standing on various personal characteristics. Clearly, the nature of people's theories and the content of their recall is much more extensive than this. Derived from their own particular experiences, people's beliefs can be relatively idiosyncratic as well as shared. Also, individuals possess many different kinds of beliefs about the nature and causes of human and nonhuman events that they can use in constructing the past.

We now turn to the study of more broadly based recollections. To begin, we review research on the childhood remembrances of depressed adults. Our purpose is twofold. Researchers often use people's memories as a basis for evaluating psychological theories of development. We discuss the potential liabilities of such retrospective analyses in the context of research on the etiology of depression. Second, we examine the possibility that people's recollections of their childhood are guided, in part, by their own beliefs about development.

Testing theories of depression through retrospection

Many theorists trace the roots of adult depression to childhood. Some theorists emphasize the importance of parental rejection; others point to the parents' disciplinary practices, associating adult depression with either too firm or too lax discipline. Researchers have typically tested theories of depression by asking depressed adults and nondepressed control subjects to recall their parents' child-rearing practices (Lewinsohn & Rosenbaum, 1987). In general, depressed adults remember less loving parents than do nondepressed adults.

Lewinsohn and Rosenbaum (1987) devised a clever test of the validity of these recollections. They examined childhood recall in three groups of subjects: adults who were currently depressed, adults who were not currently depressed but who had been depressed at earlier times in their lives, and a control group of adults who had never been depressed. The results were clear: Currently depressed adults recalled more rejecting parents than did adults who had been depressed previously, but who were now nondepressed. The latter group did not differ from controls. People whose depression was in remission did not recall rejecting parents.

On the basis of their results, Lewinsohn and Rosenbaum concluded that the parents of depressed individuals may have been no less loving than the parents of nondepressed adults. Instead, subjects' recollections can be best explained in terms of mood-dependent recall. Conceivably, people in an unpleasant mood selectively recall occasions on which their parents rejected them; in contrast, individuals in a pleasant mood may selectively recall the more positive aspects of their childhood, including incidents in which their parents demonstrated love and affection.

We suggest that the results and interpretation of this study warrant closer scrutiny. Respondents rated the behavior of their parents on 15 evaluative scales. These scales assessed parental rejection (e.g., didn't show love; hardly praised me), negative control (e.g., said I would be sorry if I was bad; wanted to control whatever I did), and the firmness of parental discipline (e.g., gave me little freedom; didn't let me stay up late). Lewinsohn and Rosenbaum obtained significant effects only on scales composing the parental rejection index. If the results simply reflect the effect of mood on recall, then why don't depressives also remember their parents as inappropriate disciplinarians or as engaging in excessive negative control? One possible answer to this question is that depressed people derogate their parents' child-rearing behaviors principally on dimensions that they believe are related to adult depression.

To provide a preliminary test of this hypothesis, Ross (unpublished data) recruited a group of undergraduates who possessed no particular knowledge of psychological analyses of depression. They ranked the parental behaviors used by Lewinsohn and Rosenbaum in terms of how likely each was to contribute to adult depression. Interestingly, these students judged the behaviors composing the parental rejection index to be significantly more implicated in adult depression than the remaining behaviors. In short, the depressives in the Lewinsohn and Rosenbaum study disparaged their parents' child-rearing practices primarily on dimensions that undergraduates associate with adult depression. We suggest that depressives may have invoked an implicit theory of depression that influenced their recall of their parents' child-rearing techniques.

Whatever the appropriate explanation may be, the results from the Lewinsohn and Rosenbaum study point to the danger of accepting long-term autobiographical recall uncritically. In the absence of corroborating evidence, researchers should treat long-term recall with a degree of caution. Although costly and time-consuming, prospective research designs offer the best and sometimes only way to answer developmental questions in a compelling manner.

The functions of personal recall

We have discussed people's recall as being partly determined by their implicit theories and the content of their memories. People's motivation for engaging in recall is another important influence. In their analyses of memory, many theorists fail to consider explicitly the impact of different goals on the content and form of people's recollections. For instance, Ross (1989) portrays the rememberer as a rather earnest soul, striving to recall the past as accurately as possible using the information that is available. In everyday life, however, individuals often use recall as a means to an end; accuracy is not necessarily their primary or only concern. Research in oral history illustrates the impact of goals other than accuracy on people's recollections. In revising the story of the creation of their state, the Gonja seemed to be attempting to legitimize their current territorial arrangement. Many social groups create mythical pasts to advance their own objectives, using history to buttress their claims for status and land

(Berg, 1980; Maines, Sugrue, & Katovich, 1983; Packard, 1980). Goals also have an impact on recall at the level of the individual. We next consider the effect of a variety of goals on the content and form of people's recollections.

Editing recall for an audience

Seldom any splendid story is wholly true.

Samuel Johnson

A great deal of people's social discourse involves the recounting of experiences. When recall is public, social context can affect the stories that individuals tell about their lives. The impact of social context can be incidental, as when other people serve as retrieval cues for specific memories. In the presence of their extended family, individuals are prompted to recall family events; similarly, when middle-aged persons encounter their former college roommates they recall shared times together, perhaps dwelling on episodes that they had not considered for years. These remembrances may be involuntary, evoked by current sights and sounds that have some link to the past (Salaman, 1970).[1]

Such context-specific recollections can also be the product of rememberers' deliberate efforts to tailor their recall for their listeners. In particular, rememberers may wish to provide accounts that are comprehensible, relevant, inoffensive, and interesting to their audiences. Thus, the recollections that people offer to their spouses, children, and therapists are likely to differ in meaningful ways. For example, a wish to be inoffensive may lead rememberers to construct accounts that are congruent with the attitudes and values of their current audience. In recalling the qualities of another individual, communicators tend to dwell on positive attributes if their audience likes the individual and on negative attributes if their audience dislikes that person (Higgins & Rholes, 1978).

A desire to be interesting or entertaining has especially intriguing implications for the stories that people tell of their pasts. The difficulty with being entertaining is that people's personal experiences are often fairly mundane. Rememberers sometimes solve this problem by offering embellished or exaggerated accounts of their adventures. In this case, the goal of telling a good story supersedes the goal of providing an accurate account. Consider that great raconteur, Toad, a character in the children's book *The Wind in the Willows* (Grahame, 1966). At the point in the story of the following quote, Toad is describing his adventures to his friend Mole.

The mole was a good listener, and Toad, with no one to check his statements or to criticize in an unfriendly spirit, rather let himself go. Indeed, much that he related belonged more properly to the category of what-might-have-happened-had-I-only-thought-of-it-in-time-instead-of-ten-minutes-afterwards. Those are always the best and the raciest adventures; and why should they not truly be ours, as much as the somewhat inadequate things that really come off? (p. 233)

Biographers are well aware that people may "improve" their stories of the past for social reasons. In his biography of Ludwig Wittgenstein, Monk (1991) obtained Bertrand Russell's initial impressions of Wittgenstein from letters Russell wrote in 1911. According to Monk, "These letters contain an almost daily record of Russell's reactions to Wittgenstein – a record which provides a useful corrective to some of the anecdotes he told about Wittgenstein in his later years, when his love of a good story frequently got the better of his concern for accuracy" (p. 37). Gould (1989) provided an example of historical embellishment in the context of scientific discovery. In the summer of 1909, Charles Walcott, head of the Smithsonian Institution, made an important fossil discovery in the Canadian Rockies. That much is certain. What is less clear is how the discovery came about. According to paleontological lore, there is a script for how major discoveries should occur. After working under difficult conditions for an extensive period of time, the paleontologist stumbles across an earthshaking find totally by accident. Walcott's story of his discovery has these attributes. After working all summer in the mountains, Walcott and his wife were heading home when her horse

slid on going down the trail and turned up a slab that at once attracted her husband's attention. Here was a great treasure – wholly strange Crustacea of Middle Cambrian time – but where in the mountain was the mother rock from which the slab had come? Snow was even then falling, and the solving of the riddle had to be left to [the next summer]. (Gould, 1989, p. 71)

Gould (1989) questioned the veracity of this story on the basis of Walcott's recordings in his daily diary. The diary provides no evidence that the discovery was attributable to a sliding horse, or that the Walcotts had to wait a year before they located the source of the fossils. The Walcotts seem to have made their important discoveries near the end of that first summer in the course of normal workdays. Over the years, the Walcotts seemingly developed a more exciting tale, one that is consistent with traditional paleontological stories of discovery.

There is an additional social influence on recall that we have not yet considered. In embellishing his adventures, Toad was trying to do more than entertain Mole; Toad was portraying himself as a brave and noble creature. Similarly, people sometimes construct stories of the past in order to influence an audience's impressions. For instance, by signaling whom they know, what they know, or what they have achieved, people endeavor to command the respect of their listeners. On the basis of years of listening to chit-chat at psychology conventions, we are tempted to infer that academics are particularly adept at forging such self-promoting tales; we lack sufficient experience in other professional settings, however, to advance this claim with confidence.

Reminiscences may provide an especially useful vehicle for managing impressions: Recollections allow individuals to project their preferred images of themselves and others in a socially acceptable manner. A friend might be embarrassed to tell us outright that she is generous or that her children are brilliant; she can offer remembrances, though, that should lead us to draw the appropriate conclusions. Personal narratives of the past are an important means by which people convey their identities and beliefs to others.

In an effort to assess the degree to which embellishment occurs in the everyday reporting of past events, Ross and Holmberg (1990) asked married couples to indicate on rating scales how they, their spouse, and most men and women describe their experiences to other people. The endpoints of the scales were labeled *almost always alter details to make a point or be entertaining* and *almost always describe events as accurately as possible*. Not surprisingly, perhaps, individuals rated themselves and their spouses as significantly more truthful than most men and women. In addition, individuals reported a sex difference in people's tendency to improve the past while engaging in public recollections. Respondents indicated that men are significantly more likely to alter details than women are, and that they and their spouse evidence this trend.

We do not know whether men are more inclined than women to alter their recollections. The finding that, on average, respondents placed themselves and their spouses toward the middle of the accuracy dimension is perhaps more important from the present perspective. People acknowledge that they alter their reminiscences in response to social factors.

Personal goals

People's recollections are influenced by personal as well as public concerns. People can study their pasts to learn about themselves and others (e.g., Bem, 1972), as well as to inform their current decisions and judgments. What people discover when they look back, however, is partly determined by their goals.

There is evidence that individuals are motivated to prefer certain types of explanations to others when accounting for past events. Gilovich (1983) found that gamblers justify their decision to continue gambling by construing their past failures in a way that allows them to deny responsibility for their losses. People may also attempt to minimize their responsibility for other negative episodes. In a book detailing his own experiences with depression, novelist William Styron (1990) suggested that the friends and families of suicide victims often refuse to accept a judgment of suicide, electing instead to view a death as accidental. If a death is deemed a suicide, then people close to the victim might have to acknowledge that they could possibly have foreseen the event and prevented it from happening. According to Styron, people support their belief in the accidental nature of a death by recalling related events that are consistent with their preferred interpretation. For example, when Abbie Hoffman died following a drug overdose, his brother appeared on television insisting that it had been an accident: Abbie "had always been careless with drugs and would never have left his family bereft" (Styron, 1990, p. 30). The coroner later reported that Hoffman had consumed the equivalent of 150 phenobarbital pills.

There are also occasions on which people seem to take excessive responsibility for negative events. For example, almost three-quarters of rape victims blame themselves, to some extent, for the rape (Janoff-Bulman, 1979). This tendency to tell a story about the rape that implicates their own behaviors (e.g., "I shouldn't have walked alone"; I shouldn't have left my window open"; "I should have locked my car") can serve an important goal: It helps people to believe that they can control their own futures. Further occurrences of the negative event ought to be avoidable if they modify their behavior. In the current context, the important point is that recall seems goal-driven. People can selectively recall and interpret events in ways that satisfy their personal needs.

Mead (1929/1964) discussed the impact of additional goals on people's recollections of both positive and negative events. He suggested that individuals seem motivated to develop coherent stories that sometimes contrast rather sharply with the ways in which their lives unfold. Life can be a jumble of independent events. As academics, spouses, and parents, we encounter many unrelated and unexpected circumstances each day. Mead suggested that people are not satisfied to remember events in the unconnected or haphazard manner in which they may occur. Imposing order and continuity, individuals construct a narrative in which they sequence and link events in meaningful patterns.

Mead (1929/1964) proposed, as well, that individuals retrospectively eliminate the breaks in continuity caused by unexpected happenings in everyday life: "The memory of the unexpected appearance of a supposedly far distant friend, or the memory of an earthquake can never recover the peculiar tang of the experience" (p. 350). In recollecting an experience, rememberers may insert explanations that diminish the surprise of the unanticipated episode. For example, a person's account of an unexpected meeting with a friend might include a description of how the friend happened to be in town at that time. In the person's original experience, however, there was no connection between the surprise meeting and the friend's travel itinerary. The meeting was totally unexpected. Mead also suggested that a rememberer will construct a plausible explanation of an unexpected event if no cause appears in memory: "The spaciotemporal connection is there to be developed as thought or imagination may refashion it" (p. 351).

We suggest that people do not always rework their pasts along the lines suggested by Mead; they do so primarily when it serves their present objectives. Mead did not discuss the psychological bases of a tendency to rework the past. We suggest two sources of motivation: (1) If recall is public, rememberers may formulate a lucid narrative in order to tell a good story. (2) People want to believe that they can predict and control their futures (Lefcourt, 1973; Seligman, 1975). If individuals can explain the past, then previous occurrences seem predictable. If, in retrospect, the past appears predictable, then people have a basis for believing that they can anticipate and control their futures. Because people are likely to be most concerned with controlling and predicting important events, they may be particularly motivated to explain past occurrences that had a significant impact on their lives. A person may devote more thought to how or why she got cancer than to how or why she caught a cold.

The impact of goals on the form of recall

People's goals can affect the form as well as the content of their recollections. In the present chapter, we consider one aspect of form, the tendency to describe events in either the third or first person. We are intrigued that people occasionally write or speak about their own past experiences in the third person. We discuss examples of third-person writing culled from academic and professional psychology, and then suggest why people may adopt this style when writing about their own experiences.

Every year the American Psychology Association bestows awards on distinguished contributors to the discipline. Appearing in the April issue of the *American Psychologist,* award announcements include a citation, which describes the major achievements of the award winner, and a biography. The biographies are spiced with humor and often include descriptions of the winners' early lives as well as of the people and circumstances that facilitated the winners' careers. The biographies all have one thing in common. They are written in the third person (the award winner is referred to by last name or by *he* or *she*), as though crafted by an outsider who has an unusually extensive knowledge of the winner and his or her career. Yet the award winners write the memoirs themselves, masking autobiographies as biographies.[2]

Why do award winners engage in this collective charade? Presumably, writing in the third person can have a liberating effect. Winners are able to emphasize their honors and achievements without appearing self-serving. Praise written in the third person appears to come from someone else. It is quite all right to receive accolades from another individual when accepting an award. Thus, pointing with pride to his "brilliant series of essays" and "more than 200 publications," one recent winner concluded that the award was a "fitting recognition" of his accomplishments. Most people would find it difficult to write such praise in the first person without experiencing acute embarrassment.

Writing in the third person may have additional purposes beyond providing anonymity and enabling individuals to avoid social disapproval. Consider two other contexts in which authors adopt the convention of writing in the third person. In clinical reports (of intake interviews, for example), clinicians often refer to themselves as "the therapist," avoiding use of their names and of the personal pronouns *I* and *me*. Therapists are not trying to mask their identity: They sign their reports. The rules for writing clinical reports are rather informal in comparison to the rules for writing journal articles in psychology, as outlined in the *Publication Manual of the American Psychological Association*. Until recently, APA style regulations discouraged use of the pronouns *I* and *my* in journal articles and encouraged psychologists to propose hypotheses as if they stemmed from an anonymous "it" (it is hypothesized that . . .), rather than the writer.

We suggest that the convention of writing in the third person arose because psychologists value impartiality in these contexts. Writing in the third person lends the appearance of, and may induce, objectivity (in both senses of the term – the writers treat themselves as objects and strive for impartiality). By referring to themselves as "the therapist" rather than "I," clinicians may be prompted to distinguish their own speculation and interpretation from the events that transpired during the interview. In journal articles written in the third person, authors adopt the same outside perspective in describing their own research as they do in describing the research of other people. Moreover, they present experimental hypotheses as following logically from theory, rather than from their own whims.

Third-person writing may thus have varied effects. When its major function is to provide anonymity, writing in the third person permits authors to avoid social disapproval. As a result, authors may feel free to write what they wish, including highly self-laudatory comments. When authorship is acknowledged, writing in the third person may encourage writers to adopt an outside perspective that leads them to present material in a relatively detached and objective fashion.

Ignoring and avoiding the past

To this point, we have implied that people dwell on their pasts with the enthusiasm of amateur historians. In an informal survey of friends and colleagues, however, we found that many claimed to disregard their pasts. They maintained that they had neither the time nor the inclination to reminisce. Next, we consider circumstances that prompt individuals to ignore or even actively suppress thinking about their pasts, as well as the possible consequences of doing so.

There is considerable evidence that people try to avoid recalling humiliating or traumatic experiences (Breuer & Freud, 1895/1966; Pennebaker, 1989; Silver, Boon, & Stones, 1983). Such avoidance can serve useful functions: It prevents individuals from being overwhelmed by negative affect and enables them to concentrate on the present. Nietzsche (1874/1983) suggested that forgetting is an important component of personal happiness: "It is possible to live almost without memory . . . but it is altogether impossible to live at all without forgetting . . . there is a degree of historical sense which is harmful and ultimately fatal to the living thing, whether this living thing be a man, a people, or a culture" (p. 62).

Although people may reduce their current distress by avoiding disturbing memories, they may suffer in other ways. Psychologists have long emphasized the debilitating consequences of inhibiting traumatic memories (e.g., Breuer & Freud, 1895/1966; Horowitz, 1976, 1987; Pennebaker, 1989). Breuer and Freud described the curative effects of encouraging people to express their pent-up emotions and emphasized the therapeutic value of prompting people to talk about the traumas that they have experienced. Other theorists have noted that traumatic experiences are disturbing, in part, because they violate some of people's core assumptions, including that their world is just, benevolent, and predictable (Janoff-Bulman, 1992; Horowitz, 1976, 1987). According to these theorists, individuals need to think through traumatic events and successfully integrate them with the beliefs that guide their lives (Horowitz, 1976, 1987). Finally, recent research indicates that the active inhibition of traumatic thoughts engenders stress that, in the long run, may make a person more vulnerable to illness (Pennebaker, 1989).

If the inhibition of traumatic experiences has deleterious effects, then liberating such thoughts should have positive health benefits. To test this hypothesis, Pennebaker (1989, 1990) asked university students to write about traumatic experiences that they had rarely discussed with others. He found that writing about such episodes increased the students' feelings of depression and guilt in the short term, but benefited their health in the long run. Students who described their traumatic experiences were less likely than controls, who wrote about neutral events, to visit a physician for illness in the months following the experimental sessions.

Writing about traumatic episodes in either the third or the first person

In a follow-up to Pennebaker's work, Fergusson and Ross (unpublished data) used writing form as an independent variable. They hypothesized that writing about traumatic events in the third person would encourage individuals to recall the details of disturbing events from an outside perspective and perhaps temper the emotional upset and embarrassment that they might otherwise experience. If writing in the third person induces a degree of detachment, then individuals may be in a better position to analyze and attain an understanding of the episode and their emotional reactions to it. Achieving this understanding may be more difficult in the first-person condition, which sets the stage for individuals to relive the event and its attendant emotions. Writing in the third person may also help people to distance or separate their current self from the self in the story, and thus put the incident behind them. All of these considerations led Fergusson and Ross to expect that individuals who wrote third-person accounts would reap greater psychological and health benefits than individuals who wrote first-person accounts of traumas.

Fergusson and Ross randomly assigned participants to write in either the third or the first person about traumatic events that they had experienced, or about neutral events (control condition). In both the third- and first-person conditions, participants were assured of anonymity; thus, writing in the third person would not provide greater anonymity, but it could prompt subjects to adopt an outside perspective. Participants writing about traumatic events were asked to describe the most distressful episodes that had occurred to them, ideally events that they had rarely if ever discussed with others in detail. They were given the opportunity to write about these events for 20 minutes on four consecutive days. They had the choice of writing about the same or different traumas during each of the sessions.

Before proceeding to the results, we should emphasize that, as in the Pennebaker studies, many of the accounts written by these working-class and middle-class university students evidenced serious tragedy and anguish. The topics included alcoholism, physical and sexual abuse, suicide, divorce, and other subjects that are fairly labeled traumas. At the present time, the data are not sufficiently analyzed to reveal how the stories told in the first person may differ from those in the third person. It is clear, however, that individuals in the third-person condition spent a significantly longer period of time writing about each specific trauma than did participants in the first-person condition. In addition, subjects stated that they ruminated less about the episode in the four weeks following the experimental sessions if they wrote about the events in the third rather than the first person. The extended reporting of each episode and the subsequent reduction in rumination suggest that individuals who wrote in the third person were more able to confront their traumas and then to put the incidents behind them. This conjecture is supported by other findings. For example, individuals who wrote in the third person reported feeling better about themselves (less guilt, less shame, more happiness, etc.) during the four weeks after the experimental sessions. Also, Fergusson and Ross examined the records of the university health center: Participants who wrote about distressful events in the third person were less likely than their counterparts in the first person condition or the control condition to visit the health center for reasons of illness in the 50 days following the last writing session.

Unlike Pennebaker, Fergusson and Ross found no particular advantages associated with writing in the first person; indeed, participants who described their traumas in the first person fared worse on some measures than controls who wrote about neutral events. This pattern of results will need to be replicated and the discrepancy with Pennebaker's findings will need to be explained. At the present time, we conclude from the Fergusson and Ross data that people do not necessarily benefit from writing about their traumas. To derive advantages from writing about the past, people must describe distressful episodes in a manner that permits them to put the events behind them. Writing in the third person may be one way of achieving this end.

Ignoring the past while predicting the future

People's wish to disregard the past is not limited to traumatic events. Researchers have found that individuals sometimes choose to ignore history even when they can improve their judgments and decisions by recalling their experiences. One striking instance concerns people's predictions about their future behavior. It is a psychological truism that past behavior predicts subsequent behavior. In a dissertation conducted at the University of Waterloo, however, Buehler (1991) found that people fail to make use of their past behavior in predicting their future actions. In this research, Buehler sought to answer two related questions that have surely puzzled most of us. Why do we frequently underestimate how long it will take us to complete a task? Why don't we learn from past experience and adjust our estimates accordingly?

Buehler found, not surprisingly, that people exaggerate the speed with which they will complete tasks in their everyday lives (including school assignments and tasks around the home). More interestingly, Buehler examined the processes that underlie people's predictions using think-aloud procedures. His subjects rarely referred to their past experiences when generating task completion estimates; instead, they focused almost entirely on the future, optimistically planning how they would complete the target activity. When Buehler explicitly asked people about their past performance on related activities, they readily admitted that they typically took longer to complete tasks than they had anticipated. Yet they remained highly confident that their current predictions were accurate.

Buehler has identified one apparent reason for this neglect of history: When people are asked to explain why they failed to complete past projects on time, they judge each of their past stumbling blocks to be relatively unique and unlikely to repeat itself. For example, they attribute their tardiness to such rare events as their computer blowing up while they were typing their last English essay. People may well be right in their judgment that a particular event is unlikely to recur. They often fail to realize, however, that a lot of things can go wrong; there are numerous potential impediments. Although many of these obstacles may have a relatively low probability of occurrence, the probabilities are additive. The likelihood that *something* will occur to slow up a person is quite high. This is the lesson that people seemingly fail to learn from past experience.

Buehler found that subjects' current task completion estimates were unrelated to their assessments of whether they had concluded previous activities on time; in contrast, the same assessments of earlier behavior predicted whether they actually finished the current activity within their estimated time period. Apparently past behavior does predict future behavior. Buehler also reported that people were less likely to underestimate completion times if they were required to take into account their past experiences while generating their estimates. Their accuracy increased when they based their predictions, in part, on their recollections of their own behavioral histories.

There are a variety of other contexts in which people seem to ignore the past while forecasting the future. For example, we have all watched individuals careen from one disastrous romance to another, seemingly not learning from their past relationships. Divorce statistics support this impression: The likelihood of divorce is greater in second than in first marriages (McKie, Prentice, & Reed, 1983). Moreover, people's tendency to fence off the past, to regard it as unrelated to present concerns, has been documented in a variety of historical contexts that go well beyond autobiographical recall. For instance, Lyndon Johnson and his advisers considered France's experience with fighting in Indochina to be largely irrelevant to predicting how the United States would fare in its own war in Vietnam. American political leaders thought that France's woes could be ignored because the United States was richer, more powerful, and more cohesive than France had been (Neustadt & May, 1986). Similarly, in 1914 Europeans distinguished their conflict from previous European wars. They apparently believed, among other things, that war had become too expensive to last long (Neustadt & May, 1986).

Perhaps it is not surprising that people deny the relevance of previous experiences, especially past failures, to future behavior and outcomes. As we have already noted, people prefer to believe that they have control over events in their lives (e.g., Langer, 1975; Lefcourt, 1973; Seligman, 1975). A desire for control may help explain a tendency to ignore the past. If people see themselves as bound to the past, they lose their sense of agency. By fencing off past failures, people can maintain the belief that they are in command of their futures, that they have the power to produce success and happiness.

There is more to it than this, however. Rather than simply ignore the past, decision makers often use it selectively to validate their choices. Victory in Vietnam was consistent with U.S. strategic objectives in Asia; for this reason, perhaps, Johnson and his advisers chose to focus on the differences and ignore the parallels between the French and American incursions into Vietnam (Neustadt & May, 1986). More recently, U.S. political leaders sought to justify American intervention in the Persian Gulf crisis of 1991. They stressed the similarities and minimized the differences between the United States' involvement in the Persian Gulf and its earlier participation in such "popular" conflicts as Korea and World War II. For example, members of President Bush's administration repeatedly compared Iraqi president Saddam Hussein to Hitler, the implication being that war with Iraq was as justifiable and necessary as war with Nazi Germany. By forging a link between the present and the past, these leaders used history to support their position, much as we have suggested that the average person invokes personal recollections to satisfy his or her present concerns.

Historians have long decried the failure of decision makers to use history objectively (e.g., Neustadt & May, 1986; Thucydides, 1954). It seems evident, however, that individuals are often not interested in using the past impartially. Instead, as in nonliterate societies, people in our culture may ignore the past or invoke it selectively in order to satisfy their current needs.

Evaluating the accuracy of recollections

We have presented research and theorizing that suggests that long-term recall is a constructive process that may be vulnerable to bias and error. We now consider whether rememberers accept this proposition, along with its implication that their personal recollections are fluid creations that change over time and differ from the remembrances of other people. As part of this discussion, we focus on the criteria that people use to evaluate the accuracy of recollections. In psychological research, investigators can assess the validity of recall by comparing participants' remembrances to a documentary record of their earlier responses. People typically lack such a record in everyday life. How then do individuals assess the accuracy of their own and other people's recollections?

People appear to exhibit greater confidence in their own recall than seems warranted by a constructivist analysis of memory. Trope (1978) found that individuals fail to adjust adequately for the fallibility of their recollections when making memory-based social judgments. In addition, there is anecdotal evidence that people express confidence in their own memories even when their recall differs markedly from that of other rememberers. Individuals insist that their own versions of history are accurate and that opposing interpretations are false. Examples of such conflicts are frequently presented in the media. Scientists in contention for Nobel Prizes sometimes offer dramatically different accounts of their relative contributions to collaborative research (Ross, 1981; Sutton, 1984). The memoirs of politicians and other public figures provoke heated debate. The same writer will be praised for his or her honesty and courage by some and accused of distorting and rearranging history by others. In the fall of 1991, a mammoth television audience watched Professor Anita Hill confront Judge Clarence Thomas, a nominee for the Supreme Court of the United States. Hill accused Thomas of sexually harassing her when she worked for him some 10 years earlier. Hill described incriminating conversations with Thomas in vivid detail. Thomas vigorously denied making the statements that Hill ascribed to him.

When conflicting accounts of the past appear in the media, the public is rarely presented with statements such as, "My memory is different from Beth's but she is as likely to be right as I am," or "Our memories differ and Beth is right." Asserting the validity of their own recollections, rememberers often profess astonishment that any sane, honest person could possibly recall the episode differently (e.g., Ross, 1981; Sutton, 1984). Obviously, we need not accept at face value these declarations of outrage reported in the media. Money, reputations, and seats on the Supreme Court may depend on whose interpretation of history is accepted by the public. Do ordinary people also tend to view others' memories of everyday incidents as more fallible than their own?

We approach this question by first examining the criteria people use to evaluate the accuracy of their own recall. We then consider how the use of these standards may lead people to favor their own accounts when their versions of the past conflict with those of other rememberers. Our analysis focuses on situations in which rememberers lack objective criteria for assessing the accuracy of differing accounts and do not knowingly or deliberately lie about the past.

Truth criteria

In many contexts, consensus serves as an especially important standard for assessing accuracy. If people's recollections of an event agree, they and others may tend to assume the validity of the remembrances. The principle of consensus is often applied in legal settings to establish the veracity of various witnesses. Consensus is also used to evaluate the historical accuracy of ancient documents. For example, in recent years many theologians have attempted to identify the parts of the gospel that are authentically historical in that they are traceable to Jesus. One approach that scholars adopt is to attribute to Jesus behavior that appears in all or most of the distinct gospel sources (Sheehan, 1988).

Nevertheless, agreement is no guarantee of accuracy. The history of science reveals that commonly accepted truths of today are sometimes overturned tomorrow. In psychology, the Ponzo and Muller-Lyer illusions are no less misleading simply because people's perceptions coincide. As well, disagreement is no proof of falsity. Conflicting accounts may both be "true" in the sense that each captures the person's original or current understanding of events.

Attempts by historians to distinguish fabrication from truth in their analyses of oral traditions also illustrate the difficulties of relying on consensus (Miller, 1980). Some historians have proposed that the points on which all narrators agree must be historically accurate. The problem with this assumption is that storytellers may "invent detail and structure along the lines of cultural consensus" (Miller, 1980, p. 20). Accordingly, "it is easy to conceive of later convergences that could produce widespread unanimity on aspects of an episode that did not descend from a single original and that had no direct relationship to the event purportedly described" (p. 20). Within our own culture, certain widely shared beliefs can be shown to be invalid. For example, people tend to overestimate the impact of the menstrual cycle on women's psychological and physical well-being (McFarland et al., 1989).

There are a number of additional criteria that people may use to evaluate the truthfulness of recollections. In a particularly relevant line of work, Marcia Johnson and her colleagues have theorized that people distinguish memories of actual episodes from memories of imagined events on the basis of features of the memories (Johnson, Foley, Suengas, & Raye, 1988; Johnson & Raye, 1981). Representations of actually experienced events include more sensory and contextual details than memories of imaginary events, and differences in detail guide people's inferences about the origins of their memories. Johnson and Raye also suggested that individuals evaluate whether a recollection represents a genuine experience by relating the content of the remembrance to other memories and to real-world knowledge. For example, most adults would relegate a recollection of flapping their arms and flying over Toronto to the realm of imagination. Research by Johnson and her colleagues, as well as others, has provided support for the Johnson and Raye analysis (e.g., Bell & Loftus, 1989; Johnson, 1988; Johnson et al., 1988; Schooler, Gerhard, & Loftus, 1986).

In a related development, a number of authors have discussed narrative truth criteria, evaluative standards that depend on people's assessments of the aesthetic quality of a story or recollection (e.g., Bruner, 1986; Spence, 1982). An account is narratively true to the extent that it is (a) vivid and detailed rather than sketchy, (b) coherent in that events are sequenced and connected in an intuitively plausible manner, and (c) characterologically consistent, with protagonists' actions seeming to stem from their personalities, intentions, and motives. Narrative truth criteria are particularly applicable to people's stories of episodes in their lives. Personal tales often include chronological descriptions of events and actions. People may judge the validity of such accounts, in part, by evaluating the narrative qualities of the story.

In summary, we suggest that individuals may examine remembrances for sensory and context information, congruence with other knowledge, vividness, coherence, and characterological consistency. Together with the consensus rule, these various standards serve as truth criteria by which individuals may evaluate the validity of recollections.

Conflicting memories

When a rememberer's recollections conflict with those of someone else, the rememberer may scrutinize the alternative accounts, assessing the degree to which each satisfies the various truth criteria. Whereas rememberers may well suppose that they are impartial in their deliberations, there is reason to suspect that they will typically come to favor their own accounts. While recalling an episode, a rememberer may have the subjective experience of hearing or seeing the event unfold once again. In reconstructing a conversation, Geoff may "hear" Megan telling him that the keys to her house are hidden under the mat.[3] Megan's subsequent denial that she made the statement cannot eliminate Geoff's sensory experience. On the other hand, Geoff lacks direct access to the vivid, sensory experience that Megan possibly derives from her own recall of the conversation. He cannot hear the sounds that reverberate in her head. Thus, people's subjective experience may often be that their own recollections are more vivid and contain more sensory information than does another person's recall of the same event.

Rememberers may also believe that their accounts better fulfill the remaining truth criteria. They may judge their own versions to be more detailed. Neither public account is likely to include all of the relevant features that the storyteller could provide, but rememberers may tacitly attach extra details to their own accounts. As well, the act of constructing a story may spontaneously induce a rememberer to recall additional memories involving parallel events and similar actions by the leading characters. Consequently, rememberers may judge their own version to be more consistent with their other memories than they would judge an alternative rendering of the story to be. Rememberers are also likely to construct a story in which the protagonists' actions are congruent with the rememberers' current attitudes and beliefs. The actions of "good guys" may be portrayed more positively than those of "bad guys." Competing depictions of the same episode may not seem as characterologically consistent: Geoff's good guys may be Megan's bad guys. Finally, rememberers are likely to judge their own accounts to be more coherent, partly because they created them and partly because they are more familiar with them. Most of us who teach or write have had the experience of generating confusion in others as we provide them with explanations that we consider to be perfectly lucid. In sum, we suggest that people will tend to rate their own stories as more plausible than conflicting descriptions because their own accounts will seem to fulfill more adequately the various truth criteria.

In a recent study, Ross, Karr, and Buehler (1992) confirmed that people are confident of the accuracy of their own recollections of everyday experiences. Undergraduates wrote accounts of a personal incident of which their memory conflicted with somebody else's. After providing detailed versions of both their own and the other person's recollection of the episode, participants assessed the historical accuracy of each statement in both accounts and evaluated the stories on a number of qualitative dimensions. Several findings are of particular interest here. First, participants judged the statements in their own accounts to be highly accurate, and substantially more accurate than conflicting statements in the other's account. Second, participants judged their own stories to be significantly more vivid, coherent, and characterologically consistent than the other person's version of the same event. Respondents seemed to deny the phenomenological reality of the other person's conflicting recollection. Finally, the higher participants estimated the vividness, coherence, and characterological consistency of their own stories to be, the more historically accurate they judged their recollections. The data suggest that people believe in the accuracy of their own recollections that satisfy the various truth criteria.

In extreme cases, rememberers may be virtually the only people who suppose that their own version of history is factual, rather than a construction of the mind. Note that we intend this comment to apply to ordinary people and their stories, not to schizophrenics or people whose tales end up on the front page of the *National Enquirer.* Consider an example of conflicting memories provided to us by a married couple describing their first encounter. The husband's account was approximately as follows: "I was sitting in ——— airport, waiting for my flight to be announced, when a woman came into the room. She chose to sit beside me even though many other seats were available. We talked, hit it off, and the rest is history." His wife's version of this episode was identical except for one detail: She recalled the waiting room as being entirely full, except for the empty seat beside her future husband. The spouses had discussed their discrepant memories on a number of occasions. Both reported that they firmly believed their own version of the story.

We have presented the airport encounter stories to a variety of audiences and asked people to judge which account they found more believable, the husband's or the wife's. The wife's account is judged to be more accurate than the husband's by almost 100% of the members of every audience. When we have probed further, audiences have offered two primary reasons for their differential acceptance of these two accounts. First, a woman would be unlikely to sit immediately next to an unfamiliar man when other seats were available. The wife's account of her own behavior is therefore judged to be more plausible because it is consistent with an audience's experiences and expectations. Incidentally, it is also more congruent with the research literature on personal space (Hall, 1966, 1974). Second, the man's story seems to flatter him more than his spouse's account seems to flatter her. In the face of conflicting accounts, audiences distrust memories that appear self-serving. They judge the story to be biased by the teller's motives, rather than a straightforward representation of historical facts.[4]

Now consider the airport story from the perspective of the husband. This intelligent, sensible human being stands virtually alone in believing the validity of his account. Presumably, he has never posed the question that audiences seem to ask themselves after hearing the two versions: Is it likely that a woman would sit immediately next to a male stranger when other seats are available? This question doesn't occur to him; he views his coherent and vivid recall as factual, rather than a hypothesis that warrants evaluation. In contrast, audiences that lack direct access to the rememberer's vivid recall are likely to judge each story on the basis of more explicit truth criteria, including whether the details are congruent with their personal and world knowledge. Thus, people may draw opposite conclusions about the validity of a recollection because they use different truth criteria.

Our discussion of truth criteria does not seem to capture fully why people remain so wedded to their own recollections. If rememberers are acting as reasonably as we propose, then one might expect them to be somewhat more swayed by conflicting evidence. It seems likely that we need to add a motivational component to our analysis. Conceivably, individuals are motivated to accept the truthfulness of recollections that score high on vividness, coherence, and so forth. A belief in the accuracy of such remembrances may be important to people's psychological well-being. If individuals can't have faith in these types of memories, what can they believe about their pasts? When forced to doubt such recollections, people may feel that they have lost touch with their own histories and, perhaps more important, with their sense of self (Baddeley, 1988).

Finally, we note that the truth criteria that people may invoke in their everyday lives to evaluate the credibility of recollections offer no assurance of success for at least two reasons. First, people may come to different conclusions on the basis of the same evidence because they use different truth criteria. Second, for the truth criteria to be effective there must be detectable, qualitative differences between accurate and inaccurate memories. Although researchers have observed some differences, the distinctions are subtle (Schooler, Gerhard, & Loftus, 1986; Schooler, Clark, & Loftus, 1987). Valid memories contain somewhat more sensory and context information; however, observers can discriminate between accurate and inaccurate memories at only slightly better than chance levels. By invoking various truth criteria, individuals may become suspicious of some accounts or believing of others, but they will not necessarily possess a definitive basis for accepting or rejecting people's stories of their pasts.

Creating Memories

The issues that we have discussed concerning people's construction and evaluation of accounts of the past come into focus in media portrayals of historical figures. Novelists, dramatists, and screenwriters deliberately blur the line between historical truth and fiction. They may sometimes do this for political reasons; for example, Shakespeare tailored the facts in his histories to suit the prejudices of the Tudor monarchs of his day. Authors may also rewrite history in order to increase dramatic tension and maintain an audience's interest. In *Amadeus*, Peter Shaffer's depiction of the characters of Mozart and Salieri, and of Salieri's possible complicity in Mozart's death, is effective drama but questionable history. Yet for many members of the audience Shaffer's account may provide the primary source of information on Mozart's life story. In this context, the reactions of audiences and reviewers to *J. F. K.*, Oliver Stone's 1991 film about the assassination of President John F. Kennedy, are interesting. Many older viewers, who lived through that event, seem annoyed by what they believe to be factual errors in the film. Younger viewers, for whom Kennedy is ancient history rather than a personal memory, appear more disposed to enjoy the film on its own terms.

Presumably most people attend films or live theater to be entertained rather than to obtain a history lesson. When the tale is set in a historical context, however, they may believe that they have received both. Such stories may be accepted as largely authentic by audiences who are unaware of alternative accounts and who use narrative truth criteria to distinguish historical fact from fiction. Consequently, the media may help shape people's collective memories.

The media also play a role in communicating the words of famous individuals to society at large and therefore in producing collective memories of their statements. Misquotations in newspapers and other print media provide intriguing examples of historical revision (Keyes, 1992). For example, baseball manager Leo Durocher is credited with saying, "Nice guys finish last." He really said, "The nice guys are all over there. In seventh place." The quote became punchier and pithier with repeated retelling. In his studies of remembering, Bartlett (1932) observed similar changes as stories were transmitted from one person to another. A second notable misquotation is associated with the comedian W. C. Fields. Fields is renowned for saying, "Any man who hates dogs and children can't be all bad." Fields didn't say it. Leo Rosten said it about Fields when he introduced the comedian at a banquet. Rosten's words were eventually attributed to the more famous person whom they described. Presumably this shift occurred because the statement expressed sentiments that Fields might well have expounded; moreover, quoters may have believed that they could impress more listeners or readers with the words of W. C. Fields than with the pronouncements of a relative unknown like Rosten. Keyes (1992) provided many other examples of quotations that change or are ascribed to the wrong person over time. Keyes was able to trace the source of the various quotations because he had access to documentary records.

Revising history to accomplish particular objectives is not the special province of professional writers. As we have emphasized in this chapter, it is also a hallmark of the average person's efforts to recall details from his or her life. In comparison to professional writers who derive their historical stories from written records, individuals may be less cognizant of their alterations as they use their present knowledge, beliefs, and goals to construct their pasts. In this sense, people's personal recollections are comparable to the oral traditions of nonliterate societies.

In closing, we should emphasize that it is perfectly healthy and normal for people to create pasts that satisfy their current needs. Such creativity probably serves us well most of the time. As Bartlett (1932) and Mead (1929/1964, 1932) stressed, the past is a resource that people can use and adapt for current purposes. People can get into trouble, however, when they underestimate the fallibility of their own memories. Perhaps the lesson of psychological research on memory is not that people should be less creative, but that they should be aware of the degree to which they author their own histories.

ACKNOWLEDGMENT

Preparation of this chapter was supported by a research grant and doctoral fellowship from the Social Sciences and Humanities Research Council of Canada.

NOTES

1 Throughout most of this essay, we present people as in control of their recall and depict memories as tools that help people accomplish their goals. Although much memory is of this sort, memory can also be involuntary, cued by current thoughts and sensations.
2 Our suspicion that this was the case was confirmed by a telephone call to the editorial office of the *American Psychologist*.
3 Novelist John Updike (1987, p. 4) uses the felicitous phrase "the acoustics of memory" to describe such experiences.
4 Audiences of psychologists have provided an additional reason for preferring the woman's account: It was she who was looking for a seat. The man would probably be less conscious of the state of the room.

REFERENCES

Alba, J. W., & Hasher, L. (1983). Is memory schematic? *Psychological Bulletin, 93*, 203–231.
Anderson, R. C., & Pichert, J. W. (1978). Recall of previously unrecallable information following a shift in perspective. *Journal of Verbal Learning and Verbal Behavior, 17*, 1–12.
Baddeley, A. (1988). But what the hell is it for? In M. M. Gruneberg, P. E. Morris, & R. N. Sykes (Eds.), *Practical aspects of memory: Current research and issues* (pp. 3–18). Chichester, England: Wiley.
Bartlett, F. C. (1932). *Remembering: A study in experimental and social psychology*. Cambridge University Press.

Bell, B. E., & Loftus, E. F. (1989). Trivial persuasion in the courtroom: The power of (a few) minor details. *Journal of Personality and Social Psychology, 56,* 669–679.

Bellezza, F. S., & Bower, G. H. (1981). Person stereotypes and memory for people. *Journal of Personality and Social Psychology, 41,* 856–865.

Bem, D. J. (1972). Self-perception theory. In L. Berkowitz (Ed.), *Advances in experimental social psychology* (Vol. 6, pp. 1–62). New York: Academic Press.

Berg, G. M. (1980). Some words about Merina historical literature. In J. C. Miller (Ed.), *The African past speaks: Essays on oral tradition and history* (pp. 221–239). Kent, England: Dawson & Sons.

Berger, P. L., & Kellner, M. (1964). Marriage and the construction of reality. *Diogenes, 46,* 1–24.

Breuer, J., & Freud, S. (1966). *Studies on hysteria.* New York: Avon. (Original work published 1895)

Bruner, J. (1986). *Actual minds, possible worlds.* Cambridge, MA: Harvard University Press.

Buehler, R. M. (1991). *Why individuals underestimate their own task completion times.* Unpublished doctoral dissertation, University of Waterloo, Ontario.

Cantor, N., & Mischel, W. (1977). Traits as prototypes: Effects on recognition memory. *Journal of Personality and Social Psychology, 35,* 38–48.

Conway, M., & Ross, M. (1984). Getting what you want by revising what you had. *Journal of Personality and Social Psychology, 47,* 738–748.

Fergusson, P. A., & Ross, M. (1991). [Disclosure, health, and well-being]. Unpublished raw data.

Gilovich, T. (1983). Biased evaluation and persistence in gambling. *Journal of Personality and Social Psychology, 44*(6), 1110–1126.

Goffman, E. (1959). *The presentation of self in everyday life.* New York: Doubleday Anchor.

Goody, J., & Watt, I. (1968). The consequences of literacy. In J. Goody (Ed.), *Literacy in traditional societies* (pp. 27–68). Cambridge University Press.

Gould, S. J. (1989). *Wonderful life: The Burgess shale and the nature of history.* New York: Norton.

Grahame, K. (1966). *The wind in the willows.* New York: Grosset & Dunlap.

Greenwald, A. G. (1980). The totalitarian ego: Fabrication and revision of personal history. *American Psychologist, 35,* 603–618.

Hall, E. T. (1966). *The hidden dimension.* Garden City, NY: Doubleday.

Hall, E. T. (1974). *Handbook for proxemic research.* Washington, DC: Social Anthropology and Visual Communication.

Hastie, R. (1981). Schematic principles in human memory. In E. T. Higgins, C. P. Herman, & M. P. Zanna (Eds.), *Social cognition: The Ontario Symposium* (Vol. 1, pp. 39–88). Hillsdale, NJ: Erlbaum.

Henige, D. (1980). The disease of writing: Ganda and Nyoro kinglists in a newly literate world. In J. C. Miller (Ed.), *The African past speaks: Essays on oral tradition and history* (pp. 240–261). Kent, England: Dawson & Sons.

Higgins, E. T., & Rholes, W. S. (1978). Saying is believing: Effects of message modification on memory and liking for the person described. *Journal of Experimental Social Psychology, 14,* 363–378.

Hirt, E. R. (1990). Do I see only what I expect? Evidence for an expectancy-guided retrieval model. *Journal of Personality and Social Psychology, 58,* 937–951.

Horowitz, M. J. (1976). *Stress response syndromes.* New York: Jacob Aronson.

Horowitz, M. J. (1987). *States of mind.* New York: Plenum.

Janoff-Bulman, R. (1979). Characterological versus behavioral self-blame: Inquiries into depression and rape. *Journal of Personality and Social Psychology, 37*, 1798–1809.

Janoff-Bulman, R. (1992). *Shattered assumptions: Towards a new psychology of trauma.* New York: Free Press.

Johnson, M. K. (1988). Reality monitoring: An experimental phenomenological approach. *Journal of Experimental Psychology: General, 117*(4), 390–394.

Johnson, M. K., Foley, M. A., Suengas, A. G., & Raye, C. L. (1988). Phenomenal characteristics of memories for perceived and imagined autobiographical events. *Journal of Experimental Psychology: General, 117*(4), 371–376.

Johnson, M. K., & Raye, C. L. (1981). Reality monitoring. *Psychological Review, 88*(1), 67–85.

Keyes, R. (1992). *Nice guys finish seventh.* New York: HarperCollins.

Langer, E. J. (1975). The illusion of control. *Journal of Personality and Social Psychology, 32*, 311–328.

Lefcourt, H. M. (1973). The functions of the illusions of control and freedom. *American Psychologist, 28*, 417–425.

Lewinsohn, P. M., & Rosenbaum, M. (1987). Recall of parental behavior by acute depressives, remitted depressives, and nondepressives. *Journal of Personality and Social Psychology, 52*(3), 611–619.

Loftus, E. F., & Loftus, G. R. (1980). On the permanence of stored information in the human brain. *American Psychologist, 35*(5), 409–420.

Loftus, E. F., Miller, D. G., & Burns, H. J. (1978). Semantic integration of verbal information into a visual memory. *Journal of Experimental Psychology: Human Learning and Memory, 4*, 19–31.

Maines, D. R., Sugrue, N. M., & Katovich, M. A. (1983). The sociological import of G. H. Mead's theory of the past. *American Sociological Review, 48*, 161–173.

Markus, H. (1977). Self-schemata and processing information about the self. *Journal of Personality and Social Psychology, 35*, 63–78.

McFarland, C., Ross, M., & DeCourville, N. (1989). Women's theories of menstruation and biases in recall of menstrual symptoms. *Journal of Personality and Social Psychology, 57*, 522–531.

McFarland, C., Ross, M., & Giltrow, M. (1992). Biased recollections in older adults: The role of implicit theories of aging. *Journal of Personality and Social Psychology, 62*, 837–850.

McKie, D. C., Prentice, B., & Reed, P. (1983). *Divorce: Law and the family in Canada.* Ottawa: Minister of Supply and Services.

Mead, G. H. (1932). *The philosophy of the present.* LaSalle, IL: Open Court.

Mead, G. H. (1964). The nature of the past. In A. J. Reck (Ed.), *Selective writings: George Herbert Mead* (pp. 345–354). Chicago: University of Chicago Press. (Original work published 1929)

Miller, J. C. (1980). Introduction: Listening for the African past. In J. C. Miller (Ed.), *The African past speaks: Essays on oral tradition and history* (pp. 1–60). Kent, England: Dawson & Sons.

Monk, R. (1991). *Ludwig Wittgenstein: The duty of genius.* London: Vintage Books.

Neisser, U. (1982). John Dean's memory: A case study. In U. Neisser (Ed.), *Memory observed: Remembering in natural contexts.* San Francisco: Freeman.

Neustadt, R. E., & May, E. R. (1986). *Thinking in time.* New York: Free Press.

Nietzsche, F. (1983). On the uses and disadvantages of history for life. In *Untimely meditations* (R. J. Hollingdale, Trans.). Cambridge University Press. (Original work published 1874)

Ong, W. J. (1982). *Orality and literacy*. New York: Methuen.

Packard, R. M. (1980). The study of historical process in African traditions of genesis: The Bashu myth of Muhiyi. In J. C. Miller (Ed.), *The African past speaks: Essays on oral tradition and history* (pp. 157–177). Kent, England: Dawson & Sons.

Pennebaker, J. W. (1989). Confession, inhibition and disease. In L. Berkowitz (Ed.), *Advances in experimental social psychology* (Vol. 22, pp. 211–240). San Diego: Academic Press.

Pennebaker, J. W. (1990). *Opening up: The healing power of confiding in others*. New York: Morrow.

Ross, M. (1981). Egocentric biases in attributions of responsibility: Antecedents and consequences. In E. T. Higgins, C. P. Herman, & M. P. Zanna (Eds.), *Social cognition: The Ontario Symposium* (Vol. 1, pp. 305–322). Hillsdale, NJ: Erlbaum.

Ross, M. (1989). Relation of implicit theories to the construction of personal histories. *Psychological Review, 96*, 341–357.

Ross, M. (1992). [Intuitive theories of depression]. Unpublished raw data.

Ross, M., & Holmberg, D. (1990). Recounting the past: Gender differences in the recall of events in the history of a close relationship. In J. M. Olson & M. P. Zanna (Eds.), *Self-inference processes: The Ontario Symposium* (Vol. 6, pp. 135–152). Hillsdale, NJ: Erlbaum.

Ross, M., Karr, J. W., & Buehler, R. M. (1992). *Assessing the authenticity of conflicting autobiographical memories*. Unpublished manuscript, University of Waterloo, Ontario.

Rothbart, M. (1981). Memory processes and social beliefs. In D. Hamilton (Ed.), *Cognitive processes in stereotyping and intergroup behavior* (pp. 145–182). Hillsdale, NJ: Erlbaum.

Salaman, E. (1970). *A collection of moments: A study of involuntary memories*. London: Longman.

Schank, R. C., & Abelson, R. P. (1977). *Scripts, plans, goals and understanding*. Hillsdale, NJ: Erlbaum.

Schooler, J. W., Clark, C. A., & Loftus, E. F. (1987). Knowing when memory is real. In M. M. Gruneberg, P. E. Morris, & R. N. Sykes (Eds.), *Practical aspects of memory: Current research and issues* (Vol. 1, pp. 83–88). New York: Wiley.

Schooler, J. W., Gerhard, D., & Loftus, E. F. (1986). Qualities of the unreal. *Journal of Personality and Social Psychology, 12*, 171–181.

Seligman, M. E. P. (1975). *Helplessness*. San Francisco: Freeman.

Sheehan, T. (1988). *The first coming*. New York: Vintage Books.

Silver, R. L., Boon, C., & Stones, M. H. (1983). Searching for meaning in misfortune: Making sense of incest. *Journal of Social Issues, 39*, 81–102.

Silver, R. L., & Wortman, C. B. (1980). Coping with undesirable life events. In J. Garber & M. E. P. Seligman (Eds.), *Human helplessness: Theory and applications* (pp. 279–375). New York: Academic Press.

Spence, D. P. (1982). *Narrative truth and historical truth: Meaning and interpretation in psychoanalysis*. New York: Norton.

Styron, W. (1990). *Darkness visible: A memoir of madness*. New York: Vintage Books.

Sutton, C. (1984). A breakdown in symmetry. *New Scientist, 26*, 34–35.

Taylor, S. E., & Crocker, J. (1981). Schematic bases of information processing. In E. T. Higgins, C. P. Herman, & M. P. Zanna (Eds.), *Social cognition: The Ontario Symposium* (Vol. 1, pp. 89–134). Hillsdale, NJ: Erlbaum.

Thucydides. (1954). *History of the Peloponnesian wars* (R. Warner, Trans.). London: Penguin.

Tice, D. (in press). Self-presentation and self-concept change. *Journal of Personality and Social Psychology*.

Trope, Y. (1978). Inferences of personal characteristics on the basis of information retrieved from one's memory. *Journal of Personality and Social Psychology, 36*, 93–106.

Updike, J. (1987). *Trust me*. New York: Knopf.

12

The remembered self and
the enacted self

ALAN BADDELEY

Willem Wagenaar's study (chap. 10 of this volume) represents an excellent example of the value of carefully planned and meticulously collected naturalistic data. Because of the quality of his earlier study, he was able to readdress the data to consider whether his memory was biased against events that cast him in an unfavorable light. The data suggest that exactly the opposite is the case, and allow a range of alternative hypotheses to be firmly rejected. I myself am convinced by this analysis, even though the pattern of observations is exactly the opposite to what one might have predicted on the basis of common wisdom, and indeed considerable data (see Baddeley, 1990, pp. 379–406, for a review). I do, however, have some misgivings over the extent to which these findings would generalize, and even more concern over Wagenaar's theoretical interpretation of them.

As Wagenaar himself emphasizes, an inevitable limitation on single-case studies is the question of generality. Despite this danger, single-case studies in neuropsychology have typically proved to generalize, and have been justifiably influential. Is there any reason to suspect that the present study will be any less general? I think there may be. Many authors have suggested that there are major differences in the ways in which individuals cope with threatening or conflicting information, with some tending to minimize such evidence (*repressors*) while others tend to focus on the discrepancy (*sensitizers*) (Byrne, 1964; Davis, 1990). One would therefore like to see a number of equally well designed studies on other subjects before generalizing too widely from these findings. Such a concern is reinforced when one considers possible alternative mechanisms that might have produced the results obtained.

A second concern is with Wagenaar's proposed explanation. Here I suggest that we can account for these findings in terms of existing models of learning, without such novel mechanisms as the tagging hypothesis proposed by Wagenaar. I should perhaps confess here to a dislike of tagging models, which lean heavily on methods of information storage in current conventional computers and seem to offer a very implausible mode of human learning and remembering. But do I have any reasons other than these prejudices for disliking the model proposed?

Problems with the tagging model

The aspects of tagging models that I dislike are first of all that they are typically all-or-none; in the present case this leaves the system with the decision to be made as to how unusual something has to be before it will be tagged. A second problem arises as to what exactly constitutes a tag. If everything that is atypical has an identical tag, then the system must surely have a problem in discriminating among such tags. A third problem concerns the information in a tag, which appears simply to mark an event as unusual. Surely it would be useful to have more information than this.

I am also a little uncomfortable with the fit of the model to the data. Very pleasant personal events occurred about as often (14 times) as very unpleasant ones (11), but were remembered *less* well than the corresponding other-related events. Why should this be? The tagging explanation also says nothing about the general trend for pleasant events to be better recollected; an account that can cover both would therefore seem preferable on grounds of parsimony.

An alternative interpretation

Although he suggests that autobiographical memory does not imply a separate system or different learning processes, Wagenaar does not attempt to use existing models. These models can, I think, explain his data relatively easily.

First of all, instead of slow and fast learning procedures, consider the broadly accepted distinction between *episodic* (or declarative or explicit) memory and *procedural* (or implicit) learning. Episodic memory often follows a single trial, and is demonstrated by the ability to recollect the events experienced at the time of learning. In procedural learning, a skill or habit is gradually acquired over a series of trials, a process that may leave the subject without any explicit recollection of the experiences that went into the learning (Richardson-Klavehn & Bjork, 1988).

The role of context

One of the problems in recollecting specific incidents is that of separating the given episode from other similar occasions. This will be possible to the extent that the incident in question has associated with it features that differentiate it from potentially competing events. Typically this will be

an association with a specific temporal and /or spatial context. The association between an event and a context is perhaps one of the essential features of episodic memory, and such contexts would seem to offer not a
single tag marking an event as exceptional, but a rich and infinitely
graded series of tags. Wagenaar's example of seeing a lion loose in a
Dutch town is likely to have sufficiently strikingly different context features to separate that scene in time very clearly from one's many other
experiences of Dutch towns and lions, without the need for an extra tagging mechanism.

Sources of bias in memory

How then do biases occur in such a system? They can in principle occur
at any of a range of points, including the initial perception, subsequent
rehearsal, storage, and eventual retrieval. We will discuss these in turn.

Perceptual Bias. There is considerable evidence to suggest that different
subjects with different values will perceive the same event in different
ways. Consider for example the classic study by Hastorf and Cantril
(1954) of a particularly violent Princeton–Dartmouth football game.
When asked to recall the game, Princeton students remembered many
more instances of illegally violent play committed by the Dartmouth
team, while the Dartmouth students showed the opposite pattern. When
instead of relying on memory, students were shown a film of the game
and asked to note any incidents of violence that occurred, essentially the
same pattern was found: Princeton students detected a preponderance
of Dartmouth violence while Dartmouth students showed the opposite
trend. Apparent differences in recollection may therefore reflect different initial perceptions. Such an interpretation cannot of course explain
the Wagenaar results, since recall involved incidents that he himself had
reported during the first part of the study.

Storage. Although I know of no convincing evidence to suggest that "dynamic" changes occur during the storage of memory traces, there is
rather more evidence to indicate that arousal may enhance the consolidation of the memory trace (Kleinsmith & Kaplan, 1963). These effects tend
not to be large, but a number of studies have confirmed that material
learned with high arousal tends to be relatively poorly recalled in the
first few minutes after learning, but may be better recalled than neutral
material after a much longer period (see Baddeley, 1990, pp. 379–406,
for a review). It is conceivable that the arousal level generated by the
embarrassing negative incidents was sufficiently high to produce this
effect, but were this so one might expect comparable results for very

positive self-related events, whereas in fact these were rather poorly recollected.

Retrieval. There is considerable evidence that highly charged emotional events may in extreme cases be very difficult to retrieve. For example, psychogenic amnesia and fugue are typically associated with the apparent need to escape from some overwhelmingly anxiety-provoking situation. A related phenomenon appears to be the amnesia frequently shown by violent criminals for the act of violence (Kopelman, 1987). However, while high levels of anxiety clearly can disrupt retrieval, such an effect would predict a result that was opposite to that observed in the Wagenaar study, where the self-related unpleasant events were of course better recollected.

Rehearsal. A more plausible interpretation is offered by the concept of rehearsal, reflecting differences in the frequency with which an event is reviewed by the subject. Linton (1978) showed that the more frequently an autobiographical incident had been retrieved, the easier it was to recall subsequently. The general tendency for pleasant events to be more easily recalled than unpleasant might thus stem at least in part from a subject's pleasure in recollecting such events, and possible avoidance of dwelling on more depressing memories. Is there any conceivable reason why Willem Wagenaar should have spent more time thinking about his few transgressions than about his more frequent pleasant experiences? Setting aside the implausible thought that Willem might simply be a Calvinist Dutchman preoccupied with sin, I would like to suggest an alternative explanation.

There is considerable evidence from Swann (1990) that people are very sensitive about feedback that appears to mismatch their perception of themselves. This preference for self-consistency is sufficiently powerful to outweigh the desire for praise, with the result that subjects who are low in self-esteem will prefer negative evaluations of themselves to positive evaluations. This is not simply an experimental laboratory phenomenon since it occurs even in the case of choice of matrimonial partner, where subjects who are low in self-esteem will report their matrimonial bond as stronger with a spouse who is critical; conversely, subjects with high self-esteem show a stronger affiliation to partners who praise them (Swann, Hixon, & De La Ronde, 1993). These effects do not occur immediately; if the subject is required to respond rapidly, then all subjects tend to prefer praise. It is only on reflection that the subjects with low self-esteem opt for criticism. This suggests very plausibly that we reflect on our experiences, and it seems not unreasonable to assume that an experience that appears to be both unpleasant and inconsistent will evoke considerably more attempts to accommodate and work through, attempts that would in fact act as rehearsals.

The autobiographical example given by Wagenaar might well have led to some probing and soul-searching. Anyone encountering the event described might reasonably ponder on whether it was merely an atypical and unfortunate anomaly, or whether it illustrated personality traits that were more characteristic than one might wish to believe. I suggest that "rehearsal" produced by this natural tendency to reflect on emotionally powerful but atypical evidence of one's personality offers a plausible explanation of Willem Wagenaar's vivid recollection of his "sins."

In conclusion then, I would suggest that differences in rehearsal pattern provide the most economical account of two features of Wagenaar's data; there is a general tendency for more pleasant events to be recollected because it is on the whole more pleasant to remember pleasant than unpleasant incidents. In addition, however, I suggest there is a tendency to ruminate on events in which one's action is clearly at odds with one's self-perception, leading to the paradoxically enhanced recall of embarrassing personal incidents.

The remembered self and the enacted self

Michael Ross and Roger Buehler are concerned with two interrelated issues: the cues that people use to decide whether an autobiographical memory is accurate, and the implications of occasions in which two people have conflicting memories of the same autobiographical event. Their account of some of the cues that allow us to decide that something is a memory rather than a confabulation is part of a growing literature concerned with this important but neglected problem. Although it, like most of the work in this area including my own, is still largely at the level of natural history, I firmly believe that this stage is an important precursor to the difficult task of exploring experimentally the use of such cues. The recent work of Jacoby and his colleagues offers some encouraging results in the investigation of such factors in laboratory situations (Jacoby & Kelley, in press). It is to be hoped that in the next few years we should be able to extend Jacoby's elegant techniques to the study of the cues to autobiographical recollection.

Those cases in which two people disagree strongly in their recollection of some jointly experienced event offer, as Ross and Buehler suggest, clues as to the reason why autobiographical memories may be important. Such events probably reflect important aspects of our self-perception, and as the previously mentioned work by Swann and his colleagues suggests, information that appears to question our perception of ourselves can appear to be particularly threatening. Swann suggests that this is because an accurate view of how the world sees us is likely to be an important tool in effective social behavior. Errors in self-perception can be very socially disruptive.

The enacted self. Our recollection of our past is clearly an important tool for predicting the future and as such is likely to affect our interaction with others. This is, however, certainly not the only way in which we project ourselves. Indeed, the remembered self is invisible to an outside observer; and yet we clearly do recognize people as coherent and continuing individuals, and indeed use expressions such as "He was not himself" and "She is back to her old self again." I suggest that such expressions are based on the observation of behavior patterns and skills, both motor and social. We know very little about what goes into such judgments, but it is certainly the case in patients suffering from brain damage that in some cases this "enacted" self is preserved even in densely amnesic patients, while in other cases the patient will be perceived to have changed. Consequently, comments like "He was not the man I married" are unfortunately not uncommon following severe brain damage (Bond, 1984).

A particularly striking example of this occurred in the case of a frontal amnesic patient, R. J. (Baddeley & Wilson, 1986). R. J. was densely amnesic and tended to confabulate quite floridly, and yet had a very distinctive and charming personality. We revisited him some years after our initial study, by which time he had deteriorated substantially as a result of a minor stroke that complicated the effects of his existing head injury. We tested him toward the end of the day when he was tired, and sadly he seemed like a deteriorated shell of his old self, not even capable of producing coherent English sentences. However, his wife reported that "on a good day" he was just the same old R. J. It was as if, perhaps following some principle such as Lashley's Mass Action, the stroke had cost him brain tissue that he could ill afford to lose. When all went well, he could apparently still function as his old self; on a bad day, however, or when heavily fatigued, his personality appeared to disintegrate.

When we had studied him previously, his autobiographical memory was distinctly and indeed on occasion bizarrely impaired, suggesting problems in the recollected self. But his enacted self allowed him to appear as a colorful and charming individual, having many of the crucial features that had attracted his wife and friends to him before his head injury. On the second occasion he had lost both remembered and enacted self, leading to a condition of personal disintegration.

It is clear from the examples given by Ross and Buehler that we do care about the way in which others perceive us, and find it somewhat disturbing when a discrepancy occurs between our personal recollection and that of someone close whom we know and trust. It seems likely that the enacted self, based on our behavior as observed by others, is likely to be at least as important a component as the remembered self in any social interaction. As such, it too is deserving of further study.

REFERENCES

Baddeley, A. D. (1990). *Human memory: Theory and practice*. London: Erlbaum.

Baddeley, A. D., & Wilson, B. (1986) Amnesia, autobiographical memory and confabulation. In D. Rubin (Ed.), *Autobiographical memory* (pp. 225–252). Cambridge University Press.

Bond, M. (1984). The psychiatry of closed head injury. In D. N. Brooks (Ed.), *Closed head injury*. Oxford: Oxford University Press.

Byrne, D. (1964). Repression – sensitization as a dimension of personality. In B. A. Maher (Ed.), *Progress in experimental personality research* (Vol. 1). New York: Academic Press.

Davis, P. J. (1990). Repression and the inaccessibility of emotional memories. In J. L. Singer (Ed.), *Repression: Defence mechanism and personality style*. Chicago: University of Chicago Press.

Hastorf, A. H., & Cantril, H. (1954). They saw a game: A case study. *Journal of Abnormal and Social Psychology, 97*, 399–401.

Jacoby, L. L., & Kelley, C. (in press). Unconscious inferences of memory: Dissociations and automaticity. In D. Milner & M. Rugg (Eds.), *The neuropsychology of consciousness*. Hillsdale, NJ: Erlbaum.

Kleinsmith, L. J., & Kaplan, S. (1963). Paired associated learning as a function of arousal and interpolated interval. *Journal of Experimental* Psychology, *65*, 190–193.

Kopelman, M. D. (1987). Amnesia: Organic and psychogenic. *British Journal of Psychiatry, 150*, 428–442.

Linton, M. (1978). Real world memory after six years: An in vivo study of very long-term memory. In M. M. Gruneberg, P. E. Morris, & R. N. Sykes (Eds.), *Practical aspects of memory* (pp. 69–76). London: Academic Press.

Richardson-Klavehn, A., & Bjork, R. A. (1988). Measures of memory. *Annual Review of Psychology, 39*, 475–543.

Swann, W. B. (1990). To be adored or to be known? The interplay of self-enhancement and self-verification. In R. M. Sorrentino & E. T. Higgins (Eds.), *Foundations of social behavior* (Vol. 2). New York: Guilford Press.

Swann, W. B., Hixon, J. G., & De La Ronde, C. (1993). *Some perversities of marital bliss: Negative self-concepts and embracing the bitter "truth."* Manuscript submitted for publication.

13

The authenticity and utility
of memories

EUGENE WINOGRAD

> I do not recall the position lucidly enough to notate it here, but
> perhaps some lover of "fairy chess" (to which type of problem
> it belongs) will look it up some day in one of those blessed li-
> braries where old newspapers are microfilmed, as all our mem-
> ories should be.
>
> Vladimir Nabokov (1966), p. 15

Accuracy implies correspondence between what is remembered and an
earlier state of affairs in the world. There are two influential points of
view that assume that memory is not, or cannot, be accurate. The first,
essentially a postmodern view of the world (see Gergen, chap. 5 of this
volume), rejects the possibility of correspondence between memory and
the event remembered on the grounds that there is no single valid interpretation of the original event against which to attempt a match. By this
view, past realities are always being constructed anew and any match is
illusory. Another view grants that a kind of accuracy is possible – events
may leave a record – but still rejects any simple correspondence model.
Memory is seen as a process of reconstruction, not reappearance (Bartlett, 1932; Neisser, 1967). By this view, it is highly unlikely that remembering will be entirely faithful to the original event. There may be occa-
sional correspondence, or accurate remembering, but normal remembering is dynamic. Still, no matter how passive or dynamic one's theory
of memory function, it would be very surprising from an evolutionary
standpoint if our memories had little to do with the events in our past at
all. As Neisser puts it while arguing for a highly constructive view of memory, "Even if the constructive nature of memory is fully acknowledged,
the fact remains that information about the past must be somehow stored
and preserved for subsequent use. Today's experience must leave some
sort of trace behind if it is to influence tomorrow's construction" (1967,
p. 280).

I want to consider here the implications for the question of memory
accuracy of Michael Ross's elegant work of the past several years, particularly his influential 1989 *Psychological Review* article. My own position on

the question of whether memory is accurate is as follows: Sometimes memory is accurate and sometimes it is inaccurate. There is not much point in debating the general question at all because instances of surprising accuracy and remarkable distortion abound. I will consider a few of these cases later. A major task for the psychology of memory is to be able to state the conditions conducive to accuracy and the conditions likely to lead to distortion. Ross and his colleagues have made a major contribution to our understanding of this difficult issue. First, to underline how important the question of memory accuracy can be, I will discuss the case of psychoanalysis.

Psychoanalysis and sexual abuse

Freud was so passionate about archaeology that his office was stuffed with relics of prehistory. He likened the task of the psychoanalyst to that of the archaeologist in that both are engaged in digging up hidden pieces of the past. For both, the task is arduous and requires skill and patience if the hidden kernels of truth are to be found. What sustains the searcher in both cases is the belief that the pieces are really there. As Donald Spence observes, Freud believed that historical truth – what really happened – was the goal. Spence (1982) argues, however, that only narrative truth is attained in psychotherapy. Spence argues that the archaeological metaphor is misleading and what emerges from the psychoanalytic process is a narrative constructed by the patient under the analyst's guidance in accord with a story line predetermined by the analyst's beliefs. The analytic process, to a large extent, consists of the analyst guiding the story of the patient by communicating to him or her what constitutes narrative truth. Historical truth, or correspondence to an earlier reality, is believed to be the outcome by the participants but it is a shared delusion.

Does it matter whether the product is historical or narrative truth? It is often argued that what the patient believes to be the truth is what is important for therapy to be successful. By this view, fantasies are as important as accurately recalled events. Remembered events have a cognitive and affective reality that is paramount; for healing to occur it is the subjective reality that must be dealt with. Yet, as can be seen from the current debate about sexual abuse in early childhood, the issue of historical truth remains. Masson (1984) has argued that Freud was correct initially when he believed the stories of his female patients being treated for hysteria. These stories involved sexual relations with adult family members at an early age. Subsequently, in a decision of great importance for the development of psychoanalytic theory and practice, Freud changed his mind about these reports and reinterpreted them as fantasies. The question of whether Freud's first or second view is correct is a question about the accuracy of memory.

The accuracy of early memories of sexual abuse is an issue that will not go away. (See also Neisser, chap. 1 of this volume.) Daniel Goleman reports in the *New York Times* (July 21, 1992) on the controversy surrounding delayed reports by adults of sexual abuse in childhood. In many cases, the claim is made that repressed memories came to consciousness only decades later. To what extent are these memory reports to be taken as accurate? How often are they a narrative construction arrived at jointly by a therapist and patient through suggestion? Goleman reports that the proliferation of these reports has led to the establishment of the False Memory Syndrome Foundation. This organization has been consulted by hundreds of parents claiming that they have been falsely accused by a grown child of having sexually molested her (most cases involve daughters) as a child. What is the status of these memory claims? Are they accurate?

What constitutes accuracy? Neisser's Pearl Harbor memory

Brown and Kulik's (1977) famous paper on "flashbulb memory" presents vivid and detailed accounts of their informants' memories for the circumstances of hearing the news of the assassination of President Kennedy 12 years earlier. Neisser (1982; Neisser & Harsch, 1992) has been appropriately critical of Brown and Kulik's undocumented assumption that these memory reports are accurate. He presents some examples of inaccurate flashbulb memories, including his own memory of hearing the news of the Japanese attack on Pearl Harbor in 1941. Neisser remembers sitting at home listening to a baseball game on the radio when the fateful news interrupted the game and recalls rushing upstairs to share the news with his mother. He reports that it took decades before he realized the absurdity of this story since no baseball game would have been played in December. It seems that this memory is inaccurate. Yet, as Thompson and Cowan (1986) and others have pointed out, a professional football game was being broadcast that day and was interrupted by the Pearl Harbor announcement. Let us assume that the young Neisser was, in fact, listening to that football game. Clearly, his memory does not correspond to the event at the level of a football game. On the other hand, it is accurate at a more general level of description: listening to a professional athletic contest that was interrupted by the profoundly important news of Pearl Harbor. The lesson here is that there are degrees of accuracy. A memory that is inaccurate at a more detailed level of description may be accurate at a more general level of event description. For some purposes, as in eyewitness identification, precise identification at the individual level is required. There are rules about what constitutes an appropriate suspect lineup: To recall a criminal as "a tall bearded white man wearing glasses" may be very useful for the police in tracking down suspects, but may not be sufficient for identification of the criminal in a lineup of six men meeting that description.

Ross's analysis of systematic inaccuracy

Ross and his colleagues have furthered our understanding of memory accuracy by trying to account in a systematic fashion for certain kinds of inaccuracy. In the typical study reviewed by Ross (1989), people are asked to recall their past standing on a personal attribute. The attribute might be their attitude toward capital punishment or abortion, how they voted in a past presidential election, how much their income was at some time in the past, or how much pain they felt on their last visit to a pain clinic. In these studies, a record of the actual previous state of affairs is available so that the investigator can assess the accuracy of later recall. Ross has shown convincingly that when recall is not accurate, it is wrong in a systematic way. Errors are not random, but are predictable from the rememberer's current beliefs and knowledge.

To be specific, the past is interpreted in accord with two principles. First, we note our present status on the attribute: How do I feel about abortion now? How will I vote in this election? How much does my back hurt at this moment? Second, we invoke a theory either of consistency (stability) or change. Guided by these two factors, we construct the past. If we err in recalling our earlier attitude toward capital punishment, it is in the direction of remembering ourselves as having been more like we are now. When we misremember how we voted, we are very likely to believe that we formerly voted in line with our current political leanings. We also are likely, when misremembering our past income, to err in the direction of our current income. If income has dramatically increased over the intervening years, remembered income is inflated; if income has declined, so does remembered income. The present influences the remembered past.

Ross's research should not be misunderstood, however. Overall, recall is often quite accurate. These systematic efforts at bringing the remembered past into line with the present do not necessarily overpower accurate remembering. For example, in the study on remembered earnings, recall errors occurred only 4% of the time and the correlation between reported income on the two occasions was .84 (Withey, 1954). However, when errors did occur, they were systematic in that people exaggerated the consistency between their past and present incomes. Thus, even when overall accuracy is high, the residual inaccuracy can be accounted for. But sometimes memory is quite elastic: Of those voters who changed party identification from 1972 to 1976 (22% of the sample), fully 91% reported not changing (Niemi, Katz, & Newman, 1980).

It is important to note that Ross provides a theory of how memory changes *when* it changes. His theory does not require that memory always be inaccurate, nor even that it be inaccurate most of the time. Rather, he offers an explanation of why it changes when it does. He offers an explanation of errors in personal memory. As he puts it,

Biases are of interest for the same reasons that perceptual psychologists study illusions and psycholinguists study grammatical errors: mental processes may be revealed *that are obscured in accurate reports*. In the current context, biases provide an indication of the implicit theory used to guide recall. (1989, p. 344, italics added)

There must be inaccuracy or there is nothing to explain. To repeat, Ross's question is, when people are not accurate, in what systematic ways are their memories inaccurate? He does not undertake to tell us whether they will be inaccurate, although his theory does point to factors predisposing us to inaccuracy.

This account is not inconsistent with a traditional account of forgetting. That is, long retention intervals, interference from similar events, massed practice at learning, and inadequate rehearsal are factors long known to be associated with forgetting. When memory is weak, constructive factors of the type described by Ross may manifest themselves.

In fact, Ross cautions us not to overemphasize the extent to which normal memory is driven by reconstructive processes. He says, "Suppose I altered the focus and examined degree of accuracy. I would then conclude that much of the research demonstrates relatively accurate recall" (1989, p. 354). In agreement with Alba and Hasher (1983), Ross suggests that there may be at least two retrieval modes available: "People can choose to engage in relatively effortless, theory-guided recall or a more effortful and extensive memory search" (p. 355). "Effortless, theory-guided recall" is the retrieval mode that leads to the kinds of inaccuracies Ross documents. It is reconstructive remembering heavily dependent on our current state. It is one kind of retrieval, but not the only kind. Sometimes we engage in "a more effortful and extensive memory search." This retrieval mode leads to accuracy but at the expense, no doubt, of gaps in the record.

If Ross is correct in proposing two kinds of retrieval, and I believe that he is, then the question is when do we engage in each type of retrieval? We are a long way from answering this fundamental question, but it seems clear that without an understanding of the functions and goals of remembering, we will never succeed. Ross and Buehler are to be commended for reminding us of the importance of function. In contexts where impression management is an important goal, "recollections allow individuals to project their preferred images of themselves," as Ross and Buehler observe. Historical truth is not crucial here, and recall would seem to be guided to a considerable degree by present needs. When testifying under oath, presumably one engages in effortful retrieval with accuracy as the goal. To be sure, the effort does not guarantee accuracy (nor does theory-guided retrieval insure distortion), but, faced with different goals, one goes about remembering in different ways.

It may be noted that Ross and Buehler are not alone in considering goals and functions in the analysis of memory (see, for example, Baddeley, 1988; Bruce, 1985; Neisser, 1988; Pillemer, 1992). Social psychologists cannot remind us too often that, in life outside the laboratory, remembering is usually a social act. As Neisser has observed, "Any actual instance of remembering falls somewhere on a continuum between two extremes: utility (using the past to accomplish some present end) and verity (using memory to recapture what really happened in the past" (1988, p. 557). Historically, psychologists have tended to see one extreme at the expense of the other. In the Ebbinghausian tradition of controlled laboratory experiments, the focus has always been on verity. Bartlett, it should be noted, saw the study of memory as part of social psychology and emphasized the constructive aspect of remembering. Ross and Buehler are to be commended for including both ends of Neisser's continuum, utility and verity, and for beginning the serious analysis of how both functions are carried out when we remember.

Memory distortion in autobiography: Nabokov's roommate

In his biography of Vladimir Nabokov, Brian Boyd (1990) describes an interesting distortion of memory in Nabokov's autobiography, *Speak, Memory* (1966), concerning the period when Nabokov roomed with his fellow Russian émigré Kalashnikov while an undergraduate at Cambridge. Nabokov states that he shared an apartment in Trinity Lane with his compatriot (not mentioned by name) for only a few months ("After a few months he left college, and I remained sole occupant of these lodgings," p. 259). But Boyd documents that the two shared rooms in Trinity College for their first few months at Cambridge, and then in January moved to the rooms in Trinity Lane, where they continued to live together until Kalashnikov failed his examinations after his second year and was forced to leave Cambridge. Thus, they lived together for a full two years. Furthermore, Boyd shows that the two were good friends; they drank together and engaged in typical undergraduate practical jokes, some of them leading to disciplinary action. They also were companions during the summer after their second year, when each visited his exiled family in Berlin. In fact, Nabokov had a love affair with Kalashnikov's young cousin during that summer in Berlin.

How can we account for this rewriting of the past? Here is a case where Ross's (1989) analysis proves fruitful. Boyd documents that as a youth at Cambridge, Kalashnikov was strongly anti-Semitic. Nabokov, we can surmise, was not anti-Semitic (his revered liberal father was well known for having fought against pogroms in Russia), but apparently he was able to tolerate anti-Semitism in others. What was Nabokov's attitude toward Jews later on? Boyd documents his hypersensitivity to real or imagined anti-Semitism. His wife was Jewish. Let us assume that while writing his autobiography in the 1950s, Nabokov detested anti-Semitism and believed in his own consistency over time. We can then interpret the distortion, 30 years later, of his association with Kalashnikov during his Cambridge years as an instance of his current attitude influencing his remembered past. There is also evidence from a 1947 letter to Edmund Wilson (Karlinsky, 1979) that Nabokov did remember Kalashnikov's anti-Semitism. What he did not remember was the extent of his association with him. Of course, it is difficult to know with certainty whether Nabokov's memory had altered over time or whether he simply chose to downplay an embarrassing friendship in his autobiography. The mature reader might try to recall his or her college roommates as an exercise.

Accuracy and distortion in diary studies

Two recent studies of autobiographical memory for everyday events have shown very accurate memory. As reported elsewhere in this volume, Willem Wagenaar kept a daily diary for four years and tested his recall of the recorded events by presenting himself with cues anywhere from shortly after the event to five years later. The cues were information about an aspect of the event, such as where it occurred or who was involved (for a description of the procedure, see Wagenaar, 1986, and chap. 10 of this volume). Remarkably, although Wagenaar demonstrated forgetting over time in that more cues were required to retrieve the events as time went by, when he did recall he was accurate. A similar finding emerged from Brewer's (1988) beeper study. Undergraduates carried beepers around that went off at random times. The participants recorded what was going on when the beeper sounded and this event record was the basis for later tests of recall. Like Wagenaar, Brewer found scarcely any cases of inaccurate recall.

Why was so little evidence of constructive retrieval found in these studies? We might classify these as cases of "more effortful and extensive memory search," echoing Ross's words, from subjects who, because they were well aware that a record existed, were avoiding "effortless, theory-guided recall." But what, then, should we make of the cases of misrecall reported by Steen Larsen (1992) in a diary study much like Wagenaar's? The Prime Minister of Sweden, Olof Palme, was assassinated during the period of time that Larsen was keeping a diary. Larsen, who is Danish, observed that this event would seem to be the kind of news "of which 'flashbulb memories' are made." Another event occurring during this period would also seem to have had flashbulb properties for a Scandinavian: the Chernobyl nuclear accident, which produced a nuclear cloud drifting toward Denmark and Sweden. Yet Larsen's recall of both events a few months later was wrong in many respects. For instance, he recalled hearing the news about Chernobyl on the radio while home alone in the morning, whereas his diary shows he heard the news "at Pia's place just after work; she was home, ill." Larsen observes that in spite of the evidence of the diary, he still has vivid false memories of both events. It might be fruitless to draw inferences from the faulty memory of one individual, but there is also Neisser and Harsch's (1992) evidence of flawed flashbulb memories of the *Challenger* space shuttle explosion. The day after the disaster, they obtained reports from undergraduates about how they heard the news. Almost three years later, when the same informants were asked the same questions again, over 40% were clearly inconsistent. So even flashbulb memories may not be accurate.

It seems to me that we have little understanding of why Wagenaar and Brewer, on the one hand, found remarkably accurate recall, while Larsen and Neisser and Harsch, on the other, found substantial distortions of memory. Nor do I have an explanation to offer. What is important is that we may have finally reached the point in the study of memory where the question of accounting for *both* accurate and inaccurate remembering is recognized as our task. Up to now, we have been predisposed by theory to regard either accuracy or distortion as reflecting "normal" remembering and therefore tended to focus on only that aspect. The work of Ross and his colleagues, by recognizing that both accurate and inaccurate remembering are part of the normal functioning of memory (although their primary goal is to account for distortions in personal recall), helps set the stage for significant progress toward an integrated understanding of the processes involved in remembering.

REFERENCES

Alba, J. W., & Hasher, L. (1983). Is memory schematic? *Psychological Bulletin, 93,* 203–231.

Baddeley, A. D. (1988). But what the hell is it for? In M. M. Gruneberg, P. E.

Morris, & R. N. Sykes (Eds.), *Practical aspects of memory: Current research and issues* (Vol. 1, pp. 3–19). Chichester, England: Wiley.

Bartlett, F. C. (1932). *Remembering: A study in experimental and social psychology.* Cambridge University Press.

Boyd, B. (1990). *Vladimir Nabokov: The Russian years.* Princeton, NJ: Princeton University Press.

Brewer, W. F. (1988). Memory for randomly sampled autobiographical events. In U. Neisser & E. Winograd (Eds.), *Remembering reconsidered: Ecological and traditional approaches to the study of memory* (pp. 21–90). Cambridge University Press.

Brown, R., & Kulik, J. (1977). Flashbulb memories. *Cognition, 5,* 73–99.

Bruce, D. (1985). The how and why of ecological memory. *Journal of Experimental Psychology: General, 114,* 78–90.

Freud, S. (1962). The aetiology of hysteria. In J. Strachey (Ed.), *The standard edition of the complete psychological works of Sigmund Freud* (Vol. 3, pp. 191–221). London: Hogarth Press. (Original work published 1896)

Freud, S. (1962). My views on the part played by sexuality in the aetiology of neuroses. In J. Strachey (Ed.), *The standard edition of the complete psychological works of Sigmund Freud* (Vol. 7, pp. 271–279). London: Hogarth Press. (Original work published 1906)

Karlinsky, S. (1979). *The Nabokov–Wilson letters.* New York: Harper & Row.

Larsen, S. F. (1992). Potential flashbulbs: Memories of ordinary news as the baseline. In E. Winograd & U. Neisser (Eds.), *Affect and accuracy: Studies of "flashbulb" memories* (pp. 32–64). Cambridge University Press.

Masson, J. M. (1984). *The assault on truth: Freud's suppression of the seduction theory.* New York: Farrar, Straus, & Giroux.

Nabokov, V. (1966). *Speak, memory: An autobiography revisited.* New York: Putnam.

Neisser, U. (1967). *Cognitive psychology.* New York: Appleton-Century Crofts.

Neisser, U. (Ed.). (1982). *Memory observed: Remembering in natural contexts.* San Francisco: Freeman.

Neisser, U. (1988). Time present and time past. In M. M. Gruneberg, P. E. Morris, & R. N. Sykes (Eds.), *Practical aspects of memory: Current research and issues* (Vol. 2, pp. 545–560). Chichester, England: Wiley.

Neisser, U., & Harsch, N. (1992). Phantom flashbulbs: False recollections of hearing the news about Challenger. In E. Winograd & U. Neisser (Eds.), *Affect and accuracy in recall: Studies of "flashbulb" memories* (pp. 9–31). Cambridge University Press.

Niemi, G., Katz, R. S., & Newman, D. (1980). Reconstructing past partisanship: The failure of party identification recall questions. *American Journal of Political Science, 24,* 633–651.

Pillemer, D. B. (1992). Remembering personal circumstances: A functional analysis. In E. Winograd & U. Neisser (Eds.), *Affect and accuracy in recall: Studies of "flashbulb" memories* (pp. 236–264). Cambridge University Press.

Ross, M. (1989). Relation of implicit theories to the construction of personal histories. *Psychological Review, 96,* 341–357.

Spence, D. P. (1982). *Narrative truth and historical truth.* New York: Norton.

Thompson, C. P., & Cowan, T. (1986). Flashbulb memories: A nicer interpretation of a Neisser recollection. *Cognition, 22,* 199–200.

Wagenaar, W. A. (1986). My memory: A study of autobiographical memory over six years. *Cognitive Psychology, 18,* 225–252.

Withey, S. B. (1954). Reliability of recall of income. *Public Opinion Quarterly, 18,* 197–204.

14

The remembered self in amnesics

WILLIAM HIRST

The *remembered self* can refer to memory of past concepts of self or to the way memory of the past structures and changes present construal of self. These two senses of the remembered self no doubt interact to give shape and definition to the present self, but a full discussion of both aspects would be more than I could accomplish in a short essay. Consequently, I want to confine the present discussion to the way memory of the past structures and changes present self-construal. Students of the self only vaguely understand this process. Probably the best articulations of the relation between memory and self grow out of work in narrative psychology (see Bruner, 1990; Howard, 1991; Spence, 1982; Viederman, 1979). From the perspective of a narrative psychologist, selves are construed through autobiographical narrating. Starting with the observation that people engage continuously in the interpretation of present and past experiences, narrative psychologists contend that this interpretation takes the form of story telling. For them, the self plays the role of both protagonist and narrator in these stories, and through these roles, people come to terms with who and what they are.

Memory contributes to self-actualizing narrative telling because it serves as the raw material for the narrative. As raw material, memories do not constitute the self. Without the interpretive molding provided by narrative telling, memories would have little chance of being much more than unconnected bits of information. My recollections of past jobs, loves, and tragedies are each fairly meaningless memories unless they can be placed in a larger context. When they can serve as ingredients for my life story, they become not just any job, love affair, or tragedy, but my job, my love affair, and my tragedy. As I interpret them in the context of a narrative telling of my life, they begin to shape my self-concept. I mold these memories into the proper narrative form, and interestingly, the narrative form will in turn dictate what memories I recollect. In this sense, "memories" can be thought of as ordinary building blocks, capable of being used in a variety of ways.

In this paper, I want to study the way in which the psychology of memory, narrative telling and self interact to effect changes in the self. The remarkable constancy of the self across a lifetime should not mask its capacity for change, indeed, its inevitable change. As many can testify, a major tragedy can profoundly alter the sense of self. From a narrative approach, the evolution of a self buffeted by experience occurs because of changes in narrative telling. People alter their concept of themselves as their life narratives shift. Thus, for a narrative psychologist, psychotherapeutic clients must work to revise their narratives (Schaffer, 1992; Spence, 1982), and people overcome by grief and tragedy must learn to construct a new narrative of their future (Viederman, 1979).

Change in the construal of self can occur in myriad ways, according to the narrative perspective. Change surfaces in part because the relation between self-construal, narrative, and memory forms a circle. The art of narrative telling determines the building blocks I use to construct the complex palace I call the *self*; it also guides the construction of this palace. Memory may serve as the raw material of autobiographical telling, and the resulting narrative may in turn guide the construal of self. The resulting construal of self will in part then determine what memories are subsequently remembered and accommodated by a new autobiographical narrative. This new narrative may in turn result in a new construal of self. The complex interactions suggested by this circle assure an ever-changing self-construal. Because one has a self, one is constantly interpreting experience. This interpretation will in turn impact on subsequent construals of self.

Self-construal, however, is not tethered to memory alone. New experiences can also change the self. From the perspective of a narrative psychologist, they do so by providing additional building blocks with which to build a narrative. If people decide to incorporate a new experience into their life narrative – often, they may feel they have no alternative but to include it – then the new experience must be interpreted in a way that "narratively" connects the present with the past. The retelling can be done straightforwardly by finding a way to weave the new experience into the old narrative without inflicting damage. Most narratives have *themes*. New memories could be incorporated in a narrative as further support for an already established theme. For instance, I may conceive of myself as a person on the rise in my company. I do not have to alter this theme to accommodate a new promotion. I need only add this new experience to the already developing theme. I was vice-president yesterday, and I am executive vice-president today.

New experience may alter self by buttressing existing themes, but often one cannot easily weave a present experience into the ongoing narrative without disturbing a narrative theme. A new experience might evoke new attitudes and beliefs, and these in turn may require new narrative themes. These new attitudes, beliefs, and themes may lead to an entire restructuring of the narrative. As psychologists of memory have noted, memories fade and change character and content, adapting to current attitudes and beliefs (Bartlett, 1932). This ebb and flow can, indeed must, shape the contours of a narrative. With new experience and a potential change in attitude and belief, new memories may surface and others may be lost or unintentionally altered. Thus, in building their life narratives, people may not only add new experiences onto already existing themes, they may forget previously remembered memories, change some recollections, and remember previously forgotten past events. These shifts in the raw material of memory may not only reinforce newly emerging narrative themes, but may in themselves create additional themes. An entirely different narrative might result from the changed mnemonic landscape. Instead of being married, one becomes a widow. The theme of how to cope with the demands of marriage changes to the theme of how to cope with grief and loneliness. Old memories are revived, others changed, others forgotten, in an attempt to deal with the new theme.

According to the narrative approach sketched here, then, changes in self can be traced to the interaction between self-construal, memory, and narrative, to the incorporation of new experiences into already existing thematic structures, and to the reconfiguration of a narrative with the establishment of new themes. This framework, while rich in its possibilities, is at best a line drawing waiting to be colored in. In this essay, I attempt to provide some color by focusing on the remembered self in a special population – brain-damaged patients with amnesia. For most people, memory, narrative, and self intertwine to create a single cord so tightly strung that it is almost impossible to separate the individual strands. With amnesics, nature has pulled apart the twisted strands. Consequently, this disorder may open a window into the dynamics of self-construction that may be difficult to peer into when studying normal adults. In particular, it may offer us the amazing circumstances of observing the possibility of change in self when people can no longer remember.

In most brain-damaged patients, the observable cognitive deficits are a complex affair, with disruptions found in a variety of cognitive domains. However, the brain damage in a small number of patients is such that the cognitive deficit is confined to memory. Language, perception, and cognition remain intact. The observed amnesia can be one of two kinds. *Anterograde amnesia* refers to the inability to remember events that occurred after the onset of the amnesia. *Retrograde amnesia* refers to the inability to remember events that occurred before the onset of the amnesia. By and large, most amnesic patients manifest some level of both retrograde and anterograde amnesia, but the densities of the two amnesias need not be correlated (Cohen & Squire, 1980; Marslen-Wilson &

Teuber, 1975; Squire, Cohen, & Nadel, 1984; Squire & Slater, 1978; Squire, Slater, & Chace, 1975; Squire, Slater, & Miller, 1981). Many anterograde amnesics have a mild retrograde amnesia, confined to a short period before the onset of the amnesia. As for retrograde amnesics, it is rare – indeed, it may be impossible – to observe an organically based retrograde amnesia without an accompanying pronounced anterograde amnesia.

Narrative psychologists, at least those who might subscribe to the framework sketched in this introduction, can offer some straightforward predications about amnesics' capacity to change their selves. Amnesics' suddenly impoverished recollection of the past should limit their ability to change their selves with experience. Anterograde amnesics could be expected to maintain self-consciousness, inasmuch as their memories for pre-onset experiences remain accessible. They should, however, feel no need to establish new narrative themes in response to new experiences inasmuch as their autobiographies should not reach beyond the onset of their amnesia. The narrative themes of the past should continue to shape their present narratives. Their selves should remain static, with evolution arrested in the period marking the onset of their amnesia. As to retrograde amnesics, one might expect a sudden transformation in their life narratives, not merely the truncated version expected with anterograde amnesics. Events that figured in pre-onset autobiographies would no longer be present in post-onset narratives. This change should, according to narrative psychologies, dramatically reshape the self.

As my story unfolds, it should become clear that these predictions rest in part on a too narrowly confined conception of self – one confined to *self-representation* – and to a too simplistic description of amnesia. These subtleties will force me to reconsider the shades and hues with which memory can color the evolving self. In particular, I will argue that one can have a dynamic changing self-concept even without personal narratives. Memories may be implicit or stored in the social setting around us. But I get ahead of myself. Let me begin with a word about the patients I will be discussing.

The four patients ranged in age from 56 to 62. Their IQs, as measured by the WAIS, ranged from 110 to 125. They had an average of 16.8 years of education. All the patients had a severe anterograde amnesia, but the density of the amnesia varied. They could recall at most one word from a ten-word list after a minute of distraction, compared to normal age-matched recall of about six. Their memory problems involved both visual and verbal memory. They recalled an average of 0.75 hard pairs in the paired associate test on the verbal portion of the Weschler Memory Scale. Their retrograde amnesia varied widely, with one patient's memory deficit stretching back almost 40 years. The others' retrograde amnesia seemed to be confined to a year or two, with one patient's retrograde amnesia remaining essentially undetectable. Thus, all the patients had great difficulty recalling events that occurred after the onset of their amnesia, but only one of the patients I am going to talk about had great difficulty with memories prior to the onset of his amnesia.

What do anterograde amnesics remember about their lives?

As I have suggested, the memory problems amnesics face are more subtle than simply not remembering anything. Consequently, before I discuss how amnesics may help us understand the remembered self, I need to describe the nature of the amnesic deficit. Such an examination will tell us what "raw material" amnesics can work with to construct their autobiographical narrative. With a grasp of the available raw material, I can consider amnesics' autobiographical narratives and ultimately their capacity to change their selves.

Several studies of amnesic memory for political events and television shows reveal a marked and sudden decline in post-onset memories when compared with pre-onset memories (see Squire, 1987). A multitude of studies of amnesia examining memory for word lists, stories, geometric patterns, and pictures reinforce the basic claim that amnesics can remember few new experiences (see Hirst, 1992). But despite this plethora of work in the laboratory, few studies have examined amnesics' memory for daily life. This dearth of research is unfortunate inasmuch as memory for daily events probably constitutes the most important raw material of any autobiographical narrative. With this in mind, Jim Satriano, working in my laboratory, decided to probe amnesics' memory by conducting a diary study with three anterograde amnesics (Satriano, 1992).

The diary study

One technique for assessing memory for daily events involves the use of diaries. Subjects can be asked to record at the end of the day the "salient" events of the day (Wagenaar, 1986), or in a more systematic manner, subjects can be given a beeper to carry and asked to record their activities each time the beeper goes off (Brewer, 1988). This latter technique is especially suited for amnesics, inasmuch as amnesics should be able to record an event as it is happening. Satriano gave three amnesics a telephone pager (beeper) and a set of index cards that would serve as event logs. The beepers were small enough to fit easily into pocket or purse or could be clipped onto a belt or strap.

Besides the three experimental subjects, there were three standard controls and three delayed controls. All six controls were matched with amnesics for age and years of education. The three standard controls followed the same diary-keeping procedure and testing conditions as the amnesics. The delayed controls followed the same diary-keeping procedure, but were tested much later than the standard controls. This delay was imposed in an attempt to equate amnesics' and controls' memory. If amnesic memory is simply a diminished normal memory – if you like, a light that has been dimmed, but not turned off – then delayed testing of controls could provide a means of equating amnesic and normal memory (Hirst, Johnson, Kim, Phelps, Risse, & Volpe, 1986; Hirst, Johnson, Phelps, & Volpe, 1988).

In the diary-keeping stage of the study, the experimenter beeped subjects seven times a day between 9:00 a.m. and 10:00 p.m. on a randomly determined schedule. The diary keeping continued for seven days. When subjects were beeped, they filled out experimenter-provided index cards, which subjects carried with them throughout the day. One side of the cards probed subjects about the *who, what, when,* and *where* of the event taking place when the beep occurred. For the *who* probe, subjects indicated the names of the participants and their relationship to the subjects. For the *what* probe, subjects provided a brief but specific description of the activity, with enough detail to distinguish frequently performed events from one another. For the *where* probe, subjects gave a specific description. They were told not just to say "home," but where in the home. Finally, for the *when* probe, subjects recorded the day, date, and time. On the opposite side of the index card, subjects indicated how frequently the event occurred on a 5-point scale, from "daily" to "rarely." They were also asked to specify the level of "emotional arousal." This latter question assessed the event's importance to the subject. They filled out the index card and placed it in an envelope. Subjects sealed the envelope at the end of each day and retained it for the experimenter.

Testing occurred 2 days after the final day of diary keeping for the amnesics and the standard controls. Testing occurred 32 days after diary keeping for the delayed controls.

Testing consisted of free recall, cued recall, recognition, and a test of temporal-order memory. In the free recall test, subjects recalled the events that they had recorded on the index cards. They were given new index cards with the same *who, when, what,* and *where* probes and asked to fill them with the details of the 49 logged events. They were told that they would successfully recall an event only if they filled out all the queries on a card. If subjects didn't recall 49 events, they were encouraged to complete the remaining cards with any event during the diary-keeping week. A correct response occurred only if the *who, what,* and *where* were correct. Both amnesics and controls had difficulty specifying the exact time and date. Inclusion of this factor would have obscured the relatively good performance of the controls. Admittedly, this test, as presently conceived, may not have fully assessed subjects' potential to recall daily activities inasmuch as it placed a somewhat artificial constraint on what could be recalled. Nevertheless, it provided a preliminary index of this potential.

In the cued recall test, subjects were probed with a *who, what, when, where,* or some combination of these and were asked to recall the unspecified features of the described event. The actual procedure was quite complicated. Satriano used as initial probes only the cues *what* and *when,* but followed up with a wide range of cues. *What* and *when* were used as the initial cues because Wagenaar (1986) reported that these probes are, respectively, the most and least powerful initial cues in eliciting memory for the entire event. The cues for *who* and *where* were counterbalanced so that each represented an equal number of second and third cues for each of the first cue type. Thus, in one condition, subjects were told the *when* of an event, then the *who,* and finally the *what.* Cueing occurred in the following orders: *what, who, where; what, where, who; when, who, where; when, where, who.* The different orders were distributed across the 49 recorded events.

The two-item forced-choice recognition tests were constructed by pairing the *who, what, when,* or *where* of one or more events, for a total of six possible pairings. The dyadic combinations were of three types: *true pairings,* in which the two elements were combined in a manner consistent with the original event, *false pairings,* in which an element describing one recorded event was combined with an element describing another recorded event, and *distractors,* in which the elements of the dyads consisted of probable but unrecorded events. For example, a distractor event might be "Shopping for fruit at Pathmark." The 72 dyads were equally divided among true pairings, false pairings, and distractors. Subjects were shown each dyad, one at a time, and indicated whether it had occurred during the diary-keeping period and assigned a confidence rating from 1 to 3 to their judgments.

Inasmuch as recognition probes memory more sensitively than does recall, it offers a more likely task with which to match amnesics and controls than does a task like recall. Indeed, in several studies involving picture memory and word-list learning, amnesic and normal recognition were equated by delaying normal testing (Hirst et al., 1986; Hirst et al., 1988; Mayes & Meudell, 1981). Several of these studies make the further point that amnesic recall is disproportionately disrupted in amnesics (Hirst et al., 1986; Hirst et al., 1988). The "dimmed light" metaphor I discussed above would suggest that the normal functional relation between recall and recognition should be preserved if amnesia is merely a diminished version of normal memory. However, severely depressed amnesic recall can be observed even when amnesic recognition reaches normal or above-normal levels. Consequently, some aspect of memory more important to recognition than recall may be preserved in amnesics, whereas another aspect of memory more important to recall than recognition may be disrupted with amnesia. Satriano hoped that by testing the delayed controls 30 days after the amnesics, he might be able to equate amnesic and control recognition for daily events and then compare their recall. Such a design would provide a more ecologically valid replication of the finding of relatively preserved recognition of amnesics than heretofore offered.

The final test examined temporal-order memory. Several reports maintain that amnesics, or at least some not fully understood subset of amnesics, have difficulty remembering the temporal order of events (Hirst & Volpe, 1982; Squire, Nadel, & Slater, 1981). In an attempt to look at this issue with ecologically valid material, we showed subjects the front of the recorded index cards for the entire event log, presented in a random order, and asked them to rearrange them in the order in which the events described on the cards occurred. In this test, the *when* information was deleted from the cards. Satriano measured performance by calculating the Spearman rank correlation between the actual order and the subject-determined order.

Satriano was concerned when beginning the experiment that it might prove too complex for amnesics. They might not remember what they were supposed to do when the beeper went off. This fear was unfounded. All the amnesics we tested complied with the instructions. The amnesics in the present study may have found the instructions memorable in part because of the beeper. Its buzzing served as a reminder that some action was necessary. Inasmuch as its operation was not part of their ordinary daily life, it offered a powerful cue. Probably, none of our amnesics' memories was so disrupted that they could not remember the instructions, once given such a powerful cue. Moreover, our amnesics were intelligent. It might not have been difficult to guess that they were to fill out the index card once the beeper went off, especially with the index cards weighing down their shirt pockets. Finally, the amnesics we tested had a support structure. If they did not remember what the beeper was for, their relatives or caretakers would. The amnesics' rate of compliance was lower than that of normals, suggesting that they may have gotten confused at some points. They also did not complete the queries on the back of the cards. Satriano inadvertently failed to put a reminder on the front of the card to flip it over and complete the back. This slip did not affect controls, but led to a high noncompliance rate for amnesics.

As Table 14.1 shows, amnesic patients recalled few items. They resisted filling out the cards, even when encouraged. This poor recall contrasts sharply with the recall of both the standard and delayed controls. For

Table 14.1. Performance on free recall test

	Amnesic	Immediate control	Delayed control
Number of event logs recorded (out of 49)			
Subject Cluster[a] I	42	44	43
Subject Cluster II	42	49	49
Subject Cluster III	46	43	41
Mean	43.3	45.3	44.3
Number of event logs freely recalled			
Subject Cluster I	5	23	8
Subject Cluster II	5	49	10
Subject Cluster III	10	34	23
Mean	6.7	35.3	13.7
Percentage of freely recalled event logs accurately recalled			
Subject Cluster I	40	65	78
Subject Cluster II	60	88	100
Subject Cluster III	40	86	61
Mean	46.7	79.7	79.7
Percentage of accurately recalled event logs out of the recorded event logs			
Subject Cluster I	5	34	14
Subject Cluster II	7	88	20
Subject Cluster III	9	67	33
Mean	7	63	23.3

[a]A subject cluster consisted of one amnesic and his or her two matched controls.

both control groups, recall was about 3 to 4 times as good as that of the amnesics. Interestingly, the few events amnesics did recall might have been guesses rather than accurate recollections, suggesting that if anything, the poor recall of amnesics might be even worse than the numbers indicate. For example, subject E2 produced three accurate remembrances. In each case, she described a recurring activity, such as watching "The Wheel of Fortune" on television with her husband. Subject E3 correctly remembered four events, three of which involved eating breakfast. He accurately stated with whom he ate breakfast in part because he had a well-established routine. For instance, on one day, he reported that his housekeeper was present, along with his son and girlfriend. His housekeeper only came on certain days, and his son habitually came home for breakfast from a nearby college on the weekends. It should be emphasized that even if I am wrong about the high rate of guessing, and amnesics were genuinely recalling these events, their recall was still dramatically below that of controls.

As Table 14.2 shows, amnesics obviously benefited from cueing. Even with this benefit, they still did not reach the overall level of performance

Table 14.2. Percentage correctly recalled out of the total recorded event logs when initially cued with *when* and *what*

	When	*What*
Amnesic I	25	75
Immediate control I	67	100
Delayed control I	42	67
Amnesic II	8	58
Immediate control II	50	100
Delayed control II	42	33
Amnesic III	42	67
Immediate control III	58	100
Delayed control III	42	92
Mean for amnesics	25	67
Mean for immediate controls	58	100
Mean for delayed controls	42	64

Table 14.3. Percentage of event logs correctly recognized out of the number recorded

	Amnesic	Immediate control	Delayed control
Subject Cluster[a] I	63	96	79
Subject Cluster II	67	96	76
Subject Cluster III	86	99	90
Mean	72	97	82

[a]A subject cluster consisted of one amnesic and his or her two matched controls.

of the standard controls. On the other hand, the *what* cue was as effective for amnesics as it was for the delayed controls (amnesics, $M = 67\%$; delayed controls, $M = 64\%$). This result does not mean that the diminished mnemonic representations of the delayed controls were the same as the amnesics' representations. Amnesics' and delayed controls' cued recall differed with the use of a *when* cue ($M = 25\%$; delayed controls, $M = 42\%$). *What* was an effective cue for both groups, but *when* was not. Whatever the nature of mnemonic representation in amnesics, past events cannot be easily accessed by stating when the event occurred. A *when* cue may be ineffective for normals, but it is still more ineffective for amnesics.

Attempts to equate amnesic recognition with the recognition of the delayed controls failed (see Table 14.3). Even after a 30-day delay, recognition of two of the three delayed controls was better than their yoked amnesics. Nevertheless, amnesic recognition was better than chance,

Table 14.4. Spearman rank correlations for temporal-order judgments

	Amnesic	Immediate control	Delayed control
Subject Cluster[a] I	.17	.83*	.71*
Subject Cluster II	.17	.99*	.70*
Subject Cluster III	.25	.97*	.64*
Mean	.20	.93	.68

[a]A subject cluster consisted of one amnesic and his or her two matched controls.
*Significant at less than .05.

suggesting, as the cued recall performance did, that despite amnesics' great difficulty in recalling material, experience is recorded and, with appropriate probes, can be accessed.

Finally, consider the temporal-order judgments. Amnesics' inability to use *when* cues would suggest that they may also have difficulty placing events in their proper temporal order. Table 14.4 clearly shows that this prediction holds: Both standard and delayed controls found it easy to order the events temporally, whereas the positive Spearman rank correlations for the amnesics could have been obtained by chance.

What then do amnesics remember about their daily lives? Even after a short retention interval of two days, they can *recall* little if anything. They nevertheless must be encoding something about their past. The *what* cues, for instance, proved surprisingly effective in eliciting memories that amnesics could not recall. And amnesics also recognized many unrecalled events. I am certain that the presently studied amnesics' ability to access memories they could not recall is not unique to them. For instance, H. M., an intensely studied and dense amnesic, could recognize pictures as well as normals with less than a minute of additional study time (Freed, Corkin, & Cohen, 1984). It would appear that amnesics can encode material in a manner that allows them to access this material under special circumstances. Free recall and temporal-order tasks remained problematic for them in almost every instance, but surprisingly good performance was found in other memory tests, as evidenced by their responsiveness to *what* cues and recognition probes. Daily events may be represented in amnesic memory, but this representation is not normal. The content of the events may be recorded, but temporal information, as well as other kinds of contextual information, may not be.

Experimental work

From this work on amnesics' autobiographical memory, it would appear that amnesics can and do store past events, but that these events can only be accessed in specific ways. Work in the laboratory using traditional verbal learning and picture memory studies has come to similar conclusions (Hirst, 1992; Squire, 1987). Amnesia is not a complete breakdown in memory functioning. Certain specific and circumscribed aspects of memory are preserved. The laboratory work has focused on three areas of preserved memory.

The first of these preserved functions was touched on in the diary study, specifically in our attempt to demonstrate relatively preserved recognition. As already noted, this ability has been amply demonstrated in the laboratory. Using word lists as stimuli, Hirst, Johnson, and their colleagues have shown that amnesic recognition is much better than would be expected given their poor recall (Hirst et al., 1986; Hirst et al., 1988). They examined amnesic free recall after they equated amnesics' and controls' recognition by extending exposure time for amnesics or delaying testing for controls, techniques that other investigators had found successful (Mayes & Meudell, 1981). They established that even when amnesic recognition was above normal recognition, amnesic free recall was still significantly worse than that of normals (but see Haist, Shimamura, & Squire, 1992). Using pictures as stimuli, a similar study on H. M. also found that with sufficient exposure, recognition can be raised to normal levels, yet recall presumably remains almost nonexistent (Freed et al., 1984; Huppert & Piercy, 1977).

The other two preserved mnemonic functions studied in the laboratory were not even hinted at in the diary study. First, there is the literature on intact skill learning. Although there is some controversy over whether all skill learning is normal in amnesics, Cohen, Squire, and others have shown that amnesics can learn a small range of skills, including mirror reading, at normal rates (Cohen & Squire, 1980; Corkin, 1968; see also Squire, 1987).

Second, there is the work on normal priming in amnesics (see Schacter, 1987). In one paradigmatic implicit memory task, subjects study a list of words, including, for example, *garage,* and then are asked to complete stems, for example, *gar.* In the implicit memory condition, subjects are asked to complete the stem with the first word that comes to mind. In the explicit memory condition, subjects are asked to complete the stem with the word from the previously presented list. Amnesics do as well as normals in the implicit memory condition, but are significantly worse than normals in the explicit memory task. Thus, when they must explicitly bring to mind a past event, amnesics suffer. However, when they are affected by past experience implicitly, they show the benefits of prior exposure as much as normals.

Laboratory work and the diary study, then, present a consistent view of amnesic mnemonic functioning. Amnesics encode experiences, but in an impoverished fashion. This encoding is enough to support some skill learning, repetition priming, and to some extent recognition, but leaves significantly depressed recall and tasks involving temporal order. This portrait has more dimensionality than the blank canvas that the traditional characterization of amnesia envisions.

Islands of preserved memory

Both the diary study and the experimental work highlight what most take to be the salient feature of anterograde amnesia: the failure to recall events shortly after they occur. They go a step further by suggesting that these events may be encoded. The events may even be accessible with the right probe. They simply cannot be free-recalled. And if supplied to the amnesic, they cannot be placed in the proper temporal order. This characterization, while probably true as a generalization, misses one important though rarely noted feature of amnesia.

When I started to study amnesia, I soon observed that in the midst of their ocean of forgetfulness lay pronounced and readily apparent islands of preserved memories. Despite a patient's failure to recall even a simple word from a short list of words, to remember even the vaguest outline of a story just read to them, or to draw from memory even a simple, just studied geometrical form, he or she could tell me the current family crisis, sometimes the major news events, and sometimes, details about what for the patient were emotional or salient events. One patient, T. F., bet heavily on sports games. Although he had a Wechsler Memory Scale score 45 points below his WAIS, he could recount as much as two or three days later the exact score and some details of the game. Another patient could provide the details of the plans for her daughter's wedding. Another could discuss her children's concerns about jobs and romance.

It is difficult to specify what it is that yields these surprisingly good memories. The salient, emotional valence of the events is striking. However, the events may be memorable simply because they are rehearsed a lot. T. F. may rehearse the results of the game until he gets paid what is owed him on the bet. The wedding plans may occupy my other amnesic's fantasy life. And the problems of children could surely be gone over and over in one's mind. Whatever the explanation, and we will explore others as the essay continues, it is clear that, unlike most daily experiences, some past events can be accessed by amnesics without much cueing.

Telling your life story

Anterograde amnesics, then, may have a few islands of preserved memory, which no doubt have some effect on their life narratives. Laboratory studies and the diary work, however, make clear that they cannot recall most events even shortly after they occur. This difficulty should directly impact on amnesics' ability to tell an autobiographical narrative of their post-onset life.

With these considerations in mind, I have been informally collecting amnesics' autobiographical tellings over the years. I have also asked Paul Shrell-Fox, a student working in my laboratory, to formally collect autobiographies from four amnesics. Few directions were given, but it was emphasized that the narrative should be detailed and cover their *entire* life, from birth to present. None of the amnesics expressed any confusion over this task. They told their stories in conventional ways. They sometimes started with a brief biography of their parents; others began with their own birth. They followed this introduction with one or two childhood episodes and then a chronicle of education. They recounted autobiographical landmarks such as marriage and the birth of children. By and large, the narratives when viewed as a whole were spotty, with many gaps between episodes. However, when amnesics described an episode, they provided many details. For instance, one woman, S., recounted an episode in her childhood in the following manner:

My sister was walking around holding a pair of scissors this way [S. gestures to show that scissors were pointing out]. We were, my cousin and I, we were throwing bunnies up into the air and she was going with the scissor to give them to my mother and this bunny came down and hit her and the scissors went into her eye. So, for years and years of my life, we took her to the city trying to save the eye. She had to wear patches on it and all. And then they finally, at a certain point, they wanted to wait until she was an adolescent so that they could remove the eye so that her face would be formed, because they were afraid otherwise, if they didn't leave it in . . . You see what happens is she kept getting infections and finally they did remove the eye and she now has an artificial eye. In a way I always felt that it was a little bit my fault because I was throwing this stupid thing in the air. But I can't go through life flagellating myself for things that . . . if I did that I would never get out of bed in the morning.

S. devoted the same level of detail to her courtship with her husband, her first job as a school teacher, and her summers in Spain. In total, her life story up to the onset of her amnesia in 1976 took up over three single-spaced transcribed pages.

As we posited, this capacity for detailed recollection disappeared for the period after the onset of S.'s amnesia. I quote her autobiographical narrative for the approximately 15-year period after onset in its entirety:

In 1976, I had the accident [in Spain, resulting in the amnesia.] I came back here [New York] and then here I did a couple of things 'cause I still had kids that were going to school. And we had to get them back in [school] and then they were going to the school up here. I was active a little here, and that's pretty much where we are.

The same sharp contrast between pre- and post-onset life stories could be seen in all the patients.

Although the diary study, as well as the work in the laboratory, dramatically demonstrated amnesics' inability to *recall* events, it also showed that they could often access memory when properly probed. *What* cues and recognition probes proved especially effective. We hypothesized that salient events that did not spontaneously appear in the amnesics' autobiographies might nevertheless be accessible if properly probed. This appeared to be the case. One patient provided even fewer details about her post-onset life than the patient quoted above, but answered questions about post-onset family events with accuracy. Although she doted on her family, she did not include in her narrative the wedding of her son Frank two years before the narrative telling. Yet when asked about the wedding, she replied:

It was very nice. Dinner, food was good, music was good. He had a two-piece band there, husband and wife. I remember her father. He ordered Dom Perignon for every table. That stuck in my mind. That was it.

When asked about her second son's wedding, which again she omitted from her extemporaneous life story, she accurately stated, although again sketchily:

He didn't have a wedding, he just went to City Hall and got married.

We see in the autobiographies the same scenario presented in the diary study: As amnesics told the story of their post-onset lives, all detail was lost. It was as if they had no raw material with which to build a narrative. Our unsystematic probing suggested that the material might be there, but it could not be easily accessed. Moreover, even when accessed it still had a vague, undetailed quality. Amnesics clearly have difficulty telling their life story when it comes to events after the onset of their amnesia.

Amnesia and self

Some brain-damaged patients with amnesia may be in such a confused state that it would be hard to say that they have a coherent self, but the amnesics that we have been discussing here did not experience such confusion. They had no difficulty thinking – some of my patients had IQs of 120 and more – they spoke fluently and clearly; they had no perceptual difficulty. No aphasias, apraxias, or agnosias. There was no doubt that these patients had a self. In my laboratory, we often discussed their personalities and the different testing demands the patients presented. Our patients had a sense of their place spatially, temporally, socially, professionally, and emotionally. Moreover, they could talk about what they liked to do – cook, watch sports, go fishing, care for their family – and they planned their lives around these activities. Such preferences are not unique to the amnesics discussed here. Again turning to H. M., even he had preferred activities. He loved, for instance, to watch the television show "The Price is Right" (Phelps, personal communication).

For the narrative psychologist, the ability of amnesics to tell a story of their life, albeit one that stops with the onset of their amnesia, probably speaks more forcefully of the amnesics' self than anything else. Their stories are detailed and well-structured. But more importantly, the stories possess a reflective quality that grows out of the amnesics' ongoing attempt to make sense of their lives. When S. told of her sister's accidental injury, she included the struggle she had in coming to terms with her own responsibility. One could see in her narrative an ongoing effort to interpret the event in a way that would preserve her current sense of self. In this respect, and other respects, the amnesics' autobiographical telling of pre-onset episodes appears normal.

I began this essay focused on the possibility of change in the amnesic's self. From a narrative psychologist's perspective, the sharp and sudden end of narration found in the autobiographies Shrell-Fox collected and to a large extent in my informal collections should indicate a static and unevolving self for amnesics. It is difficult to say whether the amnesic's self is evolving at a "normal" rate, but it is certainly not static.

First, amnesics' islands of preserved memories may exert some influence on their narrative telling and self. An anecdote involving another amnesic illustrates the dynamics of this possibility.

L. K. is a middle-class Jewish man who worked most of his life in a delicatessen. His amnesia is dense. In one experiment I did, he could not retain three words after 30 seconds of distraction, even after 50 repetitions. L. K. told me the following story two weeks after it occurred, and his wife corroborated not only the general outline, but also the details. It involved a visit to his only child one weekend. His son was living some 200 miles from home and was in his first year of medical residency. Both L. K. and his wife told me on several occasions about the financial sacrifices they had made to put their son through medical school, but they had always dreamed of him becoming a doctor and had no regrets about the sacrifices. As L. K. reported it, his son told him that weekend that he wanted to give up medicine. His memory for the entire weekend was vivid. He not only remembered what his son told him, but went on to report that his wife bought two pairs of shoes on an outing to the local mall.

L. K. did not merely report the incident. He also interpreted his island of preserved memory in a manner that reflected on his concept of himself and his son. He argued vehemently that he was to blame for his son's sudden change of heart. According to L. K., his son was upset because despite his medical training, he could not cure what was probably the most devastating medical problem his family had faced, his father's amnesia. Clearly, L. K. was doing more than merely remembering a story. He was trying to understand his son's motivations, how his son felt about himself. And he was filtering the story through his sense of self and incorporating it into the narrative he was telling about how his amnesia had not only destroyed his life, but the lives of others. The distress that L. K. showed when recounting the weekend, and the long delay between the event and the retelling, suggested that this incorporation had long-lasting, if not permanent, consequences. These consequences, however, could not be said to have radically changed his standard life narrative. The theme of the destructive nature of his amnesia figured strongly in many conversations I had with L. K. He was painfully aware that he had become, to use his words, "an inconvenience." His son's threatened action represented merely another life event in support of this theme. Clearly, islands of preserved memories can and are incorporated into the amnesic's life narrative and construal of self.

This is not to say that the only way to fit memories into a life narrative is to build on already established themes. As I noted in the beginning of this essay, some new memories can only be incorporated into an autobiographical narrative through the rejection of old themes and the development of new ones. Amnesics seem capable of such revision. A new theme, for instance, can grow out of their active attempt to come to terms with their amnesia. Immediately after onset, they are extremely depressed. They must learn to accept that they can no longer work, that they are dependent on their spouse, that they can no longer participate in life to the extent that they had. Whatever time does in curing loss, it works its effect on amnesics. My amnesic subjects have gone from seeing the self as unacceptably robbed of an essential aspect to accepting the self for what it now is. This change is due in part to the experience of living with the memory loss and in part perhaps to some other mysterious effect of time. But whatever the dynamics, in every case, they appear to have mastered their lessons.

Thus, in L. K.'s story about his son, he was not only incorporating a new memory – an island of preserved memory – into already established themes, he was also declaring that he had developed a new theme to his life story since the onset of his amnesia. Specifically, he had developed the theme of the destructive nature of his amnesia. Although I did not know L. K. before the onset of his amnesia, and consequently had no pre-onset narrative, I suspected that this new theme probably led him not only to add events to an already established narrative, but also to reconfigure the raw material of memories that formed the basis of his pre-onset narratives. His amnesia had caused a new attitude, and with this new attitude, some autobiographical memories would be forgotten, others remembered, and still others changed. The pervasiveness of L. K.'s theme of destructiveness suggested that it would have to play a role in his narrative telling.

My encounters with T. F. also underlined amnesics' potential to develop new themes and new ways of telling their life story. T. F.'s life had been and continued to be privileged and affluent. In my initial conversations with him, he could not understand why effort and money would not purchase him a new memory. He kept saying that he had always gotten what he wanted in life, if he tried for it, and now he wanted more than anything to overcome his memory problems. He did not talk about the precariousness of life and the limits to which people control their fate. A theme that continually emerged in the stories he told me was that he was the master of his fate and that he could conquer this problem.

With time, T. F. came to terms with his amnesia. His attitude shifted and the manner in which he talked about his old life changed. The old theme of omnipotence was largely dropped. He spoke more often about how one fails to get what one wants. He lowered his expectations. Again, I had no pre-onset narratives, but given his extremely successful career as a lawyer, one would have concluded that his work would have figured in any pre-onset narrative. In the autobiographical narrative collected by Shrell-Fox, T. F.'s years as a lawyer were barely mentioned. Instead he concentrated on his college days. His autobiographical narrative had a nostalgic feel, not of a man conquering the world, but of one remembering fondly an unthreatening period of his life. It was a story of a man retired before his time – desirous to repress what he had lost and focus on more pleasant material. His autobiographical narrative, in other words, had probably been reshaped to reflect his new status and attitude.

One possible effect of memory on self highlighted in our study of amnesia involved inaccessible memories and what in the memory literature is called implicit memory. The inaccessibility of many amnesics' memories can be seen in the contrast between amnesics' deficient free recall and their relatively preserved cued recall and recognition. It can also be observed in their intact skill learning and priming. In the experimental studies of priming and skill learning, the effect on behavior involves rather simple acts like completing a stem or reading a word. Yet these implicit memory effects may reach into domains of behavior more important to self-construal. Implicit memories and inaccessible explicit memories could affect self not in terms of what amnesics say about themselves, but how they act.

Consider again that classic amnesic, H. M. When a colleague asked him whether his parents were dead, H. M. replied that he thought so. His hesitant response suggested that he could not explicitly remember being told of his parents' death nor, perhaps, could he remember them dying – the hospital visit and the funeral. Given the density of his amnesia, this response was not surprising. When I had read similar reports many years ago, I thought how tragic H. M.'s life must be. Each time he learned of his parents' death he would have to grieve once again. But when my colleague asked him, he did not grieve. Indeed, he showed little or no emotion. He might not have been explicitly aware of his parents' death, but his neutral response suggested that he had incorporated this fact into his schema about himself. He was a person without parents. He did not have to suffer the loss anew, because as he conceived of himself, implicitly if not explicitly, he had already suffered the loss.

The distinction between implicit and explicit knowledge can be seen in several other incidents. Claparede (1911) reported that an amnesic patient avoided shaking his hand after Claparede had previously shocked the patient with a hand buzzer. The patient did not explicitly remember the previous encounter, but the negative valence of that encounter was incorporated into the patient's schema on how to *act* with Claparede. The patient could not say why he did not want to grasp Claparede's hand, only that he did not want to. The same point drives a story told by L. K.'s wife. L. K. had recently become interested in pottery, but his wife noticed that his interest flagged after a few weeks. She soon discovered the reason. Because he was constantly mislaying his pottery, he never completed a project. When asked why he was no longer interested in pottery, L. K. could not say. He had no explicit recollection of his frustration when looking for his half-completed work. His explicit memory of his past dealings with pottery were essentially nonexistent. Yet he had incorporated this frustration into his schemata, which in turn altered his interests.

Probably the most dramatic example of how inaccessible memories and implicit knowledge can affect the self arose during the interviewing of a patient with severe anterograde as well as retrograde amnesia. This patient had memories dating mainly before the 1940s, when as a young man he worked cutting lumber. He had since gone on to become an officer in an international company. Whereas he talked as if he still worked in a lumber camp and his friends were from the lumber camp, his demeanor was that of an executive. He dressed in medium-wale corduroy pants and a cotton polo shirt. He wore horn-rimmed glasses and topsiders. He spoke as if words counted and demanded an exactitude from the tester that came with exerting authority for many years. In other words, his actions were those of the executive he had become rather than the lumberjack he said he was. His implicit knowledge governed his behavior, but the available explicit knowledge led him to create a conflicting self-actualizing autobiographical narrative. Clearly, as with anterograde amnesia, implicit knowledge was shaping the self in this retrograde amnesic.

It would be difficult to determine the extent to which implicit or inaccessible memories shape amnesics' selves. I want to emphasize that amnesics' selves do change after the onset of the amnesia. They can incorporate the rare vividly remembered incident into their life story, develop new themes, and be guided in their actions by implicit memories.

Reflections

According to the narrative perspective sketched at the beginning of this essay, the self emerges from the autobiographical narratives people tell, giving meaning to their actions and continuity to their lives. The special nature of this interpretive process deserves added emphasis. People construct their interpretation – and hence their self – by employing the past in their understanding of their present experience, attitudes, and actions. The past provides a foundation, the structure, from which people can design their self-image. Each memory, as it is incorporated in an evolving self-image, must be relatively accessible and explicit. People fashion their autobiographical narrative from these intentionally gathered threads of the past, with the clear goal of weaving a highly textured fabric of self-construal. This fabric stretches from past to present with an uninterrupted and clearly interpretable pattern.

From this perspective, self-construals depend on relatively accessible explicit memories. Without such memories, autobiographical narratives could not shape the development of a self-image. It is inconceivable that individuals would take their autobiographical narratives as reflecting themselves if they viewed their narratives as fictions, unrelated to what they did and what they plan to do. Consequently, from the narrative perspective, my initial concerns about whether change in self is possible in amnesics seem justified. As I showed, amnesics' narratives of post-onset events resemble plain, unpatterned cloths. They do not have the texture that particular and concrete remembrances give to a narrative. By and large, their post-onset narratives consist of little more than an endless stretch of "And then I lived my life." Sometimes, islands of preserved memory may be linked to well-established themes in their narratives. This exception should not mask the sharp contrast between the lack of detail in the post-onset narratives and the clearly drawn narratives of their pre-morbid life.

But a closer look at the small group of amnesics I have studied brings into sharp relief the need to go beyond this simple rendering of the relation between memory and self. Despite the impoverished post-onset narratives, change in amnesic self appears to be possible. The sudden change in texture, from rich and colorful pre-morbid narratives to the starkly dull, undifferentiated post-onset narratives, clearly led our amnesics to reinterpret the readily accessible explicit memories of their pre-morbid life. Their depression following the onset of the amnesia speaks forcibly of such reinterpretation. With L. K., T. F., and the other amnesics I have studied, their amnesia, as well as major family events, appeared to infuse their post-onset narratives with new themes. The issues of their memory loss, their unemployment, their divorce, and other consequences of their amnesia were accommodated in the many life stories that the amnesics informally told me over seven or eight years, though they did not emerge in the autobiographies Shrell-Fox collected.

This brings me to the first concluding point I want to make. In the introduction to this essay, I stated that I wanted to understand how the psychology of memory, narrative telling, and self interact. In subsequent discussion of the psychology of memory, I adopted a widely held bias and treated memories as things that people, as individuals, have. I wrote as if the mnemonic raw material of life narratives is mined solely from the normally rich veins of individual recollections. However, analysis of the life-shaping events that affect amnesics' narratives – their illnesses, their divorces, and so on – suggests that a broader conception of memory and its impact on autobiographical telling is needed. Amnesics do not have to "remember" that they cannot remember; the evidence is always present. They are constantly reminded that they are amnesic by their own failures and the attitude of the people around them, as manifested in verbal statements and actions of friends and relatives. Similarly, they do not have to remember that they were divorced or had to change residence. The life they live and the place where they live essentially "remembers" it for them. These memories may not be represented in the amnesics' internal mechanisms – in their memory – but in others, in the amnesics' behavior, and in their physical environment.

Some of these "externalized and collective memories" may, of course, eventually be internalized. By dint of their pervasiveness, even the densest amnesic may eventually "remember" without external support the main events of his or her post-amnesic life. Amnesics might initially have difficulty remembering that their son has moved out of the house, but they must confront this fact every day in hundreds of different ways. This repeated, externally driven rehearsal should eventually lead to a rich enough encoding to permit successful recognition and, in rare cases, recall.

The post-amnesic "memories" of the amnesics, then, grow out of social interaction as well as if not more than individual mnemonic capacity. Many scholars, from George Herbert Mead (1934) to Kenneth Gergen (1991), have argued that the self is socially constructed. These thinkers maintain that the self is not something possessed by an individual, as part of his or her biological endowment, but something derived from human social interactions. I do not wish to review this large literature. Suffice it to say, scholars from this perspective rarely discuss the contribution of memory to the social construction of self. This neglect probably rests on the same individualist, internalist bias that constrained the present discussion of autobiographical narrative and memory. Although there have been a few dissenting voices, this bias is so strong in psychology that even as socially informed a memory theorist as Bartlett (1932) disavowed the possibility of a collective memory and confined his discussions to mnemonic acts within the individual.

I do not need to plumb too deeply the debate on collective memory and social remembering (see Hirst & Manier, 1993, for a review) to illustrate how memory might contribute to the *social* construction of self. Major life events become incorporated into amnesics' story telling because the social structure of their lives guarantees that memory for these events is externalized, collectivized, and eventually internalized. It is not enough to say that amnesics have difficulty remembering things and hence may not have available to them the raw material to change the themes of their autobiographical narratives. If you like, a social mechanism exists to assure that certain past events are remembered, if not individually then through external memories. Both these internal and external memories can at the very least shape the amnesics' autobiographical telling. One social contribution to self-construal, then, comes not directly through the attitudes and beliefs of others, but through the social maintenance of the past and the consequence of this preservation on the kind of autobiographies amnesics will tell.

Amnesics may place in sharp relief the need to consider social processes, but this necessity is not unique to amnesics. Social processes play an important role in the maintenance of the memories of intact individuals. Whereas intact individuals may more quickly internalize memories than do amnesics, the social machinery assuring that certain events or facts are learned and remembered can be observed in normal memory functioning as well as the impaired memory functioning of amnesics. Life-shaping events, for instance, are as ever-present for intact individuals as they are for amnesics. For amnesics, however, there may be little or no possibility that experience can be retained and subsequently affect narrative telling and self-construal without the influence of social processes. Normals may escape more easily from the need for the social, though I doubt it (Hirst & Manier, 1993). When studying either amnesics or normals, an investigation of the relation between memory and the remembered self must include not only the dynamics of individual memory, but also the workings of social memory.

I have one other concluding point. The narrative psychology articulated at the beginning of this essay maintains that the self is fashioned out of narrative telling. It is about conscious, verbalizable interpretation of the past. It uses as raw material explicit memories. And it structures these memories into a narrative form that in part represents the self. From a narrative perspective, then, self involves the representation of the past.

This rendering of the self does not fully depict the self from all possible perspectives. Action, for instance, figures only in several limited ways: Present actions may elicit and shape the telling of an autobiographical narrative, and the narrative telling, the interpretation of the past, may itself be considered an action. This discussion of action needs amplification. As William James (1890) noted, "In the widest possible sense, a man's Self is the sum total of all that he CAN call his" (p. 291). A person's action is clearly "his." These actions – from the clothes you put on in the morning to the adulterous affair you have at night – figure in self-construal as much as autobiographical narrative (see Bem, 1970). Consequently, *self-presentation* – the way people act – may not contribute to a narrative psychology of self as directly as *self-representation*, but it nevertheless bears as forcefully on the construction of a remembered self as does self-representation. (The term *self-presentation*, as used here, should not be confused with the Goffmanian presentation of self.) Although different from the intricately articulated self-representation envisioned by narrative psychologists, self-presentation depends on the past as much as self-representation. Unlike self-representation, however, self-presentation can be constituted from implicit as well as explicit memories. Self-defining actions can be primed by past experiences, even though the experiences themselves have been lost from conscious recollection. People may be predisposed to choose certain clothing, respond to queries in specific, personalized, and unique ways, even make factual claims without knowing the origins of these behaviors. People will often assert that they were abused by their fathers, yet do so without specific knowledge of any supporting episode or enough detail about dimly remembered events to evaluate the validity of the recollection.

The distinction between self-presentation and self-representation can help us understand many of the mysteries the present discussion of amnesia offered. It helps us understand Claparede's patient who acted as if he distrusted Claparede, but could not explain why. It also accounts for L. K.'s sudden loss of interest in pottery. L. K. could not explain why his interests changed, but they did. We can also see the distinction in H. M.'s failure to grieve when confronted once again about his father's death. He could not explicitly recall his father's death, nor would he presumably have included it in a life narrative. Nevertheless, his actions spoke of a man who had lost his father.

The retrograde amnesic I described also clearly illustrates the distinction between self-representation and self-presentation. His self-representation, the story he told about his life, rested on his explicit memories of a time in the remote past. He could not, however, connect in his narrative these old memories with his present actions. Whereas he represented himself in his narrative as a lumberjack, his actions, his self-presentation, was that of an executive.

My amnesics' inability to connect their actions narratively with their life stories creates a unique opportunity to observe the possibility of conflict between self-representation and self-presentation. Such conflicts, however, are not themselves unique. Indeed, a divergence between self-presentation and self-representation may rest at the core of many psychopathologies. Shapiro (1989), for instance, argues that self-deception involves a conflict between self-presentation and self-representation. And much of psychotherapy could be viewed as an attempt to narrow the gap between divergent self-presentations and self-representations. Amnesics may provide particularly dramatic examples, but the distinction between self-representation and self-presentation could figure in many discussions of self in the neurologically intact.

The study of amnesia, then, forces us to broaden the narrative psychological perspective of the relation between memory and self we outlined in the beginning of the essay. As I reflect on amnesics' remembered self, I am forced to consider two dynamics that my focus on narrative in the beginning of this essay did not bring to my attention. I must realize that any discussion of the relation between memory and self must include externalized and collective as well as individual memories. I also must distinguish between self-representation and self-presentation and consider the relation of both explicit and implicit memory to these two types of self. These realizations may supply some color to the portrait drawn by narrative psychologists, but much work still needs to be done before the remembered self is fully rendered, let alone detailed. Perhaps an even finer-grained examination of the remembered self in amnesics may provide a few more needed brush strokes.

ACKNOWLEDGMENTS

I would like to thank Stephen Hartman, David Manier, and Laura Martucci for valuable conversations, and Jim Satriano and Paul Shrell-Fox for both conversation and their considerable research effort. This research was supported by grants from the McDonnell-Pew Program in Cognitive Neuroscience and grant no. 42064 from the National Institute of Mental Health.

REFERENCES

Bartlett, F. C. (1932) *Remembering: A study in experimental and social psychology.* Cambridge University Press.

Bem, D. J. (1970). *Beliefs, attitudes, and human affairs.* Belmont, CA: Brooks/Cole.

Brewer, W. F. (1988). Memory for randomly sampled autobiographical events. In U. Neisser & E. Winograd (Eds.), *Remembering reconsidered.* Cambridge University Press.

Bruner, J. (1990). *Acts of meaning.* Cambridge, MA: Harvard University Press.

Claparede, E. (1911). Recognition et moitié. *Archieves de Psychologie, 11,* 79–90.

Cohen, N. J., & Squire, L. R. (1980). Preserved learning and retention of pattern analyzing skill in amnesia: Dissociation of knowing how and knowing that. *Science, 210,* 207–209.

Cohen, N. J., & Squire, L. R. (1981). Retrograde amnesia and remote memory improvement. *Neuropsychologia, 19,* 337–356.

Corkin, S. (1968). Acquisition of motor skills after bilateral medial temporal-lobe excision. *Neuropsychologia, 6,* 225–265.

Freed, D. M., Corkin, S., & Cohen, N. J. (1984). Rate of forgetting in HM: A reanalysis. *Society of Neuroscience Abstracts, 10,* 383.

Gergen, K. J. (1991). *The saturated self.* New York: Basic.

Haist, F., Shimamura, A. P., & Squire, L. R. (1992). On the relationship between recall and recognition memory. *Journal of Experimental Psychology: Learning, Memory, and Cognition, 18,* 691–702.

Hirst, W. (1992). *Aspects of the cognitive neuroscience of memory.* Unpublished ms.

Hirst, W., Johnson, M. K., Kim, J. K., Phelps, E. A., Risse, G., & Volpe, B. T. (1986). Recognition and recall in amnesics. *Journal of Experimental Psychology: Learning, Memory, and Cognition, 12,* 442–451.

Hirst, W., Johnson, M. K., Phelps, E. A., & Volpe, B. T. (1988). More on recognition and recall in amnesics. *Journal of Experimental Psychology: Learning, Memory, and Cognition, 14,* 758–762.

Hirst, W., & Manier, D. (1993). Putting memory in context. In K. Nelson (Ed.), *Essays in honor of Sylvia Scribner.* Cambridge University Press.

Hirst, W., & Volpe, B. T. (1982). Temporal order judgments with amnesia. *Brain and Cognition, 1,* 294–306.

Howard, G. S. (1991). Culture tales: A narrative approach to thinking, cross-cultural psychology and psychotherapy. *American Psychologist, 46,* 187–197.

Huppert, F. A., & Piercy, M. (1977). Recognition memory in amnesic patients: A defect of acquisition? *Neuropsychologia, 15,* 643–652.

James, W. (1890). *The principles of psychology* (Vol. 1). New York: Dover.

Marslen-Wilson, W. D., & Teuber, H. L. (1975). Memory for remote events in anterograde amnesia: Recognition of public figures from news photographs. *Neuropsychologia, 13,* 353.

Mayes, A. R., & Meudell, P. R. (1981). How similar is the effect of cueing in amnesic and in normal subjects following forgetting? *Cortex, 17,* 113–124.

Mead, G. H. (1934). *Mind, self, and society.* Chicago: University of Chicago Press.

Satriano, J. (1992). *Amnesic memory for daily events.* In preparation.

Schacter, D. L. (1987). Implicit memory: History and current status. *Journal of Experimental Psychology: Learning, Memory, and Cognition, 13,* 501–518.

Schaffer, R. (1992). *Retelling a life: Narration and dialogue in psychoanalysis.* New York: Basic.

Shapiro, D. (1989). *Psychotherapy of neurotic character.* New York: Basic.

Spence, D. P. (1982). *Narrative truth and historical truth.* New York: Norton.

Squire, L. R. (1987). *Memory and brain.* New York: Oxford University Press.

Squire, L. R., Cohen, N. J., & Nadel, L. (1984). The medial temporal region and memory consolidation: A new hypothesis. In H. Weingartner & E. Parker (Eds.), *Memory consolidation.* Hillsdale, N.J.: Erlbaum.

Squire, L. R., Nadel, L., & Slater, P. C. (1981). Anterograde amnesia and memory for temporal order. *Neuropsychologia, 19,* 141–145.

Squire, L. R., & Slater, P. C. (1978). Anterograde and retrograde memory impairment in chronic amnesia. *Neuropsychologia, 16,* 313–322.

Squire, L. R., Slater, P. C., & Chace, P. M. (1975). Retrograde amnesia: Temporal gradient in very long-term memory following electroconvulsive therapy. *Science, 187,* 77–79.

Squire, L. R., Slater, P. C., & Miller, P. L. (1981). Retrograde amnesia following ECT: Long-term follow-up studies. *Archives of General Psychiatry, 38,* 89–95.

Viederman, S. (1979). The analytic space: Meaning and problems. *Psychoanalytic Quarterly, 5,* 45–62.

Wagenaar, W. A. (1986). My memory: A study of autobiographical memory over six years. *Cognitive Psychology, 18,* 283–291.

15

Perception is to self as memory is to selves

EDWARD S. REED

Dualities in experience have a way of becoming dichotomies in psychological theory. What nature has linked, usually in an intricate and marvelous pattern of covariation, science often rends asunder. Scientists then find themselves deeply perplexed over problems of their own creation.

The greatest mistake in modern psychology is to treat the self-in-its-world as a self separated from its surroundings. Cognitivism, with its allegiance to the representational theory of the mind and its focus on the metaphor of mental states as internal to the mind, is particularly susceptible to this dualistic separation of self from environment. Almost all modern accounts of cognitions simply assume that cognition is a process within individuals, a process that may or may not represent the world adequately. Modern theories of memory have been affiliated with this internalist school, treating remembering as the registering, maintenance, and retrieval of internalized states. These naive assumptions not only lead to problems in understanding cognition and memory, but also tend to prevent theorists from forming an adequate conception of the individual self who is the cognizer or rememberer.

The ecological approach to cognition which I have been developing treats cognition as a process in which the individual self encounters and maintains contact with the surrounding environment, including other individuals in that environment (Reed, 1987, 1988, 1991, 1993). From this ecological point of view, memory is not just a rearousal of internal states, but is a special form of encountering the environment. Through memory, we not only encounter the past environment, but more importantly, we keep in contact with our past selves in their surroundings. Perception provides a bridging of the separation of self from environment, a means of keeping in contact with one's surroundings. Memory provides a bridging of a different sort, between earlier and later aspects of one's self. In a sense, the self of a perceiver is more unified than the self of a rememberer, and memory is the process of maintaining coordination within a multiple self. Memory thus serves an integrating function, helping to keep more or less united an individual who has engaged in numerous

278

diverse encounters, experienced many different situations, and suffered and enjoyed a whole host of feelings.

In this regard, memory functions within an individual in a way that parallels how sympathy functions between individuals. What I mean by sympathy here is all the various social cognitions and emotions that serve to unite a social group. Empathy, malice, jealousy, shared pleasure, are therefore all instances of what I am here calling sympathy – emotions with integral cognitive components that are fundamental to the processes of coordinating individuals into a coherent social group (see Scheler 1954/1970 for more on different definitions of sympathy).

My thesis is thus that memory – at least in some of its richer forms – implies a complex of selves. And I argue that memory (like sympathy) serves to coordinate diverse complex mental states without either integrating them into a single entity or dividing them into completely opposing entities. This separation without complete division I dub duality, and much of this chapter is taken up with explaining how memory requires a unique duality of the self.

This bald description of the goal of this chapter will sound odd, if not incomprehensible, to ears attuned to cognitivist ways of thinking, but I hope that by the end I will have made this odd definition of memory sound meaningful, if not plausible. To accomplish this, I shall first review selected relevant aspects of the ecological approach to perception developed by James Gibson, because it was Gibson, in his analysis of how perceiving operates over time, who first emphasized that dualities are central to all cognitive states. After illustrating the kinds of dualities found in perception, I shall explain how memory both divides and coordinates the self, creating a special duality (or even multiplicity) of the self. After a brief discussion of some of the implications of this new definition of memory and the self, I shall summarize the main points of the argument.

Perceiving the Self in the Environment

"My theory of perception is not going to be clear," wrote James Gibson to his friend Gunnar Johansson,

unless you understand that it goes hand in hand with a theory of proprioception. One cannot be aware of the world without also being more or less aware of existing in the world. . . . For me, perception is an awareness of the world. An awareness of the self accompanies it but does not contribute to it. Proprioception, as I put it, goes along with perception, but is not the same thing. There is a subjective aspect and an objective aspect to every phenomenal experience but this does not mean that there is some degree of subjective determination of objective perception. (Gibson, 1970/1982a, p. 89)

Much of what made Gibson's theory of perception so radical is contained in this brief excerpt, in which he redefined what we are said to perceive. At least in his later work (see Reed, 1986, 1988), Gibson argued that we do not perceive forms, colors, motions, shapes, or even objects and events; instead, we perceive ourselves acting within the environment. The smallest functional unit of the process of perception – if I may speak in a way not characteristic of Gibson – is the *encounter:* an agent encountering some aspect of her surroundings. The *exteroception* of objects, events, and people is accompanied by the *proprioception* of one's self actively encountering these things. The separation of self from world is bridged by the coordination of extero- and proprioception. Perceiving is dual precisely in that it serves to maintain contact between a self and what surrounds it through a coordinated double process of self- and world-perception.

For Gibson, all perceiving is dual (in this sense) and active. To perceive the world involves actively obtaining stimulation in which there is information (Gibson, 1966, chaps. 1–3). The self of which one is aware in perception is not passive, but an agent trying to do something; minimally, an agent trying to keep in contact with its environment. Because perceiving is an activity – a set of encounters – it is fallible. One may fail to obtain adequate information, or one may fail to use it correctly. Gibson's kind of perception – what he later dubbed "ambient" and "ambulatory" perception (Gibson, 1979) – is what might be called voluntary perception. And, like all acts of volition, perceiving is subject to failure. Perceiving is therefore an achievement of an individual, not a response of a physiological system to stimuli. From an ecological point of view perception is constrained and made specific by information, but it is not caused by information or stimulation, any more than other kinds of voluntary activity are caused by stimuli.

Proprioception, in Gibson's sense, is all the various ways in which we become aware of ourselves as we encounter our surroundings. Just as with exteroception, proprioception is not a response to particular stimuli, although physiologists have traditionally defined proprioception merely as the response of the central nervous system to signals from proprioceptors (e.g., inner ear, muscle and joint sensors, etc.). For an actively exploring individual there are many sources of information about the self – propriospecific information, Gibson called it (e.g., optical and auditory information about self-movement) – and all of these can contribute to self-perception. Already in *The Senses Considered as Perceptual Systems* (1966), Gibson distinguished between what he called the lower and the higher proprioceptive systems (pp. 35–40). Although both systems involve the active seeking out of information, the lower system is concerned with the regulation of postures and movements of the limbs and body

(Reed, 1982, 1989), whereas the higher system is concerned with the regulation of action (i.e., the organization and control of encounters).

Standard theories of proprioception follow standard theories of exteroception in suggesting that self-sensitivity is the result of the central nervous system's receiving and processing sensations and other sensory input. Such theories assume that perceptual (or proprioceptive) awareness is basically instantaneous or short-lived (the duration of a brief sensation), and therefore that longer-term memory plays an important role in the individual's acquisition of knowledge about either the environment or herself. By treating perception as ambulatory, Gibson suggested that perceptual awareness itself is the basis of the stream of consciousness, and not at all short-lived. Further, by emphasizing the importance of ecologically specific information, Gibson also argued that perception was a primary form of cognition – of knowledge acquisition (Reed, 1991).

When these standard theories of perception attempt to resolve the problem of how an individual distinguishes herself from the world, they run into considerable difficulties. This is because, if perceptual experience is relatively punctiform, then it is unlikely that the self–world distinction can be made within perception, without further information from memory or other modes of cognition. In this regard, it is very revealing that the most common theoretical ploy for explaining how one distinguishes self from world is to take at least some aspect of self-knowledge as infallibly given to the observer. All forms of reafference or corollary discharge theory do this. To explain, for instance, why we do not see the world as moving when we move our eyes and sweep our retinas over the visual field, these theories hold that the individual has internally given knowledge of his or her movements, and can therefore anticipate the retinal sweep and compensate for it appropriately (Gibson, 1950b, pp. 134–136; Matin, 1986). In other words, these theories invent a new kind of sensation to explain the relations between proprioception and exteroception. The idea is that one is aware of one's motor commands because of a kind of internal sensory signal they produce. (These used to be called *innervationsgefühl*, and, it should be noted, many students of this problem have also suggested that sensations from the extraocular muscles may be involved – but, of course, there is no conscious awareness of these either.) Students of memory similarly are prone to inventing hypothetical representations to explain the dualities peculiar to remembering, as I shall show below.

The duality between self and world thus engendered a dichotomy between two kinds of sensations, external and internal, the latter supposedly given in a way that makes them much less fallible than the former. (This despite the fact that there has never been any subjective evidence for the existence of such sensations, feelings, or whatever you would call them.) By rescuing the theory of external perception with the hypothesis that internal perception is a kind of given knowledge, these theories make it impossible for perceptual psychology to have much of interest to say about the self. Worse, the idea that we know ourselves best of all things, despite its great paternity (it goes back at least to Descartes's *Meditations,* and some might trace it to St. Augustine's *Confessions*), is at considerable variance with what we do know about the life of the self. From both common sense and psychology we know that people often are very poor judges of themselves, even of their own feelings, and any theory of self-knowledge that claims to be grounded in a kind of privileged access should be viewed with suspicion. It is surprising that memory researchers – all of whom know only too well that human eyewitness memory is never anything like a photograph or tape recording – nevertheless tend to assume that memory begins with sensory impressions leaving traces in a memory register, as if our remembering starts out to be photographic but simply fails to live up to its original goals.

"It is true," as Gibson (1964/1982b, p. 167) wrote, that in taking this ecological approach to perception, "a number of cherished assumptions have to be thrown overboard. We have to suppose that sensations as conscious contents are neither the causes of perception nor the components of perception, but are merely incidental." By implication, sensory impressions cannot be considered the first stage of remembering. A great deal of perception occurs without any related sensations. In particular, much of ordinary proprioception is sensationless, our awareness being firmly focused on the objective pole, not the subjective. Similarly, memory can and often is sensationless. As St. Augustine (*Confessions,* Book 10) pointed out, one can remember a past sorrow without feeling that sorrow. Where sensationless memory differs from sensationless perception is in the kind of separation being bridged in the process. In perception, what is bridged is the separation of self from surround; in memory, what is bridged is the separation of past from present encounters. Even sensationless memory is, at minimum, what Barsalou (1988) and Conway (1990) have called "direct autobiographical memory." This is memory in which one knows that one has had a particular experience or has acquired a particular piece of information. Apparently, amnesics do not even have this minimal direct autobiographical memory, for they do not reliably know that they have had a given experience, even when they can demonstrably take advantage of having had that experience (i.e., demonstrate learning; see Hirst, chap. 14 of this volume).

From the perceived self to remembered selves

I thus want to suggest a potentially radical redescription of memory. To remember – at least in the full-blown sense of personal reminiscence, as is being emphasized here – involves a duality of self not found even in ambulatory perceiving over time. Autobiographical memory is the me-experiencing-now becoming aware of a prior-me-experiencing its (prior) environment. Although I may believe these two selves to be one consistent entity, if I truly and completely identify the prior self with the present, then remembering disappears into perceiving. For instance, when I walk from one room to another, I can see the path I am taking, and can therefore see both where I have come from and where I am going, without any memory necessarily being involved (Gibson, 1979, chap. 11). Conversely, if I completely separate my present self from a prior self, memory also disappears, blurring into conjecture, inference, or even indifference. For example, if I am unsure whether I have been in a particular place (your home, say), I can attempt to "figure it out" by thinking about people I have met or events in which I have participated – perhaps concluding that I "must have been" there, because I remember some other event that I know to be associated with that place. Nevertheless, this "must have been" is an inference, and not a remembering.

These examples show how what I am here calling duality applies to memory as it relates to the self. Reminiscence requires two selves and a bridging process that unites them without identifying them, just as perception requires the bridging of a self and an object in the environment. This kind of duality may seem to be an obvious phenomenon to those familiar with the conventions of 20th-century fiction and film narrative, but it apparently comes as something of a shock to psychologists and cognitive scientists. In those fields, the standard (representationalist) theories of cognition and memory are such as to prevent one from even describing this kind of duality with any accuracy.

Memory versus learning

Representationalist theories of cognition and action tend to collapse memory and learning: Any change in one's stored knowledge or processes of retrieving knowledge is considered memory. However, from the present perspective many changes in cognition cannot be counted as memory. Any change in our capacities to encounter the environment without a corresponding change in available information should be counted as learning, not memory. Learning, at least in the present sense of the term, is an improvement in the regulation of encounters. In contrast, memory is the ability of the me-now to recollect the experiences of a prior me *without losing the distinction between present and past circumstances*.

When one learns something the duality inherent in memory is collapsed. To go through a learning process is typically to *forget*, or at least to *lose the ability to distinguish*, the learned me from the unlearned one. I can remember *that*, at a certain time, I did not know how to juggle (read, ride a bicycle, etc.), but I cannot accurately recollect that state; on the contrary, it is something that I have to infer. There "must have been" a time when I could not juggle, after all. What I remember (as opposed to infer) is learning how to juggle and it is only by remembering the act of learning that I bring my present self into cognitive contact with prior events and an earlier self who is irrevocably different from me-now. The learning as such was and is a process of change: In this case, change in my abilities to manipulate throwable objects in the environment. The memory as such involves *both* a persistence and a change: implicating a persistent self who has the ability to coordinate two experiences separated in time.

The duality in the phenomenology of memory is paralleled by a duality in memory's cognitive function. Memory in the sense being discussed here includes a reawareness of a prior state of awareness or knowledge, and is not merely a direct awareness of temporally distant events. Memory thus involves relating the knowledge state(s) of a present encounter with that of one or more previous encounters. Note that that knowledge state might be knowledge of what one was/is doing, or knowledge of what one was/is experiencing, or even knowledge of what one was/is planning. Because we are constantly learning and changing, this task of memory is by no means easy, and one would expect that forgetting is the normal accompaniment of cognitive change, not remembering.

In perceiving and acting, the attention is directed toward the information pertinent to the task and toward the relevant objects and attendant actions needed for succeeding at the task. Eleanor and James Gibson have long emphasized that there is a continual process of the education of attention. By this they mean that the organization and efficiency of the processes of information pickup undergo continual refinement merely as a result of practice (Gibson & Gibson, 1955/1982; E. Gibson, 1969; E. Gibson & Rader, 1979). If perceiving does not begin with the registering of sensory impressions, but instead with the activity of a functional system regulating our encounters with the environment, then learning can occur without the storage of traces of those impressions, without memory. This is perhaps the most difficult of the Gibsons' ideas, and deserves far more careful consideration than it has as yet received.

Representationalists have tried to account for the education of attention by making two hypotheses: first, that the self and its cognitive structures do not change once mature; and, second, that selves acquire representations – schemata or scripts, for example – and, by virtue of these novel possessions, their cognitive and performance capacities are enhanced. These two assumptions imply a third idea: that one acquires and stores the representations. Hence, according to these standard ideas, learning requires stored information or memory. Once again we have psychologists inventing mental states of which people are unaware and that have no direct connection to performance.

This kind of remembering of events is a peculiar kind of memory, however. Committing a script to memory and recalling it is something no one ever does, except when performing a play. What people do do is learn about situations and event structures, and they come to know these structures in the sense of knowing what to expect and what to do next. In a friendly tweak at Titchener, the *éminence grise* of Cornell psychology, J. J. Gibson called this learning of event structures the learning of associations.

It is safe to assume that what I am here describing as a capacity of perceptual expectation concerning familiar events is a fundamental cognitive capacity of human beings. This learning of associations occurs in toddlers as early as anyone has been able to test for it (Bauer, 1992; Bauer & Mandler, 1989, 1992; Fivush, Kuebli, & Chubb, 1992; Hudson, 1989). Fivush has pointed out (personal communication) that one partial exception to my claim that no one ever learns scripts comes from the interaction of parents and toddlers. Often a parent will rehearse an event with a toddler prior to the event. For example, a parent may tell a child what is going to happen during an imminent visit to the doctor's office. In this case, I would claim, the parent is rehearsing what might be called a script not to establish a stored representation for recall, but rather to establish a set of expectations and preparations for action. In Bauer's (1992) terms, the parent is preparing the child to notice the enabling relations that structure the forthcoming event.

According to the present account, then, one of the fundamental results of the kind of duality inherent in ambulatory perception is the learning of associations. That is, through the kind of uniting of self and world derived from perceiving, even small children derive expectations about what should happen in specific circumstances. In my household, both my children learned to perceive that the singing of "rub a dub dub" accompanied by removal of a diaper was an event that immediately preceded bathing. My two children did not learn this at 6 months of age by storing some sort of knowledge structure that enabled them to interpret various properties of the world. On the contrary, they came to perceive certain events as "things that I do" or as "things that happen to me," and they learned the structure of these events as well. There would seem to be a strong tendency for human cognitive systems to treat salient associations within an encounter as patterns to be learned. Bauer (1992) has shown that toddlers learn about and remember previously unfamiliar events, and she has shown that this learning and remembering is facilitated when those events are intrinsically organized as opposed to adventitiously structured. Bauer and Fivush (1992) have shown that 2 ½-year-olds do not learn about these intrinsically structured events via a process of familiarization and storage of a script learned through repetition. Even a single encounter with a well-structured event generalizes to different sequences that involve some of the same relations. Like Gibson's adults, these toddlers seem to learn to perceive associations; they do not seem to store instances of their experience.

In learning about event structure there is no duality of selves. One learns that there are things I do (or do not do) and situations that I encounter. This is not learned by the storage of sensory impressions organized into some sort of schema or scene, but rather due to the education of attention in perceptual systems that regulate such encounters – or so I claim. Even this simple kind of learning is dynamic and self-developing, not the insertion of static items into a static store within a static self.

In remembering events (as opposed to merely learning about them), however, there is a duality of selves because there is cognitive contact with one's own earlier self and that self's experience. After even a single experience at a birthday party, a toddler can both know something about how birthday parties "go" (in that part of the world) and also remember his or her own experiences at the party. Perhaps this is due to the storage of representations, but once again the metaphor of storage seems inappropriate. Once one truly abandons the idea that experience is some sort of sensory impression that can be stored as a trace, this whole notion of stored representations tends to look increasingly arbitrary. Is autobiographical memory the product of a system in which every encounter we have with the environment is somehow stored not only for what it is about but also for our experience during the encounter? If that is the case, then why is autobiographical memory among the most "constructive" of all facets of memory? If we really know ourselves so well, why is so much of this knowledge not in the form of photographic impressions, but much more like a story? A single encounter can – and often does – produce a measurable change in a person's cognition and in that person's self. The search for "stored traces" – even for such highly abstract stored traces as "scripts" – as the cause of these changes has obscured the more important question of what situations generate such powerful encounters.

Remembered Selves

If experience at the outset is ambulatory and dynamic, not static; if it is already the experiencing of the world by an active self, a self that has come from somewhere and that is going somewhere and is in the midst of action; if experience is as dynamic as this, then to recollect oneself is neither to rearouse an earlier experience nor to re-create an earlier experiencing, but to remember a prior encounter in the midst of a course of action. One can identify either with this prior course of action or even with the prior encounter, or one may no longer identify with them. Even when identifying with a prior course of action I am not identical with that earlier self; instead, I simply concur with the earlier action, much as I might concur with someone else's action in the present. For example, I concur strongly with my earlier self's refusal to comply with the draft, but I am no longer that 18-year-old boy – and there are many actions of that 18-year-old which I now view with chagrin, even with disgust.

A dynamic self is neither single nor multiple, it requires neither to be differentiated nor integrated. A dynamic self is complex and multiple, cohering, but only up to a point. The coherence of self is not a passive result of how items in memory are stored or integrated, but the active result of relating past and present encounters, actions, and projects. Thus it is that one can newly discover something about one's prior experiences and actions. Hirst's patient T. F. (chap. 14 of this volume) offers a poignant instance of this kind of rediscovery: In his case, a medical condition (amnesia) is a situation that leads him to reevaluate his memories of his life, and to find different meaning within them than he had before the onset of his amnesia.

There is much in any present encounter that can call to mind previous encounters – not the least of this is the fact that I am the agent of the encountering both then and now. A sudden eruption of memory or the noticing of an odd attraction or revulsion in a present encounter is often a symptom of a dynamic self making sense of all of its actions, past as well a present.

In this autobiographical striving after meaning, there is always a duality of selves, a need to reconcile present and past encounters and to see the meaning of both. Past encounters are not inert items in storage, so that a change in present circumstances can bring about a reorganization and reinterpretation of prior encounters. Children, for example, often misinterpret or simply do not understand the words and actions of their parents – and may only come to grasp their significance many years later, especially when they themselves have become parents. This is what I mean by saying that memory bridges not the self to the world, but different selves – one might say different perceiving selves. It is in this respect that memory resembles many of the fundamental processes of social relations, in which two or more people must coordinate their experiences. It may well be that memory is an intrapersonal precursor for some of these interpersonal processes. I would like to conclude this chapter with a brief review of some of these "duality of self" phenomena, phenomena that I believe are among the most central to our understanding of selves.

Dualities of the self

A number of the most important problems in psychological theory require an understanding of how the self can be separated and yet not completely divided; how it can be dual but not dichotomous. Yet, as I have emphasized in this chapter, human experimental psychologists have long resisted the idea that the self can be dual or multiple. Although theories of attention, memory, and cognition nowadays populate the mind with multiple and complex stages of information processing, modes of retrieval, and the like, there typically are two tacit assumptions of unity: first, that all basic mental states are simple and unitary (i.e., that one can isolate a percept or a memory trace or a classification), and second, that a unified agent is ultimately behind all the various psychological processes. Kant – whom some would like to believe was an early cognitivist (Kitcher, 1990) – made both these assumption explicit with his concept of a transcendental self who could, at least in principle, attach the phrase "I think – " in front of each of his mental contents.

But are selves quite so simple and unitary? Aren't there many psychological phenomena that call this assumption into question?

Akrasia, or weakness of the will.   Often we do something different from what we wish to do, or even the opposite of what we wish to do. The person giving up smoking may find herself about to light up a cigarette. We may make plans to do something but then, when the time comes, do something else. Someone trying to lose weight is rather likely to eat more than he did before the attempt. I may mean to go and get something from upstairs and find myself having gone up and down without getting it (perhaps having accomplished a different task).

These and many other examples of akrasia (Charlton, 1987) suggest that voluntary behavior itself is not the product of a simple, unified agent. Rather, it is the emergent result of many competing intentions or wills (Holt, 1915). Motivational psychology, perhaps under the influence of Freud and dynamic theories, has long known this, even though cognitivists have paid it little attention. And, it should be added, many motivation theorists insist on reducing this complexity of internal conflicts to a few simple dichotomies, such as the so-called instinctive drives, or the dichotomy of irrational versus rational thinking. I submit that such an approach offers little insight into the phenomena of akrasia; indeed, this and other dichotomous views distort such phenomena as temptation. The important thing about akrasia is how the self is in turmoil and internal conflict: There are not two coherent agencies fighting (one rational, the other not), but two (or more) partially organized courses of action competing for control of a single agency.

Empathy.   In the case of empathy one's self is not divided as it is in akrasia. When one empathizes, one perceives a situation from another's point of view without losing track of one's own point of view. We feel another's pain and may even act upon it, but it remains the other's pain, not our own (Smith, 1759/1976; Scheler, 1954/1970; Schopenhauer 1841/1965, p. 143). The cognitivist idea of perspective taking cannot capture this because it suggests a breaking down of the distinction between myself and the other. If I represent the world from your point of view, then, by hypothesis, I should experience the world as you do. In fact, such a breakdown is rarely experienced: In empathy one typically has both a strong sense of self *and* a strong sense of how the situation appears to the other. Again, this is an instance of duality – of division without separation.

Shame.   This is perhaps the most cognitive of emotions and it is therefore surprising that cognitivists have not shown much interest in it. Although infants and young children can redden, they do not blush (Darwin, 1877). To feel shame and to blush requires one not only to be aware of a situation as it appears to another (as in empathy) but to be aware of how one's self appears to another. Moreover, shame may well require some cognizance of social proprieties (Gibson, 1950a; Reed, 1988, pp. 63–66) so that one is ashamed when one is aware of another person's awareness of one's self having fallen short of a socially proper thing to do. In shame the dualities of akrasia and empathy are combined. Having done one thing, one comes to experience it as the wrong thing to have done, not necessarily from one's own point of view, but from the point of view of an empathic observer, or at least an observer attuned to our social norms. What is especially intriguing about shame is not only its developmentally late onset, but its rapid onset in some situations (despite its complexity) and its deep embodiment in the posture of all our limbs, trunk, and face, and in the vasomotor system (see Darwin, 1872). The description of shame makes it sound as if it is the result of a rather long and protracted process of ratiocination, but anyone who has ever been ashamed understands that it manifests itself instantly and deeply in everyday life.

Remorse.   In remorse as in shame one experiences one's own action as having been the wrong course to have taken. This reflective experience is not interpersonal, as in shame, but intrapersonal. One's later self reflects on the inadequacies of an earlier self. The weak-willed person (the "akratic") may come to feel both shame and remorse frequently, and almost simultaneously with his actions. Thus comes about the decidedly odd phenomenon of a person who acts in one way and, at the same time, apologizes for that action. On the other hand, remorse is one of the more powerful memory phenomena, and one can feel intense remorse (as well as shame) across years.

   The above-described psychological phenomena give a good overview of the complex nature of both the self and our everyday awareness of ourselves and, more importantly, of the central fact of duality in the stream of everyday life. From whence do these dualities arise? I would argue that they arise from a psychological phenomenon basic to human memory: that remembering often involves the capacity simultaneously to separate and coordinate a past and present self. This duality is collapsed in modern theories of memory, focusing as they do on the retention and retrieval of traces presumed to be internal to a single self. If remembering is to have present access to some mental representation of a past situation, then the past self is essentially irrelevant to memory. At best, the past self is no more than another mental representation, which may or may not be retrieved. It would seem that standard theories of cognition and memory would be hard pressed to offer even a faintly accurate description of these important psychological phenomena.

I hope to convince you that the past self should not be ignored by memory theorists, because to remember (at least in the sense of voluntary remembering) always involves a duality of awareness: an awareness of me encountering the environment now, coordinated with a previous encounter. This separation of two selves along with a coordination of the two experiences is the central duality of autobiographical memory. Although I argue that this duality appears first in autobiographical memory, it is of broad and general psychological significance, as the four examples given above should suggest. If I am right, then memory is basic to some of the most important complexities of the self, its functioning, and its organization.

REFERENCES

Augustine, Saint. (1991). *The confessions*. New York: Oxford University Press.

Barsalou, L. (1988). The content and organization of autobiographical memories. In U. Neisser & E. Winograd (Eds.), *Remembering reconsidered*. Cambridge University Press.

Bauer, P. (1992). Holding it all together: How enabling relations facilitate young children's recall. *Cognitive Development, 7*, 1–28.

Bauer, P. J., & Fivush, R. (1992). Constructing event representations: Building on a foundation of variation and enabling relations. *Cognitive Development, 7*, 381–401.

Bauer, P., & Mandler, J. (1989). One thing follows another: Effects of temporal structure on 1- to 2-year-olds' recall of events. *Developmental Psychology, 25*, 197–206.

Bauer, P., & Mandler, J. (1992). Putting the horse before the cart: The use of temporal order in recall of events by one-year-old children. *Developmental Psychology, 28*, 441–452.

Charlton, W. (1987). *Weakness of the will*. London: Blackwell.

Conway, M. (1990). Associations between autobiographical memory and concepts.

Journal of Experimental Psychology: Learning, Memory, and Cognition, 16, 799–812.

Darwin, C. R. (1872). *The expression of the emotions in man and animals.* London: Murray.

Darwin, C. R. (1877). A biographical sketch of an infant. *Mind, 2,* 285–294.

Fivush, R., Kuebli, J., & Chubb, P. (1992). The structure of events and event representations: A developmental analysis. *Child Development, 63,* 188–201.

Gibson, E. J. (1969). *Principles of perceptual learning and development.* Englewood Cliffs, NJ: Prentice Hall.

Gibson, E. J., & Rader, N. (1979). Attention: The perceiver as performer. In G. Hale & M. Lewis (Eds.), *Attention and cognitive development.* New York: Plenum.

Gibson, J. J. (1950a). The implications of learning theory for social psychology. In J. Miller (Ed.), *Experiments on social process: A symposium on social psychology.* New York: McGraw-Hill.

Gibson, J. J. (1950b). *The perception of the visual world.* Boston: Houghton Mifflin.

Gibson, J. J. (1966). *The senses considered as perceptual systems.* Boston: Houghton Mifflin.

Gibson, J. J. (1979). *The ecological approach to visual perception.* Boston: Houghton Mifflin.

Gibson, J. J. (1982a). On theories of visual space perception: A letter to Gunnar Johansson. In E. Reed & R. Jones (Eds.), *Reasons for realism: Selected essays of James J. Gibson.* Hillsdale, NJ: Erlbaum. (Original work published 1970)

Gibson, J. J. (1982b). The uses of proprioception and the detection of proprio-specific information. In E. Reed & R. Jones (Eds.), *Reasons for realism: Selected essays of James J. Gibson.* Hillsdale, NJ: Erlbaum. (Original work published 1964)

Gibson, J. J., & Gibson, E. J. (1982). Perceptual learning: Differentiation or en-richment? Reprinted in E. Reed & R. Jones (Eds.), *Reasons for realism: Selected essays of James J. Gibson.* Hillsdale, NJ: Erlbaum. (Original work published 1955)

Holt, E. B. (1915). *The Freudian wish and its place in ethics.* New York: Holt.

Hudson, J. (1990). Constructive processes in children's event memory. *Developmental Psychology, 26,* 180–187.

Kitcher, P. (1990). *Kant's transcendental psychology.* New York: Oxford University Press.

Matin, L. (1986). Visual localization and eye movements. In K. Boff, L. Kaufman, & J. Thomas (Eds.), *Handbook of human perception and performance* (Vol. 1). New York: Wiley.

Reed, E. S. (1982). An outline of a theory of action systems. *Journal of Motor Behavior, 14,* 98–134.

Reed, E. S. (1986). James Gibson's revolution in psychology: A case study in the transformation of scientific ideas. *Studies in the History and Philosophy of Science, 17,* 65–99.

Reed, E. S. (1987). Why do things look as they do? In A. Costall & A. Still (Eds.), *Cognitive psychology in question.* Brighton, England: Harvester.

Reed, E. S. (1988). *James J. Gibson and the psychology of perception.* New Haven, CT: Yale University Press.

Reed, E. S. (1989). Changing theories of postural development. In M. Woollacott & A. Shumway-Cook (Eds.), *Development of posture and gait across the life span.* Columbia: University of South Carolina Press.

Reed, E. S. (1991). Cognition as the cooperative appropriation of affordances. *Ecological Psychology, 3,* 133–158.

Reed, E. S. (1993). The intention to use a specific affordance: A conceptual framework for psychology. In R. Wozniak & K. Fischer (Eds.), *Development in context: Acting and thinking in specific environments.* Hillsdale, NJ: Erlbaum.

Scheler, M. (1970). *The nature of sympathy.* Hamden, CT: Archon Books. (Original work published 1954)

Schopenhauer, A. (1965). *On the basis of morality.* Indianapolis: Bobbs Merrill. (Original work published 1841)

Smith, A. (1976). *The moral sentiments.* New York: Oxford. (Original work published 1759)

Name index

Subject index